Family Transitions

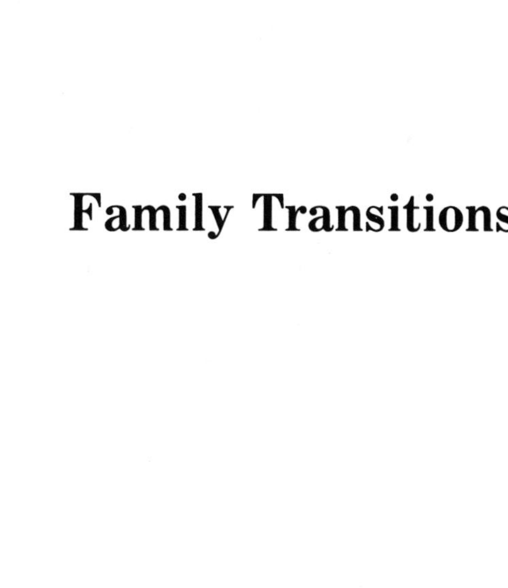

Family Research Consortium: Advances in Family Research

The Family Research Consortium was established to improve the quality of research and the breadth of collaboration in the field of family research. It has held five summer institutes for experienced researchers. The consortium designed and ran a multi-site postdoctoral training program in family process and mental health and initiated a number of collaborative research programs among its members. The consortium had 10 members: Elaine Blechman, Ph.D. (Colorado), Robert Cole, Ph.D. (Rochester), Philip Cowan, Ph.D. (Berkeley), John Gottman, Ph.D. (University of Washington), Mavis Hetherington, Ph.D. (University of Virginia), Sheppard Kellam, M.D. (Johns Hopkins University), Ross Parke, Ph.D. (University of California, Riverside), Gerald Patterson, Ph.D. (Oregon Social Learning Center), David Reiss, M.D. (George Washington University), and Irving Sigel, Ph.D. (Educational Testing Service).

The work of the consortium was supported by two NIMH grants: a research grant, 1R01MH40357 and a training grant, 1T32MH18262. Joy Schulterbrandt was project officer and played a major role in stimulating the current congress and future ones as well.

This volume is based on the second summer institute, *Understanding Normative and Non-Normative Family Transitions.* Other volumes in the Family Research Consortium series include:

Patterson, G. R. (Ed.) ***Aggression and Depression in Family Interactions*** (1990)

Cole, R., & Reiss, D. (Eds.) ***How Do Families Cope with Chronic Illness?*** (*in preparation*)

Hetherington, E.M., & Blechman, E. (Eds.) ***Stress, Coping, and Resiliency in Children and the Family*** (*in preparation*)

Parke, R., & Kellam, S. (Eds.) ***Exploring Family Relationships with Other Social Contexts*** (*in preparation*)

FAMILY TRANSITIONS

Edited by

Philip A. Cowan
University of California, Berkeley

Mavis Hetherington
University of Virginia

LEA LAWRENCE ERLBAUM ASSOCIATES, PUBLISHERS
1991 Hillsdale, New Jersey Hove and London

Lawrence Erlbaum Associates, Inc., Publishers
365 Broadway
Hillsdale, New Jersey 07642

Library of Congress Cataloging-in-Publication Data

Family transitions / edited by Philip A. Cowan, E. Mavis Hetherington
p. cm. — (Advances in family research series)
Proceedings of the second annual Summer Institute sponsored by the Family Research Consortium held in 1987 in Santa Fe, New Mexico.
Includes bibliographical references and indexes.
ISBN 0-8058-0784-5
1. Family—United States—Congresses. 2. Parenting—United States—Congresses. 3. Problem families—United States—Congresses. 4. Life cycle, Human. I. Cowan, Philip A. 1937– II. Hetherington, E. Mavis (Eileen Mavis), 1926– . III. Family Research Consortium. Summer Institute (2nd : 1987 : Santa Fe, N.M.) IV. Series.
HQ536.F3787 1990
306.85′0973—dc20 90-44479
CIP

Contents

Preface

In the Summer of 1987 a group of 60 family researches—psychologists, sociologists, psychiatrists, nurses, and an epidemiologist—spent five days together in Santa Fe, New Mexico, thinking and talking about family transitions. It was the second annual Summer Institute sponsored by the Family Research Consortium (see the chapter by Reiss & Schulterbrant in Patterson (1989), the first volume in this series). A working group of ten family researchers meeting regularly at that time over a four year period, the Consortium planned a series of five Summer Institutes, supported by funds from the National Institute of Mental Health. Each summer we came together with colleagues across the country to exchange ideas about theories, methods, and new directions in research on a specific topic relevant to family adaptation. The first year we explored depression and aggression in families (see the volume in this series edited by G. R. Patterson, 1989). This year, the focus was on family transitions.

The subject of family transitions has been a central concern of the Consortium because studies of families in motion help to highlight mechanisms leading to adaptation and dysfunction. Most research paints a portrait of families at a point in time, or follows them at arbitrarily-chosen intervals. But families are always in a process of change and reorganization as they make life choices and as they adapt to unexpected events. Coping processes that are difficult to observe in static snapshots become vivid and clear when we see individuals and families struggling with new and unfamiliar life tasks.

The Institute generated so much excitement in its morning, afternoon, and evening sessions that it kept most of us away from the wonders of Santa Fe and its surrounding attractions. Nine papers were presented by members of the Consortium and invited guests, and were formally discussed in a committee of the whole. Informal conversations occurred in small groups over breakfast, lunch, and dinner; earnest discussions of data were overheard in the jacuzzi late into the night. On the basis of both the formal and informal discussions, the nine papers were extensively re-written for the present volume, with a tenth, introductory chapter added as it became clear that a general definition of transitions was needed to provide an overarching framework for the discussion of specific transitions to follow.

Part I of this volume contains three perspectives for understanding family transitions. Philip Cowan proposes a definition of transitions that emphasizes a psychological perspective. In contrast with those who define transitions by the events that mark them (entering school, becoming a parent, divorce, unemployment), Cowan argues that for a change to be called transitional, it must involve a qualitative shift in the inner view of the self or family, and a reorganization of central roles and intimate relationships. Glen Elder provides a sociological/societal perspective, showing why family transitions across the life course must be understood in the context of the culture and the historical period in which they occur. Jason Dura and Janice Kiecolt-Glaser present some new data showing how biological processes affect and are affected by stressful psychological changes in individual and family life.

Part II presents five examples of research programs, each focused on a different kind of transition at a different period in the lifespan. Chapters 4 and 5 describe normative transitions (family formation and adolescence) while Chapters 6, 7, and 8 describe non-normative transitions (divorce and remarriage, and family dysfunction). Carolyn Cowan, Philip Cowan, Gertrude Heming and Nancy Miller describe the impact of a first child during the transition to parenthood, and the subsequent impact of family life on the child's transition to kindergarten; they also speak to the need for preventive interventions during normative family transitions. Diana Baumrind gives us an update on her longitudinal study of family socialization, reporting on effective and ineffective parenting during the early adolescent transition, and commenting on how societal changes have influenced the nature and quality of parent-adolescent relationships.

As we shift to a discussion of nonnormative transitions, Mavis Hetherington provides new data from a 6 year follow-up of the 4-year-olds in her original study of divorce. She shows how children's gender and temperament, and the characteristics of their families, contribute to children's long-term vulnerability or resilience in coping with their parents' divorce and remarriage. Gerald Patterson and Douglas Capaldi, following families with boys in grades 4 and 6 at risk for delinquency, describe intergenerational cycles in which (a) antisocial traits in the parents and grandparents (b) make the parents more vulnerable to negative life change, (c) increase the probability of ineffective parenting, thereby (d) leaving their children more vulnerable to delinquent behavior in adolescence. Elaine Blechman tackles one of the most difficult clinical problems in our society: how do we promote change and transition in multiproblem families who have been resistant to change on their own? Demonstrating that these families have profound difficulties in communication skills, she shows how specific communication techniques can facilitate both normative and nonnormative individual and family transitions.

In Part III, we return to general issues of how we conceptualize transitions and how we create statistical models capable of describing multidimensional changes in families over time. The prevailing metaphor for transition is adopted from the narrative of the journey or the individual hero's quest. Other metaphors could shed additional light on the meaning of transitional change at the family or social system level. Gottman suggests interesting analogies between family life transitions and chaos or catastrophe theory. Like unpredictable weather systems, families without internal regulating mechanisms are at risk for chaotic reactions to both normative and nonnormative life change.

Finally, our methods of measuring transitional change have not yet caught up with the concepts and metaphors that we have already developed. Describing individual differences in developmental pathways involves the mapping of multimeasure multimethod data over time. The problem is that the gathering of these data is labor intensive, and we tend to obtain a large number of measures from a relatively small number of individuals or families. Falk and Miller describe a new "soft modeling" procedure that seems to have immediate utility for the kind of data most family researchers have in mind.

We have not sampled all of the possible perspectives on family transitions in this volume. Our intent is to provide family researchers, and family health and mental health professionals, with challenging questions, theories, and methods, for thinking about how families change, or fail to change when it would be in their best interests to do so. We believe that the study of family transitions is at the core of our collective attempts to understand the mechanisms by which individuals and families adapt to the pressing issues they face at every point along their life course.

We pay special tribute here to Joy Schulterbrandt, the Chief of the Behavioral Sciences section at NIMH for her role in supporting the activities of the Consortium and the Summer Institute, David Reiss for his role as the first and only chair of the Consortium, and Judy Piemme, for her zeal in arranging the Institutes and seeing that they run so well.

P. A. Cowan
E. M. Hetherington

I PERSPECTIVES

1 Individual and Family Life Transitions: A Proposal for a New Definition

Philip A. Cowan
University of California, Berkeley

> *Americans have always been in transition. Whereas Old World families began with a place, New World families began with an act of migration. Nor did the transition from an old life to a new one end with the immigrants arrived on these shores. From place to place and job to job they kept moving.*
>
> —*(Bridges, 1980, p. 2)*

> *"Who are you?" said the Caterpillar. "I-I hardly know, Sir, just at present," Alice replied rather shyly, "at least I know who I was when I got up this morning, but I think I must have changed several times since then."*
>
> —(Carroll, from *Alice's Adventures in Wonderland*)

These two examples are used by the author of a book titled *Transitions,* to suggest that people may be "in transition" a good deal of the time (Bridges, 1980). Are Americans in fact "always in transition?" Are poor Alice's abrupt shifts of size and setting all to be regarded as transitional? It seems intuitively clear that in becoming an adolescent or a senior citizen, entering kindergarten or graduating from university, becoming a parent or contemplating an empty nest, individuals make transitions from one way of life to another. It also seems clear that some changes should *not* ordinarily be regarded as transitions—such as going on a long vacation or buying a new car. What about remodeling one's home or winning a promotion at work? Where do we draw the line between transitional and nontransitional change? Why is it important to do so?

At the beginning of any science, researchers and theorists devote most of their energies to describing relatively stable phenomena. In developmental psychology and family sociology, for example, great effort was initially devoted to classification—the identification of stable states called stages, and the presumably universal sequence in which these stages occur (Freud, 1917/1963; Mattesich & Hill, 1987; Piaget, 1968/1970). If the major interest of the theorist lies in describing a sequence through which almost all people pass, then focusing on what happens in between stages is relatively unimportant. Not until we want to explain why individuals and families differ in their rate of progress from one stage to another, or why they fail to follow the expected sequence of life changes does the search for laws of transition inevitably begin.

Are There Principles of Transition that Hold Across the Lifespan?

A primary assumption of transition theorists is that despite clear differences in the content of major life changes at different ages—adolescence or retirement, for example—general principles of transition apply to any phase of the life cycle. There are several reasons why this assumption has never been adequately tested.

1. Researchers tend to focus their studies at one age level (childhood, adulthood) and, within that age level, to investigate a single transition (school transitions, marriage, parenthood, empty nest). Comparisons between transitions, then, are usually made on the basis of data from different studies attempting to answer different questions with different methods.
2. The few investigators examining several transitions within the same study (Lowenthal, Thurner, & Chiriboga, 1976; Pearlin, 1980) use cross-sectional samples of subjects at different ages. Because the same individuals are not followed over time, we cannot know whether there is general consistency in people's adaptation to transitions across successive developmental milestones.
3. There are very real problems in the definition of transition. Most writers assume that the meaning is so obvious that it requires little explanation. Transition is loosely equated with change, sometimes qualified by *major* change. Yet, there are no guidelines to distinguish between major and minor change, or definitions of the kind of change that should be designated as transitional. If continual change implies never-ending transition, then the concept adds nothing to our understanding of development.

General principles of transition should apply equally well to children and adults. In this chapter, I examine definitions of transitions currently used in individual and family development theories and show that there are fundamental differences in the way transitions in childhood and adulthood tend to be described. My goal is to propose a formal definition that does justice to the complexity of development all along the life course.

Are There Differences Between Normative and Nonnormative Transitions?

Developmental theorists studying children, adults, and families across the lifespan have focused on what have come to be called *normative* transitions, expectable changes made by virtually every person (e.g., puberty) or by the vast majority of people in a defined population (e.g., married couples becoming parents). Other theorists have been more interested in individual or family stress and coping in the wake of *nonnormative,* often catastrophic events (war, unemployment, serious illness, loss of loved ones). I believe that theorists have blurred the distinction between normative and nonnormative transitions. I will expand on the argument by Felner, Farber, and Primavera (1983) that there has been an unfortunate tendency to focus on the life stress *events* that trigger crisis and disorganization, as if coping with the stress of becoming a parent, for example, is directly comparable to dealing with the aftermath of a tornado. (It may be, but we don't really know for certain.)

I propose instead to describe transitions as longterm *processes* that result in a qualitative reorganization of both inner life and external behavior. For a life change to be designated as transitional, it must involve a qualitative shift from the inside looking out (how the individual understands and feels about the self and the world) and from the outside looking in (reorganization of the individual's or family's level of personal competence, role arrangements, and relationships with significant others). Passing a life marker (e.g., entering school) or changing one's identity (e.g., becoming a husband or father) does not in itself signify that a transition has been completed. A central task for researchers is to determine the conditions under which both normative and nonnormative events stimulate developmental advances, produce dysfunctional crises, or leave the individual and family relatively unchanged.

I focus primarily on psychological interpretations of transitions, leaving for a final section some speculations about the biological, social, and historical contexts that help us to understand psychological adaptation and dysfunction in individuals and families as they proceed along their life course. I am responding to the challenge initiated both in conversations and written interchanges with my fellow contributors to this volume of Family Transitions. My goal is to contribute to a more precise formulation of transitions that will allow us to examine both normal and dysfunctional life change from different perspectives (biological, psychological, historical), using different levels of analysis (individual, family, societal), at any stage and phase of the lifespan.

CHILDHOOD VS. ADULTHOOD TRANSITIONS

According to Tyhurst (1957), the root meaning of *transition* is derived from two Latin words meaning "to go across." The word refers to a "passage or change from one place or state or act or set of circumstances to another" (Oxford English Dictionary). As a concept describing periods of developmental change, transition was first used in theories describing children's progress through a defined sequence of stages. It was then extended to describe individual and family changes along the adult life course.

Child Development

Developmental psychologists and psychiatrists (e.g., Freud, 1905/1953; Piaget, 1975/1985) have attempted to understand how individuals move from one stage to another, beginning with birth and extending through adolescence, with a few theorists considering transitions across the lifespan (e.g., Erikson, 1950; Jung, 1964). In these theories, changes are defined as transitions when they constitute a shift from one relatively stable form of biological or psychological organization to another. During the period when one set of *rules* for transacting with the environment (Kessen, 1962) is being replaced by a new set, the child may oscillate between two or more stages. Transition is conceived of as a time of disequilibration and internal conflict. Old cognitive/affective structures and behavior patterns are being reorganized; new patterns are not yet set. Successful resolution of the disequilibration and conflict leads to a higher, more differentiated and integrated level of adaptation. Unsuccessful resolution leads to developmental delay and regression.

Adult Development

A second group of theorists, including psychologists (Helson, Mitchell, & Moane, 1984; Levinson, 1978), psychiatrists (Gould, 1978; Vaillant, 1977), and sociologists (Havighurst, 1953; Neugarten, 1968), have been interested in development during the adult years. An individual is in transition when he or she passes a turning point in a life trajectory. Leaving home, choosing a job or career, getting married, becoming a parent, changing career directions, getting divorced, and moving into retirement all have been described as major life transitions.

The metaphoric connotation of transition for adults is a journey from one kingdom to another with no assurance of a successful passage. There are forks in the road, choices to be made, rough terrain to be crossed, risks to be faced and surmounted. There is an apparent or perceived discontinuity between the old country and the new. The traveler's eye is usually on his or her destination, focusing on what is to be gained in the new phase of life. After reaching the goal, there is sometimes disappointment about what has been left or lost along the way.

As in child development theories, the adult development literature portrays transitions as periods of change, disequilibrium, and internal conflict about gains and losses that occur between periods of stability, balance, and relative quiescence.

Family Development

Both child and adult developmentalists focus their attention on transitions made by individuals. By contrast, family sociologists (Hill & Mattesich, 1979), life course theorists (Elder, 1978), and some therapists (e.g., Carter & McGoldrick, 1988), attempt to understand transitions made by families who are in the process of formation and reorganization. Couples get married, have children, send their children to school, struggle with careers; they cope with children leaving home, retirement, the death of a parent, and widowhood.

Although stages or phases are often marked by change in individual family members, the family transition model emphasizes "multiple developmental trajectories" (Parke, 1988) or the "web of interdependencies both within the dyadic unit and across the lineage system" (Elder, Caspi, & Burton, 1989). It is critical to remember, for example, that the first day of kindergarten, nervously anticipated by both child and parents, is only one event in a long process of the child's transition to school, with implications for change in children's and parents' views of themselves, their relationships in the family, and the family's connections with community institutions (Klein & Ross, 1965; Signell, 1972). Similarly, as children enter adolescence, their parents may be in a midlife individual or marital transition of their own (Johnson & Irvin, 1983), which makes the transition to adolescence very complex indeed. Change in the life course of any one family member, dyad, or triad, then, may trigger disequilibration and reorganization of the whole family system.

Differences Between Child and Adult Transitions

Elsewhere, I have raised serious questions about whether adult developmental milestones, either individual or family, can be described as developmental *stages* in the same sense as children's movement from the preoperational to the concrete operational stage or from oral to anal stages (P. Cowan, 1988a). The criteria for the definition of stages in childhood and adulthood differ radically. Childhood developmental stages are described as occurring (a) in an invariant sequence, (b) across all cultures, (c) with qualitative differences between successive periods, (d) with each period constituting a "structured whole," defined by synchronous development in many domains and a relatively dynamic equilibrium (e) that hierarchically integrates rather than replaces previous stages (e.g., Fisher, 1983; Kohlberg, 1969).

There is some question about whether childhood stages actually fit this model (see Fisher, 1983), but no doubt that adult life changes violate most of the defining criteria (P.Cowan, 1988a; Mattessich & Hill, 1987). Not all men and women leave their families of origin; some get married before they leave home. Not all couples get married before having children, and some never marry or have children at all. There appear to be no invariant sequences in the adult life course, and little evidence, perhaps due to lack of research, that movement between one life milestone and another necessarily results in a new level of personal or relationship organization.

Although there are many distinctions to be made between child and adult transitions, I believe that one may be central. According to stage theories of child development, transitions *happen to* individuals; movement from one stage to another is not under the child's voluntary control. Transitions are triggered by changes in biological structure, psychological organization, or "the culturally controlled social agenda that determines the timing of the child's entry into various social settings such as the transition to elementary school. . ." (Parke, 1988, p. 161). There is little sense of the child consciously initiating a move toward latency or concrete operations.

In theories of adult development or the family cycle, by contrast, there is a clear emphasis on the volitional character of the change. Adolescents, decide to quit school with or without parental consent. Men and women decide to change career direction. Later in life, even if retirement is mandatory, we can choose how to prepare for retirement, and what we plan to use it for. Adult developmentalists do not characterize transitions as entirely under voluntary control, because there is a good deal of expectation and pressure involved in taking certain life steps. Nevertheless, there is a large component of choice in the journey, and the ever-present possibility of refusing to embark upon it, or of turning back even after the journey has been completed. This volitional, reversible aspect of life change is not found in descriptions of childhood stages.

At first glance, it may seem that the contrast between child and adult transitions follows from the "fact" that children's stage changes are impelled by reorganizations of biological or psychological structure, while adults' stages are self- or socially-determined and regulated. But children's stage development is also affected by social institutions (e.g., cultural differences in the meaning and timing of adolescence), and adults' life choices at the end of the life cycle are affected in part by biological regularities or irregularities in the aging process. The essential contrast between childhood and adulthood transitions, then, is not between the biological and social markers or precipitants of change, but in the person's participation in determining the direction of his or her life journey.

Childhood developmental stages, I am arguing, have metaphorical resemblance to adult development, but enough differences in core meaning to suggest that we begin to re-examine the assumption that principles of transition are constant across the lifespan. We need careful comparisons of child and adult transitions to answer some of the following questions: Can we use the same structure and process models to describe, for example, the transition to adolescence and the transition to adulthood? Do child and adult transitions trigger similar reorganizations of the nuclear and extended family system? Are there systematic differences in duration and intensity of distress in child and adult transitions? Are different coping skills needed in different transitions across the lifespan? Do voluntary and involuntary transitions function differently at each age level? Providing empirical answers to these questions presupposes a model or map of what we need to observe and measure when we assess transitional change. I return to this issue after discussing the importance of maintaining a distinction between normative and nonnormative transitions.

NORMATIVE AND NONNORMATIVE TRANSITIONS

At any point in the life course, some changes are normative; they are expected and experienced by the vast majority of individuals or families in a population (entering school, forming intimate relationships). By contrast, nonnormative transitions are associated with an unusual or unpredictable set of events (serious illness, emotional breakdowns, winning a lottery). At the present time, divorce seems to be at a midpoint in this bimodal classification. In some communities, divorce affects a majority of families, and is treated as if it were the norm. But because most couples enter marriage believing that divorce will not and should not happen to them, and because their children rarely expect it (Wallerstein & Kelly, 1980), divorce, from a societal perspective, is still a nonnormative family transition. Unfortunately, we have very little systematic information about differences between normative and nonnormative transitions because every major theoretical and empirical approach to the study of life change in adulthood blurs the distinctions between them.

Transition, Crisis, and Stress

In his description of the disequilibrium associated with the normative shift of one developmental stage into another, Erik Erikson (1950, 1959) claimed that we inevitably experience a period of crisis and intrapsychic conflict when we are faced with new and difficult developmental tasks. Crisis and conflict are temporarily incapacitating, but they are *necessary* for normal developmental growth. If the inevitable crises associated with each transition are not resolved, fixations, regressions, and other forms of psychological dysfunction may result. According to Erikson, then, normative life transitions represent both danger and opportunity, the two ideas combined in the Chinese idiograph signifying crisis.

The study of family changes resulting from catastrophic events was stimulated by Reuben Hill and his colleagues' widely used ABC-X model of crisis (Hill, 1949; Hansen & Johnson, 1982). Major life events, such as fathers' participation in World War II, produce "a sharp or decisive change for which the old patterns are inadequate. . . . the usual behavior patterns are found unrewarding, and new ones are called for immediately." The gap between what the new situation demands (A) and the current resources of the family (B), in the context of the family's definition of the event (C), produce a crisis (X). Initially, Hill focused on the disabling aspects of crisis, but he later acknowledged that the disorganization triggered by nonnormative events can be followed by reorganization and growth (Mattessich & Hill, 1987).

Just as theorists have relied on metaphoric resemblance to conclude that childrens' and adults' transitions are similar, so they seem to have felt free to equate normative and nonnormative transitions. Theorists have used Erikson's ideas to understand natural disasters, and Hill's ABC-X model to investigate passages through expectable family milestones.

Preventive Psychiatry. Concerned by the disequilibration occurring in families after one of their members is injured or killed in a natural disaster, "preventive psychiatrists" (Caplan, 1964; Lindemann, 1956, 1979), assumed that Erikson's model of normative intrapsychic crisis resolution could be applied to nonnormative events. They advocated preventive mental health services to help survivors deal with their psychological distress. Then, in an interesting "back translation" they assumed that interventions similar to those developed for families facing unexpected loss would be beneficial to individuals undergoing expectable, but stressful life changes (Rapoport, 1963). Though their model of intrapsychic disequilibrium was faithful to Erikson, their conception of transitional events was based on the catastrophe model (sudden onset, relatively quick recovery) that was the basis of their initial clinical experience. As a result, interventions designed to help individuals and families cope with life transitions (e.g., Shereshefsky & Yarrow, 1973) tended to focus on the person's psychological adaptation to inner distress. As Felner and his colleagues have indicated (Felner, Terre, & Rowlison, 1984), intervention programs based on these conceptualizations ignored the possibilities for active, interpersonally oriented interventions that could change institutional settings such as classrooms (e.g., Jason, 1980) or family environments (e.g., Cowan & Cowan, 1987b). For example, Shereshefsky and Yarrow (1973), following Caplan's suggestions, offered individual counseling sessions to pregnant women, with very little focus on their husbands; yet, their data indicated that the state of the marital relationship rather than the wife's intrapsychic distress was the best predictor of her adaptation to parenthood.

Family Sociology. In the 2 decades after Hill's seminal work, family sociologists assumed, without close scrutiny, that the ABC-X model of nonnormative transitions could easily be adapted to the understanding of normative family change. For example, LeMasters (1957), described the "normal crises" found in 83% of the couples he interviewed who had become parents for the first time. After 3 decades of controversy (see Cowan & Cowan, 1988 for a detailed review) it is still not clear whether it is appropriate to speak of wartime traumas and family transitions in the same conceptual terms.

Life Stress Events. A third approach to the study of adult life transitions completely bypasses the normative nonnormative distinction. It begins with the premise that the content of any single event is relatively unimportant; rather, it is the cumulative impact of life change that produces dysfunctional levels of stress. Holmes and Rahe (1967), using a public health epidemiological perspective, created a life change checklist, with each event weighted for level of presumptive stress by a large sample of respondents. The normative or nonnormative quality of each event was ignored. Holmes and Rahe assumed that the total weighted life change score would provide a reasonable index of the amount of stress *experienced* by the individual filling out the checklist. There have been many critiques of this point of view, including questions about Holme's and Rahe's (a) reliance on normative weightings of items rather than the unique experience of the responder, (b) failure to record the recency or positive/negative valence of the changes (Dohrenwend, 1979), and (c) tendency to focus on rather large and distant events rather than the daily hassles that influence current stress levels (Lazarus & Folkman, 1984).

Although they differ in their relative emphasis on external events and inner distress, all three approaches to the study of major life change use a natural disaster model of specific events triggering distress. None of them does justice to the alternative view that transitions are processes that unfold over time, with outcomes dependent on the nature of the processes. The extended, multiprocess description that is clearly applicable to normative life transitions (e.g., adolescence) may apply to nonnormative transitions (e.g., chronic illness of a family member) as well (Hetherington & Camara, 1984; Felner et al., 1984).

Contextual Issues in Defining Normative and Nonnormative Transitions

In arguing for systematic investigation of the differences between normative and nonnormative transitions, I do not mean to imply that the distinction between the two is absolute and clear. Definitions of "normative" and "expected" in contrast with "nonnormative" and "unexpected" always have a reference to a specific social context; we cannot distinguish normative from nonnormative transitions for any individual or family without considering what is happening in their peer group and subculture.

Deviations in the timing of life change can turn a normative transition into a nonnormative one. Some studies have shown that when individuals are "off-time," either unusually early or unusually late in comparison with their age cohort, their departures from normative *pace* of modal life journeys are associated with decreased self-esteem and increased levels of stress (e.g., Helson et al., 1984; Lowenthal, Thurner & Chiriboga, 1976; Neugarten, 1968). What is not yet known is how the disequilibration from transitions completed at the usual time compares with the stress resulting from following the beat of one's own drummer through the adult milestones.

A neglected issue in the definition of normative transitions concerns the fact that what is usual and expectable in the culture at large does not always hold in each of the subcultures. Theories of adult development focus on career choice as a marker of normative life change (e.g., Levinson, 1978), but how do we conceptualize career choice in neighborhoods where more than half the youths are unemployed and those who work are usually paid below minimum wage? Is entrance to a profession considered part of a normative life transition? The marriage–parenthood sequence is considered normative in most theories of family development. How do we conceptualize the transition to parenthood in communities where the majority of first-time parents are unmarried teenage girls?

I am raising questions to which there are, as yet, no answers. It seems to me that we need careful comparative studies of normative and nonnormative transitions, with children and adults, in a variety of social contexts. These studies will help us to decide whether a general life transition model fits the data, or whether different kinds of transitions at different ages in different social contexts require different sets of explanatory principles.

We can now return to the issues raised at the beginning of this chapter. If we are to design comparative studies of transitions, we will need to define the phenomena of transition. We must identify the core meanings of transition at a level abstract enough to encompass the range of transitional change that I have been describing, but concrete enough to guide the selection of measures appropriate to the understanding of each specific example.

A STRUCTURAL AND PROCESS MODEL OF TRANSITIONS

In agreement with others (e.g., Felner et al., 1984; Hetherington & Camara, 1984), I have argued that we should reject life event definitions of transition that document changes in the environment, and focus instead on changes in individuals and families. We need an approach that enables us to distinguish, for example, between two men, both of whom become fathers on the same day.

> The first new father describes marked changes in his sense of himself and his views of his responsibility to society. Initially, he feels somewhat out of control emotionally. He shifts his arrangement of household and employment responsibilities because he is determined to participate in the daily care of his child. He learns new skills in managing family affairs and in figuring out the needs of his

newborn. He feels more excited and involved in his marriage. Gradually, he begins to regain his emotional balance.

The second new father takes some time off during the week his son is born, and then returns, as planned, to his office. He takes pride in being a father, but his basic life pattern continues much as before.

Although the second man has become a parent, in the view of the definition I am proposing, he has not completed a *transition* to parenthood. The issue is not simply that the first man is more pleased with his new parent identity and his baby; it is possible to complete a transition in a state of serious distress. And, it is possible for the second man to delay making the transition until years later when his child is at an age that draws him back into the family (Daniels & Weingarten, 1982, 1988). The transition, is not defined by the child's date of birth, but by psychological changes in the father's inner world and in the organization of his roles and central relationships.

The dynamics or mechanisms describing the path followed and the level of adaptation achieved as each person or family makes a life transition, comprise the *process* aspects of the transition model. The description of linkages among parts of a system—the fact that aspects of self, roles, and relationships are all interconnected—constitutes the *structural* aspect of transitions. Let us examine how this proposal for a new definition of transitions incorporates both normative and nonnormative changes in individual's and families at different points in the lifespan.

The View from Within

Whether the focus is on individuals, families, or large social groups, there is evidence that transitions involve major reorganizations of each person's psychological life space; when we look inward to the self and outward to the world, we see and feel things we never experienced before. There is a perceived discontinuity between the way it was and the way it seems to be now, and, usually, this change is accompanied by some emotional turmoil.

Sense of Self. A *developmental* transition always involves a restructuring of one's psychological sense of self. Central to the child's shift from the sensorimotor stage to the preconceptual stage is a change in representation of the self from the plane of action to symbolic representation (Cowan, 1978). The question of identity—who am I and who will I be?—is raised consciously for the first time in adolescence, but remains a continuing issue at every life transition. A poignant example of change in self-view at midlife concerns a shift in perspective on one's life from "time since I was born" to "time until I die" (Neugarten, 1979).

A qualitative restructuring of one's sense of self can accompany nonnormative changes triggered solely by external forces. For example, some individuals experiencing natural disasters or severe illness begin to define themselves as victims, while others take on the complex feelings associated with viewing themselves as survivors.

Like individuals, families and social institutions have *self*-perceptions (e.g., Reiss, 1981). Couples and families have a more or less strong sense of we-ness, and a generally-agreed-upon perception or myth about the nature of their family (e.g., "The Smiths never wash their dirty linen in public"). Societies and nations, too, have a sense of identity, illustrated, by the Declarations of Independence and other, similar documents ("We hold these truths to be self-evident"). Not every individual in the system holds the same belief, but decisions and collective actions are often based on the modal self-perception. As with individual life changes, family or societal transitions leave the self-view open to question, redefinition, and reorganization. The story of cumulative transitions in our views of ourselves becomes a narrative of our own personal, familial, or cultural history.

Assumptive World. Also implicit in life transitions is a shift in what Parkes (1971) has described as one's assumptive world. Previously held premises about how the world works may no longer apply. Expectations about how roles should be defined and relationships operate may come into question. Philosophical assumptions about society and the operation of government may be seriously reexamined. Parkes does not argue that *every* aspect of one's view of the world is reorganized during what he called psycho-social transitions, but rather that in the midst of life transitions one's world will be seen through "new eyes."

These alterations in one's assumptive world can occur in the process of coping with both normative and nonnormative transitions. Progressing from Piaget's preoperational to concrete operational stage, 5- to 7-year-old children begin to shift their focus from how the world appears (things change) to how things "really are" (despite apparent change, some qualities of objects are conserved). In the normative transition to adolescence, formal operations opens the world of possibility to the teenager; in the process many adolescents begin to reconceptualize their relationships with their parents and their political system (Cowan, 1978; Turiel, 1983). Winning a lottery, losing one's job, experiencing one's parents' divorce, serious illness, or death can also result in radically altered assumptions about one's place in the universe.

Families, too, have a collective orientation to the environment, based in part on some assumptions about whether the world is a benign or threatening place (e.g., Reiss, 1981). Societies appear to adopt a collective set of assumptions that help to determine the actions of institutions and political bodies within them. During times of social change (e.g., rapid shifts in family demographics) or catastrophe (e.g., World War II), previous assumptions may be called into question and replaced by substantially altered interpretations of political and social reality.

Affect Regulation; Inner Coping. So far, my descriptions of change in self- and world-view have focused on the cognitive content of perceptions and attitudes. Left out of most contemporary accounts of transitions, or subsumed under the general heading of *stress,* is Erikson's initial emphasis on the inner emotional upheaval that accompanies the attempt to cope with new and ambiguous life tasks. When old patterns no longer work, when old assumptions are no longer valid, there is often a precarious feeling of standing on shifting sands. Tension, anxiety, and depression are common not just after layoffs and divorces, but after weddings and promotions. In reading clinical case histories, I have been struck by how often a detailed account of a patient or family's severe turmoil and distress includes an incidental mention of a major life change (a new sib, a relationship loss, a move across country).

Adaptive coping with inner emotional arousal involves achieving a balance between two competing tendencies. First, in order to mobilize the appropriate psychological defenses and problem-solving skills, it seems to be necessary for us to *experience* some of the disruption instead of blocking it out or ignoring it (cf. C. Cowan, 1988). Second, it is necessary to develop some strategies for self-regulation so that our feelings do not totally overwhelm and incapacitate us. This shifting balance between experiencing and controlling emotion has recently been described as emotional regulation, and occurs, as we shall see, in interpersonal as well as intrapsychic domains (Gottman & Krokoff, 1989; Levenson & Gottman, 1983).

In sum, from the inner perspective, transitions involve a qualitative shift in perceptions of oneself and the world, and an imbalance usually, but not always, followed by rebalance in our emotional equilibrium. *Some* change in all of these aspects of the self must occur before we describe a life change as a transition.

The View from Outside

We cannot afford to rest the definition and assessment of transitions solely on the person's inner point of view. Successful navigation of transitions requires new forms of adaptive behavior—concrete, observable external actions and readjustments to cope with new developmental tasks and social/interpersonal demands. In addition to studies of inner coping and defense during transitions (see Boss, 1987 for a review), sociologists and psychologists have explored the consequences of reorganizing roles, and the changes in personal-social competence stimulated by attempts to master the developmental tasks that new roles demand.

Role Reorganization. There is no absolute distinction to be made between what belongs to one's sense of self (the inner view) and what belongs to one's roles (the view from outside). A woman thinks of herself as a high-powered manager at the same time that she is involved in carrying out her role at the office. Similarly, it is not easy to distinguish between roles and relationships, since roles are usually defined in relational terms: employer implies employee, teacher implies student, parent implies child, husband implies wife. In general, *role* refers to the definition of appropriate behaviors for a person occupying a given position, while *relationship* refers to the dynamics or qualities of the interaction between two or more people as they carry out their various roles. Parenthood is a role. It implies a large set of caretaking, guiding, and socializing behaviors initiated from parent to child. Parents carry out their roles in different ways. Baumrind's description of authoritative, authoritarian, and permissive parenting (this volume) represents one type of role behavior. But because authoritative is defined as demanding and responsive, authoritarian as demanding and unresponsive, and permissive as undemanding and responsive, these categories also describe different qualities of relationship between parents and their children.

During transitions, roles can change in three ways:

1. Roles can be added or subtracted, entered or left: a child enters school and becomes a student; one spouse dies and the other becomes a widow or widower.
2. The set of expectations and behaviors that determine how the role is to be enacted can be redefined or reconceptualized: a child leaves kindergarten and enters the "serious work" of the first grade, a woman who has been a full-time homemaker makes changes in her household role after entering the labor force.
3. A transitional change may involve marked shifts in the salience of an already-existing role: an adolescent stops "playing the field" and becomes involved in one serious relationship; a man becomes more psychologically invested in fatherhood as his children grow older.

Note again that the psychological aspects of role changes may not shift at the time of the external event used to mark the transition. Individuals anticipating becoming parents begin to think of themselves in the parent role and to behave as they imagine parents should (e.g., more responsibly) during pregnancy, or even before. A woman whose husband has left or died may be psychologically involved in a relationship with him for many years after her formal role as wife has ended.

Change in one major role through addition, redefinition, or a shift in salience, usually affects the organization of existing role arrangements. New roles must be integrated and coordinated with old ones. Role losses, whether sudden and unexpected or long-planned for, may stimulate a search for new roles to take their place. The changes are often disequilibrating and stressful. Within the person, the pushes and pulls associated with conflicting role demands can result in severe role strain (Goode, 1960). Within the family, the addition and redefinition of roles can create new or increased interpersonal conflict (Cowan et al., 1985). Even when only one family member changes roles, other people are forced to make shifts in their own role expectations and behaviors. For example, when a teenage girl becomes a mother but decides to go back to work, her role transition may have serious consequences for her mother or grandmother who may now take on a role as primary caretaker of the baby, which may, in turn, affect the relationships between the new mother and other members of her family (Elder et al., 1989).

The concept of role provides a bridge between a focus on individuals and a focus on their relationships. A change in one major role (e.g., from student to employee) may improve a man's or woman's self-esteem and encourage him or her to consider commitment to a longterm romance. A change in a major relationship (e.g., divorce) not only alters a central role but may also put a large dent in one's self-confidence.

Restructuring Personal Competence. The crises associated with transition may be triggered by internal reorganizations, by external challenges, or by a combination of the two. Whatever the precipitating cause, the individual, couple, or family must adopt new strategies, skills, and patterns of behavior to solve new problems. In the transition to junior or senior high school, for instance, adolescents face a new school organization; teachers place greater demands on students' academic self-direction, and a complex new social network taxes students' interpersonal resources at a time when relationships with peers are increasingly important to their well-being (Felner, Ginter, & Primavera, 1982). In addition, parents may be experiencing their own transitional crises (Johnson & Irwin, 1983). If a new level of skills is achieved, we assume that the transition has been resolved successfully. If personal disorganization continues, the negative consequences may have longterm effects, especially when new normative or nonnormative life transitions come along.

Reorganization of Relationships. Individual life transitions, normative and nonnormative, involve disequilibration and reorganization of one's family relationships. As children enter school for the first time, their interactions with their parents may change (Klein & Ross, 1965). As men and women become parents, they describe marked transformations in the quality of their relationships with their own parents, in their relationship with each other, and, of course, in their relationships with their child (Cowan, Cowan, Heming, & Miller, this volume). Similarly, divorce and remarriage not only alter the nature of the couple relationship, but also the relationships between parents and children, and between parents and their own parents (Hetherington, this volume; Hetherington & Camara, 1984).

Life transitions also involve reorganization in the relationships between family members and their social networks outside the family. Children's preadolescent cognitive changes probably accompany their ability to form more intense, long-lasting and complex relationships with groups of peers (Coie & Dodge, 1983; Gottman & Parker, 1986). The last child's entrance to school may have an immediate impact on his or her mother's involvement in the workplace. Sudden accidents or illnesses may lead to unexpected shifts in the network of people one turns to for comfort and support.

Affect Regulation: Interpersonal Coping. In discussing the internal view of transitional change, I described the need for individuals to achieve an inner balance between experiencing feelings and avoiding being overwhelmed. Affect regulation is an essential aspect of adaptation in the interpersonal domain, too. Gottman and Levenson (1989; Levenson & Gottman, 1983) describe graphically how maritally dissatisfied couples tend to escalate negative affect until their exchanges are out of control, in contrast with couples in more satisfying marriages who are able to express negative affect without impairing the relationship.

Most of the chapters in this volume describe individual and family transition periods as times of new and heightened affective arousal. Presumably, then, transitions should increase the risk of affect disregulation, and increase the probability that intimate relationships will change in a negative direction, at least temporarily (cf. Cowan et al.; Dura & Kieckolt-Glaser; Hetherington; Patterson & Capaldi; all in this volume). One way of documenting the role of transitions in psychological distress would be an examination of therapy patients and controls to see whether clinically distressed individuals and families experience more than their share of life transitions. A more comprehensive approach to this issue would be large-scale epidemiological studies, to determine the association between life transitions and the emergence of psychopathology. At present, though we know that some psychiatric disorders tend to occur more frequently in a specific age period (DSM-III-R, 1987), we know little about the direct connection between normative transitions and diagnosable psychological distress, except, perhaps, for the study of postpartum psychosis (cf. Kumar & Robson, 1984).

This account of multiple, qualitative reorganizations of the person's inner life and relationships constitutes the *structural* definition of life transitions. Are there changes that we would regard as transitions that do not involve structural alteration? If we focus on what are described as life transitions, I believe not. There are certainly differences in the timing, duration, magnitude, and complexity of the changes as we examine different individuals or families in the course of different transitions. But, a shift in role (e.g., from one rank to another at work) that did *not* involve a shift in one's inner view of self and world *and* in some major relationships, should not qualify as a life transition. It would signify that whatever changes occurred in the individual and his or her life circumstances, a developmental advance or regression would be unlikely.

The Process: Phases Within Transitions

I assume that reorganizations of the psychological sense of self, world-view, and internal affect regulation, roles, relationships and interpersonal affect regulation do not always occur simultaneously. It is more likely that individuals and families go through a period of *de-organization* in which almost everything is out-of-sync. Roles may change first (e.g., unemployment), followed by lowered self-esteem, depression, marital distress and a jaundiced view of governmental incompetence (cf. Liem & Liem, in press). Or, marital conflict may lead to role reorganization, which, in turn, stimulates a reconsideration of one's identity as a married person. One process sets other changes in motion. Lack of synchrony during a period of change constitutes an essential defining characteristic of transitions (see Reigel, 1975). It is precisely because asynchrony is disequilibrating that it contains the potential for stimulating developmental growth or dysfunction.

Parkes (1971) suggests that there may be a lawful sequence within transitions, beginning with an early phase of conflict, loss, uncertainty, proceeding through a middle phase of testing new alternatives, and entering a late phase involving a return toward a previous equilibrium or to the establishment of a new equilibrium. This description seems to fit childhood normative transitions, and some adult normative transitions (e.g., parenthood, divorce). It remains to be seen whether this within-transition sequence applies to a wider range of examples, and whether we can identify the conditions affecting the rate of movement through each phase.

The structure and process model of transitions I am proposing underlines a central premise in the study of transitions that is often disregarded or minimized by sardonic references to mid-life crisis. Despite the emphasis in the theories I have presented on the stress and disequilibrium of both normative and nonnormative transitions, there seems to be a public belief that those who are at risk for psychological distress are at the extremes of socioeconomic deprivation and clinically diagnosable psychopathology. The picture of transitions that I have summarized makes it clear that many of us (we don't yet know how many) experience stressful changes in our sense of themselves and in our relationships, and that we may need assistance if we are to make normal developmental progress. As a first step in any planning of preventive interventions, we must begin to identify individuals, couples, and families, who are more likely than others to have difficulty in coping with transitional change.

VULNERABILITY AND RISK, RESILIENCE AND PROTECTION

There is substantial support for the hypothesis that there is continuity of adaptation over time and across transitions—some individuals and families are generally vulnerable, while others are usually resilient. But pretransition adaptation is not the only determinant of how they will feel after their transitional journeys. A number of researchers have begun to identify (1) risk factors that increase the probability of dysfunction during and after transitions, and (2) protective factors that reduce the severity of successful or unsuccessful outcomes (Boss, 1987; Clausen, 1972; Felner et al., 1983; Hetherington, 1989; McCubbin & McCubbin, 1988; Moos & Schaefer, 1986; Rutter, 1987). I comment first on continuities in vulnerability and resilience, and then discuss the more general issues of risk and protective factors affecting major life transitions. increase or decrease resilient, and then

Vulnerability and Resilience: The Continuity Inherent in Transitions

The emphasis in defining transitions here and in most other accounts is on change and discontinuity. However, it is important to remember that individuals and families do not become unrecognizable as they move from one life period to another. In studies of the transition to parenthood, Belsky and his colleagues (Belsky, Spanier, & Rovine, 1983; Belsky, Lang, & Rovine, 1985; Heinicke and his colleagues (1986). Lewis, Owen, and Cox (1988) and Carolyn Cowan and I have made the point that despite consistent change from before to after the birth of a first child, the best predictors of who copes well with the transition are indicators of individual and couple adaptation before the baby arrived. As a working hypothesis, I suggest that this principle applies in all transitions; the transition amplifies processes already in motion before the transition begins.

This hypothesis reflects a general assumption about both transitions and crises that has not received an empirical test. It is widely believed that how individuals or families handle current transitions or crises is a direct reflection of how they have handled transitions or crises in the past. It is a bedrock belief held by psychodynamically oriented therapists following Freud and Erikson, that the key to understanding patients' present intrapsychic conflicts can be found in their history of unresolved early conflicts or traumas, and that resolution of past long-standing distress will allow development to proceed more normally. We have rich longitudinal data sets demonstrating that early adaptation is related to later adaptation (Baumrind, this volume; Block & Block, 1980; Eichorn, Clausen, Haan, Honzik, & Mussen, 1981). We have new evidence that the cycle of maladaptation is transmitted across three generations (Main & Goldwyn, 1984; Patterson & Capaldi, this volume) or even four (Caspi & Elder, 1989). Surprisingly, though, we do not know whether the link between early and later distress is shaped in part or in whole by difficulties in coping with *transitions*. There are virtually no longitudinal studies following individuals and families through more than one transition (rather than simply through more than one age period) to show the cumulative effect of failure to adapt to normative or nonnormative transitional change.

Risk and Protective Factors in Transitions

The fact of continuity in vulnerability and resilience constitutes only one part of our understanding of the risk factors that increase the probability of distress, and the protective factors that help individuals to manage transitions successfully. Most investigators conceptualize categories of risk and protection similar to the one that Hill proposed in his ABC-X model (1949). Transitions are more or less successful depending on (a) the nature of the physical and social demands faced by the individual in coping with the life change, (b) the availability of personal resources including social support and guidance, and (c) the meaning of the transition to the individual or family (Boss, 1987; Felner et al., 1983; McCubbin & McCubbin, 1988).

(a) Demands. Presumably, the fewer new skills demanded by the transition, the fewer obstacles in the environment (e.g., poverty) and the longer one has to prepare, the easier the transition (e.g., Boss, 1987). What is not yet known is whether some transitions are inherently more difficult than others. For example, widowhood has been compared with divorce (cf. Kitson, Babri, Roach, & Placidi, 1989); perhaps because it is difficult to equate resources and meanings of these two nonnormative transitions, no clear-cut conclusions about their relative difficulty have emerged.

(b) Resources. There is no question that personal resources make transitions easier. In addition to the personal psychological coping resources I have been describing, transitions are easier when there are individuals and institutions available to provide instrumental and emotional support (e.g., Heller & Swindle, 1983; Hetherington, Stanley-Hagan, & Anderson, 1989). It seems reasonable to expect that different sets of coping skills and social resources will function as protective factors at different points in the lifespan (McCubbin & McCubbin, 1988).

As a supplement to traditional resources for those already in distress, new options have been generated by preventive programs to: (i) help students adjust to a school transition (Bogat, Jones, & Jason, 1980; Durlak & Jason, 1984; Felner, Ginter, & Primavera, 1982), (ii) work with first-time parents in coping with childrearing (Matese, Schorr, & Jason, 1980) and with strains in their marital relationship (Cowan & Cowan, 1987b; C. Cowan, 1988) during the transition to parenthood, (iii) help families minimize the traumatic effects of divorce (Emery,

Hetherington, & Fisher, 1984), and (iv) assist widows and widowers in coping with the impact of losing a spouse (Osterweis, Solomon, & Green, 1984). These interventions, and others, have demonstrated positive effects, not necessarily in preventing distress but in minimizing its negative consequences. Given the risk potential of even the most positive life transitions, it seems reasonable to make them more available to individuals and families. Unfortunately, preventive services addressed to the general population are still relatively rare.

(c) Meanings. Consistent with a dual focus on inner and external aspects of transition is the recognition that how individuals and families interpret (Hill, 1949) or appraise (Lazarus & Folkman, 1984) their situations determines to a large extent how stressful they are, or how successfully they react to stress. For example, in our follow-up of a preventive intervention designed to reduce marital strain during the transition to parenthood (C. Cowan, 1988b), couples who had taken part in groups with trained leaders were less likely than the no-treatment controls to separate or divorce for the first 3 years after having a baby. This effect on marriage occurred despite the fact that there were few differences between the intervention and no-intervention couples in self-view, and in their family arrangements. It appeared that partners' *interpretations* of those changes, and the fact that the intervention couples did not attribute their negative changes directly to the marriage, contributed to less negative change in marital satisfaction, and greater marital stability.

Elder (this volume) argues that we must understand the risks and protections of transitional change in the context of time. He suggests that *when* the transition occurs in the individual's or family' life trajectory has as great deal to do with the outcome. Marriage or widowhood have different risks if they occur at age 20 or at age 70 (the on-time off-time issue). Having an adolescent child affects parents entering mid-life or facing retirement in different ways. And, historical change, too, alters the nature of risk, for example, in children's transitions to adolescence (Baumrind, this volume).

Life Transitions Highlight Individual and Family Adaptive Processes

We have seen that life transitions bring to the foreground issues of individual and family adaptation. That is, subtle processes observable in day-to-day lives are heightened by the stress and challenge of dealing with major life change. Transitions can be seen as "naturally-occurring experiments" that provide a strategic opportunity to highlight mechanisms of individual or group development (Cowan & Cowan, 1990, Elder, this volume).

If life transitions are considered as *natural experiments,* then psychotherapy and other forms of psychological intervention with individuals, families, and social systems, may be conceptualized as *planned experiments.* Successful interventions (a) remove barriers to the operation of normal transition processes, and (b) facilitate adaptive change in the client's psychological sense of self, affect regulation, roles, and relationships (see C. Cowan et al., this volume, for an example of preventive intervention with nonclinic families, and Blechman, this volume, for examples of interventions promoting life transitions with multi-problem families). We need further systematic research to understand whether those who participate in interventions make changes similar to people who manage life transitions without the assistance of mental health professionals. Just as the answer to this question could help to establish a comprehensive theory of transitions, it would also be at the heart of a unified theory encompassing both adaptive and maladaptive development.

WIDER PERSPECTIVES FOR THE CONCEPT OF TRANSITIONS

A Biological Perspective

I have focused almost entirely on psychological and social variables in defining transitions. It is clear that a generic theory of adaptation and dysfunction must also encompass biological levels of analysis (e.g., P. Cowan, 1988b). Like psychological variables, biological variables function as (a) causes, (b) consequences, and (c) mediators of life transitions.

(a) Causes/Precipitants. Freud surmised that progression through the psychosexual stages is precipitated by biological shifts in the locus of pleasure. Piaget (1968/1970) assumed that at least some of the shifts in cognitive stages are accompanied by qualitative transformations of neurological organizations. Adolescence is marked by, sometimes even defined by, the physical and hormonal manifestations of puberty. Physical, hormonal, and neurological malfunctions can precipitate illness and major life change.

(b) Consequences. New research on psycho-neuro-immunology (Kieckolt-Glaser, Fisher, Ogrocki, Stout, Speicher, & Glaser, 1987, Dura & Kieckolt-Glaser, this volume) suggests that stressful life transitions may trigger biological changes in hormonal function and in the immune system.

(c) Mediators. Biological functions participate in interactive systems that amplify or reduce the impact of environmental, psychological, or behavioral events. It is likely, then, that both temporary and long-lasting biological characteristics of the organism are involved in determining the timing, duration, and adaptational outcomes of each life transition.

Transitions in Historical Perspective

Lifespan transitions must be understood in a historical context (Baumrind, this volume; Elder, this volume; Hareven, 1978). Historical changes in the timing of children's entrance into school, in the role of adolescents in society, in age of marriage, in the technology of birth control, and in women's entrances and exists from the labor force, shape the potential meaning of these life transitions to the individuals and families who experience them and to the researchers who study them. School entrances and exits had different meaning in times when schooling was not universal and compulsory. Unemployment in the 1930s is not the same phenomenon as it is in the 1990s. Taking the historical period into account helps to define what is normative and nonnormative both from the point of view of the observer and from the perspective of the person involved in the life transition.

Like developmental theorists, historians write about change and transitions without defining what a transition *is*. As a working hypothesis, I would like to suggest that the redefinition I have proposed might apply to historical transitions. That is, historical transitions may be said to have occurred when a significant proportion of the population undergoes change in their sense of themselves, in their assumptive worlds, in their approach to solving problems, in the organization of their central roles, and in the structure of their relationships. Simple changes in the demographics of households, school attendance, or marriage patterns, would constitute insufficient evidence of a historical transition in the organization of family life. Like life events, these data are markers of *potential* historical transitions, but they must be supplemented by information about change in the worlds of the individuals and families being studied (cf. Elder's classic account of the impact of the Great Depression on family life and individual development, [1974]).

CONCLUSIONS

We need longitudinal comparative studies of normative and nonnormative transitions at different points in the lifespan, to test the usefulness of defining transition as a *structural* change in inner life (shifts in the psychological sense of self, world-view, and affect regulation) and in the interpersonal world (role reorganization, personal competence, interpersonal relationships, and the management of emotions in relationships with others). Measurements at closely spaced intervals will be necessary to describe the unfolding *process* of transitions, and the mechanisms that link pretransition status to posttransition outcomes. Studies of multiple transitions will ultimately help us to describe and understand similarities and differences in the principles governing individual and family transitions at different chronological ages and in different historical circumstances.

In conclusion, I comment briefly on three pieces of unfinished business. First,

I have described the areas that should be assessed in life transitions, but I have not indicated how we know when a transition begins and when it ends. It is clear that not all of the changes in the inner world and observable behavior occur at once, or even within a short period of time. It is also clear that change in one of the domains interacts with change in the others in a circular rather than linear mode of influence. I believe that the mutual influence of one family subsystem on another during a transition is what helps individuals and families define their the subjective experiences of disequilibration. Given the fact that two or more transitions can be simultaneous (fatherhood, job change), overlapping (late adolescence, career choice), or sequential (marriage, parenthood, or vice versa), it would seem difficult to find two periods of stability that a transition is supposed to bridge. My tentative conclusion is that stability and change are relative terms. Life may never seem quiescent, but there are periods in which multidomain change appears to be accelerated and periods in which it slows down. We have tended to let researchers be the sole definers of transition. We need to integrate the views of the subjects we follow longitudinally; their responses to interviews and questionnaires may inform us about how *they* mark off periods of stability and change as they move from the past, through the present, toward the future.

Second, there are interesting issues to be resolved concerning the metaphors that we choose to describe transitions. The prevailing metaphor for transition is adopted from the narrative of the journey or the individual hero's quest. Other metaphors could shed additional light on the meaning of transitional change at the family or social system level. Gottman (this volume) describes concepts from chaos or catastrophe theory (Gleick, 1987) that may help us to understand transitions in and out of family system chaos. The point I make here is not that chaos theory should replace other transition metaphors, but that we must remain open to new and better ways of capturing both the process and structure of family change. Finally, our methods of measuring transitional change have not yet caught up with the concepts and metaphors that we have already developed. We need to find more suitable ways of mapping the pathways traversed by the individuals and families as they pass through multiple transitions in the course of living out the triumphs and tragedies of their lives (see Falk and Miller, this volume, for a description of one new path analytic technique—"soft modeling").

We have a substantial set of tasks ahead of us in the investigation of family transitions that will stretch our minds and tax our endurance. I have suggested that we must follow families over multiple transitions, with large enough samples to support the multivariate complexity of assessing change in self-view, roles and relationships, getting close enough to measure biological function and observe micro-interactions, and back far enough to take societal context and historical time into account. Clearly, these are not tasks that a single researcher can hope to accomplish alone. Perhaps more than other fields, family research must be a collaborative endeavor, in which researchers from different disciplines, attempting to understand different life periods, will bring their perspectives to bear on similar problems. Bringing family adaptation into the spotlight, the special advantages of focusing on transitions, will more than justify the effort of setting ourselves such a difficult and complex task.

ACKNOWLEDGMENT

Preparation of this chapter was supported in part by grants to Philip and Carolyn Cowan from NIMH (R01-MH 31109) and from the Spencer Foundation. Carolyn Cowan's ideas and editorial contributions are evident in every section of this chapter.

REFERENCES

Belsky, J., Lang, M. E., & Rovine, M. (1985). Stability and change in marriage across the transition to parenthood: A second study. *Journal of Marriage and the Family, 47,* 855–865.

Belsky, J., Spanier, G. B., & Rovine, M. (1983). Stability and change in marriage across the transition to parenthood. *Journal of Marriage and Family, 45,* 567–577.

Block, J. H., & Block, J. (1980). The role of ego-control and ego-resiliency in the organization of behavior. In W. A. Collins (Ed.), *Minnesota symposium on child psychology* (Vol. 13). Hillsdale, NJ: Lawrence Erlbaum Associates.

Bogat, G. A., Jones, J. W., & Jason, L. A. (1980). School transitions: Preventive intervention following an elementary school closing. *Journal of community psychology, 8,* 343–352.

Boss, P. (1987). Family stress. In M. B. Sussman & S. K. Steinmetz (Eds.), *Handbook of marriage and family development* (pp. 695–724). New York: Plenum.

Bridges, W. (1980). *Transitions: Making sense of life's changes.* Reading, MA: Addison-Wesley.

Caplan, G. (1964). *Principles of preventive psychiatry.* New York: Basic Books.

Carter, B., & McGoldrick, M. (Eds.). (1988). *The changing family life cycle: A framework for family therapy* (2nd ed.). New York: Gardner.

Caspi, A., & Elder, G. (1989). Emergent family patterns: The intergenerational construction of problem behavior and relationships. In R. Hinde & J. Stevenson-Hinde (Eds.), *Understanding family dynamics.* New York: Oxford University Press.

Clausen, J. A. (1972). The life course of individuals. In M. W. Riley, M. Johnson, & A. Foner (Eds.), *Aging and society* (Vol. 3) New York: Russell Sage Foundation.

Coie, J. D., & Dodge, K. K. (1983). Continuities and changes in children's social status: A five-year longitudinal study. *Merrill-Palmer Quarterly, 29,* 261–282.

Cowan, C. P. (1988). Working with men becoming fathers: The impact of a couples group intervention. In P. Bronstein & C. P. Cowan (Eds.), *Fatherhood today: Men's changing role in the family.* New York: Wiley.

Cowan, C. P., & Cowan, P. A. (1987a). Men's involvement in parenthood: Identifying the antecedents and understanding the barriers. In P. Berman & F. Pedersen (Eds.), *Men's transition to parenthood.* Hillsdale, NJ: Lawrence Erlbaum Associates.

Cowan, C. P., & Cowan, P. A. (1987b). A preventive intervention for couples becoming parents. In C. F. Z. Boukydis (Ed.), *Research on support for parents and infants in the postnatal period.* Norwood, NJ: Ablex.

Cowan, C. P., Cowan, P. A., Heming, G., Garrett, E., Coysh, W. S., Curtis-Boles, H., & Boles, A.

J. (1985). Transitions to parenthood: His, hers, and theirs. *Journal of Family Issues, 6,* 451–481.

Cowan, P. A. (1978). *Piaget: With feeling.* New York: Holt, Rinehart & Winston.

Cowan, P. A. (1988a). Becoming a father: A time of change, an opportunity for development. In P. Bronstein & C. P. Cowan (Eds.), *Fatherhood today: Men's changing role in the family.* New York: Wiley.

Cowan, P. A. (1988b). Developmental psychopathology: A nine-cell map of the territory. In E. Nannis & P. Cowan (Eds.), *Developmental psychopathology and its treatment. New directions for child development* (Number 39, pp. 5–30). San Francisco: Jossey-Bass.

Cowan, P. A., & Cowan, C. P. (1988). Changes in marriage during the transition to parenthood: Must we blame the baby? In G. Y. Michaels & W. A. Goldberg (Eds.), *The transition to parenthood: Current theory and research.* Cambridge, England: Cambridge University Press.

Cowan, P. A., & Cowan, C. P. (1990). Becoming a family: Research and intervention. In I. Sigel & E. Brody (Eds.), *Family research, Vol. I.* Hillsdale, NJ: Lawrence Erlbaum Associates.

Daniels, P., & Weingarten, K. (1982). *Sooner or later: The timing of parenthood in adult lives.* New York: Norton.

Daniels, P. D., & Weingarten, K. (1988). The fatherhood click: The timing of parenthood in men's lives. In P. Bronstein & C. P. Cowan (Eds.), *Fatherhood today: Men's changing role in the family.* New York: Wiley.

Dohrenwend, B. (1979). Stressful life events and psychopathology: Some issues of theory and method. In J. E. Barrett (Ed.), *Stress and mental disorder.* New York: Raven Press.

DSM-III-R (1987). *Diagnostica and statistical manual of mental disorders* (3rd ed. revised). Washington, D.C.: American Psychiatric Association.

Durlak, J. A., & Jason, L. A. (1984). Preventive programs for school-aged children and adolescents. In M. C. Roberts & L. Peterson (Eds.), *Prevention of problems in childhood; Psychological research and application* (pp. 103–132). New York: Wiley.

Eichorn, D. H., Clausen, J. A., Haan, N., Honzik, M. P., & Mussen, P. H. (Eds.) (1981). *Present and past in middle life.* New York: Academic Press.

Elder, G. H., Jr. (1974). *Children of the great depression.* Chicago: University of Chicago Press.

Elder, G. H., Jr., (1978). Family history and the life course. In T. K. Hareven (Ed.), *Transitions: the family and the life course in historical perspective* (pp. 17–64). New York: Academic Press.

Elder, G. H., Jr., Caspi, A., & Burton, L. (1989). Adolescent transitions in developmental perspective: Sociological and historical insights. In M. Gunnar (Eds.), *Minnesota symposium on child psychology* (Vol. 21, pp. 151–179). Hillsdale, NJ: Lawrence Erlbaum Associates.

Emery, R. E., Hetherington, E. M., & Fisher L. (1984). Divorce, children, and social policy. In H. Stevenson & A. Siesal (Eds.), *Social policy and children* (pp. 189–266). Chicago: University of Chicago Press.

Erikson, E. (1950). *Childhood and society.* New York: W. W. Norton.

Erikson, E. (1959). Identity and the life cycle. *Psychological Issues, 1,* 1–171.

Felner, R. D., Farber, S. S., & Primavera, J. (1983). Transitions and stressful life events: A model for primary prevention. In R. D. Felner, L. A. Jason, J. N. Moritsugu, & S. S. Farber (Eds.), *Preventive psychology: Theory, research, and practice.* New York: Pergamon.

Felner, R. D., Ginter, M., & Primavera, J. (1982). Primary prevention during school transitions: Social support and environmental structure. *American Journal of Community Psychology, 10,* 277–290.

Felner, R. D., Terre, L., & Rowlison, R. T. (1984). A life transition framework for understanding marital dissolution and family reorganization. In S. A. Wolchik & P. Karoly (Eds.), *Children of divorce: Perspectives on adjustment* New York: Guilford.

Fisher, K. W. (1983). Developmental levels as periods of discontinuity. In K. W. Fisher (Ed.), *Levels and transitions in children's development. New directions for child development* (No. 21). San Francisco: Jossey-Bass.

Freud, S. (1905/1953). Three essays on the theory of sexuality. In *Standard editions of the complete psychological works of Sigmund Freud* (Vol. 7). London: Hogarth Press.

Freud, S. (1917/1963). Introductory lectures on psychoanalysis, Part III: General theory of neuroses. In *Standard editions of the complete psychological works of Sigmund Freud* (Vol. 16). London: Hogarth Press.

Gleick, J. (1987). *Chaos*. New York: Penguin.

Goode, W. J. (1960). A theory of role strain. *American Sociological Review, 41,* 483–496.

Gottman, J. M., & Krokoff, L. J. (1989). Marital interaction and satisfaction: A longitudinal view. *Journal of Consulting and Clinical Psychology, 57.*

Gottman, J. M., & Levenson, R. W. (1989). The social psychophysiology of marriage. In P. Noller & M. A. Fitzpatrick (Eds.), *Perspectives on marital interaction*. San Diego, CA.: College Hill Press.

Gottman, J. M., & Parker, J. G. (1986). *Conversations of friends: Speculations on affective development*. Cambridge, England: Cambridge University Press.

Gould, R. (1978). *Transformations: Growth and change in adult life*. New York: Simon & Schuster.

Hansen, D., & Johnson, V. (1979). Rethinking family stress theory: Definitional aspects. In W. R. Burr, R. Hill, F. I. Nye, & I. L. Reiss (Eds.), *Contemporary theories about the family: Research-based theories* (Vol. I). New York: Free Press.

Hareven, T. K. (1978). Introduction: The historical study of the life course. In T. K. Hareven (Ed.), *Transitions: The family and the life course in historical perspective* (pp. 1–16). New York: Academic Press.

Havighurst, R. J. (1953). *Human development and education*. New York: Longmans, Green.

Heinicke, C. M., Diskin, S. D., Ramsay-Klee, D. M., & Oates, D. S. (1986). Pre- and postbirth antecedents of 2-year-old attention, capacity for relationships and verbal expressiveness. (1986). *Developmental Psychology, 22,* 777–787.

Heller, K., & Swindle, R. W. (1983). Social networks, social support and coping with stress. In R. D. Felner, L. A. Jason, J. Moritsugu, & S. S. Farber (Eds.), *Preventive psychology: Theory, research, and practice*. New York: Pergamon.

Helson, R., Mitchell, V., & Moane, G. (1984). Personality patterns of adherence and nonadherence to the social clock. *Journal of Personality and Social Psychology, 46,* 1079–1096.

Hetherington, E. M. (1989). Coping with family transitions: Winners, losers, and survivors. *Child Development, 60,* 1–14.

Hetherington, E. M., & Camara, K. A. (1984). Families in transition: The process of dissolution and reconstitution. In R. D. Parke (Ed.), *Review of child development research: The family* (Vol. VII). Chicago: University of Chicago Press.

Hetherington, E. M., Stanley-Hagan, & Anderson, E. R. (1989). Marital transitions: A child's perspective. *American Psychologist, 44,* 303–312.

Hill, R. (Ed.). (1949). *Families under stress*. New York: Harper.

Hill, R., & Mattesich, P. (1979). Family development theory and life-span development. In P. Baltes, (Ed.), *Life-span development and behavior* (Vol. 2). New York: Academic Press.

Hobbs, D. F., Jr. (1968). Transition to parenthood: A replication and an extension. *Journal of Marriage and the Family, 30,* 413–417.

Holmes, T. H., & Rahe, R. H. (1967). The social readjustment rating scale. *Journal of Psychosomatic Research, 22,* 324–331.

Jason, L. A. (1980). Prevention in the schools: Behavioral approaches. In R. H. Price, R. F. Ketterer, B. C. Bader, & J. Monohan (Eds.), *Prevention in mental health: Research, policy and practice* (pp. 109–134). Beverly Hills: Sage.

Johnson, C. L., & Irvin, F. S. (1983). Depressive potentials: Interface between adolescence and midlife. In H. L. Morrison (Ed.), *Children of depressed parents*. New York: Grune & Stratton.

Jung, C. (1964). *Man and his symbols,* New York: Doubleday.

Kessen, W. (1962). "Stage" and "structure" in the study of children. In W. C. Kessen & C. Kuhlman (Eds.), Thought in the young child. *Child Development Monographs, 27,* 65–82.

Kiecolt-Glaser, J., Fisher, L., Ogrocki, P., Stout, J., Speicher, C., & Glaser, R. (1987). Marital quality, marital disruption, and immune function. *Psychosomatic Medicine, 49,* 13–34.

Kitson, G. C., Babri, K. B., Roach, M. J., & Placidi, K. (1989). Adjustment to widowhood and divorce: A review. *Journal of Family Issues, 10,* 5–32.

Klein, D. C., & Ross, A. (1965). Kindergarten entry: A study of role transition. In H. J. Parad (Ed.), *Crisis intervention: Selected readings.* New York: Family Service Association.

Kohlberg, L. (1969). Stage and sequence: The cognitive-developmental approach to socialization. In D. Goslin (Ed.), *Handbook of socialization theory and research.* Chicago: University of Chicago Press.

Kumar, R., & Robson, K. M. (1984). A prospective study of emotional disorders in childbearing women. *British Journal of Psychiatry. 144,* 35–47.

Lazarus, R., & Folkman, S. (1984). *Stress, appraisal, and coping.* New York: Springer.

LeMasters, E. E. (1957). Parenthood as crisis. *Marriage and Family Living, 19,* 352–355.

Levinson, D. J. (1978). *The seasons of a man's life,* New York: A. A. Knopf.

Levenson, R. W., & Gottman, J. G. (1983). Marital interaction: Physiological linkage and affective exchange. *Journal of Personality and Social Psychology, 45,* 587–597.

Lewis, J. M., Owen, M. T., & Cox, M. J. (1988). The transition to parenthood: III. Incorporation of the child into the family. *Family Process, 27,* 411–421.

Liem, R., & Liem, J. H. (in press). The psychological effects of unemployment on workers and their families. In D. Dooley & R. Catalano (Eds.), *Journal of Social Issues.*

Lindemann, E. (1956). The meaning of crisis in individual and family living. *Teachers College Record, 57,* 310–315.

Lindemann, E. (1979). *Beyond grief: Studies in crisis intervention.* New York: Jason Aronson.

Lowenthal, M. F., Thurner, M., & Chiriboga, D. (1976). *Four stages of life,* San Francisco: Jossey-Bass.

Main, M., & Goldwyn, R. (1984). Predicting rejection of her infant from mother's representation of her own experience: Implications for the abused-abusing intergenerational cycle. *Child Abuse and Neglect, 8,* 203–217.

Matese, F., Shorr, S., & Jason, L. A. (1982). Behavioral and community interventions during transition to parenthood. In A. Jeger & R. Slotnick (Eds.), *Community mental health: A behavioral-ecological perspective.* New York: Plenum.

Mattessich, P., & Hill, R. (1987). Life cycle and family development. In M. B. Sussman & S. K. Steinmetz (Eds.), *Handbook of marriage and family development* (pp. 695–724). New York: Plenum.

McCubbin, H. I., & McCubbin, M. A. (1988). Typologies of resilient families; Emerging roles of social class and ethnicity. *Family Relations, 37,* 247–256.

Moos, R. H., & Schaefer, J. E. (1986). Life transitions and crises. In R. H. Moos (Ed.), *Coping with life crises: An integrated approach.* New York: Plenum.

Neugarten, B. L. (1968). Adult personality: Toward a psychology of the life cycle. In B. L. Neugarten (Ed.), *Middle age and aging: A reader in social psychology.* Chicago: University of Chicago Press.

Neugarten, B. L. (1979). Time, age, and the life cycle. *American Journal of Psychiatry, 136,* 887–894.

Osterweis, M., Solomon, F., & Green, M. (Eds.). (1984). *Bereavement: Reactions, consequences, and care.* Washington, D.C.: National Academy Press.

Parke, R. D. (1988). Families in life-span perspective: A multilevel developmental approach. In E. M. Hetherington, R. M. Lerner, & M. Perlmutter (Eds.), *Child development in lifespan development.* Hillsdale, NJ: Lawrence Erlbaum Associates.

Parkes, C. M. (1971). Psycho-social transitions: a field for study. *Social Science and Medicine, 5,* 101–115.

Pearlin, L. (1980). Life strains and psychological distress. In N. J. Smelser & E. E. Erikson (Eds.), *Themes of work and love in adulthood* (pp. 174–192). Cambridge, MA: Harvard University Press.

Piaget, J. (1968/1970). *Structuralism.* New York: Basic Books.

Piaget, J. (T. Brown & K. J. Thampy, trans.) (1985). *The equilibration of cognitive structures: The central problem of intellectual development.* Chicago: University of Chicago Press. (Originally published 1975).

Rapoport, R. (1963). Normal crises, family structure, and mental health. *Family Process, 2,* 68–80.

Reigel, K. F. (1975). Toward a dialectical theory of development. *Human Development, 18,* 50–64.

Reiss, D. (1981). *The family's construction of reality.* Cambridge, MA: Harvard University Press.

Rutter, M. (1987). Psychosocial resilience and protective factors. *American Journal of Orthopsychiatry, 57,* 316–332.

Shereshefsky, P., & Yarrow, L. J. (Eds.). (1973). *Psychological aspects of a first pregnancy and early postnatal adaptation.* New York: Raven Press.

Signell, K. A. (1972). Kindergarten entry: A preventive approach to community mental health. *Community Mental Health Journal, 8,* 60–71.

Turiel, E. (1983). *The development of social knowledge: Morality and convention.* Cambridge, England: Cambridge University Press.

Tyhurst, J. S. (1957). The role of transition states—including disasters—in mental illness. *Symposium on preventive and social psychiatry.* Washington, D.C.: Government Printing Office.

Vaillant, G. (1977). *Adaptation to life.* Boston: Little Brown.

Wallerstein, J., & Kelly, J. (1980). *Surviving the breakup.* New York: Basic Books.

2 Family Transitions, Cycles, and Social Change

Glen H. Elder, Jr.
University of North Carolina at Chapel Hill

Family studies represent an expanding area of lively ideas and empirical work across the social sciences.[1] A central feature of this development appears in the growing prominence of three conceptual distinctions, those of time, process, and context. Out of such work has come a deeper appreciation for the complexity and diversity of family life and change.[2] This chapter explores new ways of thinking about family dynamics in a changing society, with emphasis on transitions.

Transitions are one of the most popular topics of study in the family area. Instead of comparing families at different stages of the family cycle, research questions are now more likely to center on pathways from one stage or state to another, such as the transitions to marriage, divorce, and remarriage (Elder, 1978a; Elder, Caspi, & Burton, 1988; Hareven, 1978). What factors account for their occurrence, timing, and duration? Adaptations to any transition are influenced by life history, by the nature of the event in question, and by its meaning. Studies today extend beyond the single transition and its probabilities to multiple, interlocking events (Hogan & Astone, 1986). Family transitions are also embedded in the course of family life, the individual's life span, and the larger environment.

Transitions within the family serve as a bridge between lives and social change. The significance of this bridge stems in large measure from a notable

[1]A useful collection of such work has just been published in the *Journal of Family History*, Summer, 1987, Issues 3–4.

[2]See Elder (1981) on "History and the Family: The Discovery of Complexity" and Hareven's *Family Time and Industrial Time* (1982).

convergence in social science between the study of life-span development and the study of social change (Riley, 1985). We now realize that neither the individual nor social change can be understood fully apart from the other. Moreover, their interconnections are played out most completely within the family.

What can be learned by studying family transitions? Three answers seem especially compelling. First, we learn much about social accommodation because transitions pull people apart from situations. In doing so, they provide insight into family process and adaptation. Second, transitions enable us to observe processes of family growth and breakdown, the formation of relationships and their dissolution (Hetherington, 1979). Third, family transitions represent potential areas of contact between social change and the individual, such as through income losses of families in the 1930s.

I begin the chapter with some ways of thinking about family development and then turn to the task of relating family patterns to social change. The first way of thinking involves the question of event occurrence. Research projects still ask little more than whether a particular event ever occurred. We argue that other distinctions are needed to specify the meaning of family change. For example, transitions vary in duration, as seen in protracted separations of husband and wife and sudden breaks. Timing and sequence are other distinctions that are now commonplace in life course studies. For the most part, these concepts are most effectively put to work in various combinations.

I conclude the section by giving more thought to process models that specify multiple choice points and phases. An example is the multiphase model of divorce. In William Goode's pioneering study (1956), the divorce process is marked by phases of disenchantment, consideration of divorce, and adjustments within the framework of marriage, separation, and postdivorce adaptations. The transition from one phase to another typically involves a different set of causal factors. Few studies ask why particular transitions are relevant to certain outcomes, and yet this approach, as we note, is the most effective option for expanding current understanding of the implications of family change within the life course and social history.

FAMILY TRANSITIONS IN PERSPECTIVE

Temporal views of the family include both the long duration of a trajectory and the short span of a transition. Lives and families evolve over an extended time span, a trajectory of work, marriage or parenting; and they evolve through entry into and exit from a particular state, such as that of the widow or divorcée. Transitions of this kind are elements of family trajectories and acquire meaning from them. Part of this meaning also depends on where the transition occurs within a trajectory. Contrast, for example, the early and old age death of a mother and father.

Ordinarily, family transitions refer to changes in state that are publicly known or recognized—they have social meaning or significance. In a cultural sense, rites of passage ensure that transitions are a public or shared fact. However, a good many private events within the family setting never enter the public domain owing to diligent efforts to preserve family standing. Thus, a teenage daughter's pregnancy might be denied public recognition by her family's decision to send her to another city for the remainder of the pregnancy. Over time, such private transitions or secrets can become known and thereby change the status of individuals and families. Adopted children who discover their status in adulthood illustrate a process that alters relationships, status, and identities.

From the 1960s to the present, transition studies have become a useful way to investigate the life course. At time of publication in 1972, *Aging and Society* (Riley, Johnson, & Foner, 1972) represented the most comprehensive statement on the life course. Clausen's chapter in the volume (1972) brought together a diverse body of literature which generally describes multiple "ways in which age gives patterning to the life span and to the sequence of roles, relationships, and activities that make up the life course." He refers to the "largely unintegrated" empirical facts and concludes that our best chance for a theoretical advance is likely to be found among "types of role transitions in different kinds of social settings" (p. 512). At the time, Glaser and Strauss (1971) made this forecast look promising with publication of a formal theory of status passages in general.

A decade after *Aging and Society,* three new monographs symbolized a new look at family transitions in a changing society: Hogan's *Transitions and Social Change* (1981), Entwisle and Doering's *The First Birth* (1981), and Hareven's *Family Time and Industrial Time* (1982). Using survey data on a nationwide sample of American men, Hogan examines the patterning of events in the transition to adulthood across successive cohorts, giving particular emphasis to their order and disorder. With multiwave data on a longitudinal sample, Entwisle and Doering assess the process by which a first birth influences each parent and their marital relationship. Hareven's ambitious project investigates the impact of industrial growth and decline in the textile community of Manchester, New Hampshire (circa 1900–1934) on workers and their families. This study actually links family transitions and historical change.

These and other studies must necessarily begin with the question of whether a specified event or transition has been experienced. Occurrence represents the *first* and most basic property of a transition. In family surveys, we collect this information by merely asking the respondent whether they ever married, had a child, or divorced. Clearly, some potentially important facts are ignored by focusing solely on the occurrence of an event. In the case of divorce, we do not know how long the person has been divorced, whether it was the first or second divorce, or whether the event occurred immediately after marriage or many years later. No information is collected on the context of the divorce, economic or otherwise. Despite this incomplete account, a number of studies continue to rely on it.

A prominent example of this empirical tradition is known as the Social Readjustment Rating Scale of Holmes and Rahe (1967). Up to the 1980s, over a thousand studies (Dohrenwend & Dohrenwend, 1983) used this scale of life change in research. The 43 life events making up the inventory are known to have different frequency distributions by age (Brim & Ryff, 1980). Some are concentrated in the early years of adulthood, such as loss of job and divorce, while others typically occur over the last quarter of the life span—deaths, for example. Distributional variations of this kind mean that identical scores from the inventory can result from markedly different life changes for men and women across stages of the life span.

Such differences raise many questions about what the scores mean. Other questions are raised by the scoring procedure. Holmes and Rahe weight the life events according to social adjustment requirements and they sum the scores to provide a life change value. By using a single array of weights for the events, they assume that marriage, divorce, widowhood, and unemployment all have invariant meaning across the life span. The empirical literature solidly refutes this premise as we make clear in the remainder of the chapter.

Duration and Timing

Family transitions take place over time and thus lead to matters of duration, a second conceptual distinction. Duration has special relevance for understanding family separations and resulting adaptations. The more abrupt the departure, the less adequate the anticipatory adjustment (cf. Cottrell, 1942), and the greater the risk of prolonged and maladaptive responses to the loss.

When a separation takes place over a long span, family members have more time to work through the painful reality before the separation actually occurs, such as the death of a family member. The severity of this event has much to do with its lack of conformity to age norms and suddenness. Drawing on a large sample of cases, Ronald Knapp (1986) observes that "child death, from any cause and under any circumstances, is so inappropriate, unnatural, and unacceptable in our modern society that it often is not fully comprehended. This is particularly true where the death is sudden and unexpected" (p. 31).

Duration also tells us something about transitions when we use it to refer to "time in state." The duration of marriage is linked to marital permanence, and residential duration predicts residential permanence. Likewise, as one's life as a single person increases, prospects for marriage decrease. In statistical terms, we speak of transitions, whether entry or exit, as duration dependent. The probability of a change in state depends on one's duration. But what is the behavioral meaning of a short or long duration? What is taking place? Pressures for socialization and conformity may be involved, as well as deepening social attachments, commitments, and widely recognized identities.[3]

A third conceptual distinction on family transitions concerns timing and its relation to the social meanings of age. Age expectations define appropriate times for major life events and transitions: there is an appropriate age for leaving home, for marriage and bearing children, for the postparental years, retirement, and old age. Violation of age norms has its consequences. Thus, while the death of a loved one is painful at any age (Knapp, 1986), it is most traumatic when the loss involves a young child with a full life to live. Across the life span, a general awareness of timely and untimely transitions is maintained through shared understandings, rationales, and informal sanctions.

Timing refers to both a stage of the life course and to variations within a life stage. From a conventional perspective, we know that most first marriages occur during young adulthood. This stage represents the appropriate time for marriage, but even within the stage we can speak of men and women who marry early or late relative to the marriage distribution. What are the consequences of marriage relatively early or late? One consequence for women is suggested by the marriage market and mating options.

From those marrying early to late brides, women's conjugal decisions are made in an ever-shrinking marriage market. The field of age-eligible men becomes more restricted. Coupled with this change is the educational gain of women who marry late. From these observations, one might expect late brides to marry younger men who have less education, in contrast to those who marry relatively early. The latter would be more apt to marry older men who are better educated than they are. Empirical support for these patterns comes from a cohort of women who grew up in the San Francisco Bay area (Elder, 1974) and from a nationwide cohort of American women (Elder & Rockwell, 1976). Both samples of women have birth years in the 1920s.

The variable timing of marriage introduces the problem of career options and synchronization. Early marriage is marked typically by an economic squeeze, owing in part to the young age of the husband and his lack of work skills, whereas late marriage generally brings an economic advantage. Among women born in the 1920s, early marriage (before age 19) anticipated a life course of relative deprivation for women—limited formal education, marriage into the lower strata, a heavy child-care burden, and inadequate material resources. The young wives were more likely than other women to combine family and employment, a double track. Even when similar on education, those marrying late were more likely to expand their range of social opportunities and contacts

[3]Some durations in state are socially expected (Merton, 1984). Depending on the culture, waiting times for marriage are socially patterned, such as the announced intent to marry and the wedding itself.

through marriage to successful men. Compared with other women, the older brides occupied a position of economic advantage at time of marriage and in 1970. Whether high or low in education, these women most often followed a conventional pattern in which they remained employed only up to marriage or their first birth.

These contrasts provide a number of reasons as to why marriage timing matters to women and the family. From the perspective of middle age, women in the large cohort tended to endorse a timing schedule which seemed neither too late nor too early (Elder & Rockwell, 1976). Those marrying younger voted overwhelmingly for a later marriage in the lives of daughters, and for a childbearing pattern that is on time. "In the minds of all women in the cohort, there is clearly an optimal time for marriage and children, a time which frequently differs from the life schedule they followed" (p. 51). Since completion of this research, studies of parenthood timing (Cox, 1985; Marini, 1984) add greater significance to the life course implications of such timing.

One of the more significant issues on family timing concerns the age difference between women and their children. The later the first birth, the larger the age gap between mother and child. This difference has increasing implications as larger number of women postpone their first birth, including the probability that its meaning and correlates vary across the life course. An age difference of 35 or 40 years between mother and infant may have positive value through the mother's maturity and yet in 20 or 30 years become a source of intergenerational estrangement (Rossi, 1980). The older mother would be nearing retirement age when her daughter reaches the age of majority.

The social timing of family transitions represents the most important of conceptual distinctions in our discussion up this point, and it is one of the more innovative conceptual features of the monographic studies by Entwisle and Doering (1981), Hareven (1982), and Hogan (1981). Hogan analyzes the differential timing of life events in the transition to adulthood, Entwisle and Doering focus on the timing of parenthood within a specific historical context, and Hareven vividly shows that industrial change had different consequences for textile workers of differing age in Manchester, New Hampshire (circa, 1900–1930). Across these studies, all evidence suggests that "the timing of an event may be as consequential for life experience as whether the event occurs and the degree or type of change" (Elder, 1978a, p. 21). Moreover, timed or dated events can be ordered as well.

Timing and Sequence

The order of events represents a familiar perspective on the family and lives. In life histories, for example, events or transitions are typically arranged in chronological order. The notion of career or career line also presents a chronology of experience, whether of marriage, parenthood, or work. A career line of work is marked by entry and exit points relative to jobs and employers. Perhaps the most common sequence model for studies of the family is known as the family cycle (Elder, 1978a; Hill, 1970). This cycle refers to a set of ordered stages which are defined primarily by variations in family composition and size.

Major points of change include marriage, the birth of the first and last child, age-graded transitions in the lives of dependent offspring (such as entrance into grade school), departure of the eldest and youngest children from the parental home, withdrawal of one or both parents from the labor force, and marital dissolution through the death of one spouse. The expansion phase, which ends with birth of the last child, is followed by a period of stability up to the departure of the last child and the last phase of contraction.

As readily noted, the common theme across the family stages is that of a timetable of parenthood—before children, the active phase of parenting, the departure of children, and the empty nest. Moreover, the stages follow a preferred script of a marriage that bears children and survives to old age, an increasingly rare specimen in contemporary society. Stages of parenthood today are becoming less connected to marriage through high rates of birth and marital dissolution. In addition, the launching of older children has become a more transitory operation in the marketplace of young adult initiatives. Competitive pressures and failures in marriage and work can and frequently do lead back to the parental household, producing multigenerational households. Family diversity has replaced the preferred scripts of the family cycle as a representation of family life over the life course.

Life histories, careers, and the family cycle arrange events and transitions in order without attention to their duration and timing or temporal location. In their analysis of event disorder and the transition to parenthood, Rindfuss, Swicegood, and Rosenfeld (1987) conclude that "understanding the nature and importance of sequence in the life course requires analyzing what the roles themselves mean and how they are causally linked" (p. 27). This meaning derives in large part from knowledge of the duration and timing of events. For example, a series of marriages becomes interesting when we learn that a first marriage lasted nearly 25 years for one person and only 2 years for the other individual.

Differences in duration can and do alter the implications of a sequence. In the case of parenting, we know that the childbearing span determines in part the implications of being a parent and of being a second child. A rapid sequence of births produces a very different family dynamic in terms of demands and pressures from that of widely dispersed births. But we also need to know the mother's life stage in order to make sense of a birth sequence. A rapid sequence has more severe implications for the young mother than for a mother 10 or 15 years older.

The sequential perspective of the family cycle offers little for analysis of family transitions, since it orders stages or states and typically neglects their duration and the timing of entry and exit in a person's life. Couples who eventually have children are marched through the stages without noting their ages at marriage and child births. With sharply different ages at first marriage or cohabitation, marital pairs experience each stage at a different age in life. The range of ages at first birth for American women, which extends from sexual maturity to age 40 or so, identifies qualitatively different stages of parenthood defined by parent's age. The specifics of timing thus have critical significance if we are to examine the interplay between family experience and individual development. Each stage of the family cycle derives meaning from the life histories and developmental status of the parents.

The Family Cycle and Interdependent Transitions

Models of the family cycle, as stages of parenthood, became popular in the postwar era of family studies, a time when static models prevailed over dynamic models in the social sciences and when families seemed to follow a well-trod path from marriage to the empty nest and old age. Questions today center more on the dynamics of family life than on stages, and contend with unparalleled diversity in family patterns. Nearly half of the White children born during the 1970s are not likely to attain their 18th birthday in a household with their two parents, and the percentage is approximately 80% for Black children (Hofferth, 1985). A conventional sequence of family stages may fit the world that was, but it has little use on the contemporary scene.

Even so, the family cycle does help to place family transitions in an intergenerational context, the evolving relations between successive generations and the process by which one generation is replaced by another. Any model of parenthood stages depicts a process of generational replacement. In an age of lengthening lives, this process involves up to four or five generations and defines a family system with interlocking cycles (Hagestad, 1982). The four-generational system links child and parent, the parent and grandparent, and the grandparent and great-grandparent. The concept of interlocking cycles links transitions among members of different generations and underscores the more general pattern of interdependence in families and lives.

The challenge in assessing the influence of any transition is to determine its consequences amidst other transitions. Divorce is a prime example, since it frequently involves multiple transitions—in residence, income, and marital status, along with changes in kin relations. When children live with mother after a divorce, they may experience a drop of 50% or more in living standard, a residential change to less desirable housing, a marked reduction in contact with father, and a change in grandparent contacts. Owing to the usual custody pattern, ties are likely to become stronger between children and their maternal grandparents. Contacts generally weaken with the paternal grandparents (Cherlin & Furstenberg, 1986). The influence of divorce on children, then, involves an understanding of these initiated transitions as well.

How might one proceed in assessing the implications of divorce for parents and children when so many correlated events are part of the picture? The most important step is to unpack the life changes according to a model of divorce, its consequences, and related coping adaptations. Divorce entails a variable change in family income, and both factors establish the survival and recovery terms of the new situation. The sexual and material deprivations associated with divorce might be resolved through remarriage or through a combination of male friends and economic adaptations—cutting back on expenditures and efforts to generate more income through loans and employment.

One of the clearest cases of interlocking transitions across the generations comes from a study of 41 female lineages among Black families in Los Angeles (Burton, 1985; Burton & Bengtson, 1985). The purpose of the study is to assess the effects of early parenthood from one generation to the next. The young daughter becomes a parent, her mother becomes a grandparent, and her grandmother becomes a great-grandmother. This ripple effect has deprivational implications when the birth occurs in early adolescence across two successive generations instead of during the usual ages of parenthood. The infant of a 14-year-old mother may have a 28-year-old grandmother.

An early birth to the teenage daughter of a young mother creates a disparity between age and kinship status, in particular, between being young in age and facing the prospects of grandparental status. As a 31-year-old grandmother observed: "I'm just too young to be a grandmother. That's something for old folks, not for me." Four out of five of the mothers of young mothers actually refused to accept their new obligations as a grandmother. Their refusal shifted the grandmother burden in child care up the generational ladder to the great-grandmother who in many cases was carrying a heavy load. By comparison, the women who became grandmothers in their late 40s or so were eager for the new role. In this lineage, a timely transition to motherhood by the daughter meant a timely transition to grandmotherhood by her mother. Timely and untimely parental events have ripple effects across the generations.

Family transitions across the life span are undoubtedly linked together in ways that are only vaguely understood at this time. Consider, for example, the link between family formation and old age. Historically, traditional thinking about family size centered around the social and material needs of old age. Children were needed to ensure a viable old age. Using data from the Retirement History Study, Angela O'Rand (1982) found that women's delayed and interrupted work patterns, resulting in part from family obligations, generally delayed their retirement, depressed their retirement income levels, and limited options for retirement income. Among unmarried women in the later years, childbearing delayed retirement, even with adjustments for work history, pension status, and health characteristics.

Transitions as a Social Process

Issues of timing, order, and duration are part of a dynamic view of family transitions, but what are the properties of this evolving process? One way to answer this question is to focus on a specific transition project, such as Frank Furstenberg's (1976) longitudinal study of unwed parenthood among Black teenagers in Baltimore. Consistent with the general literature on family events at the time, the event of unwed motherhood was typically portrayed as a sharp transition from one status to another. Analysts sought an answer as to why some teenage girls had a child out of wedlock and others did not. The research task centered on specific *kinds of people* and not on their life histories and settings.

Challenging this static account, Furstenberg, along with others (Rains, 1971), showed that an illegitimate birth is part of a multiphase career marked by a sequence of choice points. At each stage young women have the option of premarital sex or not, contraception or not, abortion or not, and marriage or not. Only a handful of possible pathways lead to an illegitimate birth. After the young girls become mothers, they face a number of other decisions, such as whether to ask for their own mothers' help in child care or to put the child up for adoption, to marry or remain single, to have more births out of wedlock, to pursue educational advancement and employment possibilities, or to enter into the welfare system. In Furstenberg's formulation, the influence of an illegitimate birth varies according to options chosen. Some options blend well together in favoring promising outcomes, such as mother's help, return for more schooling, and effective birth control.

Employment increased prospects for a better life, but the young Baltimore mothers entered the labor market with a substantial handicap in education and experience. They were younger than their competitors and a good many had not completed their high school education. They suffered labor market discrimination against women, and because most were Black, they also faced racial discrimination. The jobs they obtained often did not even cover the expenses of child care and maintenance of a family.

The availability of mother's child care made a big difference under these circumstances, for it enabled the young mother to finish school and achieve reasonable earnings. Additional births typically ruled out this path of recovery. From all of these choice points and pathways, we see that persistent economic dependency turned not on the event of an illegitimate birth but instead on which of several pathways (see Fig. 2.1) the young mothers followed across the life course.

Figure 2.1 presents the life course of unwed motherhood as sketched from Furstenberg's study. Each point of decision occurs at a different stage in the young female's career and each requires a different explanation. Consider, for example, initiation of sexual intercourse versus the decision to abstain. Hofferth (1987a, p. 11) outlines a model of sexual activity that shows the interplay between biological and social factors. The biological process of physical development includes physical capacities, such as motor skills, hormonally linked sex motivation, and physical maturation. The psychosocial component stresses family and peer influences.

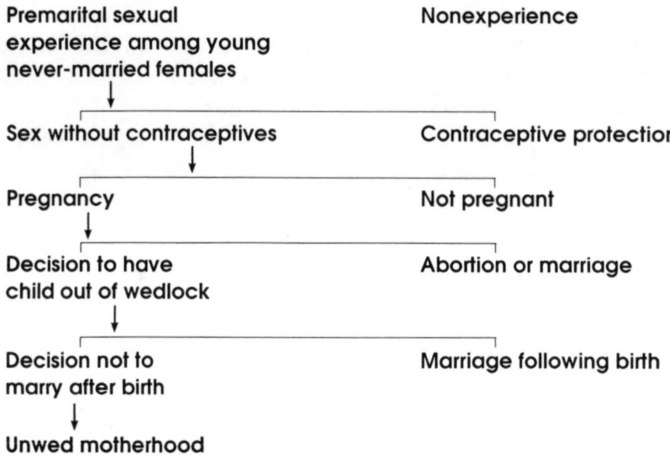

FIG. 2.1. The life course of unwed motherhood.

In a following chapter on contraceptive decision making among adolescents, Hofferth (1987b) presents a summary of the literature which is organized around proximate determinants: frequency of intercourse, perceived probability of pregnancy, willingness to use abortion as back-up if pregnancy occurs, and both positive and negative consequences of pregnancy and contraception. In a subsequent essay, Hofferth (1987c) focuses on the next step in the decision-making tree, pregnant versus not pregnant, and concludes with an overview of the decision points, their respective explanatory processes, and implications for intervention.

> . . . in order to become a teen mother, a young woman must first become sexually active, next, not use contraception or fail in its use in some way (including experiencing method failure), and finally, once pregnant, decide to bear and raise the child herself. There are several points at which alternatives present themselves. Some teens choose one way, others choose another. Thus the agency has several possible points at which to target its interventions: at initiation of sexual activity, at contraception use, or, at the resolution of a pregnancy. (p. 78)

The significance of this multiphase model of the life course is readily noted for research, theory, and intervention by returning to a time when we thought of unwed motherhood as an event undifferentiated by time and ordered choice points. This simplistic view promoted misunderstandings and ensured failure among intervention efforts. Behavioral scientists did not begin to make progress in this field until their problem statements were informed by a process model, as outlined by Hofferth.

Some research benefits of a dynamic model are suggested by a follow-up of the Baltimore teen mothers in their mid-30s (Furstenberg, Brooks-Gunn, & Morgan, 1987). At the time, the children of the teen mothers were approaching adolescence. Contrary to the usual predictions, a disadvantaged life course was not a certain outcome among the young mothers. Education provided the most viable escape route, as forecast many years earlier. The young mothers who managed to complete high school were half as likely to be receiving public assistance and twice as likely to be economically secure in adulthood. Fertility control defined another important adaptation. Women who did not have more children after the birth of their first child were three and a half times more likely to be economically secure in 1984.

Fertility control enabled the young women to continue their education, obtain a full-time job, and marry. Those who married were more likely than other women to achieve economic security. By adapting to teenage motherhood in various ways, the teen mothers constructed life courses with varying prospects.

One of the most pioneering aspects of this study is its effort to connect the mother's life course with their children's lives. Overall, the teenage mothers' decisions and choices strongly influenced the environment in which their children were raised, and the costs of teenage parenthood were often reproduced in the lives of their offspring. For example, the children of these parents displayed more symptoms of maladjustment than did adolescents whose mothers were older when they had their first child. The consequences of additional births clearly damaged the developmental prospects of the children. The more additional births, the higher the risk of long-term developmental impairment. By their early adolescence, a number of the daughters of the teenage mothers were sexually active and at substantial risk of a pregnancy in adolescence.

The Baltimore study illustrates a process by which transitions to unmarried parenthood are linked across the generations. In both generations, the transition represents a multiphase process of decision making (Elder, 1978a). This means that in childbearing, each birth occurs in a different context and is thus influenced by a different set of conditions. A child's birth order is linked to parental skill and attitudes, socioeconomic conditions, work-life prospects, and consumption priorities. Consequently, the assumption that couples make a fixed decision about how many children to have at the time of marriage is largely fiction. Rather, the decision process involves multiple decisions, each one dealing with "the addition of a (another) child to the family" (Namboodiri, 1972, p. 198). For example, White and Kim (1987) found that the wife's career success becomes a more powerful constraint on childbearing across successive parities, but especially in discouraging a second child.

Increasingly, studies show that processes of entry and exit vary among social roles over the life course (see Goldscheider & Waite, [1986] on marriage; Sørensen [1983] on women's employment). Among married women, husband's occupational status is a more important source of attitudes across the childbearing and child-rearing years than their own education (Clausen & Gilens, 1990). Educational level becomes more influential during the later years, once family pressures decline.

This evolving picture of different processes by life stage clearly favors analytic techniques for modeling transitions and variant causal sequences (cf. Tuma & Hannan, 1984). At this point we do not know which antecedents or outcomes of family transitions are invariant across the life span and which are variable. Indeed, we are merely beginning to understand the social dynamics of families and lives over the life span. But one message is clear. Family transitions are a social process and should be modeled accordingly. In this respect, the Baltimore study has implications that extend beyond the field of unwed motherhood to other transitions, from marriage to departure of children from the household, retirement, and loss of a spouse.

The Analytic Model and Research Question

Family transitions represent a social process with important temporal and contextual features: an evolving life course and its properties, such as the career of the unwed adolescent mother. By placing the birth of an illegitimate child at the end of a series of choice points, we gain a clearer picture of the paths by which some girls reach this status and others do not. Temporal distinctions matter in a number of respects, especially in terms of marking ages at sexual activity, pregnancy, and child birth, as well as the larger temporal setting of historical time and place. Duration tells how long adolescents spend in each stage and bears on the likelihood of subsequent life changes.

Two sets of research questions largely define the field of family transitions. One focuses on the antecedents of a transition, such as marriage or divorce, and the second type views a specific transition as an antecedent of certain outcomes, social or psychological. In the first category, we find questions about influences on entry into marriage, divorce, and remarriage; the departure and return of grown children; and the addition of aged parents to the household of the eldest child. The second type of question inquires about the consequences of these changes. What are the implications of early or late marriage, the departure of the last child from the household, and retirement? Transition experiences can of course be antecedents and consequences in a particular analysis. Loss of employment may increase the risk of marital breakdown, while the latter increases the risk of ill health.

Frequently, family transitions are concurrent with other transitions. Transition to adolescence often entails changes in family support, associations with peers, educational demands, and physical development (Brooks-Gunn & Petersen, 1983). A Milwaukee study (Simmons & Blyth, 1987) found that developmental risks among adolescents correlated with the rapid cumulation of life events or transitions, including residential change, a parental divorce, the transition from grade school to junior high, and menarche. These risks tend to be greatest for girls who mature early and for boys with a below-average record in academics and athletics. Multiple transitions, as during entry into adolescence, underscore the implications of appropriate timing. The transition to secondary school and its acute heterosexual pressures are ill timed for girls with an accelerated rate of physical maturation.

Whatever the type of question and the complexity of the transition, a statement of the problem for investigation provides a general outline of relations between constructs. An analytic model specifies the full meaning of these constructs and their association—a conceptual map of the principal lines and boundaries for the study. A complete discussion of the model includes a set of theoretical statements that provide rationales or explanations for specific relations among constructs. A model is most helpful when it clarifies the meaning of constructs, sketches out theoretical linkages and central hypotheses, and makes underlying assumptions explicit.

To illustrate this conceptual operation, consider the link between the departure of the youngest son from the home and marital quality. Why do we have reason to believe that this transition has implications for the quality of marital relations? One line of explanatory analysis might focus on an increase in the frequency and quality of shared recreational activity between husband and wife. With no children at home for supervision, meals and clean clothes, husband and wife are more free to establish their own agenda of joint activities. A second line of inquiry might center on the emotional dynamics of a change from triadic to dyadic interaction. A third avenue for exploration involves the effect of the departure on marital privacy. These and other potential linkages come to mind from observation and the literature.

Linkages between the younger child's departure and marital quality would center on the pattern of shared activity, and would provide an account of why the two constructs should be related (Elder, 1973). The same procedure can be followed in tracing the implications of this departure for change in the emotional dynamics of the household and for marital privacy. An explanatory model with linkages of this sort structures measurement and the statistical analysis. Empirical results should enhance knowledge of whether and how the departure of the youngest child influences marital relations.

Instead of starting with the transition and asking about its implications, one might begin with an outcome and work back to various influences, including perhaps a family transition. This latter option was chosen by Menaghan (1984) in a panel study of over 1000 adults from the Chicago area using interviews from 1972 and 1976. Ten transitional experiences were identified and compared on feelings of marital equity and affection–fulfillment. Eight of the experiences included adults with a single transition, such as becoming a parent for the first time, having a later child, seeing the youngest become a teen, and seeing the oldest leave home. The transitional groups were matched as closely as possible with stable adults.

The only significant outcomes involved the youngest child. Menaghan notes the "consistent lack of explanatory power of the transitional variable" in her data and asks "are family transitions in themselves all that important in shaping marital experience?" (p. 382). Many factors, methodological and other, could account for the unpromising results, and Menaghan thoroughly evaluates them in her concluding discussion. But one question remains: Why were the effects concentrated only among adults who experienced changes in the youngest child's status? In particular, why did the departure of the youngest child generally improve feelings of equity in marriage? Menaghan (1984) closes her report with a recommendation for a different kind of study, one that examines the implications of a family transition for family behavior.

> It is now time for researchers to specify more carefully what the key dimensions in these related role areas are and how we expect them to shape one another. By carefully conceptualizing the separable threads currently combined in these categorizations, assessing them independently, and examining their interrelationships, empirical researchers will be in a far stronger position to advance our knowledge about the impact that changes in children's lives may exert on the lives of their parents. (p. 384)

This recommendation calls for research in which transitions become a point of departure (see Elder, 1987b) for explicating their influence on behavior. It is time, as Menaghan puts it, for researchers to identify the basic aspects of transitional experiences and to make clear how and why they are relevant for the behavior in question. Theoretical development is the first order of business. The task is to make sense of the connection among family transitions and relationships or behavior patterns. As a rule, greater understanding of a transition's influence tends to generate a range of potential effects and their linking processes. The model begins with an antecedent transition and branches out toward multiple outcomes.

When the objective is to account for a single outcome, such as maritial stress, family transitions become only one of the potential determinants. Social origins, education, work life, and timing of family events might all be included in the appraisal of determinants. This outcome design is broad in the range of potential antecedents and narrowly focused on a single effect. By limiting her analysis of influences mainly to family transitions, Menaghan does not take full advantage of this design, since other variables are known to be more powerful. She also misses the strong point of the transition perspective by not developing the full conceptual relevance of specific transitions and their linkages for family behavior.

This distinction between types of models plays an important role in accounts of family transitions and historical change. Only by focusing on the conceptual relevance of particular changes for family behavior can we explain the family effects of such change.

LINKING TRANSITIONS AND HISTORICAL CHANGE

Family transitions take place in a changing society, though little is known about whether and how these changes are related. Indeed, attempts to trace family patterns to social change are rare and typically unsatisfying (Tilly, 1987). One explanation for this unhappy state refers to a general failure to extend research to the causal processes linking events and times (Elder, 1987b). What are the connections between an economic collapse and family hardship or between education trends and family structure? Questions of this kind are seldom asked by studies of families and lives.

Over the years family studies have focused on what might be called the interior of family process and individual personality. In sociology, this bias extends across the work of Ernest Burgess, one of the founding figures of this area of study (Elder, 1984, 1985). Instead of placing families in the larger environment of cultural, institutional, and historical forces, Burgess trained his eyes on the interactional dynamics of families and on the "unity of interacting personalities." Other studies relate families to socioeconomic conditions and religion, but much of this work pays no attention to the historical changes taking place. A full-scale approach to these changes in the experience of families establishes a causal link between the macro level of distal forces and the micro level of family life.

Macro-level studies of family transitions in history illustrate important contributions of this approach and major limitations. One of the more important limitations involves a design in which explanatory analysis of specific social changes is subordinated to a description of family events over time. I discuss related problems in the context of specific projects, and then move to a more cross-level approach that begins with a changing environment and explores its implications for family change.

The Macroscopic World of Family Transitions

One of the most dramatic developments among American families in this century involves a change in the timing of transitions, marital and parental (Cherlin, 1981). Much of this change is associated with the "baby boom" over the postwar years. Cohort studies document the shifting pattern of family transitions, but they do so without direct attempts to measure social change. Instead, they present estimates of historical influence in the form of cohort and period effects (Glenn, 1983). The latter refers to a case where social change differentiates the family or life patterns of successive cohorts. Thus, youth experienced the family hardships of the Great Depression in different ways than did adults or younger children (Elder, 1979). A period effect refers to the influence of a change or event that is relatively uniform across successive cohorts. Some of the most prominent family changes in this century are period effects. Examples include first marriage trends, marital dissolution, and the baby boom.

Consider for example the cohort research of Rodgers and Thornton (1985), a comparative study of first marriage rates across cohorts of American men and women in the 20th century. Data were obtained from censuses and sample surveys. World War I, the Great Depression, and World War II influenced marriage rates in dramatic fashion. Both wars preceded an upswing. Downswings occurred in the early years of the Great Depression and in the midst of World War II. From these findings the researchers conclude that "most of the change in marriage rates observed during this century are the consequences of period characteristics" (Rodgers & Thornton, 1985, p. 276), and the same conclusion applies to rates of marital instability across the decades. The precise nature of the period forces is unknown and consequently remains a matter of speculation.

A similar picture emerges from a program of study on the first birth transition among Americans in this century. Using birth cohorts from 1915–1939, Rindfuss, Morgan, and Swicegood (1984) found evidence of strong historical variations that were expressed as cohort and period effects. In particular, a strategy of delayed childbearing appears among American women in two epochs of economic depression and pressure, the 1930s and the 1970s. The latter decade coupled greater employment opportunities for women with soaring housing prices, high inflation, and an active women's rights movement. In the final analysis, the study identifies critical times for historical forces but does not proceed beyond this point to more explanatory research.

These macroscopic studies offer a reconnaissance of the territory which more precisely identifies the temporal and ecological boundaries for research that explicates historical influences on families. Only recently have studies identified the major sources of variations in family events and pinpointed the historical setting for micro-level investigations of precise historical changes.

Over 25 years ago, we began a series of investigations along this line at the Institute of Human Development, University of California at Berkeley. The first part examined the influence of the Great Depression on men and women who were born during the early 1920s and attended school in the city of Oakland, California. The family became the connecting link between the macro event of an economic collapse in society and the life experience of the children. The second part of the project extended our analysis to a younger cohort of men and women who were born just prior to the Great Depression, the Berkeley Guidance Study. Selected comparisons were made between the two cohorts. The third and last phase views war mobilization and experience during World War II and the Korean conflict as influences on the life course and family.

From Macro to Micro

The early years of social science are marked by major events of a rapidly changing society, and thoughts about this change were shaped by Thomas and Znaniecki's *The Polish Peasant in Europe and America* (1918–20), a multivolume study of migration to urban-industrial areas in Poland, Germany, and the

United States. This work and Thomas's other writings outlined a processual view of family and individual experience in changing times, a view that attends to this experience without losing sight of the larger forces and historical vision. The principal aim of *The Polish Peasant* is to explicate the process by which change occurring in a family patterns the lives of its members.

Before work began on *The Polish Peasant,* Thomas (see Elder, 1978b) discussed an approach to the family in crisis situations that offered a fruitful way of viewing the family as a bridge between general social change and individual experience. Crises represent a loss of control over outcomes and arise from a disparity between family expectations or claims and outcomes. In this sense, a crisis involves a "disturbance of habit"; the family loses its balance or equilibrium. Any rupture of the old ways heightens attentional capacities and mobilizes efforts for effective solutions, perhaps leading to a revision of conventional methods of control. Adaptations to the new situation and its demands represent efforts to restore control over life under terms of the new situation.

This perspective seems made to order for making sense out of the ups and downs of family experience during the general economic crisis of the 1930s. Heavy income losses and unemployment placed families in a deprivational situation that called for new ways of living. These experiences were common to members of the Oakland Growth Study at the Institute of Human Development, Berkeley, California. All members of the Oakland project were born in the early 1920s, grew up in the northeastern section of the city of Oakland, and were followed into the middle years through a series of interviews and personality assessments. Over half of the families came from the middle class, and a majority lost more than a third of their 1929 income by the end of 1933. All families with losses below 35% up to 1933, qualified as nondeprived families; deprived families lost more than 34% of their 1929 income. Overall, the theoretical model depicts the family and its adaptations as a link between the general economic decline of the community and the life experience of the child.

With the explanatory focus on socioeconomic change, the study led to a variety of outcomes in the lives of the Oakland children, a branching tree made up of three micro-theories or models on the mediating role of the family. First, the family became more labor intensive—the need for new forms of economic maintenance increased labor-intensive activity in the household and altered the productive roles of family members, shifting responsibilities to mother and older children. Second, family relationships changed in response to father's loss of job and income, with mother becoming more central as a figure of authority and affection. Third, hardship increased social and emotional strain and discord—social ambiguity, conflicts between husband and wife, as well as friction between parents and children.

The study traced all deprivational effects through these modes of family adaptation and change to the experience of the children. Each model represents an account of the process by which drastic income loss made a difference in the lives and transitions of the Oakland children. One of the clearest examples involves the link between the Great Depression and an accelerated passage to the adult years. The Oakland children became more valuable as conditions worsened for their families. They were called on to meet the increased labor and economic needs of deprived households, and a significant number managed tasks in the family or earned money on paid jobs. In most cases, a portion of this money went to family needs.

The adolescents who obtained paid jobs were judged more responsible in financial matters by mother when compared with nonworking adolescents. Such work in the 1930s resembled "odd jobs" in the adult world, from running errands and clerking to waiting on tables, but it carried the significant implication that other people counted on them. Observers considered the employed to be more industrious and energetic than the unemployed. A mother of one of these adolescent workers described him as having "one driving interest after another, usually a practical one" (Elder, 1974, p. 145). With additional responsibilities in the household, these adolescents experienced the obligations of adult status. Indeed, to observers who knew them well, they appeared to be more adult oriented in values, interests, and activities, when compared with other youth.

This accelerated pathway to adult status varied between boys and girls according to their predominant role in the family economy of deprived households. Work roles were more common among boys and tended to enhance their freedom from traditional constraints of parental control. The work pattern among boys extended into the adult years through an early crystallization of their work life and less floundering from one job to another. Moreover, adolescents with paid employment during their Depression years were most likely to favor industry as a quality in their children at midlife when compared with other men.

Girls were primarily involved in household responsibilities, a social adaptation that reinforced family ties and dependency while orienting them to domestic interests and roles in the adult world. As we move to the adult years of the Oakland adolescents, this household change acquired significance as an explanation of why women from hard-pressed families tended to value homemaking, family activity, and responsibility for parenting. When compared with other Oakland women, the household career of deprived women included relatively early family events (marriage, children), especially among those of middle-class origins and a preference for family values at mid-life.

By lowering adult-like responsibilities toward the childhood years, the Great Depression accelerated the passage to adult roles. The same acceleration has been noted among contemporary children in one-parent households and in paid jobs. As Weiss (1979) puts it, children in these households "grow up faster." The contemporary work experience of teenage Americans may have adverse consequences, from premature affluence to less investment in schooling (Greenberger & Steinberg, 1986), but these effects do not appear in our data on the Oakland cohort. A plausible reason for this difference involves the effect of hard times on families; the shift of households from capital to labor intensive made room for the valued contributions of children.

> These children had productive roles to perform. But in a more general sense, they were needed, and, in being needed, they had the chance and responsibility to make a real contribution to the welfare of others. Being needed gives rise to a sense of belonging and place, of being committed to something larger than the self. However onerous the task may be, there is gratification and even personal growth to be gained in being challenged by a real undertaking if it is not excessive or exploitative. (Elder, 1974, p. 291).

Deprivational conditions among Oakland adolescents favored an accelerated pace toward adult status, a pace responsive to the "downward extension of adult-like obligations" in hard times and also produced families that resembled an undermanned environment. An "undermanned" family is one with an excess of tasks relative to able members. Here, young and old have multiple opportunities for work and responsibility. Indeed, in a series of field studies, Barker (1968) found that inhabitants of undermanned settings to be involved in more challenging and consequential actions when compared with occupants of overmanned environments; they are "busier, more vigorous, more versatile, and more oriented vis-à-vis the settings they inhabit, and more interdependent" (p. 190).

We observed this adverse effect of an undermanned family in the life experiences of a younger cohort of Californians who were born just before the Great Depression, 1928–29. In the Berkeley Guidance sample, the economic crisis was magnified by childhood dependence on family nurturance and vulnerability to an unstable family environment (Elder, Caspi, & Downey, 1986; Elder, Caspi, & Van Nguyen, 1986). Among the boys in particular, the economically deprived turned out to be less hopeful, self-directed, and confident about their future when compared with the nondeprived.

This dysphoric outlook is one element of a behavioral syndrome that emerged from personality ratings—personal and social inadequacy, feelings of victimization, and self-defeating behavior. In addition, deprived boys held lower aspirations than children from nondeprived families, and their scholastic performance in adolescence fell well below that of adolescents from nondeprived homes. The disadvantage of growing up deprived continued in adulthood, limiting formal education among the sons of both middle- and working-class parents. Whereas deprivation among older Oakland boys led to greater mobilization of effort and ambition for adult work and family security, the same conditions among the younger Berkeley boys lowered expectations and achievements.

These studies of the Depression's influence extend well beyond the substantive domains we have noted, though all findings support the life stage principle and its implications for the *timeliness* of timing. The principle refers to the differential implications of historical change for people of different ages. The experience of historical change depends on one's location among the life course. In reference to this principle, the Oakland children were too old to be solely dependent on the fortunes of their hard-pressed families in the 1930s, and they were too young to be forced into an unreceptive labor market before the onset of World War II and its mobilization.

Perhaps reflecting this timing, the Depression's legacy of impaired well-being was not generally observed in the adult lives of the Oakland men and women. Concluding the analysis, I noted that "if one were to select an optimum age at which to pass through the Depression decade, it would not differ much from that of the Oakland sample" (Elder, 1974, p. 273). This statement could not be made for the younger Berkeley cohort of boys. Their prospects had much to do with the misfortunes of hard-pressed families, but even in this group Depression hardships were barely in evidence by the 1970s.

What can we say about the discontinuity between childhood misfortune and adult well-being in a large number of cases? How did this occur? As we focused more thought on such matters, our analyses considered turning points. A prominent candidate is that of mobilization into World War II. All of the men, Oakland and Berkeley, passed through this war, and about 90% of the Oakland men actually served. The Berkeley men were teenagers in the war, though approximately 70 served at some point. A turning point refers to a mechanism that enables a redirection of life trajectory, a recasting of life chances (Elder, 1986, 1987a; Elder & Bailey, 1987). Military service qualifies as this kind of recasting experience, particularly when entry came at a formative time in a man's life—immediately after completion of high school.

Early entry into the service, in particular, could extend the transition to adulthood, postpone family events and responsibilities, and provide a route to future opportunities through separation from home, exposure to new places and people, and access to educational benefits. Historically, this route has been linked to self-improvement and greater opportunity. The data show that perceptions of this kind were most common among young men in both cohorts with a history of family hardship through the Depression years, a record of school difficulty, and evidence of self-inadequacy in adolescence. They were most likely to join the service at the earliest possible age.

Military service generally entailed a delay in the timing of marriage and first birth among veterans in both cohorts and especially among the early entrants (less than age 22). By contrast, the late entrants more often encountered the costs of leaving an established family and career. As a whole, the early servicemen tended to follow a less conventional path of adult achievement than the late group in both cohorts. With less education, they did not fare as well on occupational achievement by midlife. However, they frequently acquired more education after military service and narrowed the gap in life achievement relative to the late entrants.

In both cohorts, the "developmental path" seems to apply most notably to the veterans who entered the armed forces at an early age. From the evidence at hand, these men show the greatest development and career achievement when measured from baseline. Military service became a turning point in many cases.

The disadvantaged origins of men who entered the service at an early age do not favor marital stability or occupational achievement, when compared with the life course of men who entered the service at a later time. But in both cohorts the early veterans were more likely to achieve a stable marriage, and their marriages ranked higher on perceived quality when compared with those of the late entrants. Late mobilization increased the risk of marital discord and divorce by separating men from their families. Very few of the early entrants were married when they joined the service. Recent interviews with Oakland and Berkeley veterans who served in World War II and Korea tend to underscore the degree to which late entry fosters marital instability (Elder, 1987a). Separation from loved ones and economic problems were cited far more often by late than by early entrants when they were asked about the costs of their term in the service. Time of mobilization within the life course is a matter of some importance in relation to the family and its transitions.

The differential timetable of the Oakland and Berkeley cohorts tells much about their legacies from the Great Depression and World War II. The Depression crisis drew the Oakland men and women into the service of their households, a social experience with lasting consequences for their adult lives. The enterprise they learned and displayed in the 1930s became a vital resource in their war efforts of the 1940s, on the home front and on the battlefield.

The younger Berkeley boys were impaired by the economic and emotional crises of Depression families, a legacy that had something to do with their attraction to and service in the military. As countervailing influences, the Depression and war dramatically changed the lives of the Berkeley males, more so than any other cohort or group. Though identical in age, the Berkeley girls had little in common with the boys. They were spared the pain of family deprivation by the support of mother and military duty by cultural preference.

As we bring this section to a close, several observations are worth repeating. First, macro studies of families and family transitions perform a valuable function in studies of social change and families by mapping the general territory of historical time. But to understand how specific social changes influence the family, we must shift attention to cross-level connections between macro and micro events or processes. Depression studies of families help to make sense of the marital instability rates of the 1930s by linking drastic income loss to family patterns.

Another point has to do with timing. The link between a specific event and family outcomes depends on the temporal position of the family and its members at the time of change. Are the families headed by older or younger men? Lastly, studies that seek to understand the influence of social change on families must eventually include this change as variables in the model. Speculation is not a worthy alternative. In the words of C. W. Mills (1959), a social science investigation is incomplete until it attends to "problems of biography, of history, and of their intersections within society" (p. 6).

CONCLUSION

No development in family studies over the past 25 years is more striking than the growing prominence of approaches that view families in structured situations and over time. The new social history of the family is part of this movement and so is research on the life course, its trajectories and transitions. Family transitions across the life course represent an especially active field of empirical research, from marriage and parenthood through divorce, remarriage, and widowhood. This chapter identifies some distinctive features of a life course model of family transitions and explores way of linking transitions to social change.

Popularity of transitions as research foci has much to do with the insights they offer about family patterns. In W. I. Thomas's terminology, transitions have something of the character of crises that produce "disturbances on habit." Transitions also entail processes of development and breakdown, such as building a relationship through marriage and its breakdown through separation and formal divorce. Lastly, family transitions represent connections between people and their changing environment.

Duration, timing, and sequence are three distinctions that clarify the social meaning of a family transition. When duration refers to time in a situation, it sheds light on forces that restrict life change. Duration of marriage is linked to marital permanence, and residential duration predicts residential permanence. Timing refers to both a stage of the life course in which a transition occurs and to variations within a stage. The consequences of timing are vividly documented in marriage, early versus late, and parenthood. Sequence or order is expressed in the family cycle, but its stages of parenthood need to be clarified in terms of timing and duration.

Transitions are social processes that require models that adequately represent process. Divorce illustrates this evolving dynamic, beginning with the phase of disenchantment and extending to post-divorce adjustments. Another example is unwed motherhood, a life course punctuated by ordered choice-points and their pathways. An illegitimate birth represents one aspect of a multiphase career. At each point, young women have a choice among options, such as premarital sex or abstention and the use of birth control or not. Different factors influence decision making at each choice point.

Many studies of family transitions conclude without an account of why such changes make a difference in behavior. Some of this work focuses on a particular outcome and looks for relevant antecedent factors. More productive is research that begins with a transition, such as departure of the youngest child from the home. By answering the question of why the transition should matter for family relations, the analyst develops an account of explanatory processes and likely outcomes. The very same design applies in tracing out the implications of historical change for family behavior.

Little is known at present about how family transitions are influenced by social trends and historical forces, and this is owing in large part to the descriptive nature of cohort studies on the macro level. These studies document the shifting pattern of first marriages and births in the United States, but they do so without actually measuring the influence of social change. Instead they provide estimates of unspecified historical factors as in the 1940s or 1950s. More promising alternatives include studies that link macro changes with micro events in the family. Transitions within the family are symptomatic of historical and life-span changes.

REFERENCES

Barker, R. (1968). *Ecological psychology*. Stanford, CA: Stanford University Press.

Brim, O. G., & Ryff, C. (1980). On the properties of life events. In P. B. Baltes & O. G. Brim, Jr. (Eds.), *Life-span development and behavior* (Vol. 3, pp. 368–387). New York: Academic Press.

Brooks-Gunn, J. & Petersen, A. C. (Eds.). (1983). *Girls at puberty*. New York: Plenum.

Burton, L. M. (1985). *Early and on-time grandmotherhood in multigenerational black families*. Unpublished doctoral dissertation, University of Southern California.

Burton, L. M., & Bengtson, V. L. (1985). Black grandmothers: Issues of timing and continuity of roles. In V. L. Bengtson & J. F. Robertson (Eds.), *Grandparenthood* (pp. 61–77). Beverly Hills, CA: Sage.

Cherlin, A. J. (1981). *Marriage, divorce, and remarriage*. Cambridge, MA: Harvard University Press.

Cherlin, A. J., & Furstenberg, F. F., Jr. (1986). *The new American grandparent: A place in the family, a life apart*. New York: Basic Books.

Clausen, J. A. (1972). The life course of individuals. In M. W. Riley, M. Johnson, & A. Foner (Eds.), *Aging and society: A sociology of age stratification*. New York: Russell Sage Foundation.

Clausen, J. A., & Gilens, M. A. (1990). Personality and Labor Force Participation Across the Life Course: A Longitudinal Study of Women's Careers. *Sociological Forum*, in press.

Cottrell, L. S., Jr. (1942). The adjustment of the individual to his age and sex roles. *American Sociological Review*, *7* 617–620.

Cox, M. J. (Ed.). (1985). The transition to parenthood. *Journal of Family Issues*, *6* (December).

Dohrenwend, B. S., & Dohrenwend, B. P. (Eds.). (1983). *Stressful life events and their contexts*. New Brunswick, NJ: Rutgers University Press.

Elder, G. H., Jr. (1973). On linking social structure and personality. *American Behavioral Scientist*, *16*, 785–800.

Elder, G. H., Jr. (1974). *Children of the Great Depression*. Chicago: University of Chicago Press.

Elder, G. H., Jr. (1978a). Family history and the life course. In T. Hareven (Ed.), *Transitions* (pp. 17–64). New York: Academic Press.

Elder, G. H., Jr. (1978b). Approaches to social change and the family. In S. Boocock & J. Demos (Eds.), *Turning points* (pp. 1–38). Chicago: University of Chicago Press. (A Special Supplement to the *American Journal of Sociology*, Vol. 84).

Elder, G. H., Jr. (1979). Historical change in life patterns and personality. In P. Baltes & O. Brim, Jr. (Eds.), *Life-span development and behavior* (Vol. 2, pp. 117–159). New York: Academic Press.

Elder, G. H., Jr. (1981). History and the family: The discovery of complexity. *Journal of Marriage and the Family, 43,* 489–519.

Elder, G. H., Jr. (1984). Families, kin, and the life course: A sociological perspective. In R. Parke (Ed.), *Review of child development research: The family.* Chicago: University of Chicago Press.

Elder, G. H., Jr. (1985). Household, kinship, and the life course: Perspectives on black families and children. In M. Spencer, G. Brookins, & W. Allen (Eds.), *Beginnings: The social and affective development of black children* (pp. 29–43). Hillsdale, NJ: Lawrence Erlbaum Associates.

Elder, G. H., Jr. (1986). Military times and turning points in men's lives. *Developmental Psychology, 22*(2), 233–245.

Elder, G. H., Jr. (1987a). War mobilization and the life course. *Sociological Forum 2*(3), 449–472.

Elder, G. H., Jr. (1987b). Families and lives: Developments in life course studies. *Journal of Family History, 12,* 179–199.

Elder, G. H., Jr., & Bailey, S. (1987). The timing of military service in men's lives. In J. Aldous & O. Klein (Eds.), *Social stress and family development.* New York: Guilford.

Elder, G. H., Jr., Caspi, A., & Burton, L. (1988). Adolescent transitions in developmental perspective: Sociological and historical insights on adolescence. In M. R. Gunnar (Ed.), *Minnesota symposia on child psychology* (Vol. 21). Hillsdale, NJ: Lawrence Erlbaum Associates.

Elder, G. H., Jr., Caspi, A., & Downey, G. (1986). Problem behavior and family relationships: Life course and intergenerational themes. In A. Sørensen, F. Weinert, & L. Sherrod (Eds.), *Human development: Multidisciplinary perspectives* (pp. 293–340). Hillsdale, NJ: Lawrence Erlbaum Associates.

Elder, G. H., Jr., Caspi, A., & Van Nguyen, T. (1986). Resourceful and vulnerable children: Family influences in hard times. In R. Silbereisen & H. Eyferth (Eds.), *Development in context* (pp. 167–86). Berlin: Springer.

Elder, G. H., Jr., & Rockwell, R. (1976). Marital timing in women's life patterns. *Journal of Family History, 1,* 34–53.

Entwisle, D. R., & Doering, S. G. (1981). *The first birth: A family turning point.* Baltimore, MD: Johns Hopkins University Press.

Furstenberg, F., Jr. (1976). *Unplanned parenthood.* New York: Free Press.

Furstenberg, F. F., Jr., Brooks-Gunn, J., & Morgan, P. J. (1987). *Adolescent mothers in later life.* New York: Cambridge University Press.

Glenn, N. (1983). *Cohort analysis.* Beverly Hills, CA: Sage.

Glaser, B. G., & Strauss, A. L. (1971). *A theory of status Passage.* Chicago: Aldine.

Goldscheider, F. K., & Waite, L. J. (1986). Sex differences in the entry into marriage. *American Journal of Sociology, 92,* 91–109.

Goode, W. J. (1956). *After divorce.* Glencoe, IL: Free Press.

Greenberger, E., & Steinberg, L. (1986). *When teenagers work: The psychological and social costs of adolescent employment.* New York: Basic Books.

Hagestad, G. O. (1982). Parent and child: Generations in the family. In I. Field, H. Huston, L. Quay, & G. Finley (Eds.), *Review of human development.* New York: Wiley.

Hareven, T. K. (1982). *Family time and industrial time: The relationship between family and work in a New England industrial community.* New York: Cambridge University Press.

Hareven, T. K. (1978). *Transitions: The family and the life course in historical perspective.* New York: Academic Press.

Hetherington, E. M. (1979). Family interaction and the social, emotional and cognitive development of children after divorce. In T. B. Brazelton & V. C. Vaughn (Eds.), *The family: Setting priorities* (pp. 71–87). New York: Science & Medicine Publishing.

Hetherington, E. M. (1988). Parents, children, and siblings six years after divorce. In R. Hinde & J.

Stephenson-Hinde (Eds.), *Relationships Within Families: Mutual Influences* (pp. 311–331). New York: Oxford University Press.

Hill, R. (1970). *Family development in three generations*. Cambridge, MA: Schenkman.

Hofferth, S. L. (1985). Children's life course: Family structure and living arrangements in cohort perspective. In G. H. Elder, Jr. (Ed.), *Life course dynamics: Trajectories and transitions, 1968–1980* (pp. 75–112). Ithaca, NY: Cornell University Press.

Hofferth, S. L. (1987a). Factors affecting initiation of sexual intercourse. In S. Hofferth & C. Hayes (Eds.), *Risking the future: Adolescent sexuality, pregnancy, and childbearing* (Vol. 2, pp. 7–35). Washington, DC: National Academy Press.

Hofferth, S. L. (1987b). Contraceptive decision-making among adolescents. In S. Hofferth & C. Hayes (Eds.), *Risking the future: Adolescent sexuality, pregnancy, and childbearing* (Vol. 2, pp. 56–77). Washington, DC: National Academy Press.

Hofferth, S. L. (1987c). Teenage pregnancy and its resolution. In S. Hofferth and C. Hayes (Eds.), *Risking the future: Adolescent sexuality, pregnancy, and childbearing* (Vol. 2). Washington, DC: National Academy Press.

Hogan, D. P. (1981). *Transitions and social change*. New York: Academic Press.

Hogan, D. P., & Astone, N. M. (1986). The transition to adulthood. In R. Turner & J. Short (Eds.), *Annual review of sociology* (pp. 109–130). Palo Alto, CA: Annual Review.

Holmes, T. H., & Rahe, R. H. (1967). The social readjustment rating scale. *Journal of Psychosomatic Research, 11,* 213–218.

Knapp, R. J. (1986). *Beyond endurance: When a child dies*. New York: Schocken.

Marini, M. M. (1984). Women's educational attainment and the timing of entry into parenthood. *American Sociological Review, 49,* 491–511.

Menaghan, E. (1984). Marital stress and family transitions: A panel analysis. *Journal of Marriage and the Family, 46,* 371–386.

Merton, R. K. (1984). Socially expected durations: A case study of concept formation in sociology. In W. W. Powell & R. Robbins (Eds.), *Conflict and consensus: A festschrift for Lewis A. Coser* (pp. 262–283). New York: Free Press.

Mills, C. W. (1959). *The sociological imagination*. New York: Oxford University Press.

Namboodiri, N. K. (1972). The integrative potential of a fertility model: An analytical test. *Population Studies, 26,* 465–485.

O'Rand, A. (1982). *The determinants of retirement among older women*. Final Report to the National Institute of Aging.

Rains, P. M. (1971). *Becoming an unwed mother*. Chicago: Aldine.

Riley, M. W. (1985). Age strata in social systems. In R. H. Binstock & E. Shanas (Eds.), *Handbook of aging and the social sciences* (pp. 369–411). New York: Van Nostrand.

Riley, M. W., Johnson, M., & Foner, A. (1972). *Aging and society: A sociology of age stratification*. Beverly Hills, CA: Sage.

Rindfuss, R. R., Morgan, S. P., & Swicegood, C. G. (1984). The transition to motherhood: The intersection of structure and temporal dimension. *American Sociological Review, 49,* 359–372.

Rindfuss, R. R., Swicegood, C. G., & Rosenfeld, R. (1987). Disorder in the life course: How common and does it matter? *American Sociological Review, 52,* 785–801.

Rodgers, W., & Thornton, A. (1985). Changing patterns of first marriage in the United States. *Demography, 22,* 265–279.

Rossi, A. S. (1980). Aging and parenthood in the middle years. In P. Baltes & O. Brim, Jr. (Eds.), *Life-span development and behavior* (Vol. 3, pp. 137–205). New York: Academic Press.

Simmons, R. G., & Blyth, D. A. (1987). *Moving into adolescence: The impact of pubertal change and school context*. New York: Aldine de Guyter.

Sørensen, A. (1983). Women's employment patterns after marriage. *Journal of Marriage and the Family, 45,* 311–321.

Thomas, W. I., & Znaniecki, F. (1918–1920). *The Polish peasant in Europe and America*. Chicago: University of Chicago Press.

Tilly, C. (1987). Family history, social history, and social change. *Journal of Family History, 12*, 319–330.

Tuma, N. B., & Hannan, M. (1984). *Social dynamics: Models and methods*. New York: Academic Press.

Weiss, R. (1979). Growing up a little faster: The experience of growing up in a single-parent household. *Journal of Social Issues, 35*, 97–111.

White, L. K., & Kim, H. (1987). The family-building process: Childbearing choices by parity. *Journal of Marriage and the Family, 49*, 271–279.

3 Family Transitions, Stress, and Health

Jason R. Dura
Janice K. Kiecolt-Glaser
The Ohio State University College of Medicine

Considerable literature has documented the psychological and physiological impact of both acute and chronic stressors on individuals. In contrast, only limited research has addressed the impact of stress on family members' health. It seems reasonable to assume that family transitions could have both positive and negative effects on family members. In this chapter, several negative family transitions that may produce adverse physiological and emotional changes in family members and alter family processes are discussed.

We have chosen to discuss two common kinds of transitions and their sequelae that appear to have untoward mental and physical health effects. Caregiving for an ill family member is the first of these, and marital disruption in the form of discord, separation, divorce, or bereavement follows. Although the actual incidence of each form of transition is not known most families will experience at least one of these transitional events.

Our discussion of physiological data will highlight evidence linking familial stressors and the functioning of the immune system, the body's defense against infectious and malignant disease. We suggest that these data provide some insight into possible mechanisms through which family relationships might influence infectious disease morbidity and perhaps mortality. Family process is assumed to change during transitions both as a function of, and a precursor to, changes in immune function. Behavioral immunological literature and family systems theory are combined in discussions of transitional changes. The major emphasis throughout is the link between the stressful nature of transitions and health.

BEHAVIORAL IMMUNOLOGY

It is important to summarize the conceptual framework that underlies the behavioral immunology research discussed in this chapter, since the model provides the basis for the interpretation and discussion of data. We suggest that an increase in psychological distress, sustained over time, can lead to potentially maladaptive immunological changes. Interactions between the endocrinological and immunological systems provide a physiological pathway through which major and minor life events could lead to an increased incidence of infectious disease; the endocrine system is very responsive to psychological stimuli (Baum, Grunberg, & Singer, 1982), and there are clear endocrinological influences on immunity (O'Dorisio, Wood, & O'Dorisio, 1985).

It is well known, however, that most individuals who undergo major negative life changes do not become ill, or they only experience brief illness episodes. These individual differences in the number of infectious disease episodes are a function of differential exposure to pathogens, as well as the prior health of the individual, especially in regard to immune system function. Thus, across individuals who have equal exposure to an infectious agent like a virus, the probability that they will become ill, as well as the intensity and duration of the illness, is (in part) a product of the status of the individual's immune system. Presumably, the individuals who are most likely to become ill during stressful periods would be those whose immune system is already compromised to some extent, either by an immunosuppressive disease like AIDS, by a natural process like aging that is associated with impaired immune function, or by longer-term immunological changes that may appear in chronically distressed individuals. These kinds of individuals are more likely to have poorer immunological defenses at the onset of a stressful event, so that smaller stress-associated immunological decrements could have more important consequences.

In summary, while many individuals will show stress-related immunological changes in response to a negative life event, actual physical illness is more likely in individuals who are already vulnerable, either because their immune system is already compromised by a natural process like aging, or (more speculatively) through more chronic stress-related alterations. The model suggests that stress modulates endocrine function which leads to altered immune function and greater vulnerability to illness. Literature is reviewed that establishes the stressful nature of the negative transition and, where possible, the link between the transition and health. Within our model changes in transaction patterns between family members are not an endpoint. Instead, these changes collude to produce chronic arousal leading to decrements in immune function and, potentially, health.

CAREGIVING FOR FAMILY MEMBERS

When an individual in a family becomes ill, another family member usually becomes the primary caregiver. If the disease is short-lived, the costs of caregiving are usually limited. However, prolonged illness in a family member may lead to profound changes in interaction patterns, roles, and responsibilities within a family. Moreover, there is evidence suggesting that prolonged caregiving may have adverse physiological and psychological effects. Different facets of the caregiving literature are reviewed, with an emphasis on the association between familial stress and physical and emotional illness.

Chronically Ill Children

There are approximately 10 million chronically ill children in the United States (Perrin, 1985). While there are wide differences in parental caregiving related to differences in illness, there are a number of common issues and fears, and most studies describe parental distress related to the illness and/or their caregiving responsibilities. Caregiving within a family presents the dilemma of focusing disproportionate amounts of family resources on a single member while simultaneously maintaining some sense of equilibrium within the family. For children, a primary goal of development is establishing autonomy. The parent-child conflicts that commonly surround the management of diabetes are used to illustrate the difficulties attendant when chronic illness and needs for autonomy collide. Representative studies illustrating the alterations in family process across a variety of chronic illnesses follow.

The existence of considerable fear and worry in parents of chronically ill children has been documented across diseases. For example, Cosper and Erickson (1985) studied 45 mothers of asthmatic children. Three-quarters of mothers reported worrying about their child's health when separated from their child. Similarly, 60% reported fear of a fatal asthma attack. They found that two-thirds reported intermittent dysphoria and feelings of helplessness related to their child's illness. No differences were found related to time since onset.

Research exploring familial response to cystic fibrosis has produced similar results. Cystic fibrosis is a potentially fatal genetically transmitted endocrine disorder. The course of the disease varies widely; repeated hospitalizations and a need for daily treatment are common. In research exploring the effect of a child's cystic fibrosis on the family, Hymovich and Dillon-Baker (1985) found much of the parents' concern focused on the child's situation, and 64% of parents reported moderate to considerable concern regarding their child's future. Additionally, 30% of mothers and 18% of fathers reported chronic fatigue due to caregiving or worry.

King and Hanson (1986) reviewed research on the impact of juvenile rheumatoid arthritis on families. Chronic worry and anxiety about the illness were common findings, as well as some indications of maternal depression. Other work has addressed the effects on nonimpaired siblings; in a well-designed study of psychosocial functioning in children with both severe and mild forms of rheumatic disease, Billings, Moos, Miller, and Gottlieb (1987) found that the siblings of rheumatic disease patients generally functioned as well as the siblings of healthy children; however, the former did report significantly more allergies and asthma. Related work has suggested that cohesive and expressive family environments are associated with better adaptation among nonimpaired siblings (Daniels, Miller, Billings, & Moos, 1986).

The negative effects of a child's chronic illness also include conflict that may be centered on the management of the illness. Often times normal family conflict engendered by the child's struggle for autonomy with the parent's struggle for control is played out in situations where noncompliance can have life-threatening consequences. Management of diabetes in children serves as a good example, and is characteristically associated with dysphoria and conflict. In a study of mother-daughter interactions and treatment adherence among diabetic adolescents, a common pattern included highly emotional engagement and chronic worry in both mothers and daughters (Bobrow, AvRuskin, & Siller, 1985). Neither mothers or daughters showed much flexibility, and both appeared to use compliance as an arena for attempting coercive control of the other (Bobrow et al., 1985).

The literature on parental caregiving for chronically ill children has supported the stressful nature of caregiving and linked these stressors to alterations in emotional health. However, few published studies have specifically addressed caregiving for a chronically ill child and the parents' or siblings' physical health. One of the ways in which caregiving for chronically ill children may have indirect but significant effects on the family may be through the disruption of family relationships, particularly the marital relationship. Reviewing literature on neurological diseases and the impact on the family, Kerns and Curley (1985) noted that a number of studies have suggested a relationship between marital discord and the presence of a family member with a neurological disease. Later in this chapter we take up the issue of marital discord and its association with poorer emotional and physical health.

Caregiving for a Mentally Ill Family Member

The disruption of family process is not specific to parents caring for medically ill young children. When mental illness occurs in a family it is often associated with major alterations in family life. Mentally ill individuals can display a number of disruptive behaviors, including mood swings, socially inappropriate behavior, paranoia, and apathy. The strains of managing these disruptive behaviors can have significant adverse effects on the family; since 30–50% of mentally ill adults live with their parents (Lefley, 1987), sizable numbers of families are affected.

Parents caring for their mentally ill adult offspring have consistently reported changes in household routine, relationships with friends and relatives, and curtailment of social activities; moreover, the family's focus on the patient may result in neglect of other family members' needs (Lefley, 1987; Smith & Birchwood, 1987). In one study of over 1000 family caregivers, 38% reported their mentally ill relative was assaultive and destructive in their home either sometimes or frequently (Swan & Lavitt, 1986). Parents reported they restricted their own behavior in an attempt to avoid confrontation, and thus their social and recreational activities were concomitantly restricted.

Jacob, Frank, Kupfer, and Carpenter (1987) studied the distress experienced by family members or close friends of individuals who had repeated episodes of major depression. The majority of interviewees reported considerable distress related to the patients' depression, with 43% stating that they personally experienced dysphoric mood as a result. Not surprisingly, individuals living with the patient reported more personal distress than those who lived elsewhere.

In a similar study, Noh and Turner (1987) interviewed 163 spouses and 48 parents who lived with recently discharged patients who had a psychotic diagnosis. They found considerable variability in family members' emotional distress, with the level of caregiver distress showing little relationship to the patients' behavioral problems. A subgroup within the sample was apparent, in which feelings of personal control were low and distress was high; these individuals appeared to be at significantly greater risk for developing psychological problems themselves.

Sainsbury and Grad de Alarcon (1970) studied the effects of community care on the families of elderly psychiatric patients; their sample included multiple psychiatric diagnoses. Using psychiatrists' ratings of the impact of caregiving on family members' physical health, they found substantial negative changes. Similarly, Lefley (1987) used anonymous self-reports to assess family stress and coping strategies in 84 mental health professionals who had a family member with schizophrenia (66%), affective disorder (19%), or an unspecified disorder (16%). Three-quarters of the sample reported emergency contact with treatment service providers, and 73% reported a hospitalization during the most recent year. Family members described the experience as chronically stressful: Psychological problems were reported by 67% of the caregivers, and 72% reported using psychotherapy to assist themselves in coping with their family situation. Similar to the Sainsbury and Grad de Alarcon (1970) data, they noted that 32% of caregivers reported ill health as a consequence of caregiving.

Caregiving for a mentally ill family member differs from caregiving for a chronically ill child in many ways. The nature of the tasks, the caregivers' concerns, and the relationships between caregiver and patient are different. However, extended caregiving in both cases is linked to marital discord, financial concerns, and fears of disease recurrence or progression (Jacob et al., 1987), all factors that could contribute to the observed decrements in emotional health.

Caregiving for a Family Member with Progressive Dementia

In discussing the caregiving literature, we have progressed on a developmental continuum. First parental care of children, then parental care of adult children were reviewed. Now, we come full circle to the case of caregiving in progressive dementia where adult children provide care for aged parents.

The adjustment to aging parents is described as the last developmental task of middle age (Havighurst, 1948). For adult child caregivers this inevitably requires compromises in need satisfaction for both parent and child. Thus, as an adult child works through his or her own aging process he or she is simultaneously faced with the aging process in their parents (Robinson & Thurner, 1979). Privacy and freedom for caregiver and care-receiver are compromised and this loss is a documented stressor (Scharlach, 1987).

The most common progressive dementia is Alzheimer's Disease (AD). The course of the AD is unpredictable and uncontrollable, and deterioration may extend over 20 or more years (Heston, Mastri, Anderson, & White, 1981). The illness culminates in profound cognitive and behavioral changes including disorientation, bowel and bladder incontinence, and an inability to assist in activities of daily living (Reisberg, 1983; Heckler, 1985). Thus, prolonged caregiving for a demented family member may be conceptualized as a chronically stressful situation (Fiore, Becker, & Coppel, 1983). The loss associated with cognitive decline in a family member has been referred to as a "partial death" in which closure is prevented and grieving exists as a chronic state within the family (Woods, Neiderehe, & Fruge, 1985). A recent discussion of care-receiving emphasized how the provision and reception of care alters transactions within a family (Rakowski & Clark, 1985). In this study the provision of care was linked to decreases in quality of future outlook. From a practical perspective, chronic care provision or reception appears to restrict positive future-oriented fantasy. In other words, caregiving may rob a family of the ability to dream of better things, and instead lock the family into a perpetual focus on the present.

Little data is available detailing caregiver and care-receivers interactions. This is especially true during the early stages of dementia when the effects are subtle and the diagnosis remains tentative. Robinson and Thurnher (1979) explored the process transformations from the perspective of the adult child caregiver. They interviewed caregivers of demented and nondemented (frail) parents at baseline, 18 months, and 5 years. Dementia in a parent was linked to negative descriptions of the parent. The transition from positive to more negative attitudes appeared almost exclusively with care for a demented parent. It appeared that the caregivers were unable to attribute negative changes in their parent's behavior to the effects of the disease. Additionally, care provision was described as interfering with caregivers' retirement and financial plans, with frustration a frequent result. One important potential confound that was not discussed in the foregoing study is prior relationship between the parent and the caregiver. The role of history in parent-child interactions cannot be ignored. Finding oneself in the role of caregiver or care-receiver may reactivate previously dormant conflicts (Kuypers & Bengtson, 1983; Norris & Forbes, 1987).

The dilemma adult child caregivers face has been widely heralded as the "sandwich effect," with adult children caught between responsibilities for their own children and aging parents. Yet both adult children and spousal caregivers for a demented family member suffer from the time demands of caregiving. Several studies suggest that they have less time for personal interests and fewer social contacts (Barnes, Raskind, Scott, & Murphy, 1981). Thus, paradoxically, caregivers' needs for interpersonal support are often increasing while their caregiving responsibilities may limit contacts. Moreover, friends may be less willing to visit because of their discomfort in the presence of the demented person, and/or family members' own embarrassment may lead them to curtail contacts with others. Thus, the spouses or adult children who most often serve as AD caregivers may be doubly disadvantaged.

There is good evidence that these chronic stresses associated with caregiving for a demented family member may have significant consequences for caregivers' mental health. Cross-sectional data from several laboratories suggest that the stresses of AD caregiving leave family members at high risk for depression (Crook & Miller, 1985; Eisdorfer, Kennedy, Wisnieski, & Cohen, 1983). In one study of 44 spousal caregivers, 73% either currently met RDC criteria for depression or had met the criteria earlier in the spouse's illness (Fiore et al., 1983). Similarly, 81% of the caregivers in another sample met DSM-III criteria for major depression (Drinka & Smith, 1983).

George and Gwyther (1984) found substantial deterioration in the well-being of caregivers who provided continuous at-home care in two measures taken a year apart. Caregivers reported lower life satisfaction, less time for social activities, and increased levels of stress-related psychiatric symptoms than they had reported a year previously. These data were particularly noteworthy, given the face that baseline measures were already quite low.

While these mental health consequences of caregiving for a demented relative have been well-documented, the health-related consequences of this chronic stressor have not been studied as intensively. George and Gwyther (1984), however, found substantial deterioration in self-rated health measures taken one year apart in caregivers who provided continuous at-home care. Brocklehurst, Morris, Andrews, Richards, and Laycock (1981) studied caregivers of another cognitively impaired population, stroke victims. They found that the number of caregivers self-reporting poor health tripled in the year after they begin caregiving for a stroke patient, while those who reported receiving medical treatment increased from 33% to 40%. Finally, comparisons of 44 primary caregivers of AD patients and 44 matched controls showed that the former reported poorer health, more prescription medication use, and higher utilization of health care than the latter (Haley, Levine, Brown, Berry, & Hughes, 1987).

Researchers have begun to address possible pathways through which caregiving stresses could lead to increased risk for physical illness. Kiecolt-Glaser et al. (1987b) explored the immunologic correlates of caregiving in 34 family caregivers of AD victims; these data were contrasted with a sociodemographically-matched sample of 34 individuals without similar responsibilities. AD family caregivers were more distressed and had significantly poorer immune function across most of a battery of qualitative and quantitative indices of immune function. The data suggest that caregiving may accrue some risk to caregiver's physical and mental well-being.

Commonalities in Caregiving Research

As yet, few attempts have been made to integrate research on caregiving across such diverse populations as chronically ill children, mentally ill adults, and demented elderly. However, in a 2-year study of AD and cancer patient caregiver well-being, Rabins, Fitting, Eastham, and Zabora (1987) found no significant differences between the two caregiver groups. Both caregiver groups showed decreases in anger and anxiety over time, while measures of guilt and depression remained stable. Guilt and negative mood decreased most among those AD caregivers who placed their AD family member in a nursing home during the study.

As was stated earlier, a major goal for family members is differentiation (Minuchin, 1974). Family dysfunction is assumed to be secondary to a lack of differentiation. When a child, spouse, or aged parent becomes ill, the transformation into caregiver and care-receiver requires crossing boundaries of independence. Loss of privacy and freedom are commonly lamented by caregiver and receiver. From a family systems perspective these new roles inherently establish a behavioral, if not emotional, enmeshment (Norris & Forbes, 1987).

Problems with decreased time for oneself, fewer social contacts and increased (yet often unmet) desires for interpersonal support appear to exist as common themes in the various literatures. All of these factors combine to form the concept of "burden," a central theme across the diverse family caregiving literature (George & Gwyther, 1986).

At the simplest level, caregiving burden is measured by dividing burden into objective and subjective realms. Objective burden refers to concrete, observable aspects of the caregiving experience that can be measured quantitatively, including the amount of time spent in caregiving activities, the nature and quantity of caregiving activities, and the nature and frequency of behavior problems manifested by the impaired family member, e.g., wandering or catastrophic reactions (Montgomery, Gonyea, & Hooyman, 1985).

Subjective burden refers to the extent to which family members are distressed by the behaviors of their impaired relative. Not surprisingly, these measures may vary widely across individuals within a family, even when objective burden does not (Montgomery et al., 1985).

In general, the amount of objectively measured burden does not predict caregivers' distress (Noh & Turner, 1987; Zarit, Reever, & Bach-Peterson, 1980). For example, the level of behavioral and cognitive deterioration in the AD victim seems to be only mildly predictive of the level of caregiver distress (Haley,

Levine, Brown, & Bartolucci, in press; Zarit, et al., 1980), and the physical and mental health of caregivers appear to be affected independently of objective dysfunction in the impaired family member.

In contrast, subjectively perceived burden seems to be a much better predictor of distress among caregivers. The predictive power of subjective burden likely exists as a function of its role as a dependent variable, somewhat equivalent to measures of distress. When a caregiver reports a large subjective sense of burden, they may be assumed to be experiencing the sense of burden relative to some internal sense of inability to accommodate the burden. As such, the lack of correspondence between objective burden and distress follows, with the objective level of burden varying independently of coping ability. While there may be some ultimate or absolute limit of objective burden that combines intensive and extended objective caregiving demands, the limits of individual caregivers vary widely across levels of objective burden.

The modest relationships between objective burden and distress may also be due to mediation of objective burden effects by variables such as social support. For example, Fiore et al. (1983) examined social support provided to 44 AD caregivers in an attempt to predict self-reported depression. They found that upsettingness within the social network was the best predictor of self-reported depression in their sample, either because of unhelpful assistance, unmet expectations, or some other variable(s). Similarly, Zarit et al. (1980) found caregivers who received social support in the form of calls and visits from family members felt less burdened than those who did not. Other researchers have reported similar findings.

A further difficulty that arises when attempts are made to measure caregiving burden is that these measures explicitly focus on caregiving per se, and thus cannot be administered to noncaregivers (George & Gwyther, 1986). When very specific burden measures are used, the extent to which the burden experienced by caregivers compares to other life burdens such as high stress occupations, working long hours, and/or existing within an environment with limited social support is unclear.

One method of equating burden across situations involves assessing the extent of interference with desired activities using a standard instrument. The question then becomes how such roles as caregiver, mother, or untenured assistant professor interfere with one's ability to recreate, engage in social activities, pursue vocational interests, or attend to family responsibilities. Previous research has supported the predictive value of this for both individual and family distress with diverse conditions (Dura & Beck, in press).

Finally, research is largely absent that compares caregiving either between types of conditions and/or compares caregivers with a healthy comparison group. Before statements can be made about relative risk, studies of this nature are required.

MARITAL DISRUPTION

The second major category of negative life transitions that we review includes interference with the marital relationship through death, divorce or separation, and discord. A high level of emotional support is expected and frequently forthcoming from marriages in our culture; indeed, many persons list their spouse as their closest confidant (Lee, 1988). The rest of the chapter discusses how negative marital transitions affect emotional well-being, immune function, health, and mortality.

Bereavement

The irreversible loss of a close companion begins a process of grief and extended transition for the surviving spouse. Bereaved individuals are clearly at increased risk for emotional disturbance compared to their nonbereaved community counterparts (Bloom, Asher, & White, 1978). Moreover, these effects may persist several years or more for a significant number of individuals (Zisook & Schuchter, 1985).

Research on spousal bereavement has shown increased morbidity and mortality among survivors (Jacobs & Ostfeld, 1977; Stroebe & Stroebe, 1983; Windholz, Marmar, & Horowitz, 1985). In one of the more striking studies in the literature, Rees and Lutkins (1967) followed a group of 903 survivors (spouses, parents, children, and siblings) for 6 years following the death of their family member. Mortality was seven times greater among survivors than among 878 well-matched comparison subjects in the first year following bereavement. Although not statistically significant, mortality rates for the bereaved subjects were also higher in the second and third years as well.

In an effort to explore possible physiological mediators underlying these differences in morbidity and mortality, several laboratories have assessed immune and endocrine function. In a sample of 56 persons who were acutely bereaved or threatened with a loss, those individuals whose separation anxiety increased over a period of a month after the event had higher urinary free cortisol output than individuals whose grief decreased (Jacobs et al., 1987).

Bartrop and colleagues showed that bereaved spouses had a poorer lymphocyte proliferative response to mitogen stimulation two to six weeks after their spouses' death than nonbereaved comparison subjects (Bartrop, Luckhurst, Lazarus, Kiloh, & Penny, 1977). In a subsequent prospective study of bereavement, men whose wives were dying of breast cancer were assessed before and after their wives' deaths (Schleifer, Keller, Camerino, Thornton, & Stein, 1983). These men had a poorer lymphocyte proliferative response following the death of their spouses, compared to data obtained prior to bereavement. These data suggest that the loss of a spouse can have immunological consequences even when the loss is anticipated, a hardly surprising finding given the psychological sequelae of bereavement described earlier.

Irwin, Daniels, Bloom, Smith and Weiner (1987) examined immune function in three groups: 16 women whose husbands were undergoing treatment for metastatic lung cancer, 10 women whose husbands had died of lung cancer 1 to 6 months prior to their research participation, and 11 women whose husbands were in good health. Multiple samples were collected for each subject. Widows showed the greatest depression and impairments in immune function, consistent with the data from Schleifer et al. (1983).

Although there is good evidence that bereavement is associated with poorer health, there may also be some important differences in spousal health before bereavement. In a survey of 678 elderly residents of Alamada County, California, respondents who reported that their spouses were ill within the last 6 months were also more likely to describe their own health as poorer than individuals whose spouses had not been ill (Satariano, Minkler, & Langhauser, 1984). In fact, the spouse's health was the best predictor of the respondent's health.

Marital Separation and Divorce

Some of the strongest evidence linking family transitions with poorer mental and physical health comes from epidemiological studies of separation and divorce. While the related studies on bereavement are better known, the psychological and physical morbidity and mortality associated with separation and divorce reliably exceed those associated with bereavement (Bloom et al., 1978; Verbrugge, 1979). Several studies specifically show differences in infectious disease and are thus directly relevant to the immunological data that have been collected. For example, separated and divorced men have six times as many deaths from pneumonia as married men (Lynch, 1977). Additionally, separated women reported 30% more acute illnesses and physician visits than their married peers (Somers, 1979). Summarizing the evidence for differences in health, Verbrugge (1979) concluded "Separated women are strongly disadvantages, compared to married ones, for acute incidence, all short-term disability measures, major activity limitations, and partial work disability . . . Divorced women are also strongly disfavored. . ." (p. 283).

These epidemiological data demonstrate a strong association between marital disruption and poorer health. In order to assess the possibility that there were concomitant immunological alterations associated with separation and divorce, 38 separated or divorced women and 38 sociodemographically-matched married comparison women completed questionnaires and allowed blood samples to be drawn for immunological and nutritional assays (Kiecolt-Glaser et al., 1987a). The immunological assays included three qualitative or functional assays and three quantitative or enumerative measures.

The experimental hypotheses were derived from attachment theory, the primary conceptual framework used in the divorce literature to explain the differences in post-separation symptomatology (Bowlby, 1975; Weiss, 1975). Within this framework, continued preoccupation with the inaccessible spouse (including either positive or negative affect) leads to "separation distress" and the associated distress-related symptoms. Not surprisingly, attachment feelings generally decline as separation time increases; however, there is considerable variability in the amount of continued attachment in separated and divorced individuals, even for those separated for similar time periods. Based on these factors, both shorter separation periods and stronger feelings of attachment were expected to be inversely related to immune function. These predictions were supported.

In addition, two sets of comparisons were of interest for the separated/divorced and married women. The separated/divorced group had separation times ranging from 3 months to 6 years, with a mean of 1.72 years. The 16 women who had been separated a year or less had significantly poorer immune function on five of the six assays than 16 sociodemographically-matched married women.

Overall group differences were not predicted since the average time since separation in the marital disruption group was almost 2 years. However, comparisons of data from all of the 38 separated/divorced women and the 38 married women showed significantly poorer immune function across three of the six immunological assays in the former, with significantly greater distress in the former as well.

In a similar study, Kiecolt-Glaser, Kennedy, Malkoff, Fisher, Speicher, and Glaser (1988) compared self-report data and blood samples obtained from 32 separated or divorced men and 32 sociodemographically-matched married men. Separated/divorced men were more distressed and lonelier, and reported significantly more recent illnesses than married men; the former also had significantly poorer values on two functional indices of immunity, while not differing on quantitative indices. Those separated/divorced men who had separated within the last year and who had initiated the separation were less distressed, reported better health, and had a better performance on one functional immunological assay than noninitiators.

The discussion thus far has focused on the health related consequences for (ex)spouses; although less well understood, there is some evidence that children may also have health impairments following their parents' divorce. Guidubaldi and Cleminshaw (1985) compared parent ratings of child health in 341 children whose parents were divorced to ratings of 358 children from intact families. Children of divorced parents had significantly poorer health and more behavior problems than their peers from intact families.

It is clear that marital disruption (either through divorce or bereavement) can be associated with poorer health. These data are perhaps the most striking examples of greater morbidity and mortality associated with family transitions. Moreover, both endocrinological and immunological changes have been demonstrated through convergent data from several laboratories.

Marital Quality

Although data from marital disruption studies have shown that even the termination of a troubled relationship can have adverse physical and emotional consequences, the simple presence of a spouse is not a panacea. Unhappy marriages are reliably associated with increased distress: on the average, unmarried persons are less distressed than those in troubled marriages (Glenn & Weaver, 1981; Pearlin & Lieberman, 1979). Having a close confidant who is not the spouse is associated with lower marital satisfaction as well as lower emotional well-being (Lee, 1988). In addition, poorer marital quality has been associated with poorer health; in a study by Renne (1971), unhappily married people reported poorer health than either divorced or happily married individuals of the same age, sex, and race.

Data from Levenson and Gottman (1985) provide evidence of a physiological pathway through which chronically abrasive relationships could affect health. They found that greater autonomic arousal in interacting married couples was strongly predictive of larger declines in marital satisfaction 3 years later; greater marital satisfaction decrements were also strongly correlated with self-ratings of poorer health. If a spouse's presence in a disturbed relationship is associated with relatively consistent physiological arousal, then there could be concurrent endocrinological alterations that could have an impact on the immune response (O'Dorisio et al., 1985).

In the studies on marital disruption and immunity described earlier (Kiecolt-Glaser et al., 1987a; Kiecolt-Glaser et al., 1988) relationships between marital quality and immune function were also assessed. For women, poorer marital quality was significantly associated with greater depression and loneliness in hierarchical multiple regression equations, after entering the subject's education, her husband's socioeconomic status, and the number of negative life events on previous steps. Poorer marital quality was also associated with poorer responses on functional immunological measures. Similar results were obtained with men.

A Final Note on Stress and Health Related to Family Transitions

There is good evidence for greater health impairment in more distressed populations, in individuals whose marital relationship has been disrupted through divorce or death, and in older adults whose interpersonal relationships are less satisfactory and/or less numerous. Moreover, some of the more provocative evidence suggesting that family interactions may have health consequences comes from research on utilization of medical care following family therapy. Doherty (1985) reviewed studies suggesting that there were declines in health care utilization among patients who received family therapy for emotional problems as compared to matched controls. However, there are a number of other factors to be considered in interpreting these data.

Methodological problems that are common in many of the studies discussed in this chapter include few longitudinal or prospective designs, a paucity of control or comparison groups for understanding the actual impact of the stressors, heavy reliance on correlational designs, and the infrequent use of rigorous subject or case selection criteria. Thus, the psychological and physiological processes that may underlie any observed differences cannot easily be assessed.

In addition, many of the studies assessed health by self-report, frequently by such methods as asking individuals to rate their health as excellent, good, fair, or poor. It is well-known that individuals that are more distressed tend to focus more on somatic symptoms, so that health ratings in this context are difficult to interpret.

Furthermore, there may be other explanations for much of the data described. For example, in discussing alternative explanations for the findings that respondents whose spouses were ill describe their own health as poor (Satarariano et al., 1984), several possible explanations were proposed. First, individuals who share the same environment and lifestyle may also share greater risk for certain health problems. Second, in the case of marriage, those individuals who are already in poor physical or emotional health may select mates who share similar poorer health characteristics (Bloom et al., 1978). Finally, illness in a spouse or other significant family member may create strains that cause a caregiver to alter his/her perceptions of his/her own health, i.e., the presence of an ill family member may alter the family norms for health and well-being.

In addition, many of the transitions described in this chapter are associated with financial strains; for example, many caregivers suffer financial losses related to the medical expenses of the patient, as well as through a decreased ability to work outside the home. Similarly, bereavement and divorce are often associated with downward financial alterations as well. Thus, individuals in these circumstances may have less money for their own medical treatment, leading to the neglect of less severe symptoms. Similarly, the focus on a more seriously ill individual within a family may lessen attention to less serious medical problems in other family members.

Health risks related to family transitions may be mediated by a number of other variables as well. For example, it has been suggested that marital disruption or other major life changes might have adverse effects on health because of differences in risk-related health behaviors; e.g., more distressed individuals may drink, smoke or use alcohol and drugs more than their less distressed, counterparts, and/or they might have poorer diets and get less sleep (Verbrugge,

1979). These behaviors undoubtedly contribute to the health differences consistently reported in epidemiological studies. However, researchers in behavioral immunology normally use good health and the absence of prescription or nonprescription drug use as screening criteria; subjects are excluded who report excessive alcoholic consumption. Differences have not been found in sleep or nutritional status that are of sufficient magnitude to account for the observed immunological differences (Chandra & Newberne, 1977) in the populations studied to date. Thus, while some of the differences in the epidemiological literature may reflect risk-related life style variables, it is also possible that there are persistent distress-related physiological changes that could make an additional contribution to the observed health difference.

A final caveat is in order with respect to the immunological data. While it is reasonable to assume that both transient and more chronic immunosuppression may have adverse health consequences, the longitudinal studies that are essential for providing information on the magnitude of these effects and their association with the incidence, duration, and intensity of infectious disease are largely absent from the literature. The critical connections between stress-related immunosuppression and actual health changes are not well-established, with a few exceptions (Glaser et al., 1987; Kasl, Evans, & Niederman, 1979; Pennebaker, Kiecolt-Glaser, & Glaser, 1988). These kinds of studies are essential for our understanding of family-related stressors, transitions, and health.

ACKNOWLEDGMENTS

Work on this paper was supported in part by grant R01 MH42096 from the National Institute on Mental Health to Dr. Kiecolt-Glaser.

REFERENCES

Barnes, R. F., Raskind, M. A., Scott, M., & Murphy, C. (1981). Problems of families caring for Alzheimer's patients: Use of a support group. *Journal of the American Geriatrics Society, 29,* 80–85.

Baum, A., Grunberg, N., & Singer, J. (1982). The use of psychological and neuroendocrinological measurements in the study of stress. *Health Psychology, 1,* 217–236.

Bartrop, R., Luckhurst, E., Lazarus, L., Kiloh, L. G., & Penny, R. (1977). Depressed lymphocyte function after bereavement. *Lancet, 1,* 374–377.

Billings, A., Moos, R., Miller, J. J., & Gottlieb, J. (1987). Psychosocial adaptation in juvenile rheumatic disease: A controlled evaluation. *Health Psychology, 6,* 343–359.

Bloom, B. L., Asher, S. J., & White, S. W. (1978). Marital disruption as a stressor: A review and analysis. *Psychological Bulletin, 85,* 867–894.

Bobrow, E., AvRuskin, T., & Siller, J. (1985). Mother-daughter interactions and adherence to diabetes regimens. *Diabetes Care, 8,* 146–151.

Bowlby, J. (1975). *Attachment and Loss: 1.* Attachment. New York: Basic Books.

Brocklehurst, J., Morris, P., Andrews, K., Richards, B., & Laycock, P. (1981). The social effects of stroke. *Social Science Medicine, 15A,* 35–39.

Chandra, R. K., & Newberne, P. M. (1977). *Nutrition, immunity and infection: Mechanisms of interactions.* New York: Plenum Press.

Cosper, M., & Erickson, M. (1985). The psychological, social, and medical needs of lower socioeconomic status mothers of asthmatic children. *Journal of Asthma, 22,* 145–148.

Crook, T., & Miller, N. (1985). The challenge of Alzheimer's Disease. *American Psychologist, 40,* 1245–1250.

Daniels, D., Miller, J., Billings, A., & Moos, R. (1986). Psychosocial functioning of siblings of children with rheumatic disease. *Journal of Pediatrics, 109,* 379–383.

Doherty, W. (1985). Family interventions in health care. *Family Relations, 34,* 129–137.

Drinka, T., & Smith, J. (1983). Depression in caregivers of demented patients. *Gerontologist, 23,* 115–116.

Dura, J., & Beck, S. (1988). A comparison of family function when mothers have chronic pain. *Pain, 35,* 79–89.

Eisdorfer, C., Kennedy, G., Wisnieski, W., & Cohen, D. (1983). Depression and attributional style in families coping with the stress of caring for a relative with Alzheimer's Disease. *Gerontologist, 23,* 115–116.

Fiore, J., Becker, J., & Coppel, D. (1983). Social network interactions: A buffer or a stress. *American Journal of Community Psychology, 11,* 423–439.

George, L., & Gwyther, L. (1984). *The dynamics of caregiver burden: Changes in caregiver well-being over time.* Paper presented at the annual meeting of the Gerontological Society of America, San Antonio.

George, L., & Gwyther, L. (1986). Caregiver well-being: A multidimensional examination of family caregivers of demented adults. *Gerontologist, 26,* 253–259.

Glaser, R., Rice, J., Sheridan, J., Fertel, R., Stout, J., Speicher, C., Pinsky, D., Kotur, M., Post, A., Beck, M., & Kiecolt-Glaser, J. (1987). Stress-related immune suppression: Health implications. *Brain, Behavior, and Immunity, 1,* 7–20.

Glenn, N. D., & Weaver, C. N. (1981). The contribution of marital happiness to global happiness. *Journal of Marriage and Family, 43,* 161–168.

Guidbaldi, J., & Cleminshaw, H. (1985). Divorce, family health, and child adjustment. *Family Relations, 34,* 35–41.

Haley, W., Levine, E., Brown, S., & Bartolucci, A. (1987). Stress, appraisal, coping and social support as predictors of adaptational outcome and dementia caregivers. *Psychology and Aging, 2,* 323–330.

Haley, W., Levine, E., Brown, L., Berry, J., & Hughes, G. (1987). Psychological, social, and health consequences of caring for a relative with senile dementia. *Journal of Aging and Geriatric Society, 35,* 405–411.

Havighurst, R. J. (1948). *Developmental tasks and education,* Chicago: University of Chicago Press.

Heckler, M. (1985). The fight against Alzheimer's Disease. *American Psychologist, 40,* 1240–1244.

Heston, L., Mastri, A., Anderson, V., & White, G. (1981). Dementia of the Alzheimer type. *Archives of General Psychiatry, 38,* 1085–1091.

Hymovich, D., & Dillon-Baker, C. (1985). The needs, concerns and coping of parents of children with cystic fibrosis. *Family Relations, 34,* 91–97.

Irwin, M., Daniels, M., Bloom, E., Smith, T., & Weiner, H. (1987). Life events, depressive symptoms, and immune function. *American Journal of Psychiatry, 144,* 437–441.

Jacob, M., Frank, E., Kupfer, D., & Carpenter, L. (1987). Recurrent depression: An assessment of family burden and family attitudes. *Journal of Clinical Psychiatry, 48,* 395–400.

Jacobs, S., Mason, J., Kosten, T., Kasl, S., Ostfeld, A., & Wahby, V. (1987). Urinary free cortisol and separation anxiety early in the course of bereavement and threatened loss. *Biological Psychiatry, 22,* 148–152.

Jacobs, S., & Ostfeld, A. (1977). An epidemiological review of mortality of bereavement. *Psychosomatic Medicine, 39,* 344–356.

Kasl, S. V., Evans, A. S., & Niederman, J. C. (1979). Psychosocial risk factors in the development of infectious mononucleosis. *Psychosomatic Medicine, 41,* 445–466.

Kerns, R., & Curley, A. (1985). A biopsychosocial approach to illness and the family: Neurological diseases across the life span. In D. C. Turk, & R. D. Kerns (Eds.), *Health, illness, and families; A life-span perspective* (pp. 146–182). New York: Wiley.

Kiecolt-Glaser, J., Fisher, L., Ogrocki, P., Stout, J., Speicher, C., & Glaser, R. (1987a). Marital quality, marital disruption, and immune function. *Psychosomatic Medicine, 49,* 13–34.

Kiecolt-Glaser, J., Glaser, R., Shuttleworth, C., Dyer, C., Ogrocki, B., & Speicher, C. (1987b). Chronic stress and immunity in family caregivers of Alzheimer's Disease victims. *Psychosomatic Medicine, 49,* 523–535.

Kiecolt-Glaser, J., Kennedy, S., Malkoff, S., Fisher, L., Speicher, C., & Glaser, R. (1988). Marital discord and immunity in males. *Psychosomatic Medicine, 50,* 213–229.

King, K., & Hanson, V. (1986). Psychosocial aspects of juvenile rheumatoid arthritis. *Pediatric Clinics of North America, 33,* 1221–1237.

Kuypers, J., & Bengtson, U. (1983). Toward competence in the older family. In T. Brubaker (Ed.), *Family relations in later life.* Beverly Hills, CA: Sage.

Lee, G. R. (1988). Marital intimacy among older persons: The spouse as a confidant. *Journal of Family Issues, 9,* 273–284.

Lefley, H. (1987). Impact of mental illness in families of mental health professionals. *The Journal of Nervous and Mental Disease, 175,* 613–619.

Levenson, R. W., & Gottman, J. M. (1985). Physiological and affective predictors of change in relationship satisfaction. *Journal of Personality and Social Psychology, 49,* 85–94.

Lynch, J. (1977). *The broken heart.* New York: Basic Books. Minuchin, S. (1974). *Families and family therapy.* Cambridge, MA: Harvard University Press.

Montgomery, R., Gonyea, J., & Hooyman, N. (1985). Caregiving and the experience of subjective and objective burden. *Family Relations, 34,* 19–26.

Noh, S., & Turner, R. J. (1987). Living with psychiatric patients: Implications for the mental health of family members. *Social Science Medicine, 25,* 263–271.

Norris, J. E., & Forbes, S. J. (1987, November). *Cohesion and adaptability in caregiving families.* Paper presented at the annual meeting of the Gerontological Society of America. Washington, D.C.

O'Dorisio, M. S., Wood, C. L., & O'Dorisio, T. M. (1985). Vasoactive intestinal peptide and neuropeptide modulation of the immune response. *Journal of Immunology, 135,* 792s–796s.

Pearlin, L. I., & Lieberman, M. A. (1979). Social sources of emotional distress. In R. Simmons (Ed.), *Research in community and mental health.* Greenwich CN: JAI Press.

Pennebaker, J. W., Kiecolt-Glaser, J. K., & Glaser, R. (1988). Disclosure of traumas and immune function: Health implications for psychotherapy. *Journal of Consulting and Clinical Psychology, 56,* 239–245.

Perrin, J. (1985). Chronically ill children in America. *Caring, 4,* 16–22.

Rabins, P., Fitting, J., Eastham, S., & Zabora, J. (1987, May). *Emotional adaptation over time in caregivers for the chronically ill.* Presented at the annual meeting of the American Psychiatric Association, Chicago.

Rakowski, W., & Clark, N. M. (1985). Future outlook, caregiving, and care-receiving in the family context. *Gerontologist, 25,* 618–623.

Renne, K. S. (1971). Health and marital experience in an urban population. *Journal of Marriage and Family, 23,* 338–350.

Rees, W., & Lutkins, S. (1967). Mortality of bereavement. *British Medical Journal, 4,* 13–16.

Reisberg, B. (Ed.). (1983). *Alzheimer's disease: The standard reference.* New York: Free Press.

Robinson, B., & Thurner, M. (1979). Taking care of aged parents: A family cycle transition. *The Gerontologist, 19,* 586–593.

Sainsbury, P., & Grad de Alarcon, J. (1970). The psychiatrist and the geriatric patient: The effects of community care on the family of the geriatric patient. *Journal of Geriatric Psychiatry, 4,* 23–41.

Satariano, W., Minkler, M., & Langhauser, C. (1984.) The significance of an ill spouse for assessing health differences in an elderly population. *Journal of the American Geriatrics Society, 32,* 187–190.

Scharlach, A. E. (1987). Role strain in mother-daughter relationships in later life. *Gerontologist, 27,* 627–631.

Schleifer, S., Keller, S., Camerino, M., Thornton, J. C., & Stein, M. (1983). Suppression of lymphocyte stimulation following bereavement. *Journal of the American Medical Association, 250,* 374–377.

Smith, J. V., & Birchwood, M. (1987). Specific and non-specific effects of educational intervention with families living with a schizophrenic relative. *British Journal of Psychiatry, 150,* 645–652.

Somers, A. R. (1979). Marital status, health, and use of health services. *Journal of the American Medical Association, 241,* 1818–1822.

Stroebe, M., & Stroebe, W. (1983). Who suffers more? Sex differences in health risks of the widowed. *Psychological Bulletin, 93,* 279–301.

Swan, R., & Lavitt, M. (1986). *Patterns of adjustment to violence in families of the mentally ill.* Elizabeth Wisner Research Center, Tulane University School of Social Work.

Verbrugge, L. M. (1979). Marital status and health. *Journal of Marriage and Family, 41,* 267–285.

Weiss, R. S. (1975). *Marital separation.* New York: Basic Books.

Windholz, M., Marmar, C., & Horowitz, M. (1985). A review of the research on conjugal bereavement: Impact on health and efficacy of intervention. *Comprehensive Psychiatry, 26,* 433–447.

Woods, A. M., Nederhe, G., & Fruge, E. (1985). Dementia: A family systems perspective. *Generations, 10,* 19–22.

Zarit, S., Orr, N., & Zarit, J. (1985). *The hidden victims of Alzheimer's disease: Families under stress.* New York: New York University Press.

Zarit, S., Reever, K., & Bach-Peterson, J. (1980). Relatives of the impaired elderly: Correlates of feelings of burden. *Gerontologist, 20,* 649–655.

Zarit, S., & Zarit, J. (1982). Families under stress: Interventions for caregivers of senile dementia patients. *Psychotherapy: Theory, Research and Practice, 19,* 461.

Zisook, S., & Shuchter, S. (1985). Time course of spousal bereavement. *General Hospital Psychiatry, 7,* 95–100.

II NORMATIVE AND NONNORMATIVE TRANSITIONS

4 Becoming a Family: Marriage, Parenting, and Child Development

Carolyn Pape Cowan
Philip A. Cowan
Gertrude Heming
Nancy B. Miller
University of California, Berkeley

The transition from being a couple to becoming a family has been a focus of study and controversy since LeMasters' (1957) apparently startling assertion that the birth of a first child constituted a "crisis" for 83% of the couples in his study. Drawing conclusions from his intensive retrospective interview data, LeMasters argued that this normative transition, typically seen as a time of joy and optimism, could also be a time of significant strain for new parents. For the next 2 decades, other investigators published skeptical rejoinders to LeMasters' conclusions. The researchers were mostly sociologists who used cross-sectional or postbirth samples of new mothers and fathers completing brief checklists or answering a few simple survey questions (e.g., Hobbs, 1965, 1968; Hobbs & Wimbish, 1977). Their results were interpreted as minimizing the incidence, prevalence, and seriousness of distress in new parents and their marriages, and led the investigators to suggest, as Hobbs and Cole (1976) put it, that "initiating parenthood may be slightly difficult, but not sufficiently difficult to warrant calling it a crisis experience for parents whose first child is still an infant" (p. 729).

Despite these early conclusions minimizing the effects of becoming parents, three separate lines of research continue to suggest that there are significant risks associated with this major normative life transition—for individual men and women and for their relationship as a couple:

a. Cross-sectional surveys indicate that marital satisfaction declines during the years of childbearing and childrearing (Blood & Wolfe, 1960; Spanier & Lewis, 1980).

b. With very few exceptions, recent short-term longitudinal studies have shown that couples who have had a first child are less satisfied with their marriage during the first postpartum year than they were in late pregnancy (Belsky, Lang, & Rovine, 1985; Clulow, 1982; Cox et al., 1985; Cowan et al., 1985; Duncan & Markman, 1988; Feldman & Nash, 1984; Grossman, Eichler, & Winickoff, 1980; Heinicke, Diskin, Ramsay-Klee, & Oates, 1986; Lewis, 1988; Osofsky & Osofsky, 1984; Shereshefsky & Yarrow, 1973; Snowden, Schott, Awalt, & Gillis-Knox, 1988). In two studies that use nonparent controls, it is evident that the decline in satisfaction with marriage is not a function of time alone; it is greater in new parents than in childless couples followed over a comparable period (Belsky & Pensky, 1988; Cowan et al., 1985).

c. Epidemiological data on postpartum distress in women, along with findings from several studies of new fathers, indicate that both men and women who have recently become parents are at increased risk for psychosis, depression, and the "blues" (e.g., Brockington et al., 1981; Davenport & Adland, 1982; Fedele, Golding, Grossman, & Pollack, 1988; Zaslow et al., 1981). Whereas postpartum psychosis is a rare occurrence, however it is defined, the incidence of postpartum blues in some studies approaches 50%.

While the most serious after-effects of becoming a family may happen to a small minority of individudals or couples, there is no doubt that Hobbs' and Wimbish's conclusion that "parenthood may be slightly difficult" was off the mark. Furthermore, in all of this debate about whether the transition to parenthood has negative effects on men, women, and marriage, the search for the *mechanisms* leading to positive or negative change during the transition to parenthood has barely begun.

Because of the way evidence of individual and marital distress in the early postpartum period is reported, it is being used both by researchers and the general public to blame babies for their parents' tension and distress in the early years of family life. We have quite another view (Cowan & Cowan, 1988a). While we too find pervasive negative changes in partners as they become parents, we also find a notable degree of continuity and predictability of individual and marital adaptation from before to after the first child's birth. We have found that babies certainly have an impact on the lives of their parents, but the prebaby state of the parents and their marriage contributes much more than the baby does to their postbirth adaptation levels (Heming, 1985, 1987). The transition to parenthood seems to increase the stress in parents' lives, amplify the differences between the spouses, and thereby increase their level of marital dissatisfaction.

During the 1980s, researchers have gone beyond documenting the impact of becoming a family on the parents to exploring the pathways from mothers' and fathers' pre- and postbaby adjustment to the later quality of their marriages, their parenting styles, and the early developmental progress of their children. In this chapter, we examine how parents' adaptation to a major life transition—becoming a family—has longterm consequences extending from the first child's birth to his or her entrance to kindergarten. Drawing primarily on data from our longitudinal study of couples becoming parents, we provide evidence for three assertions:

1. The transition to parenthood, which is experienced by 90% of married couples (Houseknecht, 1988), is a time of heightened risk for distress in men, women, and marriage.
2. Marital distress in the early childbearing years is accompanied by less optimal parent-child relationships and slower progress in the child's cognitive and social development at home, in the laboratory, and at school.
3. Given the risks associated with the transition to parenthood for parents and their children, we should be designing preventive interventions aimed at strengthening couple relationships and creating family environments more conducive to children's early development and psychological well-being.

Overview of the Study

Participants. We began the Becoming a Family Project with 72 couples expecting a first baby and 24 comparable couples who had not yet decided whether to become parents. We recruited them from a range of obstetric-gynecology practices, both private and clinic, and through several San Francisco Bay area-wide newsletters. When we first met them, the participants ranged in age from 21 to 49 years; the mean age of the expectant mothers was 29 years, and of the fathers, 30. The childless spouses were, on the average, 1 year younger. Most of the couples were married when they joined the study, anywhere from 8 months to 12 years, with an average length of relationship of 4 years. A few of the couples have married since they joined the study. They lived in 28 different cities and towns in northern California within a 40 mile radius of the University of California at Berkeley, and spanned a wide range of background and training. They had all completed high school, and some had extensive training beyond. The men and women include carpenters, teachers, architects, writers, doctors, nurses, postal workers, professors, lawyers, retail store clerks, mental health professionals, an airline mechanic, an electrician, a clothes designer and seamstress, a caterer, and a cable car driver. Fifteen percent of the participants are Black, Asian-American, or Hispanic, and 85% are Caucasian.

Design. At the beginning of the study, one-third of the 72 expectant couples, randomly selected, were offered a 6-month-long couples group intervention conducted by predoctoral clinical psychology students or postdoctoral level clinical psychologists; 85% of the couples accepted. Each participating couple was interviewed and filled out a battery of questionnaires before attending a group with four expectant couples and one trained leader couple. For 6 months, from late pregnancy through the early months of parenthood, each group met weekly to talk about what was happening to the men, the women, and their relationships as couples.

A second set of 24 couples was assessed at the same time as the couples in the groups, but not offered the intervention. In order to evaluate the impact of completing the questionnaires before having a baby, we interviewed a third set of 24 couples prior to birth, but did not ask them to fill out questionnaires until the after-birth assessment periods.

Finally, because we expected all couple relationships to change over time, we included a comparison sample of 24 couples who had not yet decided whether to have a baby. We have complete data from 15 of these couples who remained childless and were followed over a 2-year period equivalent to the pregnancy-to-18-months-postpartum assessments of the new parents.

Assessments of the couples were done in (1) late pregnancy; (2) 6 months after birth; (3) 18 months after birth; (4) when the children were 3½; and (5) during the kindergarten year, when they were 5½ to 6-years-old. At each of these points we have analyzed responses to individually completed questionnaires from the parents—some standard ones developed by others and some developed by us—and in-depth interviews conducted with each couple at their home or at the University.

At the 3½ and 5½-year points, families came to our playroom laboratory for play and work sessions in 4 situations: the child alone (with experimenters), with mother, with father, and with both parents. Observations of these sessions by our staff were done by separate male-female teams who were blind to the rest of the data obtained from the family.

A 5-domain Structural Model of the Family with a First Child

In attempting to synthesize schemes from our own earlier studies and from the work of other researchers following couples through the transition to parenthood (e.g., Belsky, 1984; Heinicke, 1984; Parke & Tinsley, 1982), we have developed a 5-domain model of family structure. With variables assessing each of these aspects of new parents' lives, we try to understand what leads to family distress and adaptation:

1. the characteristics of each individual in the family, including self-concept, self-esteem, symptoms of depression, and emotional distress;
2. the parents' marriage, with special emphasis on their division of labor and patterns of communication;
3. the quality of relationship between each parent and the child;
4. the intergenerational relationships among grandparents, parents, and grandchildren; and

5. the relationship between nuclear family members and individuals or institutions outside the family, with an emphasis on work, school, and the balance between life stresses and social supports.

This model is consistent with Bronfenbrenner's (1979) ecological approach. To understand what happens to family members and relationships during major life transitions, it is necessary to examine the interconnections among all 5 domains.

In contrast with family research focusing either on individuals *or* on the system as a whole, the Becoming a Family Project assumed that individual, dyadic, triadic, three-generational, and extra-family domains each contribute unique information to our understanding of the quality of relationships parents develop with each other and with their children. If and when second or third children become part of the family, the relationships between the siblings, and between the parents and siblings, constitute a sixth domain that contributes to the level of family adaptation.

WHAT HAPPENS TO THE MARRIAGE WHEN PARTNERS BECOME PARENTS?

When we compared the changes in couples who became parents with those who remained childless over a similar period of time, we found that the childless couples showed change in several of the 5 domains, but *the new parents showed change in all of them* (Cowan et al., 1985; Cowan & Cowan, 1987a; Cowan & Cowan, 1990a).

Sense of Self. The data from a questionnaire we call *The Pie* (Cowan & Cowan, 1990b) illustrate the dilemmas faced by men and women as they experience change in their self concept and identity from before to after becoming a parent. Each partner makes a list of the salient or important aspects of self and divides a circle 4 inches in diameter to reflect the "psychological salience" of each "piece" (how large it *feels,* rather than the amount of time spent in that role). As we might expect, "father" and "mother" become an increasingly larger part of men's and women's self descriptions in the first 18 months after having a baby. What gets squeezed in this process, for both men and women, are the "husband/wife/lover" aspects of self. To complicate matters further, *women's* sense of self as "worker" or "student" becomes a much smaller part of their identity, but *men's* remains virtually unchanged. (Cowan & Cowan, 1988b) It is our opinion that one of the major challenges for couples in the early family years is coping with the impact of these psychological changes—and with the fact that men and women experience them differently.

Marital Roles and Communication. Quality of life in the couple domain showed significant shifts. On our *Who Does What?* questionnaire (Cowan & Cowan, 1990c), we found a growing traditionalization of gender roles, with women assuming greater responsibility for household tasks and care of the child than either partner predicted. Not surprisingly, couples also reported a *decline* in satisfaction with the "who does what?" of life, and an *increase* in marital disagreement and conflict (Cowan et al., 1985). Support for the link between shifting roles and marital conflict comes from the fact that both husbands and wives reported that the division of family labor was the issue most likely to cause arguments between them.

Parent-Child Relationships. The most obvious aspects of becoming a family is the shift from fantasies about what it will be like to have a child to the hands-on caring for the baby. We initially reported little systematic change in ideas about parenting (Cowan et al., 1985), but a refactoring of Heming's *Ideas about Parenting* scale (Heming, Cowan, & Cowan, 1990) reveals a few important shifts from before to after the birth of a first child. Men's view of the child as a separate and autonomous being declines significantly over time. Both men and women become more child-centered, saying that adults should suspend their own satisfactions in favor of the child, yet mothers of 18-month-olds believe even more strongly than they did in pregnancy that parent care is better than other sources of child care, while fathers begin to shift in the opposite direction. This ideological parting of the ways provides fertile soil for the growth of conflict between the parents. Because our main focus during the first 18 months postpartum was on the parents, we did not have any way of knowing how these shifting ideas and beliefs about parenthood were being translated into actual parenting behavior at that time.

Three-Generation Relationships. In interviews with all 96 couples in the study and in ongoing discussion with partners in the intervention groups, we learned that men's and women's relationships with their own parents were undergoing marked change as they themselves entered parenthood. For some, the becoming a family period seemed to be an intense period of reconciliation and reconnection with their parents, but others were faced with a reawakening of earlier tensions and family struggles.

Life Stress/Social Support/Employment. For new parents, connections between the nuclear family and the outside world shift quickly and radically. The major change in most cases is that women leave their studies or their jobs to stay home for at least a few months of virtually full-time care of the babies. In our sample, half the women were still at home 18 months after their babies were born; this proportion appears to be similar to national trends. Men, too, experienced change in their jobs or career directions as they became fathers, but their involvement in paid work tended to increase.

Despite the fact that there were significant changes in their work involvement, self-concept, roles, communication, parenting ideas, and relationships with their own parents, husbands and wives showed no overall increase in their life stress scores over the first 18 months of parenthood. They showed an increase in social support from friends, neighbors, family, and coworkers between pregnancy and 6 months postpartum, and then a decline over the next year of parenthood.

Why Does Marital Satisfaction Decline?

The decline in marital satisfaction that we measured was not correlated with the life changes we have described. We found that the key to understanding the shifts in marital quality that new parents described lies in the fact that the transition to parenthood widens *already-existing differences between the partners.* Although men and women showed many similar changes, there are, to paraphrase Jessie Bernard (1974), both "his" and "her" transitions to parenthood (Cowan et al., 1985). The decrease in the partner/lover aspect of self was twice as large for women as it was for men. Women's decline in satisfaction with "who does what?" was greater than men's, and, as we have noted, women's involvement in paid work decreased markedly, while their husbands' work involvement tended to remain the same or increase. The negative impact of these changes on the marriage was delayed for men; mothers' greatest decline in marital satisfaction occurred from pregnancy to 6 months after birth, whereas fathers reported an even larger drop between 6- and 18-months-postpartum.

The fact that husbands and wives change at different rates and in different directions appears to have important consequences for the relationship between them. Based on our interviews and the ongoing couples group meetings, we began to suspect that differences between partners lead to their feeling distant, that feeling distant tends to stimulate conflict in their relationship, and that increased conflict, in turn, affects both partners' feelings about their overall marriage. We constructed an index based on absolute differences *between spouses* on their descriptions of (a) themselves, (b) their marriage, (c) their families of origin, (d) their ideas about parenting, and (e) their balance between life stress and social support. Using multiple regression analyses, we found that partners who described more differences *between* them and greater increases in marital conflict from pregnancy to 6 months postpartum, showed more decline in satisfaction with the overall marriage from pregnancy to 18 months after birth ($R = .64$ for men and .61 for women).

Between-partner differences were not the only predictors of decline in satisfaction with marriage. Belsky, Ward, and Rovine (in press) and Garrett (1983) note that unfulfilled expectations may have a negative impact on marital quality. We found that when there was a larger discrepancy between wives' predictions of their husbands' involvement in the care of the babies and the men's actual involvement, the wives showed a greater decline in marital satisfaction from pregnancy to 18 months postpartum (r = .65).

The metaphors from Festinger's cognitive dissonance theory (1957) help describe, if not explain, how marital distress can build during a generally positive life transition. Each partner is confronted daily by a spouse who has different ideas about how to do things, is performing a different family role, and is less available than he or she was only a few months before. Unprepared for this stark reality of life with a baby, each partner is jolted by frequent unexpected, and often surprisingly powerful emotions. The disequilibration results from the violation of each partner's expectations, and from increasingly noticeable differences and discrepancies between their perceptions and their realities. The dissonance within and between partners, we believe, may combine to produce increasing distress *within* each spouse that is often attributed to things going on *between* them—especially if neither spouse is getting enough sleep or caring attention.

Continuity and the Early Identification of Risk

Despite some clear and expectable shifts, we found significant continuity and consistency in individual and couple adaptation over the 2-year period from pregnancy to 18 months postpartum. We have documented findings of consistency in self-concept, self-esteem, adjustment, role arrangements, communication patterns, perceptions of the family of origin, life stress, social support, and marital satisfaction over time (Cowan et al., 1985; Cowan & Cowan, 1987a, 1987b), as have others studying this transition (Belsky, Lang, & Rovine, 1985; Cox et al., 1985; Feldman, 1987; Fleming et al., 1988; Grossman et al., 1980). Longitudinal data, then, help confirm the hypothesis that despite significant changes in mean scores, individuals and couples remain in roughly the same rank order on our measures of adaptation and distress as they move from being a couple to becoming a family.

Predicting Who Will Become Most Distressed with Parenthood. Gertrude Heming (1985, 1987) used the information that parents in the Becoming a Family Project gave about themselves and their lives during pregnancy to predict the parents' well being or distress 2 years later when their babies were 1½ years old. In regression analyses, she looked at 4 indices of parents' 18-months-postpartum well-being or distress:

a. Symptoms of *depression,* as measured by the Center for Epidemiological Studies in Depression scale (CES-D; Radloff, 1977);

b. *Parenting stress,* using Abidin's (1981) Parenting Stress Index

c. *Marital distress,* as measured by partners' Locke-Wallace (1959) self-reports about the state of the overall marriage, and

d. *Level of functioning as a couple,* using our staff couple's clinical rating of the couple's relationship after interviewing them. The 5-point clinical rating created by Heming (1985) describes the couples' relationships on a continuum from very well functioning to poorly functioning.

To summarize her findings very briefly, Heming (1985, 1987) found that from 22% to 53% of the variance in new mothers' and fathers' depression, parenting stress, marital distress, and level of functioning as a couple could be predicted from parents' descriptions of themselves and their life as a couple before their baby was born. For example, 53% of the variance in the couple's observed level of functioning at 18 months postpartum could be predicted by a combination of her rating of the couple's problem-solving effectiveness, his level of self-esteem and dissatisfaction with the amount of affection he was receiving, *and* his negative feelings about having a baby—as reported in late pregnancy. In other words, husbands and wives who made the best adaptation to new parenthood were those who were doing better *as couples* and had a husband feeling ready to become a parent.

Direct and Indirect Pathways to Adaptation and Distress. So far, we have been describing how pretest measures correlate directly with criteria of adaptation or distress at 18 months postpartum. We used path analyses to determine whether there are indirect effects as well. In her recently completed dissertation, Marsha Kline (1988) found, as expected, *direct* paths between pregnancy and a number of 18-month-postpartum indices of well-being: self-esteem, marital satisfaction, role satisfaction, family cohesion, and job satisfaction. Kline also found that in every case, there was a significant *indirect* path through parenting stress. That is, the men and women who were more dissatisfied with themselves, their marriage, or their jobs before becoming parents, were more stressed *as parents,* and their parenting stress contributed to their dissatisfaction with themselves and their marriage over and above their prebaby levels of dissatisfaction.

In sum, we have shown there is an underlying continuity of adaptation in the parents during a time of profound individual and relationship change in the structure and function of their family. Negative and positive outcomes of the transition to parenthood appear to be predictable from parents' prebaby levels of distress and adaptation, but the stresses involved in parenting make an additional contribution to their later feelings about themselves and their marriage. These data support our 5-dimensional structural model of the family in that we can account for parents' individual or marital distress and well-being fairly well with a combination of measures from different domains of family life.

Transition and the Issue of Normative Distress

Change within a framework of continuity in these partners becoming parents certainly fits the defining criteria for life transitions outlined by P. Cowan (this volume). He suggests that a life transition has occurred when there are qualitative reorganizations of the person's inner experience (psychological sense of self, world-view, and emotional balance) and his or her interpersonal life (role structure, personal competence and problem solving, and central relationships). Clearly, men and women becoming parents demonstrated significant shifts in most or all of these aspects of their lives.

Two issues about the nature of this particular transition remain to be addressed. First, neither the beginning nor end markers defining the transition to parenthood have been clearly identified. Second, returning to the initial controversy about "crisis" that began more than 3 decades ago between LeMasters and Hobbs, it is not yet clear what we should be saying abut the extent of personal and marital distress associated with this normative change in couples' lives.

When Does the Transition Begin and End? It is traditional for researchers to begin studies of the transition to parenthood in late pregnancy and to end them between 9 and 18 months after the birth of the first child. Our clinical interviews suggest that for some couples the beginning of the transition occurs long before conception, and many have "not quite got the hang of being parents" by the time their first child enters kindergarten. Others identify a much more limited transition period. From the participants' point of view, then, there seems to be great variability and idiosyncrasy about when the transition begins and ends.

As observers, we believe that it makes sense to describe the end of the transition to parenthood as occurring, *on the average,* when the first child is about 2-years-old. New data from our 3½ year follow-ups indicate that between 1½ and 3½ years postpartum, there is some stabilization of both actual and psychological involvement in household and childcare roles for the parents, but marital conflict and marital *dis*satisfaction show a small increase. The *rate* of parents' negative change, so marked at the 18 month follow-up assessments, begins to decline considerably. The children are entering a new phase of life, with the increased physical mobility of walking and the intellectual mobility inherent in the use of language. At the same time, the births of second children, parents' job changes, and other positive and negative life events begin to stimulate new individual and family transitions. There is no clear endpoint to family change, but our provisional hypothesis is that the transition involved in *becoming* a parent ends by the time the first child is 2-years-old.

We note with interest that a 2-year period demarcating a major life transition has also been described in families who have experienced divorce (Wallerstein & Kelly, 1980; Hetherington & Camara, 1984), though not in families in which one of the parents has remarried (Hetherington, personal communication). It is clear that further investigation throughout the life course is necessary to determine how best to define the onset and termination of transitions at each major turning point in the life of a family.

What Should we Conclude About "Normative" Distress? We have found in presenting our findings over the past few years that it is difficult to convey to some audiences how much distress parents of young children are experiencing these days. We find that in the new burst of interest in "families at risk," many researchers have been focusing on problems of poverty, alcohol, and a variety of DSM-III disorders—schizophrenia, depression, and antisocial disorders. What is getting lost in this crisis orientation, we feel, is an appreciation of the real vulnerability of ordinary people creating new families.

Readers seem to assume that because the families in our study were volunteers, well-educated, and not from a sample in treatment, the parents would be relatively well-functioning as individuals, couples, and parents, and would have a low divorce rate. Our experience with emergent families in the past 12 years suggests quite another story. Let us counter these assumptions with some additional and surprising facts from our longitudinal study:

I. As we followed our sample of first-time expectant parents over a period of almost 7 years, the percentage of Locke-Wallace Marital Adjustment scores that fell into the risk of clinical distress range (under 100) was as follows: (Note that the proportion of scores indicating marriages in distress is *over and above the 20% of the sample that has already divorced by 66 months postpartum.)*

	Pregnancy	*Postpartum*			
	3rd trimester	*6 months*	*18 months*	*42 months*	*66 months*
Men	14%	16%	22%	27%	28%
Women	9%	18%	24%	24%	35%

II. The proportion of parents' scores on the Center for Epidemiological Studies of Depression Scale (CES-D) that fell into the clinical depression range (above 15) was as follows:

	Postpartum		
	18 months	*42 months*	*66 months*
Men	30%	30%	34%
Women	30%	20%	29%

III. New data from a recent paper (Cowan & Cowan, 1988c) indicate that 20% of the children in our study have a least one parent who is an Adult Child of an Alcoholic (ACA). While very few of the parents in our study are themselves alcoholics, those whose parents had serious alcoholic problems showed significantly greater difficulty navigating the transition to parenthood. Furthermore, the children of ACAs (the grandchildren of alcoholics) were more often identified by their kindergarten teachers as having academic and internalizing problems than the children of nonACAs—especially the boys. These findings make it clear that these nonclinic families in our volunteer sample show a sequence of risk and difficulty spanning three generations.

We are concerned about focusing so much of our attention on the data about the negative outcomes associated with having a child. After all, our own experiences (three of the four authors are parents), those of the couples we interviewed, and data from national surveys indicate that having children is one of the most rewarding and fulfilling aspects of life. Nevertheless, because so many new parents in "normal" samples are describing unexpected distress, we feel compelled to counteract Hobbs' widely cited attempt to minimize the difficulties and underestimate the risks. Glossing over potential problems does a disservice to ordinary people who experience family-making as stressful: it misleads mental health researchers, service providers, and policy makers who can then conclude that no help is necessary for "normal" couples traversing normative transitions.

We think that the case for early intervention with couples creating new families can be made even more effectively with recent evidence from our 6-year follow-ups of the families. The longitudinal data show that the parents' individual adjustment and marital quality affects the quality of their relationships with the child, and the tone of the relationships between parents and their children shapes the children's cognitive, social, and emotional development.

THE FAMILY SYSTEM AND CHILD DEVELOPMENT

The data in this section are based on preliminary analyses of our family assessments when the children were 3½ and 5½ years old. Now we can flesh out our 5-domain model of family adaptation by tracing the pathways from (a) the individual parents' characteristics, (b) the quality of the marriage, (c) the 3-generational family patterns, and (d) life stresses and social supports to (e) the parents' behavior when they work and play with their child, to (f) the child's development.

Correlational studies of parents and preschoolers have begun to suggest that parents' individual personalities and their satisfaction with marriage contribute to variations in the degree of warmth, structure, and effectiveness of their interactions with their children (Belsky, Robins, & Gamble, 1985; Goldberg, & Easterbrooks, 1984; Parke, 1979). These family determinants of parenting style become centrally important when we remember that parenting style is one of the chief influences on the rate and quality of the child's developmental progress. Baumrind (1979; this volume) and other investigators have established the fact that a combination of parents' warmth/responsiveness and structure/limit-setting/maturity-demands has positive effects on the development of intellectual and social competence in their children from preschool through adolescence. By and large, parents who are authoritative tend to have children who show more positive developmental progress than children of parents who are permissive (warm but not structuring), authoritarian (structuring but cold and critical), or disengaged (neither warm nor structuring).

Studies of families in clinical populations are beginning to provide evidence that when parents are in some form of psychological distress, their children are also at risk. Children of depressed mothers, for example, tend not to experience the kind of authoritative parenting that tends to lead to optimal social and intellectual development. More frequently than children of nondepressed mothers, they show signs of psychological dysfunction across a wide range of difficulties that are not limited to depressive symptoms or syndromes (Beardslee, Bemparad, Keller, & Klerman, 1983). Most clinically based studies focus on the psychopathology of the mother, and ignore the fact that (1) when women are depressed, their marriages are often in distress (Weissman & Klerman, 1977), and (2) nondepressed but maritally distressed fathers may be contributing to the difficulties experienced by the child (Hops, Sherman, & Biglan, 1989).

In the studies we have cited in this section, it is difficult to interpret the meaning of correlations between parents' individual or marital states and their parenting style. Since studies usually begin after the child is a member of the family, it is impossible to tease apart the contributions of the parents' and the child's characteristics to what happens when parents and children interact. Seven longitudinal studies, including ours, have addressed the problem of understanding how parents and children influence each other by tracing the links between parents' adaptation *before the child was born* and the quality of the parent-child relationships in the early childrearing years (Belsky, Lang, & Rovine, 1985; Cowan & Cowan, 1987a; Fleming et al., 1988; Grossman et al., 1980; Heinicke et al., 1986; Lewis, Owen, & Cox, 1988). Six of these research teams have shown that mothers' and fathers' psychological adaptation and marital quality before they become parents predict the quality of their parenting behavior during the first year or two of the child's life. Our study extends those findings by tracing links between the parents' psychological and marital well-being in pregnancy and the quality of the parent-child relationships *4 and 6 years later*. We also found, as others have, that we can add to our understanding of parents' and children's current adaptation with information about the quality of the relationships in the parents' families of origin (Cox et al., 1985; Main, Kaplan, & Cassidy, 1985; Ransom, 1988) and the parents' level of current life stress and social support (Crockenberg, 1981; Heming, 1985, 1987).

Methods

Of the original 72 expectant couples entering our study, we retained 87% at the 18-month follow-up, 70% at the 42-month follow-up, and 80% at 66 months postpartum (subject travel funds were responsible for this increase). Only 10% of the sample refused to continue their participation, with most attrition occurring because families had moved from the state. Except for a tendency toward lower marital satisfaction scores at earlier assessments for dropouts, there appear to be few differences between those who dropped out and those who continued to be involved in the study.

At each follow-up, we repeated the interviews and self-report assessments of the parents, as described earlier. In addition, we did some comprehensive assessments of the child—alone, with father, with mother, and with both parents. In the parent-child interaction sessions, children were taken out of the playroom and told a story by one of the experimenters; the parents were asked to have the child tell them the story when they returned to the playroom. Children were also given some rather difficult tasks that the parents were told they could help with as much as they ordinarily would (Block & Block, 1980), and then in each visit, parents and children were invited to "make a world together in the sand" using a sand tray and miniature people, animals, fences, trees, and a variety of manufactured objects. Parent-child interaction around both convergent and divergent tasks and the sandworld task were sampled in these procedures.

A. Parenting

Our general strategy has been to use global ratings to establish the "big picture" of how parent behavior is related to child outcomes, and these are the results we report here. We have also begun to perform microanalyses to help us understand the mechanisms or processes by which parents affect their children's competence and distress (Levine, 1988; Pratt, Kerig, Cowan, & Cowan, 1988).

(1) *Parenting style.* Experimenter-observers, blind to other data from the study, provided global ratings of each individual within the mother-child or father-child dyads (e.g., warmth, anger, interactiveness, responsiveness, and clarity of both parent and child). Seventeen parenting scales, based on our review of the central dimensions in socialization research, assessed both the *typical* level of the specified behavior over the whole session, and the *highest* level of the behavior observed. The 17 scales were factor analyzed and five orthogonal factors were derived: positive emotion, warmth-responsiveness, limits-maturity demands, engagement, and structure-clarity. In addition to analyses performed with the factors taken separately, we examined a bipolar *authoritative-disengaged* "superscale" created by z-scoring the items from each factor and compositing them (i.e., to combine warmth-responsiveness and structure-limits). At its high end the scale described parents who were warm, responsive, and structuring of the tasks; at its low end were parents rated as cold and uninvolved. A bipolar *authoritarian-permissive* superscale was created by inverting positive emotion, warmth/responsiveness, and engagement, and adding the inverted scores (z-scores) to limit setting and structure. At its high end this scale described parents who were cold, critical, nonresponsive, and limit setting; at the low end were parents who were observed to be warm and responsive but who set few limits and made few demands.

(2) *Co-parenting.* The team also rated the behavior of the mothers and fathers *towards one another* in the whole-family sessions. A factor analysis of 12 items yielded 5 factors, but here we will focus on one—observed couple conflict—because of its identification as an important correlate of children's adaptation (Emery, 1982; Rutter, 1983).

B. Child Behavior and Development

(1) *Global ratings.* Parallel to the 17 dimensions of parent behavior were 17 dimensions of child behavior rated by independent teams of experimenter-observers of the child (a) alone, (b) with each parent, and (c) with both parents. We are in the process of factoring these ratings, which seem to cluster into factors describing the child's relationship with the tasks (engaged, nonengaged) and with the parents (cooperative, hostile/resistant).

(2) *Laboratory tasks and tests.* Consistent with our approach to the selection of ratings, we chose tasks reflecting well-established theoretical conceptions of development, including Piagetian cognitive measures of *classification* and *seriation* (the precursors of number concepts), *role-taking* (related to social interaction), and 4 tasks developed by Jack and Jeanne Block (1980) to measure two aspects of the child's ego development—*ego-resiliency* (the child's adaptive resourceful response to challenge) and *ego-control* (the ability to control impulses and delay gratification). We used the same set of four laboratory tasks to measure these dimensions that Arend, Gove, and Sroufe (1979) had used in their study, in which they showed that early attachment and competence predict the child's ego-resiliency and control at 3- and 5-years-of-age. The laboratory tasks are cognitive in nature, but they are related to non-laboratory measures of personality and social competence.

(3) *Parents' descriptions of the child.* When the children were 3½, each parent filled out the *Minnesota Child Development Index* (MCDI; Ireton & Thwing, 1972), a checklist of developmental milestones that is correlated with Binet IQ and pre-school teacher ratings of child behavior, and O'Donnell and Van Tuinen's (1979) adaptation of the *Quay-Peterson Behavior Problem Checklist.* When children were 5½, parents completed both the *MCDI* and Schaefer's (1983) *Child Adaptive Behavior Inventory* (CABI), a 60-item inventory expanded with behavior problem items from other sources.

(4) *Teacher ratings* (5½-year follow-up only). In order to gain a sense of the child in the context of his or her classroom, we used a unique approach to teacher ratings. We asked the teachers of the children in our study to rate all of the children in their class on the CABI, without our identifying which child was in our study. We received Fall and Spring rating data from an astonishing 95% of the teachers including those of out-of-state children. A conceptual and correlational grouping produced 20 3- to 5-item scales (e.g., intelligent, outgoing, tense, depressed, kind, somaticizing). Scale scores factored neatly into four

major factors: *externalizing behavior; academic competence; shy/withdrawn behavior; and physical symptoms.*

(5) *Child test and interview data* (5½-year follow-up only). Another independent assessment was obtained from 2 different sessions with each individual child: Staff members who were blind to any other family data administered the *Peabody Individual Achievement Test* (PIAT), and *Harter's Self Esteem Scale* (1978).

The Family with a 3½-year-old Child

Details of the links between various family domains and specific aspects of child development will be presented in a set of forthcoming papers. Here we present some generalizations and examples based on a preliminary analysis of the full data set.

Parents' Depression and Child Development. Contrary to our expectations, simple correlations revealed that the number of connections between mothers' and fathers' self-reported symptoms of depression (CES-D, SCL-90, Parenting Stress Index depression scale) and measures of their children's developmental status (cognitive development, personality development, parent-reported behavior problems) did not exceed the number we would expect by chance.

Parenting Style—A Beginning Structural Model of the Mediating Process. While there were few direct connections between parents' reports of distress as individuals or couples and their children's developmental outcomes, the quality of their interactions with their child, as rated by observers in our laboratory, functioned as a link between parents' and children's adaptation.

We have begun to develop a structural model to describe the paths from parents' to children's adaptation. Structural modeling has become much more common in family studies during the last few years (e.g., Patterson & Capaldi, this volume). However, many intensive family studies have too few subjects to satisfy the relatively rigorous assumptions of LISREL (Joreskog & Sorbom, 1985). Fortunately there is an alternative modeling method. Nancy Miller (Miller, Cowan, Cowan, & Hetherington, unpublished manuscript) has constructed and tested a theoretical path model using Latent Variable Path Analyses with Partial Least Squares ("soft modeling"—Falk, 1987; Falk & Miller, this volume; Wold, 1982), using data from our 3½-year after birth follow-up.

The first goal of this model is to understand the family factors in the development of children's externalizing behavior (anger, hostility, fighting, disobedience) in the preschool period. Externalizing serves as an important example, in part because early antisocial behavior appears to have longterm negative consequences for children's development (Kellam, Simon, & Ensminger, 1982). All variables at each step of this model are latent variable composites. That is, they are, in essence, "factors" composed of multiple measures of each construct. With the exception of the depression variable, all of the composites assessing marriage, parenting, and child outcome include both self- or parent-report and observational data. Patterson and Bank (1986) have recommended this multimethod combination as a powerful technique for the building of structural models of family adaptation.

1. The latent variable for parents' depression summarizes three self-report instruments (the CES-D, Hopkins Symptom Checklist depression scale, and the Parenting Stress Index depression subscale).

2. For the latent variables representing the parents' marriage, Miller created both positive (satisfaction, observed cooperation) and negative (dissatisfaction, observed conflict) indices, as she did for

3. parenting style (parenting warmth and control), to investigate the possibility that each contributes differently to variations in children's externalizing behavior.

4. The latent variable representing the children's externalizing behavior included parents' descriptions of the child on the Quay-Peterson Behavior Problem Checklist scales that included externalizing and hyperactive behavior, and with observers' ratings of the child's negative emotions when he or she interacted with both parents in the laboratory.

The general model, then, looks like this:

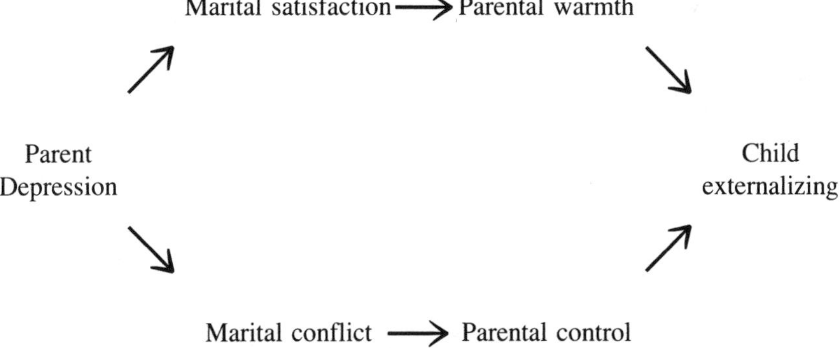

Miller's analyses of 44 families with 3½-year-olds show that there seem to be two pathways to preschoolers' externalizing behavior, one through low marital satisfaction and low parenting warmth, and another through high marital conflict and low parental control. The models for mothers and fathers are somewhat different in their details, with the mother's model accounting for 48% of the variance in the child's externalizing behavior, and the fathers' model accounting for 58% of the variance at the 3½-year postpartum assessment.

A model combining data from both parents, shows two paths to children's angry aggressive behavior:

(a) a positive path from less depression in the parents to higher marital satisfaction, to greater parenting warmth—to less externalizing behavior in the child, and

(b) a negative path from more depressive symptoms in the parents, to more marital conflict, to less parental control—to more externalizing in the child. This combined model accounts for an impressive 65% of the variance in preschool children's externalizing behavior.

These data show that marital distress contributes to negative mother-child or father-child interactions *over and above* the contribution of either parent's depression.[1] In other words, it is important to take *both mothers' and fathers'* individual and marital distress into account in explaining individual differences in their children's developmental status. The data are consistent with two versions of a buffering hypothesis. First, protective factors in one domain of family life (e.g., the marriage) can buffer the negative effects of one parent's depression on the child. Second, given the 2 pathways to child externalizing, it is likely, as Rutter suggests (1983), that one well-functioning parent can protect the child from the negative outcomes of interaction with the other distressed parent. So far, we have described only one outcome—the child's externalizing behavior—but other concurrent correlational analyses corroborate the general pattern of these findings.

The Family Context of Parenting: Predictability Over Time. The patterns of concurrent correlations among parents' depression, marital quality, and parenting style and the child's adaptation raise the issue of whether the parents are reacting to qualities of the child or whether the parent-child relationship is affecting the parents' perceptions of themselves, their marriage, and the child. Our longitudinal patterns of correlations indicate that at least some of the qualities we observe in parenting style grow out of the preexisting individual and family context.

(a) Consistency of self-reports. The consistency we reported earlier in the self-report measures from pregnancy to 18-months postpartum continued at least until the first child's kindergarten year. Correlations between pregnancy and 6, 18, 42, and 66 months postpartum averaged between .54 and .64 for both men and women on measures of self-esteem, marital satisfaction, role satisfaction, and depression. Correlations across the whole 6-year period were only slightly lower than those between adjacent periods.

---

[1]In her Master's research, Rachel Conrad is finding both direct and indirect connections between the parents' self-reported symptoms of depression and the microanalytically coded observations of mothers', fathers', and children's behavior as they work and play together in our laboratory playroom visits.

(b) Predicting parenting style at 3½ years postpartum. A multiple correlation of pregnancy measures of fathers' marital satisfaction, role satisfaction, perception of positive relationships in their families of origin, favorable balance between life stress and social support, and natural rather than C-section delivery predicted 45% of the variance in *fathers'* authoritative parenting of their preschoolers almost 4 years later. The same variables (assessed in pregnancy) predicted from 30% to 37% of the variance in *the couple's* co-parenting style (rated warmth, cooperation, and conflict) when they were interacting with their 3½ year olds. Although the data analyses are not yet complete, similar relationships emerged when we correlated prebirth data with parenting styles 6 years later, when the children were 5½-years-old and into elementary school classrooms.

Of course, the kind of child one has influences the parenting one does. But we have found in this study that a large component of parenting behavior is set in motion before the child comes along, arising from how parents feel about themselves and each other, and from the kind of family environment the couple has already established to receive the child.

The Family and Kindergarten Adaptation

Concurrent Analyses. Simple correlations based on our partial data set at 5½ years postpartum suggest that the early patterns of individual, marital, parenting, and child outcome from our assessment during the preschool period are replicated in general form, even if not always in specific detail, when the children are in kindergarten. Let us describe several new findings that demonstrate how the earlier family data predict the teachers' observations of the children's adaptation to kindergarten.

Teachers' ratings were standardized within their own classrooms so that the target child could be assigned scores on each factor *relative to his or her peers.* Although this procedure minimizes the rating biases of teachers, it does not deal with the possibility that some classrooms differ systematically from others in the general level of adaptive and maladaptive behavior (Kellam, personal communication). First, parents' and teachers' descriptions of the child on our adaptation of Schaefer's (1983) Child Adaptive Behavior Inventory were significantly correlated (averaging .48 for mother–teacher and .35 for father–teacher agreement). These correlations seem low until we remember that most studies find no correspondence between parent and teacher ratings of children. Second, there were consistent correlations between our staff observations of parenting in the laboratory and the teachers' observations of child developmental "outcomes," as the following examples demonstrate:

The *sons* of more permissive *fathers* (laboratory global rating composite) were described by their kindergarten teachers as more negative (.45), hostile (.44), and antisocial (.42), and less fair (.50) and kind (.59).

The *sons* of more permissive *mothers* were described by their teachers as more tense (.49) and negative (.47), and less fair (.43).

The *daughters* of more permissive *fathers* were described by their teachers as less symptomatic (.49), less distractible (.51), and less somaticizing (.37).

The *daughters* of more permissive *mothers* were described by their teachers as less hostile (.56), less victimized (.41), less creative (.49), and less task oriented (.53).

Permissive parenting may have quite different effects on sons and daughters. Furthermore, correlations between our staff ratings of *couple conflict* during the family session and the teacher's rating of the child's adaptation in the classroom were even higher than these associations between parenting styles and teachers' ratings of the child: the more the parents appeared to our observers to be in conflict with one another in our family playroom situation, the more the teacher described the child as having some difficulty adapting to the social and academic demands of being in the kindergarten classroom.

Predicting the Child's Adaptation to Kindergarten. Studies of family influences on children's school adaptation require longitudinal data to untangle the direction of influence. Here we find that family conditions occurring long before the child enters kindergarten predict the child's academic and social adaptation to school—as assessed by an individually administered achievement test (Peabody), and by the teacher's ratings on the Child Adaptive Behavior Inventory (Schaefer, 1983).

(a) From Preschool to Kindergarten. Parenting style observed in our lab when the child was a preschooler predicted reading comprehension scores on the Peabody at the end of the child's kindergarten year. When mothers were more actively engaged (r = .59) and fathers were warmer and more responsive (r = .45) with their preschool boys, the boys were better at reading 2-years later. When fathers showed more positive emotion (r = .62), warmth, responsiveness (r = .49), engagement (r = .49), and authoritativeness (r = .53) with their daughters during the preschool period, the girls had higher total Peabody achievement scores. Similarly, mothers who were more positive (r = .45), warm, responsive (r = .43), and authoritative (r = .38) with their daughters, had daughters with higher total Peabody scores.

(b) From Pre-*birth* to Kindergarten. Finally, we have begun to test the hypothesis that the parents' adaptation to the transition to parenthood predicts their child's later adaptation to school. We created an index of the amount of decline in parents' self-esteem or marital satisfaction between pregnancy and 18 months after birth (a change score). Parents with less decline in self-esteem during the transition to parenthood were more authoritative in the parent-child interaction sessions 6 years later (r = .42 fathers; .36 mothers). Similarly, parents who showed less decline in marital satisfaction over the transition to parenthood tended to have sons who were rated by their kindergarten teachers as less shy (.59 for fathers; .54 for mothers) and daughters who were described as more academically competent (.45 for fathers; .47 for mothers) as they made their transitions to elementary school.

There is impressive continuity, then, between parents' adaptation to the transition to parenthood and their children's later adjustment to the demands of elementary school. The patterns are consistent with our model, showing links that center on the ways in which each parent's well-being or distress is carried over to his or her style of relating to the child.

We are not the first researchers to have demonstrated relationships between parents' adaptation or parenting styles and child outcomes. What our model adds, we think, is the importance of the quality of the couple relationship to both the parent-child relationships and the child's own developmental status. The couple relationship appears to form a background out of which each parent's relationship with the child develops. While psychodynamic theory has helped trace parenting practices to roots in the quality of relationships in parents' families of origin, our data suggest that these links may be mediated by the quality of marital attachments that husbands' and wives' early experiences allow them to form in their adult years.

TRANSITION AND INTERVENTION

The first three authors are clinical psychologists, the fourth a sociologist. All of us believe that providing fuller descriptions of families in distress is only part of the researcher's task. We are also concerned about trying to understand how to buffer or alleviate some of that distress before it spills over into all of the relationships in the family. When we began this study, we believed that there was sufficient evidence of couples having a difficult time of family-making to warrant the design of a preventive intervention. The longitudinal data support this view. Furthermore, our findings showing that couple relationship quality is implicated in the child's early social, emotional, and cognitive development and adaptation provide even greater force to the argument that families may benefit from psychological help while they are facing the challenges of complex normative transitions.

In addition to the practical goals that could be served by developing interventions with families before they feel the need of psychological services, interventions are useful for testing our theoretical models of family process. Our correlations suggest that certain variables are interconnected. Interventions that can affect certain parts of "the model" can provide a critical test of whether those covariations involve dynamic connections.

More than 20 years ago, Caplan (1964) and his colleagues suggested that the transition to parenthood was an ideal time to provide preventive interventions, although their attention was focused primarily on expectant *mothers.* Very few clinicians and researchers have put this suggestion into practice. We are aware of only two preventive intervention projects focusing on the transition to parenthood in addition to the one we are reporting here, and only one was focused on the parents' marital relationship. The first, designed in the United States (Shereshefsy & Yarrow, 1973), involved individual counseling of expectant mothers by mental health professionals during the last trimester of pregnancy. The second project, developed in London, England, focused on expectant couples (Clulow, 1982), and involved 6 once-a-month meetings of both partners in couples groups. Unfortunately, it is difficult to evaluate the effects of the British couples groups, because there were no systematic before or after assessments of the couples' marriages.

There is a very strong tendency for parents of young children to relegate their own needs as individuals and as couples to the proverbial "back burner" while they cope with the extraordinary demands of a helpless and demanding infant, one or two jobs outside the family, and all of the increased needs of maintaining an increasingly complex household. We felt that if parents could learn that this is par for the course during family formation, their strain might feel more manageable—and that might free them to use their strengths as a couple to make their lives fit their own and their babies' needs.

In part because of the relative isolation of contemporary couples, we envisioned couples *groups* in which trained leaders would help to draw out and contain what we had come to understand were the expectable anxieties and conflicts for partners becoming parents. Based on our pilot study (Cowan et al., 1978), the first 2 authors trained 2 other married couples (graduate students in Clinical psychology at the time) by forming a small couples group made up of the 3 staff couples. All of us used the questionnaires from the project to describe ourselves as individuals and as couples. Then, over a period of 3 months, we met together weekly to talk about how the day-to-day issues in our lives as individuals and as couples led us to feel close, distant, satisfied, disenchanted, and so on. Over time, we began to see how our feelings about ourselves, our role arrangements as a couple, and the ways we went about working on the problems in our lives affected how we felt about ourselves and about our relationships as couples.

This staff couples group modeled the form and process of the groups we later offered the expectant couples. The groups combined some of the qualities of support, consciousness-raising, and therapy groups. They were semistructured in the sense that part of each evening was planned by us for discussing the aspects of life covered by our conceptual model and the study questionnaires. We used partners' responses to the questionnaires as a focus for discussion. The unstructured part of each evening was a time when any of the participants could raise questions, concerns, or issues that were on their minds. When an issue or problem was being described by a group member, our role as coleaders was to ask each spouse, in essence, "What does this mean for you?" and "How is this affecting you as a couple?" During the late pregnancy months, men and women slowly began to explore their dreams and their concerns about creating an "ideal" family. They talked a little about the families they grew up in, a great deal about the impending birth, and everyone had trouble imagining anything after the day of birth.

As the babies were born, each couple returned to the group to tell their birth story. Our focus was soon diverted by everyone's fascination with the four newborns who had joined the group. It was difficult to complete a sentence without being distracted by the distinctive cries, hiccups, and gurgles of the babies. We felt as if we were part of a "living laboratory" in which we as group leaders could reflect on what we were seeing—that neither husbands or wives were getting an opportunity to rest or explore a feeling or an idea since their babies' births. The concern that group participants began to show for one another was poignant. Each week, we shared laughter at the delightful parts of watching the babies' personalities come alive—and not infrequently some tears as overwhelmed mothers and fathers tried to find their way in the common dilemmas and conflicts of being a family. Who would work, who would give up what, how to keep the relationship between the parents viable and look after the infant's never-ending needs became a serious challenge. As planned, the groups ended when the babies were about 3-months-old, just as some of the parents were beginning to feel competent. Phase 1 of the study included a follow-up of every couple in the study—those with and without a couples group—with individually completed questionnaires and staff interviews with each couple when their babies were 6- and 18-months-old.

Effects of the Intervention: Early on. At our 18-month postpartum follow-ups, the results of the couples group intervention were encouraging (see Cowan & Cowan, 1987b and C. Cowan, 1988 for more detail). Compared to parents without an intervention, fathers who had been in a couples group described themselves as more psychologically involved in the parent role when their children were 1½-years-old, and mothers had retained more of their sense of self as workers or students. The intervention fathers were more satisfied with their role in caring for their children, and they described less decline in social support, and less negative change in their sexual relationship than fathers without the intervention. The mothers from the intervention sample had also maintained their satisfaction with the couple's division of labor (no-intervention mothers' satisfaction had declined), increased their positive balance of social support and life stress, and, like their partners, experienced fewer negative changes in their sexual relationship than their no-intervention counterparts.

Did the intervention groups affect the marriage? Although both intervention and no-intervention couples showed a decline in marital satisfaction from pregnancy to 6 months after birth, the decline in the intervention couples was smaller. Then, over the next year of family life, from 6- to 18-months postpartum, the marital satisfaction of the intervention couples remained stable, while the no-intervention couples' satisfaction declined again, even more steeply than it had earlier. Intervention couples' descriptions of marital quality remained stable despite the fact that their conflict had increased and their role satisfaction had decreased. It is as if the group experience helped to keep partners from attributing their negative change and distress to failures in their relationships as couples.

Our separation and divorce data on all couples in the study support the argument that the intervention had some ongoing positive effects. Two years after the study began, 16% (4/24) of the couples who had *not* had a baby were separated or divorced. At the same time, 18 months after giving birth, 12.5% (4/48) of the new parent couples without an intervention had separated or divorced. The marriages of *all* of the parents who had participated in a couples group during their transition to parenthood were still intact. Thus, in the short run, the intervention appeared to buffer the marital strain, disappointment, and dissolution experienced by childless couples and new parents without an intervention.

How can we explain the separation/divorce effects for the intervention couples? The intervention seems to "unhook" the relationships between many of the variables and satisfaction with marriage. For a number of the pregnancy risk factors, variables that predicted marital declines in the no-intervention couples (low income, ambivalence about wanting the child, and high marital conflict) were not significantly related to later marital satisfaction for the couples who had participated in the intervention. As a result, marital quality for the intervention couples, as rated by both husbands and wives, was highly consistent from pre-baby days to 4 years later ($r = .70$), but the aftertransition levels were not predictable for couples without the intervention.

In the Longer Run. When the children were between 3½ and 4-years-of-age, the rate of separation and divorce in the nonintervention families had increased to 15%, and the first couple from the intervention sub sample had separated (4%)—samples too small to test for statistically significant differences but a still noticeable difference between the subsamples more than 3 years after the intervention ended. The percentage of no-treatment couples who had divorced by the time their first child was 3 is comparable to Eiduson's (1982) finding in a traditional-to-nontraditional sample of couples, 15% of whom had divorced by 3 years after their first child's birth, and comparable to the rates of marital dissolution in a national study of divorce by Bumpass and Rindfuss (1979). This makes our intervention sample's low rate of divorce almost 4 years after birth especially noteworthy.

New continuous self-reports from parents about their life in each of our family domains suggest that the positive effects of the intervention were beginning to wane during this preschool period. Satisfaction with the overall marriage, which declined steadily in the no-treatment couples from pregnancy to 3½ years after birth, had now begun to drop in the treatment couples as well.

When the children were 3½, we compared the families in which the parents had participated in the intervention and those who had not, looking for differences in parenting style or in the children's adaptation. Even though we found a few significant differences that favored the families who had participated in a couples group during the transition to parenthood, in light of the number of statistical tests that were done, the number of differences may not have exceeded those expected to occur by chance.

Our preliminary data at the kindergarten year follow-up 2 years later suggest that the positive effects of the intervention have disappeared. The couples who became parents are still more likely to be in intact marriages than couples remaining childless, whose rate of separation and divorce is now at 50%. But the rate of separation and divorce in all of the parent couples with or without the intervention, is now the same—19.5%. We return to the issue of the high rate of divorce in childless couples shortly.

Clearly, the intervention effects do not last forever—nor would we expect them to. Despite the help from working with mental health professionals on marital disenchantment and conflict as it occurs, the early promising effects on the parents have eroded with the passage of time and the strains of other challenging family transitions. By the time we interviewed the parents in the preschool period, many had moved, changed jobs, given birth to second or third children, or suffered illnesses in their immediate or extended families. It is clear that an early intervention of this kind is helpful but not sufficient for keeping the disenchantment that many spouses feel with their partners from leading to divorce (cf. Epperson, 1987).

The results so far suggest to us that a "booster shot" intervention when the first child is two could address the issues that seem to lead to parents' later declines in marital satisfaction. As the early data suggest, if we can help to keep the parents' marital disenchantment to a tolerable minimum, we may able to affect the child's early developmental progress and adaptation to school through fostering less tension-filled parenting.

Conclusions

With these comprehensive longitudinal data on the transition to parenthood, we have been able to establish that it is possible to identify partners and couples who will be at risk for distress two years later from their descriptions of themselves, their spouses, and their marriages before they give birth. Those in most distress as individuals and couples once they become parents tend in the next year or two to show more tension, and less warmth and structure as they work and play with their preschool children. The preliminary analyses we have reported here provide encouraging support for our 5-domain model of individual and family functioning.

Since couples who were in most distress during pregnancy tended to be in most distress after they became parents, and since 15% of the parents without an intervention had separated or divorced by the time their first child was 3½, it seems critical that mental health professionals begin to develop interventions for working with distressed couples as they are forming new families.

We have argued that the consistent average declines in new parents' satisfaction with their role arrangements and their overall marriage suggests that there are risks associated with the transition to parenthood. What, then, do we make of the fact that 5 years after the study began, about half of the couples *remaining childless* were divorced? The data in our study are quite consistent with census data on this point: having a young child functions as a protective factor in preserving the marriage during the early years of childrearing (Glick, 1979; Houseknecht, 1987). But in the marriages that remain intact, there is a decided deterioration in both the quantity of partners' time together and the quality of their relationships as couples. There seem to be marital risks along each of these life pathways. It is not surprising to us that disenchanted partners with preschool age children are slower to divorce than childless couples. But we do continue to be surprised at the extent of distress reported by these parents of young children as they take stock of the realities of their life as couples and families.

Although not all of the couples experienced distress during this couple-to-family transition, our findings strengthen our determination to continue to develop and systematically evaluate preventive interventions targeted to helping parents cope with the strains of this major adult transition. The data linking the parents' well-being with their children's adaptation suggest that it will be costly—for the parents and their children—to wait until the parents feel distressed enough to seek relief from therapists or divorce lawyers. Even when the parents stay together, their dissatisfaction with their relationship as a couple tends to color the quality of their relationships with their preschool age children. And, as we have seen, the state of family life in the preschool years appears to foreshadow the children's adaptation their first year of elementary school. Our correlational data imply that family-based interventions focused on both marital and parenting issues—and addressed to both mothers and fathers—would be a fertile area for mental health professionals to pursue.

ACKNOWLEDGMENTS

This study has been supported throughout by NIMH grant MH 31109. Preparation of this chapter was supported in part by funds from the Spencer foundation. We also want to acknowledge major contributions to the longitudinal study by other members of the research team: Dena Cowan, Barbara Epperson, Beth

Schoenberger, and Marc Schulz processed the data; Ellen Garrett and William S. Coysh, Harriet Curtis-Boles and Abner Boles III, along with the Cowans, followed families over the first years and led intervention groups; Laura Mason Gordon and David Gordon did follow-up interviews with some couples in the last three years. Sacha Bunge, Michael Blum, Julia Levine, David Chavez, Marc Schulz, and Joanna Cowan worked with the children in the study; Linda Kastelowitz, Victor Lieberman, Marsha Kline, and Charles Soulé conducted the parent-child and family visits; Laurie Leventhal-Belfer and Elaine Ransom collected the teachers' ratings. Finally, we are indebted to Profs. Michael Pratt and Yona Teichman, whose collaboration from afar has proved invaluable.

REFERENCES

Abidin, R. (1981). *The parenting stress index: A concurrent validity study using medical utilization data.* Unpublished manuscript, Institute of Clinical Psychology, University of Virginia.

Arend, R., Gove, F. L., & Sroufe, A. (1979). Continuity of individual adaptation from infancy to Kindergarten: A predictive study of ego-resiliency and curiosity in preschoolers. *Child Development, 50,* 950–959.

Baumrind, D. (1979). The development of instrumental competence through socialization. In A. D. Pick (Ed.), *Minnesota symposia on child psychology* (Vol. 7). Minneapolis: University of Minnesota Press.

Beardslee, W. R., Bemporad, J., Keller, M. B., & Klerman, G. L. (1983). Children of parents with major affective disorder: A review. *American Journal of Psychiatry, 140,* 825–832.

Belsky, J. (1984). The determinants of parenting: A process model. *Child Development, 55,* 83–96.

Belsky, J., & Pensky, E. (1988). Developmental history, personality, and family relationships: Toward an emergent family system. In R. Hinde & J. Stevenson-Hinde (Eds.). *The interrelationship of family relationships.* London: Cambridge University Press.

Belsky, J., Robins, E., & Gamble, W. (1985). The determinants of parental competence: Toward a contextual theory. In M. Lewis & L. Roseblum (Eds.). *Beyond the dyad.* New York: Plenum.

Belsky, J., Lang, M. E., & Rovine, M. (1985). Stability and change in marriage across the transition to parenthood: A second study. *Journal of Marriage and the Family, 47,* 855–865.

Belsky, J., Ward, M., & Rovine, M. (in press). Prenatal expectations, postnatal experiences, and the transition to parenthood. In R. Ashmore & D. Brodzinsky (Eds.), *Perspectives on the family.* Hillsdale, NJ: Lawrence Erlbaum Associates.

Bernard, J. (1974). *The future of marriage.* New York: World.

Block, J. H., & Block, J. (1980). The role of ego-control and ego-resiliency in the organization of behavior. In W. A. Collins (Ed.), *Minnesota symposia on child psychology* (Vol. 13). Hillsdale, NJ: Lawrence Erlbaum Associates.

Blood, R. O., & Wolfe, D. M. (1960). *Husbands and wives: The dynamics of married living.* Glencoe, IL: The Free Press.

Brockington, F., Crnic, K. F., Schonfield, E. M., Downing, A. R., Francis, A. F., & Keelan, C. (1981). Puerperal psychosis: Phenomena and diagnosis. *Archives of General Psychiatry, 38,* 839–833.

Bronfenbrenner, U. (1979). *The ecology of human development.* Cambridge, MA: Harvard University Press.

Bumpass, L., & Rindfuss, R. R. (1979). Children's experiences of marital disruption. *American Journal of Sociology, 85,* 49–65.

Caplan, G. (1964). *Principles of preventive psychiatry.* New York: Basic Books.

Clulow, C. F. (1982). *To have and to hold: Marriage, the first baby and preparing couples for parenthood.* Aberdeen: Aberdeen University Press.

Cowan, C. P. (1988). Working with men becoming fathers: The impact of a couples group intervention. In P. Bronstein & C. P. Cowan (Eds.), *Fatherhood today: Men's changing role in the family.* New York: Wiley.

Cowan, C. P., & Cowan, P. A. (1987a). Men's involvement in parenthood: Identifying the antecedents and understanding the barriers. In P. Berman & F. A. Pedersen (Eds.), *Men's transition to parenthood.* Hillsdale, NJ: Lawrence Erlbaum Associates.

Cowan, C. P., & Cowan, P. A. (1987b). A preventive intervention for couples becoming parents. In C. F. Z. Boukydis (Ed.), *Research on support for parents and infants in the postnatal period.* Norwood, NJ: Ablex.

Cowan, C. P., & Cowan, P. A. (1988b). Who does what when partners become parents: Implicatons for men, women, and marriage. *Marriage & Family Review, 13,* 1 & 2.

Cowan, C. P., & Cowan, P. A. (November, 1988c). *Adult children of alcoholics: What happens when they form new families?* Paper presented at the National Council on Family Relations, Philadelphia, PA.

Cowan, C. P., & Cowan, P. A. (1990b). The pie. In J. Touliatos, B. F. Perlmutter, & M. A. Straus (Eds.), *Handbook of family measurement techniques.* Newbury Park, CA: Sage.

Cowan, C. P., & Cowan, P. A. (1990c). Who does what? In J. Touliatos, B. F. Perlmutter, & M. A. Straus (Eds.), *Handbook of family measurement techniques.* Newbury Park, CA: Sage.

Cowan, C. P., Cowan, P. A., Heming, G., Garrett, E., Coysh, W. S., Curtis-Boles, H., & Boles, A. J. (1985). Transitions to parenthood: His, hers, and theirs. *Journal of Family Issues, 6,* 451–481.

Cowan, C. P., Cowan, P. A., Coie, L., & Coie, J. D. (1978). Becoming a family: The impact of a first child's birth on the couple's relationship. In W. B. Miller & L. F. Newman (Eds.), *The first child and family formation.* Chapel Hill, N.C.: Carolina Population Center.

Cowan, P. A. (1988). Becoming a father: A time of change, an opportunity for development. In P. Bronstein & C. P. Cowan (Eds.), *Fatherhood today: Men's changing role in the family.* New York: Wiley.

Cowan, P. A., & Cowan, C. P. (1988a). Changes in marriage during the transition to parenthood: Must we blame the baby? In G. Y. Michaels & W. A. Goldberg (Eds.), *The transition to parenthood: Current theory and research.* Cambridge: Cambridge University Press.

Cowan, P. A., & Cowan, C. P. (1990a). Becoming a Family: Research and Intervention. In I. Sigel & G. Brody, G. (Eds.), *Family research, Vol. I.* Hillsdale, NJ: Lawrence Erlbaum Associates.

Cox, M. J., Owen, M. T., Lewis, J. M., Riedel, C., Scalf-McIver, L., & Suster, A. (1985). Intergenerational influences on the parent-infant relationship in the transition to parenthood. In M. J. Cox (Ed.), *Journal of Family Issues, Vol. 6, No. 4,* 543–564.

Crockenberg, S. B. (1981). Infant irritability, mother responsiveness, and social support infuences on the security of infant-mother attachment. *Child Development, 52,* 857–865.

Davenport, Y. B., & Adland, M. L. (1982). Postpartum psychoses in female and male bipolar manic depressive patients. *American Journal of Orthopsychiatry, 52,* 288–297.

Duncan, S. W., & Markman, H. J. (1988). Intervention programs for the transition to parenthood: Current status from a preventive perspective. In G. Y. Michaels & W. A. Goldberg (Eds.), *Transition to parenthood: Current theory and research.* Cambridge, England: Cambridge University Press.

Eiduson, B. T. (1981,April). *Parent/child relationships in alternative families and socioemotional development of children at 3 years of age.* Paper presented at Society for Research in Child Development Meetings, Boston, MA.

Emery, R. E. (1982). Interparental conflict and the children of discord and divorce. *Psychological Bulletin, 92,* 310–330.

Epperson, B. (1987). *Predicting divorce.* Unpublished manuscript, University of California, Berkeley.

Falk, F. (1987). *A primer for soft modeling.* Institute of Human Development, University of California, Berkeley.

Fedele, N. M., Golding, E. R., Grossman, F. K., & Pollack, W. S. (1988). Psychological issues in adjustment to first parenthood. In G. Michaels & W. Goldberg, (Eds.), *The transition to parenthood: Current theory and research.* Cambridge, England: Cambridge University Press.

Feldman, S. S. (1987). Predicting strain in mothers and fathers of 6-month-old infants: A short-term longitudinal study. In P. W. Berman & F. A. Pedersen (Eds.), *Men's transitions to parenthood: Longitudinal studies of early family experience.* Hillsdale, NJ: Lawrence Erlbaum Associates.

Feldman, S. S., & Nash, S. C. (1984). The transition from expectancy to parenthood: Impact of the firstborn child on men and women. *Sex Roles, 11,* 84–96.

Festinger, L. (1957). *A theory of cognitive dissonance.* Evanston, IL: Row, Peterson.

Fleming, A. S., Ruble, D. N., Flett, G. L., & Shaul, D. L. (1988). Postpartum adjustment in first-time mothers: Relations between mood, maternal attitudes, and mother-infant interaction. *Developmental Psychology, 24*(1), 71–81.

Garrett, E. T. (1983, August). *Women's experiences of early parenthood: Expectation vs. reality.* Paper presented at the American Psychological Association Meetings, Anaheim, CA.

Glick, P. (1979). *Who are the children in one-parent households?* Paper delivered at Wayne State University, Detroit, Michigan.

Goldberg, W. A., & Easterbrooks, M. A. (1984). The role of marital quality in toddler development. *Developmental Psychology, 20,* 504–514.

Grossman, F. Eichler, L., & Winickoff, S. (1980). *Pregnancy, brith, and parenthood.* San Francisco: Jossey-Bass.

Harter, S. (1978). *Perceived competence scale for children.* Manual. Colorado seminary: University of Denver.

Heinicke, C. (1984). Impact of prebirth parent personality and marital functioning on family development: A Framework and suggestions for further study. *Developmental Psychology, 20,* 1044–1053.

Heinicke, C. M., Diskin, S. D., Ramsay-Klee, D. M., & Oates, D. S. (1986). Pre- and postbirth antecedents of 2-year-old attention, capacity for relationships and verbal expressiveness. *Developmental Psychology, 22,* 777–787.

Heming, G. (1985). *Predicting adaptation in the transition to parenthood.* Unpublished doctoral dissertation, University of California, Berkeley.

Heming, G. (1987, April). *Predicting adaptation to parenthood.* Paper presented to Society for Research in Child Development. Baltimore, MD.

Heming, G., Cowan, P. A., & Cowan, C. P. (1990). Ideas about parenting. In J. Touliatos, B. F. Perlmutter, & M. A. Straus (Eds.), *Handbook of family measurement techniques.* Newbury Park, CA: Sage.

Hetherington, E. M., & Camara, K. A. (1984). Families in transition: the process of dissolution and reconstitution. In R. D. Parke (Ed.), *Review of child development research: The family.* Vol. VII. Chicago: University of Chicago Press.

Hobbs, D. F. Jr. (1965). Parenthood as crisis: A third study. *Journal of Marriage and the Family, 27,* 367–372.

Hobbs, D. F. Jr. (1968). Transition to parenthood: A replication and an extension. *Journal of Marriage and the Family, 30,* 413–417.

Hobbs, D. F., & Cole, S. (1976). Transition to parenthood: A decade replication. *Journal of Marriage and the Family, 38,* 723–731.

Hobbs, D. F., & Wimbish, J. M. (1977). Transition to parenthood by black couples. *Journal of Marriage and the Family, 39,* 677–689.

Hops, H., Sherman, L., & Biglan, A. (1989). Maternal depression, marital discord, and children's behavior: A developmental perspective. In G. R. Patterson (Ed.), *Advances in Family Research, Vol. 1. Depression and aggression: Two facets of family interactions*. Hillsdale, NJ: Lawrence Erlbaum Associates.

Houseknecht, S. K. (1987). Voluntary childlessness. In M. B. Sussman & S. K. Steinmetz (Eds.), *Handbook of marriage and the family*. New York: Plenum.

Ireton, H. R., & Thwing, E. J. (1972). *Minnesota Child Development Inventory Manual*. Minneapolis: Interpretive Scoring Systems.

Joreskog, K. G., & Sorbom, D. (1985). *LISREL-V Program manual*. Chicago. International Educational Services.

Kellam, S. G., Simon, M. B., & Ensminger, M. E. (1982). Antecedents in first grade of teenage drug use and psychological well-being: A ten-year community-wide prospective study. In D. Ricks & B. Dohrenwend (Eds.), *Origins of psychopathology: Research and public policy*. New York: Cambridge University Press.

Kline, M. (1988). *Family work, employment work, and well-being during the transition to parenthood*. Unpublished doctoral dissertation. University of California, Berkeley.

LeMasters, E. E. (1957). Parenthood as crisis. *Marriage and Family Living, 19,* 352–355.

Levine, J. (1988). *Play in the context of the family*. Unpublished doctoral dissertation. University of California, Berkeley.

Lewis, J. M. (1988). The transition to parenthood: II. Stability and change in marital structure. *Family Process, 27,* 273–284.

Lewis, J. M., Owen, M. T., & Cox, M. J. (1988). The transition to parenthood: III. Incorporation of the child into the family. *Family Process, 27,* 411–421.

Locke, H., & Wallace, K. (1959). Short marital adjustment and prediction tests: Their reliability and validity. *Marriage and Family Living, 21,* 251–255.

Main, M., Kaplan, N., & Cassidy, J. (1985). Security in infancy, childhood, and adulthood: A move to the level of representation. In I. Bretherton & E. Waters (Eds.), *Growing points of attachment theory and research. Monographs of the Society for Research in Child Development, 50,* Serial No. 209, pp. 66–106.

Miller, N. B., Cowan, P. A., Cowan, C. P., & Hetherington, E. M. *Parents' depression, marital quality, and parenting style, and externalizing behavior in preschoolers and adolescents*. Unpublished manuscript, University of Akron.

O'Donnell, J. P., & Van Tuinen, M. V. (1979). Behavior problems of preschool children: Dimensions and congenital correlates. *Journal of Abnormal Child Psychology, 7,* 61–75.

Osofsky, J. D., & Osofsky, H. J. (1984). Psychological and developmental perspectives on expectant and new parenthood. In R. D. Parke (Ed.), *Review of child development research 7: The family*. Chicago: University of Chicago Press.

Parke, R. (1979). Perspectives on father-infant interaction. In J. Osofsky (Ed.), *Handbook of infant development* (pp. 549–590). New York: Wiley.

Parke, R. D., & Tinsley, B. (1982). The early environment of the at-risk infant: Expanding the social context. In D. D. Bricker (Ed.), *Intervention with at-risk and handicapped infants*. Baltimore: University Park Press.

Patterson, G. R., & Bank, L. (1986). Bootstrapping your way in the nomological thicket. *Behavioral Assessment, 8,* 49–73.

Pratt, M., Kerig, P., Cowan, P. A., & Cowan, C. P. (1988). Mothers and fathers teaching three year-olds: Authoritative parenting and adult scaffolding of young children's learning. *Developmental Psychology, 24*(6), 832–839.

Radloff, L. (1977). Sex differences in depression: The effects of occupation and marital status. *Sex Roles, 1,* 249–265.

Ransom, E. (1988). *Parents' childhood memories: How are they related to their own children's development?* Unpublished dissertation, University of California, Berkeley.

Rutter, M. (1983). Stress, coping and development: Some issues and some questions. In N. Garmezy & M. Rutter (Eds.), *Stress, coping and development in children* (pp. 1–42). New York: McGraw-Hill.

Schaefer, E. S. (1983). *Classroom Behavior Inventory*. Unpublished instrument. University of North Carolina at Chapel Hill.

Shereshefsky, P., & Yarrow, L. J. (Eds.). (1973). *Psychological aspects of a first pregnancy and early postnatal adaptation*. New York: Raven Press.

Snowden, L. R., & Schott, T. L., Awalt, S. J., & Gillis-Knox, J. (1988). Marital satisfaction in pregnancy: Stability and change. *Journal of Marriage and the Family, 50,* 325–333.

Spanier, G. R., & Lewis, G. B. (1980). Marital quality: A review of the seventies. *Journal of Marriage and the Family, 42,* 825–839.

Wallerstein, J. S., & Kelly, J. B. (1980). *Surviving the breakup: How children and parents cope with divorce*. New York: Basic Books.

Weissman, M. M., & Klerman, G. L. (1977). Sex differences and the epidemiology of depression. *Archives of General Psychiatry, 34,* 98–112.

Wold, H. (1982). Systems under indirect observation using PLS. In C. Fornell (Ed.), *A second generation of multivariate analysis* (pp. 325–347). New York: Praeger.

Zaslow, M., Pedersen, F., Kramer, E., Cain, R., Suwalsky, J., & Fivel, M. I. (1981, April). *Depressed mood in new fathers: Interview and behavioral correlates*. Paper presented at the Society for Research in Child Development, Boston, MA.

5 Effective Parenting During the Early Adolescent Transition

Diana Baumrind
University of California, Berkeley

In this paper I develop a conceptual framework for predicting the impact on adolescents of various facets of parental demandingness and responsiveness. My focus is on effective parenting during the early adolescent transition when Time 3 data were collected as part of the *Family Socialization and Developmental Competence Project* (FSP), a longitudinal program of research. I first discuss sociopolitical and developmental features that impact on the adolescent-parent relationship and then contrast two views of the parent-adolescent bond which are dubbed "classic" and "contemporary." FSP findings on effective parenting are presented, followed by a discussion of the implications of the early adolescent data for the classic and contemporary views.

ADOLESCENCE AND ADOLESCENTS IN TRANSITION

In this section I discuss both secular changes that affect adolescents differently from other age groups, and developmental changes that take place within the individual during adolescence.

By adolescence I refer to an age span roughly between ages 10 and 21, heralded by the accelerating physical changes accompanying puberty that result in sexual maturity and identity formation, and eventuate in emancipation from childhood dependency. Ages 10 to 15, which are often used to bracket early adolescence, correspond to the ages of children attending middle school (4th through 6th grades) and junior high school (7th through 8th or 9th grades) in the United States. Ages 15 to 18, which bracket midadolescence, correspond to the ages of children attending high school. Late adolescence extends from high school graduation to entry into young adult status by which time the individual should have made crucial, but not irreversible, decisions concerning school, love, and work; and be fully emancipated from parental authority, although not from parental influence.

In all human societies adolescence is the developmental period in which the physical and social status of *child* changes to that of *adult*. Our culture has no rites of passage to demarcate the change in status from child to adult, but has instead a long transitional period between puberty and adulthood that we call adolescence. The normative adolescent stage-transition includes major role changes in the individual's position relative to others, a shift in loyalties towards peers if not away from family, and a different mix of entitlements and obligations within the family and larger society. However, developmental *progress* is not guaranteed. Successful stage-transition, resulting in a more differentiated and integrated level of adaptation in young adulthood can occur only through personal commitment to courses of thought and action that depart from early, more stable and secure patterns; and accommodation by parents and other significant adults to the changing status of the child. Developmental progress may be retarded either when action is curtailed and interaction with a disequilibrating environment reduced, for example by repressive or overly protective parents; or when adolescents engage in experiences, such as drug abuse, that reduce full presence of mind. In any event, the individual changes occurring within the adolescent may (and indeed should) stimulate disequilibrium and reorganization of the family system. These changes in roles and relationships may scarcely be noticed by family members, or they may be experienced as stressful crises.

Adolescence in Transition

Adolescents are the only age group in the United States in which mortality has increased since 1960 with three-quarters of these deaths due to accidents, suicides, and homicides (Brown, 1979). Substance use and abuse (Johnston, Bachman, & O'Malley, 1980) and the consequences of nonresponsible sexual activity (Furstenberg, 1981; Shafer & Irwin, 1983) have had a profound impact on the early adult and long-range health of youth (U.S. Department of Health, Education, and Welfare, 1979). Although there has been an overall decline in *reported* drug use (Johnston et al., 1985), underreporting of drug use may now be prevalent because of a change in social climate less favorable to drug experimentation (Warner, 1978).

Unlike traditional societies which offer guidelines to human behavior that remain relevant across many generations, contemporary American society presents adolescents with a plenitude of frequently contradictory values, extreme mobility, and a dearth of extended support groups. These social factors may prolong unduly the adolescent transition, requiring a crisis (e.g., anorexia or acting out) to resolve. On the other hand, premature rejection of, or ejection from, the protective environment of the family may increase the risk of anomie, confusion, and exclusive dependence on the peer group for affiliation and self-esteem.

Contemporary American sociopolitical factors impacts unfavorably on youthful development in at least three ways:

1. First, rapidly accelerating demographic and socioeconomic changes have resulted, according to Bronfenbrenner (1985), in an "unravelling of the social fabric in which families, schools, and other immediate contexts of development are embedded" (p. 337). This breakdown in tradition is reflected in symptoms of despair and disaffiliation among a sizeable minority of our adolescents.

2. Second, in the United States today, adolescents are effectively excluded from adult society and have no normative niche of their own. The gap between puberty and psychosocial maturity is wider than ever before, and is likely to remain so since puberty is reached at an earlier age today than it was in the past, and the sagging economy cannot employ all the young people the society produces. Thus, entry into the adult world of commitment and responsibility is often delayed for affluent youth and may be denied to a growing proportion of this generation's poor.

3. Third, and perhaps most critical, the social role of women has been permanently altered placing women at greater risk themselves and less able to perform their traditional role as conservators of health. The changes brought about by the women's movement—as liberating as they have been to adults—do have at least four expectably negative consequences for adolescent development: First, to the extent that maternal presence in the home has been an essential part of traditional upbringing, the traditional conservative and countervailing force to unbridled risk-taking behavior is diminished; second, the benefits of having an adult in the home to supervise the activities of adolescents and to provide them with comfort and solace is forfeited; third, commitment to vocation may be accompanied by lessened commitment to parenting for many mothers; and fourth, young women are likely to engage in increasingly greater risk-taking problem behavior symbolic of their liberated status, such as use of tobacco and acts of violence.

Furthermore, beginning in the 1950s and continuing for at least 2 decades, a strong contingent of children's rights advocates in the fields of education and childrearing, with some success, promoted the notion that the effects on the child of adult authority are inhibiting, neurotogenic, and indefensible ethically (Friedenberg, 1971; Goodman, 1964; Holt, 1974; Maslow, 1954; Neill, 1964; Rogers, 1960). Worsfold (1974), basing his argument on John Rawls' universalistic metaethic (1972), argued that since in their fundamental rights children and adults are the same, children have the moral right and should have the legal power to do what they choose when it conflicts with what their parents or society prefer. Presumably then the best adults could do for adolescents was to free them from oppressive adult rule. Both the psychoanalytic emphasis on separation from the family as a precondition for the process of individuation to take place, and the Piagetian emphasis on the peer group as the appropriate social context in which true autonomy develops provide theoretical justification for the rapid withdrawal of adult engagement and supervision during the adolescent transition. Bronfenbrenner and myself, among others, have been vocal opponents of this trend.

In a provocative essay entitled, "Freedom and Discipline Across the Decades," Bronfenbrenner (1985) pointed out that the "permissiveness" of the 1960s and 1970s was quite extreme by the standards of the 1930s. Taking a historical perspective, Bronfenbrenner posited that the optimal ratio of control relative to freedom within the family increases as the modal level of stability and structure in the larger society decreases. Because the social fabric in which families are embedded has become increasingly unstable over the last 40 years, there has been a correspondingly increased need for family structure, engagement, and discipline. Bronfenbrenner conjectures, and I concur, that the consequences of permissiveness became increasingly more negative in the 1960s and 1970s because the imbalance in favor of freedom and the degree of social instability increased simultaneously.

The population from which our sample was drawn, predominantly Berkeley families, were harbingers of such secular changes. It follows from Bronfenbrenner's analysis that in a context of social instability, caregivers are required to sustain a higher level of supervision than would be needed in a period of stability. The level of adult supervision required to be protective in a period of social instability may be experienced as constraining by many adolescents who feel ready to explore new social relationships and stimuli, unless parents are simultaneously responsive and nonintrusive.

Adolescents in Transition

I summarize briefly those features of adolescent development that are most likely to impact on the adolescent-parent relationship (for more extended discussion see Baumrind, 1987; Baumrind & Moselle, 1985). As I see it, the central issues faced by adolescents include: identity formation and alienation; cognitive and moral development; and changes in systems of family power and the role of the peer group.

The core developmental task at adolescence is *identity formation,* to negotiate the transition between the literal safe reality of childhood and the complex, indeterminate reality of adulthood. By identity, I mean the adolescent's ability to conserve a sense of continuity through the act of validating simultaneously the interest of personal emancipation and individuation, and the claims of other individuals and mutually shared social norms. Lowered self-esteem presents a special risk to young adolescents, with stabilization in self-ideal congruence beginning around the 9th grade and recovery occurring by age 18 (Backman, Green, & Wirtanen, 1971; Jorgensen & Howell, 1969; Nickols, 1963; Yamenoto, Thomas, & Karnes, 1969). Dramatic discontinuities in body image occur as a result of pubertal changes, so that youngsters may actually be less physically attractive precisely when their awareness of self and others is developing. The adolescent identity crisis, when it occurs, is a disequilibrating conflict during which individuals question the heretofore accepted values of their parents and other adult authorities before arriving at a set of principles capable of reconciling what are, or may appear to be, disparate points of view characterizing their own and their parents' generations. Adolescents who undertake the transitional passage but do not negotiate it successfully may remain in limbo with diffuse identity, suffering symptoms of prolonged aimlessness and lack of clarity about goals. Adolescents who do not undergo a process of emancipation in some form are said by Erikson (1959) and Marcia (1980) to have a "foreclosed identity": They remain willing pawns of others, with an external locus of control, unwilling to accept responsibility for who they are or want to be or for the consequences of their actions. However, a developmental transformation is disequilibrating and disrupting, and thus replete with opportunities for experiences that are both dangerous and growth enhancing.

The emphasis in the American character on personal freedom and autonomy, while contributing to our material prosperity and democratic traditions, also leaves us vulnerable to *alienation*. Alienation describes a psychological state in which a human being feels like an outsider in the community, unable to find a shared interest and a consensually validated way to contribute to society. From a sociological perspective, adolescents are in fact outsiders in modern western societies. Some adolescent problem behaviors including becoming pregnant, can be viewed not as accidental, but rather as a purposive strategy for attaining adult status, in order to secure a sense of belonging and being needed. If adolescents cannot see their own interests and needs reflected in external social norms, compliance with such norms becomes equated with estrangement from the self, entailing a sacrifice of the self to society. Conversely, when adolescents cannot or will not recognize the extent to which social conventions inevitably mediate their perceptions of what they view as intrinsic personal characteristics, their personal lives become alienated from the collective. Unless an ethic of private fulfillment and radical autonomy is balanced by an ethic of civic commitment and interpersonal caring a sense of alienation often accompanied by apathetic withdrawal results (Bellah, Madsen, Sullivan, Swidler, & Tipton, 1985; Lasch, 1979). In view of the opportunities for health-endangering behavior available to adolescents today, premature emancipation is perhaps a greater threat to mature identity formation than delayed separation from family attachments. Early separation from family bonds of attachment in the interest of furthering their individuation may leave adolescents vulnerable to loneliness, despair, and uncritical dependence on peer group norms. To reduce such risks, emancipation from adult authority is best accomplished as a gradual process leading to a capacity for interdependence rather than an exaggerated stance of independence.

Substance abuse is a prototypic symptom of adolescent alienation. It may contribute further to such alienation by delaying or distorting personal identity formation such that a sense of personal continuity becomes antithetical to identification with others, inducing a phantasmic perception of social reality, and contributing to a break in intergenerational continuity both in transmission of values and in maintenance of a viable parent-child relationship. The social consequences of drug use may confirm the adolescent's sense of vulnerability, powerlessness, and external locus of control contributing to the psychological experience of alienation and resulting in disengagement from the social institutions of the family, school, and community.

The "amotivational syndrome" describes a pattern of apathetic withdrawal of energy and interest from effortful activity, an uncertainty about long-range goals with resultant mental and physical lethargy, a loss of creativity, and social withdrawal from demanding social stimuli. These symptoms, descriptive of adolescent alienation, may result from the experience of exclusion from the peer group, or from substance abuse, which typically causes serious mutual estrangement between adolescents and their parents.

The *cognitive and moral advances* accompanying puberty enable adolescents to conceive of themselves as individuated and self-regulating beings. Capable now of hypothecating possibilities beyond the concrete experiences of their past, adolescents who have achieved formal operations may construct a moral vision of an ideal world in which inequities are resolved justly, and peers nourish and care for each other in mutual love and interdependence. These new potentialities for critical ideation and action enable some adolescents to develop enduring commitments to lovers, work, and transcendent ideals but also place other adolescents—those who prematurely reject the norms of their parents or conventional society—at risk in contemporary America.

Parent-adolescent conflict typically increases immediately following puberty, but abates in midadolescence. In giving up a view of parental authority as absolute and unquestionably valid, adolescents in the process of emancipation do not typically develop a negative identity that totally rejects parental values. Instead, adolescent negation of convention usually expresses simultaneous emulation and rejection of parental standards. Parents' willingness and ability to allow conflictual interchange to develop and be resolved while sustaining an affective climate of support and mutual respect should facilitate cognitive and social development during adolescence (Powers, Hauser, Schwartz, Noam, & Jacobson, 1983), at least in youths who are not regular drug users.

Turiel (1978) identified seven levels of *social-conventional reasoning* through analyses of children's and adolescents' responses to a probing (Piagetian) clinical interview. He found that prior to ages 12 or 13, adherence to convention is based on concrete rules and authoritative expectations. Later, with the early adolescent transition (to Turiel's fourth stage), children typically come to question parental authority and social expectation as bases for following convention. Conventions that serve to maintain the dominant social order but that are not seen as intrinsically good (e.g., dress codes) tend to be viewed as arbitrary, and therefore rules or laws supporting such conventions are asserted to be invalid. From 14 to 16, with the transition to Turiel's fifth stage, systematic concepts of social structure typically emerge and adult-supported conventions are once again affirmed, now however justified by their regulative function.

Increased symmetry of power typically characterizes family role structure following puberty. During childhood, power is asymmetrical in the family unit. As Dubin and Dubin (1963) point out, by experiencing the imposition of parental authority in the early years children learn to express their social individuality within the confines of what the culture will accept. However, the attainment of sexual maturation and full stature signaled by puberty liberates adolescents and their parents from the asymmetrical dependence-nurturance bond of childhood. While unilateral exercise of kindly authority is well accepted by juveniles during the authority inception period, it is likely to be resisted by most adolescents. Following puberty, a renegotiation of entitlements and obligations, and of roles and responsibilities among family members often will enable adolescents to accept reasonable parental control without sacrificing self-esteem and social assertiveness within the peer group.

Beginning in early adolescence, the *peer group becomes increasingly significant* as a socializing context, but the effect of the family, though diminished, is by no means eradicated. The intensification of peer relationships and need for social approval that adolescents have is developmentally appropriate. It serves the vital function of consolidating a sense of self, both distinct from, and belonging to, a social reference group. However, unless checked by internal moral standards, adolescents can accede to peer pressure to engage in thrilling, but unhealthy, novel experiences. Adolescents conform to peer standards that deviate from adult norms up to a point to achieve status and identity within the peer group. However, influence on long-range educational aspirations and occupational plans appears to remain the province of parents (Brittain, 1968; Douvan & Adelson, 1966); and family environment variables predict adolescent aspirations (Davies & Kandel, 1981), as well as later adverse outcomes in school or with the police (Langner, Gersten, Wills, & Simcha-Fagan, 1983). As the importance of parental approval wanes with the increasing importance of peer approbation, high-achievers can be faced with a dilemma—namely that the approval of their age-mates may be based not so much on high academic achievement as on conformity to group standards of behavior, standards which the high-achiever may at first be reluctant to adopt. However, if they fail to meet their own high academic standards or if they suffer the rejection of their peers, the high achiever may then suffer a loss of self-esteem (Gordon, 1972) and seek solace in groups which, by adult standards, are deviant (Kaplan, 1980).

THE ROLE OF PARENTS

A substantial body of empirical literature is beginning to accumulate that focuses on the nature and function of the parent-adolescent relationship in the successive phases of the adolescent transition. Of particular interest are issues of attachment and separation. The classic view derived from psychoanalytically oriented theoretical and clinical literature, was perhaps more appropriate in an earlier social climate. By contrast, an antithesis of the classic view, and a contemporary synthesis, both of which are derived largely from recent empirical studies seem better suited to the social realities of contemporary life.

The Classic View

The central task of the adolescent stage of development has traditionally been conceptualized as one of separation from family leading in its final step to a sense of identity. The Western emphasis on individualism at the expense of interdependence has shaped our presuppositions about the process of adolescent individuation. Based upon early psychoanalytic formulations and clinical experience (Freud, 1969), it was widely accepted that the process of adolescent individuation required loosening of family ties and infantile object attachments. Current clinical formulations (Beiser, 1980; Bloom, 1980; Blos, 1979; Coleman, 1978; Haley, 1980; Spotts & Shontz, 1985; Stierlin, 1981), while less apt to place blame for adolescent problems on overprotective mothers, still emphasize the need for emotional separation from parents as a precondition of adolescent individuation and normal establishment of intimate bonds with peers. As conceived by Blos (1962), the process of individuation entails rebellious, oppositional, and resistive strivings, and testing of limits by excess—all part of a gradual severance of emotional ties with one's family of origin. The view that it is natural and desirable for adolescents to transfer emotional attachments from parents to peers is supported by Piaget's distinction (1932/1965) between heteronomous and autonomous morality: According to Piagetians, a young child's heteronomous view of authority as unilateral and role bound is supplanted during adolescence by an autonomous view of authority arising from symmetrical and reciprocal relationships established among peers.

The Antithesis of the Classic View

The classic view that adolescents who remain emotionally attached to parents and respectful of their authority suffer foreclosed identity contrasts sharply with that of contemporary researchers concerned with the prevention of problem behavior (e.g., Jessor & Jessor, 1977, 1978). The developmental pattern descriptive of adolescent drug users that Jessor and Jessor (1978) refer to as "transition-proneness" and label as deviant (pp. 58–59) includes such developmentally appropriate elements as higher value on independence, increased social and political activism, decreased religiosity, increased reliance on friends relative to parents, and perceived relaxation of parents' standards. These are all indices of what Blos, Erikson, and indeed most developmentalists, would regard as appropriate individuation, and mature rather than premature transitional processes. But in addition, transition-proneness as a syndrome includes such problem behaviors as lowered achievement values, substance use, and early sexual experience that are not beneficial per se, and which may retard rather than promote growth. In opposition to the message of classic (Freudian or Piagetian stage) theorists who emphasize the importance of letting go, the message of clinicians and researchers concerned with preventing such problem behaviors is to contain youth within childhood bonds of authority in order to delay psychosocial adolescence. Their data suggest that traditional values and restrictive practices can avert the problems associated with psychosocial adolescence by postponing the movement toward independence and intensification of peer relations. However, retarding normal adolescent social development in order to prevent adolescent problem behavior is not a viable strategy for preventing adolescent deviance from the norms adults have set for adolescents. Transitional processes are to be negotiated carefully but certainly not to be prevented or circumvented.

Parents are caught on the horns of a dilemma—adolescents, in order to become self-regulated, individuated, competent individuals, require both freedom to explore and experiment; and protection from experiences that are clearly dangerous. The classic view emphasized the importance of the former; its antithesis the importance of the latter. To use Cowan's apt metaphor (this volume) there is "rough terrain that must be crossed, risks that must be faced and surmounted" and "the successful outcome of the journey is not assured."

The Contemporary View

There is a contemporary view that has sought to resolve this dilemma. In a paper that presaged what I refer to here as the contemporary view, Beatrix Hamburg (1974) delineated adolescence into three phases each requiring a different mix of parental control and encouragement of emancipation: In early adolescence, coinciding with the middle school and junior high school periods, young people assume an exaggerated pseudoindependent stance which parents should respond to by continuing to enforce age-appropriate limits; the mid-adolescent period, coinciding with the high school years, brings forth cognitive and social gains that enable parents to increase both responsibilities and rights in the domains of money management and individual liberty; only in late adolescence, following graduation from high school, sometimes with an intervening moratorium in the form of college or apprenticeship, does emancipation become the central developmental issue and a nearly symmetrical parent-child relationship become a meaningful possibility.

Several teams of investigators are focusing on the importance of security of attachment in facilitating adolescent individuation. This theme has been enunciated by Willard Hartup (1979) and by John Hill (1980), and developed further by Hill and Holmbeck (1986) in an article on attachment and autonomy in adolescence. In place of the traditional emphasis on emotional detachment from parents as the sine qua non that defines adolescent maturity and moves individuals towards the interdependence of late adolescence and young adulthood, these investigators stress the *balance* between agency and communion, between separation and connectedness, and between conflict and harmony in family relationships.

Even in late adolescence, some investigators find a positive association between feelings of closeness to parents and social competence in populations where achievement and independence are valued by parents (Bell, Avery, Jenkins, Feld, & Schoenrock, 1985; Greenberger, 1984; Kenny, 1987). Steinberg and Silverberg (1986), suggest that for boys, a subjective sense of self-reliance develops out of family relations that are neither very close nor very distant, and that resistance to peer pressure is facilitated by close family ties. Steinberg (1985) claims that emotional distance from parents results not in social competence but rather in heightened susceptibility to antisocial peer influences. Earlier data from our study also show that amount of drug use is positively related to desire to please peers, and negatively related to desire to please adults: Amount of adolescent drug use correlated *negatively* with endorsement of items on the Crandall Social Desirability Questionnaire (Crandall, Crandall, & Katkovsky, 1965) aimed at obtaining the approval of adults ($r = -.39$), but *positively* with endorsement of items aimed at obtaining the approval of peers ($r = .37$). Similarly, contributors to a recent conference sponsored by the Office of Science of the National Institute on Drug Abuse (NIDA) (Hawkins, Lishner, & Catalano, 1985) proposed that youths are more susceptible to negative peer influences when the social bonds of attachment and commitment to prosocial others, especially parents, are weakened. They concluded that parents who use authoritative management skills including effective and open communication, consistent support, and firm enforcement of mutually agreed upon rules that respect the developmental needs of adolescents, are better able to prevent adolescent drug abuse than parents who are either more lenient or more restrictive.

The contemporary view that adolescent individuation should take place in a context of continued attachment within the family setting owes much to the feminist emphasis on communion and connectedness. The feminist perspective is framed largely in neopsychoanalytic terms by theorists such as Chodorow (1978), Dinnerstein (1977), Gilligan (1982), and Josselson (1973); and more recently by Marta Zahaykevich and colleagues (Zahaykevich, Sirey, & Lortie, 1987; Zahaykevish, Sirey, & Sprik, 1987). Carol Gilligan (e.g., Gilligan & Wiggins, 1987) has written eloquently about the continuity into adolescence of two dimensions of early childhood relationships—inequality reflected in the child's awareness of being less capable and powerful than adults, and attachment reflected in the child's awareness of being able to have an effect on others because they care about you. She asserts that when either (a) the striving to gain power in order to become equal (agency), or (b) the need to sustain attachments when these are threatened (communion) becomes too strong relative to the other, the core of moral wisdom is threatened. Gilligan argues that adolescent girls' resistance to detachment, far from being a failure of separation and occurring at the expense of their intellectual and moral growth, makes possible a mature ethic of care and compassion. She asserts that the adolescent's tendency to messianic egocentrism can be countered only by the development of genuine intellectual commitments and deep emotional attachments.

Josselson differentiates the process of individuation into two phases. In the first, called the "practicing" phase and characterized by an unambivalent assertion of will, adolescents revel in feelings of separateness and autonomy, defining themselves oppositionally to their parents and other authority figures. But in the second "rapprochement" phase, feeling safer from regressive childhood impulses, adolescents attempt to reestablish bonds with parents. Provided that parents (mothers in particular) provide recognition of their adolescents' (daughters in particular) autonomy, an amicable relationship can be restored.

In two conceptionally interesting (unpublished) studies along similar lines, Marta Zahaykevich and colleagues (Zahaykevich, Sirey, & Lortie, 1987; Zahaykevich, Sirey, & Sprik, 1987) investigated the legitimation of maternal claims on daughters in conflict situations in early and midadolescence (i.e., in 7th and in 9th graders), distinguishing between the effects of two forms of maternal control: (a) overt power assertion, and (b) covert control exercised through projection (e.g., by the mother guilt-tripping or appealing to her own wishes and needs). Zahaykevich, Sirey, and Lortie found that the premenarcheal 7th graders were more actively hostile and negativistic than the older, postmenarcheal 9th graders; and that mothers' convert exercise of control through projection increased at menarche and was associated with compliance only in the oldest group, the 9th graders. They interpreted these findings as supportive of Josselson's distinction between oppositional behavior shown by girls in the *practicing* phase and renewed attachment in the *rapprochement* phase. Zahaykevich, Sirey, and Sprik distinguished between two kinds of legitimation of maternal authority: (1) One kind consistent with authoritative parents, in which mothers give reasonable and principled explanations for rules *they* formulate and enforce, but not with the objective of building mutual consensus; and (2) the second kind, which the investigators regarded as a *higher* level, in which mothers attempt to build consensus through discourse that results in *mutual* decision making and conflict resolution. This postulated higher level of consensus did not appear even among the families of their 9th graders. Operationally, therefore, consensus was defined not as mutual decision making, but rather as increased understanding of the other's position, after active discussion in which mothers explained their rules, and daughters explained their objections to conforming with these rules. Such consensus was reached (for 9th graders only) when daughters used personal legitimation (e.g., "I need to spend more time with my friends") but mothers did not, and instead legitimated their claims by referring to the developmental goals they had for their adolescents such as gaining in competence, or to moral and social-conventional principles such as fairness and mutual obligation.

Noteworthy among the interesting ideas Zahaykevich and colleagues bring forth are:

1. The adolescent individuation process comprises at least two phases—an initial *practicing* phase of differentiation from the mother marked by oppositional behavior, and a *rapprochement* phase marked by reconciliation initiated by those daughters who have received support and recognition from their mothers;

2. Maternal legitimation of her authority can occur through two different processes—through reason in the early practicing stage when the power relations are still quite asymmetrical, and through the building of parent-child consensus based on mutual influence much later in the adolescent's development; and

3. Finally, their emphasis on the need that adolescents have throughout the transition from childhood to adult status for parents to acknowledge, support, and respond positively to their rational objections and arguments, rather than to attempt to control them by coercion or appeals to their own personal needs and vulnerabilities. It would appear that mothers are most effective when they conform to higher levels of moral judgments than they require of their adolescents.

I would add that a truly symmetrical intellectual relationship is *not* experienced as genuinely appropriate by mothers or their daughters until quite late in the adolescent transition, and perhaps not until young adulthood. Power relations between adolescents and their parents in the practicing phase of adolescence are typically still asymmetrical. Conflictual rational discourse presupposes a symmetrical intellectual relationship that cannot be achieved between parents and their adolescents until adolescents are secure in their capacity for rational reflection and are emotionally prepared to evaluate dispassionately their parents' perspective in terms of its adequacy. Paradoxically, young adolescents may feel less on the defensive and better able to respond positively when parents legitimate their own position by rational argument rather than when they seek consensus in egalitarian rational discourse. Therefore, truly egalitarian argumentative discourse is unlikely to occur prior to the rapprochement phase and typically will not predominate until late adolescence or early adulthood.

The importance to adolescents of parental support is underscored by the findings of Powers, Hauser, and their colleagues (1983). These investigators focus on early adolescence as the period in which power and role relations within the family are renegotiated. They hypothesized that adolescent ego development would be enhanced by exposure to conflicting points of view within the family as well as by opportunities to share one's own perspective and take the role of others. They expected to find that by disequilibrating adolescents' expectations, cognitive conflicts would accelerate their ego development. Instead, these investigators found that the parent behaviors hypothesized to be cognitively stimulating, (challenging and focusing) were not related positively to adolescent ego development but rather that acknowledgment and support of the adolescent's perspective were related strongly to the adolescent's ego development. They concluded however that challenging and cognitively stimulating behaviors do have a salutary effect when they occur within a context of acceptance and support. Also it should be noted that their analyses were not conducted within-sex. Our own results reported in a later section indicate that (maternal) confronting behavior has more consistently positive effects for girls than for boys.

Cooper, Grotevant, and Condon (1982, 1983) describe the effective family system as one that avoids both enmeshment, in which individuality is discouraged in favor of exaggerated family harmony; and disengagement, in which family members are so separate that they have little effect on each other. They refer to the individuated adolescent as one who displays a *balance* between individuality and connectedness. By individuality they mean (a) self-assertion or the clear presentation of one's own point of view, and (b) separateness or the ability to differentiate one's point of view from those of others (particularly from one's parents). By connectedness they mean (a) permeability or responsiveness to the views of others, and (b) mutuality or respect for the ideas of others. Family processes that balance expressions of individuality with expressions of connectedness are thought by these investigators to be most effective in generating competence. In their studies, in contrast to those of Zahaykevich and colleagues, or Powers, Hauser, and colleagues, cognitive conflict or what we call "confronts" (e.g., mother's self-assertion and challenges) correlated positively with identity exploration in such areas as choice of vocation, religion, and politics. It should be noted however that, by contrast with the findings of Zahaykevich, and of Hauser and colleagues, Cooper, Grotevant, and colleagues found that mother's assertive behavior clearly took place in an affective context of compromise and support (as is true in our study; e.g., r between Confronts and Supportive = .39 for mothers). However, girls' identity exploration and mothers' permeability were *negatively* correlated, perhaps because maternal permeability indexes oversolicitous concern, by contrast with mutuality which indexes mothers' respect for herself as well as for her daughter. Thus, confrontation and mutuality rather than child-centeredness and laxness were associated in girls with mature identity exploration.

All studies cited agreed that mothers are more centrally involved than fathers in conflict with their adolescents of both sexes, and that they suffer more than fathers during the adolescent transition (cf. Papini & Sebby, 1985). Mothers suffer a loss of intimacy with daughters if and when emotional separation does occur, and they suffer a loss of status and power with sons following puberty. Steinberg (1987) found that immediately following puberty, that is during the *practicing* phase, both sons and daughters report less cohesion with their mothers. Also, Steinberg (1981) found that during the *rapprochement* phase of the individuation process, boys assume a dominant role with mothers. Fathers, on the other hand, maintain their dominance over both mothers and adolescents of either sex. It follows that without strong support from their husbands, mothers of adolescent children may become disillusioned with the mothering process, and sad and insecure about their own personal development. To the extent that their own needs are not met or that they are unjustly treated in the family setting, mothers may well elect either to detach emotionally, leaving adolescents too much on their own, or alternatively to seek to sustain a level of intimacy that enmeshes and "castrates" their daughters or sons.

Effective Parenting During Early Adolescence

Research evidence is now emerging that successful negotiation of the adolescent transition lies not in asserting independence for the purpose of overcoming the dependency of childhood, but rather in establishing modes of interdependence through familial reorganization of rights, responsibilities, and personal relationships. The ability of the late adolescent to become financially and emotionally independent may require in early and midadolescence continued emotional attachment and monitoring within a context of increasing empowerment and self-governance (Moore, 1987).

Although early adolescents are still in need of firm guidance and sustained emotional support, unlike themselves as children, adolescents can differentiate between legitimate and illegitimate authority and justify their claim to greater participation in decisions that affect them. In early adolescence, as privacy issues surface, children are more likely to regard as personal and private issues that their parents regard as important conventional matters still under their jurisdiction. This mismatch may result in conflict.

Middle-class adolescents have been shown to value self-reliance and the ability to make their own decisions extremely higher (Feather, 1980; Greenberger, 1984). As Kandel and Lesser (1972) have shown, adolescents who feel that their parents give them enough freedom are more likely to feel close to their parents and to respect their wishes. While at all ages a control attempt by one person towards another results in psychological forces both to comply and to resist, by adolescence the forces to resist are legitimated by accelerated capacity for, and value placed on, self-reliance. Those mothers who are concerned about the adverse consequences of girls' sexual behavior and who are ambivalent about separation may become increasingly vigilant precisely when their daughters are seeking greater freedom, resulting in an increase in conflict. This should be a special problem for early-maturing girls and their mothers.

The fundamental changes taking place in adolescents' social and cognitive capabilities are acknowledged when parents show willingness to negotiate and to explain the rationale for their decisions. What we have termed "authoritative" control (responsive and negotiated) should be well-accepted (i.e., viewed as legitimate) whereas "authoritarian" control (status-oriented and nonnegotiated) should be rejected (i.e., viewed as illegitimate). Authority viewed by adolescents as illegitimate should have adverse effects on their self-esteem, competence, and individuation. Therefore, authoritarian methods should have more adverse effects on adolescents' than on young children's functional competence, even though they are also expected to deter externalizing problem behavior.

The dramatic changes that take place during adolescence disequilibrate parents as persons and the family as a system. Parental attributes and childrearing practices along the communal-responsive axis are expected to be more important than those along the agentic-demanding axis in contrast to the findings at earlier time periods when parental demandingness was expected to, and did, have prepotent positive effects. Parental practices that change in the direction of greater responsiveness and independence-granting are expected to facilitate the development of competence following puberty. However, such changes presuppose earlier firm control. Thus *early* permissiveness is expected to be harmful at adolescence: If maintained, the adolescent will have no limits to test and as a consequence may behave irresponsibly or diffusely; if formerly permissive parents become strict, the adolescent may rebel because a freedom heretofore granted has been curtailed. It is hypothesized therefore that parents who were permissive in childhood will be dissatisfied with the way their adolescents behave and as a consequence either abdicate their parental responsibilities altogether or become authoritarian. Even if permissive parents should become more authoritative rather than more authoritarian, adolescents are expected to demonstrate "reactance." Therefore, adolescents whose parents were permissive in childhood may be expected to reject parental authority and to show problem behavior during adolescence, even if they were well-adjusted earlier.

By adolescence (with the possible exception of hard-core miscreants) behavior management using rewards and punishment is less appropriate developmentally than use of reason, discussion of values, and modeling. Ideally, during adolescence parents act more as mentors, exemplars, and supervisors, than as disciplinarians. Adolescents' lack of respect for, and attachment to, parents should impair formation of a positive identity, sense of self-esteem, and transmission of prosocial values. Parents' respect and consideration for each other and for their adolescents should be associated with a positive identity and prosocial values, whereas family disorganization and parents' lack of impulse control should undermine adolescents' respect for them, and be associated with dysphoria and low communion.

EARLY ADOLESCENT FINDINGS FROM THE FAMILY SOCIALIZATION AND DEVELOPMENTAL COMPETENCE PROJECT (FSP)

Prior to discussing the adolescent-parent correlational analyses, I provide a context by summarizing findings from the earlier time periods.

Historical Overview of the FSP

I began my ongoing work on childrearing in 1959 with the first of three studies, using as participants Caucasian, middle-class parents and their preschool children enrolled in one of 13 nursery schools in Berkeley and Oakland, California. The population from which my sample was drawn is more educationally and socially advantaged than the general population. However, investigators such as Reginald Clark (1983), and Sanford Dornbusch and colleagues (1987) have shown that our basic findings contrasting the impact on young children of authoritative, authoritarian, permissive, and rejecting–neglecting families have wide applicability to a demographically more heterogeneous population.

My long-range objective was to identify the familial antecedents of optimal competence in children and adolescents. At each of three developmental periods—preschool (T1), middle school (T2), and early adolescence (T3)—we collected comprehensive data from ecologically valid sources. These sources consisted of direct observation in naturalistic and laboratory settings, intensive structured interviews, and standardized and Project-designed psychological tests. With each successive developmental stage, additional measures were included in the battery to match the increasingly differentiated status of the maturing child. At all three time periods, the subsequent observations and ratings of parents and children were collected by separate teams of observers. The Q-sorts and Likert-type rating scales based on the observations and interviews for children were reduced via cluster and factor analyses to two primary interpersonal modalities assessing "agency" and "communion." For parents, these two underlying modalities are called "demandingness" and "responsiveness."

In the psychological literature (for example, Bakan, 1966), agency refers to the drive for independence, individuality, and self-aggrandizement, and in the sex-role literature (for example, Spence & Helmreich, 1978) it is identified as the masculine principle; whereas communion refers to the need to be of service and to be included and connected, and is identified as the feminine principle. The social dimensions of status (dominance, power) and love (solidarity, affiliation) that emerge as the two orthogonal axes from almost all factor analyses of human behavior (for example, Baumrind & Black, 1967; Leary, 1957; Lonner, 1980; Schaefer, 1959; Wiggins, 1979) are manifestations of agency and communion.

The basic typological constructs were derived from two separate samples of preschool children and their families. The first small sample of 32 families was selected from a larger sample after prolonged observations in the nursery school setting of the children's pattern of behavior. The three prototypic patterns of parental authority—Authoritative, Authoritarian, and Permissive—associated with each of three child types emerged from this study (Baumrind, 1967). The second and more comprehensive study of preschool children also constitutes the first wave of the ongoing longitudinal study. The 134 Caucasian, middle-class children in this longitudinal sample were born in 1964 and were first studied in 1968–69 when they were 4 to 5 years-of-age. Whereas in the pilot study, families were selected on the basis of their children's pattern of behavior and their parents were then compared, in the longitudinal study the families were classified on the basis of the parents' pattern of behavior, and their children were then compared. The parent classification was theory-based and included variations of the three prototypic patterns that had emerged previously from the pilot study: Authoritarian, Authoritative, and Permissive.

The complex results from the longitudinal study (Baumrind, 1971), as they pertain to the three major prototypes are summarized as follows:

Authoritarian parents attempt to shape, control, and evaluate the behavior and attitudes of their children in accordance with a set standard of conduct, usually an absolute standard, theologically motivated or formulated by a higher secular authority. They attempt to inculcate such conventional values as respect for authority, work, and preservation of order and traditional structure. They do not encourage verbal give and take, believing that children should accept their parents' word for what is right. Couples were assigned to the Authoritarian pattern if they had high scores on the clusters measuring firm enforcement and maturity demands, and low scores on the clusters measuring responsiveness and psychological differentiation.

Children of Authoritarian couples did not have a distinctive profile when compared to children from Permissive homes. However, when children from Authoritarian homes were compared specifically with their same-sex peers from Authoritative homes, boys from the Authoritarian households were found to be relatively hostile and resistive, and girls were found to be relatively dependent and submissive.

Authoritative parents, by contrast with Authoritarian parents, attempt to direct their children's activities in a rational, issue-oriented manner. They encourage verbal give and take, and share with their children the reasoning behind their policy. They value both expressive and instrumental attributes, both autonomous self-will and disciplined conformity. Therefore, they exert firm control at points of parent-child divergence, but do not hem their children in with restrictions.

Authoritative parents are demanding in that they guide their children's activities firmly and consistently and require them to contribute to family functioning by helping with household tasks. They confront their children directly, state their values clearly, and expect their children to respect their norms. Authoritative parents are responsive affectively in the sense of being loving, supportive, and committed; and responsive cognitively in the sense of providing a stimulating and challenging environment. They are protective but not intrusive. They do not base their decisions on group consensus or on the individual child's desires; but also, do not regard themselves as infallible or divinely inspired. Couples assigned to the Authoritative pattern, like Authoritarian parents, had scores high on firm enforcement and maturity demands. But by contrast with Authoritarian parents, Authoritative parents were responsive and psychologically differentiated.

Preschool children from Authoritative homes were consistently and significantly more competent than other children. For girls, Authoritative parental behavior was associated with purposive, dominant, and achievement-oriented behavior; and for boys, with friendly, cooperative behavior.

Permissive parents, were less controlling than they were warm and autonomy-granting. Permissive parents attempt to behave in a nonpunitive, acceptant, and affirmative manner toward their children's impulses, desires, and actions. They consult with their children about policy decisions and give explanations for family rules. They make few maturity demands. They allow their children to regulate their own activities as much as possible, and attempt to use reason or covert suggestion, but not confrontation or overt power to accomplish their ends.

Preschool children of Permissive couples did not differ significantly from children of Authoritarian couples. However, compared to children from Authoritative homes, girls were markedly less socially assertive and both sexes were less achievement oriented.

The similarities between children of Permissive and Authoritarian parents, and their lack of competence by comparison with children from Authoritative homes underscores the importance of examining the effects of warmth and control jointly. Although girls in particular were adversely affected by lax control, optimum competence was generated by parents who were actively involved, and who *balanced* high warmth and firm control.

At Time 2 when the children were 9-years-of-age, we collected a second wave of data. The sample consisted of 164 children and their parents, 104 of whom had been studied at Time 1, and 60 of whom had been added in order to provide an enhanced sample for future waves. Based on their scores on the child and parent clusters, child and parent types were identified. The results are too complex to be summarized here. However, Table 5.1 provides a convenient summary of comparisons across five prototypic parent types for three groups of girls and boys distinguished by their level of competence. The five parent prototypes include three that we discussed earlier—Authoritative, Authoritarian, and Per-

TABLE 5.1
Parent Prototype by Child Competence Levels

	Optimally Competent		*Partially[a] Competent*		*Incompetent*		*N*	
Parent Prototype	*Girls*	*Boys*	*Girls*	*Boys*	*Girls*	*Boys*	*Girls*	*Boys*
Authoritative	86%(6)	83%(5)	14%(1)	17%(1)	00%(0)	00%(0)	7	6
Traditional	50%(3)	43%(6)	33%(2)	57%(8)	17%(1)	00%(0)	6	14
Authoritarian	42%(5)	18%(2)	58%(7)	55%(6)	00%(0)	27%(3)	12	11
Pemissive	00%(0)	20%(1)	71%(5)	60%(3)	29%(2)	20%(1)	7	5
Rejecting-Neglecting	00%(0)	00%(0)	63%(5)	33%(3)	27%(3)	67%(6)	8	9

Note. Based on Table VI-10 from "Familial Antecedents of Social Competence in Middle Childhood" (Baumrind, under review).
[a] The three child types--Oversocialized, Undersocialized, and Average--were combined into partially Competent in order to convert the types into competence levels.

missive. In addition, we identified Rejecting–Neglecting parents who were neither responsive nor demanding; and Traditional parents who differed from the other prototypes in that mothers and fathers enacted sex-stereotyped roles. In Traditional families mothers were significantly more responsive than they were demanding; and fathers were significantly more demanding than they were responsive. The child groups are: The Optimally Competent, those who are highly agentic *and* communal (that is, "socially assertive" and "socially responsible"); Incompetent, those who are neither agentic nor communal; and Partially Competent, those who either obtained (a) average scores on both dimensions, or (b) high scores on one dimension and low scores on the other dimension.

Comparisons of the children's competence levels across the five parent prototypes using the Kruskal-Wallis test were highly significant for girls ($chi^2 = 17.43$; $p < .002$) and boys ($chi^2 = 19.31$; $p < .001$). No child raised by an Authoritative couple, or girl raised by an Authoritarian couple, or boy raised by a Traditional couple was Incompetent. No child raised by a Rejecting-Neglecting couple, or girl raised by a Permissive couple was Optimally Competent. By contrast, 67% of boys raised by Rejecting-Neglecting couples were Incompetent, and over 85% of children raised by Authoritative couples were Optimally Competent. Compared to each other, more children from nondemanding families (Permissive + Rejecting-Neglecting) were Incompetent and more children from demanding families (Authoritative + Traditional + Authoritarian) were Optimally Competent (Fisher Exact test for girls, $p < .001$ and for boys, $p < .008$).

In addition to the typological analyses, dimensional analyses examining the effects of parental demandingness and parental responsiveness were completed. Demanding parenting was highly related to general competence for both sexes, and was a sufficient condition for the acquisition of a high level of social agency for girls. High responsiveness and low demandingness accentuated social responsibility for girls. High responsiveness paired with high demandingness appeared to facilitate, perhaps by reinforcing, the effect of demandingness on girls; but even when highly demanding parents were not responsive, their daughters were more socially assertive than other girls. However, for boys to be optimally competent or to behave communally, it was necessary for parents to be responsive as well as demanding. When their parents were neither responsive nor demanding, both girls and boys tended to be either incompetent or sex-normed.

Parent-Adolescent Relations

At Time 3 when the adolescents were about 14½ years-of-age (1978–1980), 139 of the 164 subjects seen at previous time periods were again assessed.

Measures and Procedures

At Time 3 an even more comprehensive assessment of parents and adolescents occurred than at previous periods. The adolescents were observed twice for 2 hours, once in school and again in an informal extracurricular peer context of their choice. They were interviewed three times: One interview focused on health and substance use, the second on personal development and individuation, and the third on moral issues. Teachers were interviewed about the adolescents behavior in school.

On the bases of transcripts of the entire battery of interview and observational procedures, two psychologists independently rated each adolescent on 90 Q-sort items and 47 Likert-type rating scales, a problem checklist summary, and several alcohol and drug use scales. The Adolescent Q-Sort is an ipsative rating procedure designed to assess constructs included at the two previous time periods together with dimensions of ego strength and individuation relevant to adolescent development. The Adolescent Rating Scale is a normative rating system designed to reflect the adolescent's functioning with respect to sex, society, parents, cognition, and physical fitness. In addition to the Q-sort and rating items a number of other measures were collected on the adolescents. Included in this chapter are some measures developed and widely used by other investigators to assess: intelligence, traditionality, locus of control, and moral reasoning; as well as additional measures developed by the project to assess self-concept, characterological functioning, perception of parents, and problem behaviors.

Each parent was interviewed twice—about their socialization and health practices, and about moral issues. Parents were also observed in interaction with their children during a home visit and a structured family interaction that was videotaped. These interviews and observations were summarized by the Parent Behavior Rating Items (82 items), and Personal Attribute Ratings (71 items). The project also developed measures to examine parents' health, substance use, characterological functioning, and problem behavior.

Scale Construction and Data Reduction

A large number of measures contributed to the observers' assessments of adolescents and their parents that are not included in this report because they are ancillary to its focus, or not yet fully analyzed. The majority of the adolescent and parent measures included here are derived from observers' ratings. Several self-report scales are also included. The ratings and Q-sorts were reduced to a number of scales via principal component and cluster analyses. Cluster analyses rather than principal component analyses were used for the Adolescent Q-sort because of the common metric used in the Q-sort items. Scales for the Q-sort items contain all items falling into each cluster. In the principal component analyses used for the other adolescent and parent measures the number of components extracted was determined by the scree test (Cattell, 1966). Scales contain items with loadings solely on each component or items with similar loadings on multiple components (Gorsuch, 1974). The Parent Behavior Ratings and Personal Attribute Ratings were analyzed separately by sex of parent.

For both adolescents and parents the scales were further reduced by second order principal component analyses, with the number of components extracted determined by a scree test. For both adolescents and parents a two factor solution was found. These two factor solutions were used to help organize the scales for the adolescents or their parents into a circumplex according to the procedure outlined by Wiggins (1979, 1980). After the adolescent and parent circumplexes were constructed, other measures were graphed onto each circumplex based on their correlations with the axes (second order principal components) and defining scales. These secondary measures not used to construct the circumplex, but which filled *gaps* in the circumplex were self-report measures, problem behaviors, and ratings of adolescents' perceptions of adults.

Adolescent Scales. The data reduction for the Adolescent Q-sort yielded 9 scales, and the reduction of the Adolescent Ratings Scales yielded 3 scales. These 12 scales were used to construct the adolescent circumplex, which was defined by an *Agentic axis* and a *Communal axis*. These 12 scales all have acceptable reliabilities (Chronbach's alpha is presented in parenthesis following the scale labels below) and describe adolescents' social agency, general competence, communion and sex-stereotyped behavior:

Emancipated (alpha = .89)—values and actions are not under adult control
Explorative (alpha = .89)—takes risks and is a leader in peer group
Socially conscious (alpha = .84)—idealistic and socially active

Gregarious (alpha = .91)—popular and sociable

Individuated (alpha = .94)—possesses a well-formulated sense of identity, internal locus of control, social charisma and articulate self-expression

Optimistic (alpha = .80)—buoyant, cheerful and enthusiastic

Resilient (alpha = .88)—flexible adaptive, socially responsive and copes well with stress

Cognitively motivated (alpha = .95)—challenges self intellectually

Self-Regulated (alpha = .95)—self-contained, self-controlled, intrinsically motivated, and takes perspective of others

Achievement-Oriented (alpha = .94)—scholastically successful and motivated to achieve

Socially Responsible (alpha = .88)—facilitative, considerate, and friendly with peers and adults

Sex Stereotyped (alpha = .74)—sex-typed interests, manners and gestures.

In addition to these 12 primary scales, 19 other scales were graphed onto the circumplex and are described next:

The *Adolescent Optimum Competence* scale was constructed by averaging the judgments of five male and five female psychologists who used the Adolescent Behavior Q-sort to describe an optimally competent 15-year-old girl and boy. After ascertaining that there were few sex differences attributable to sex of child or sex of rater, the twenty *ideal* Q-sorts were averaged.

Another six of the additional scales refer to observers' assessments of adolescents' perceptions of their mother and father as (a) *Effective Enforcers* (alpha = .91), that is, knowledgeable about and aware of the adolescent's lifestyle, substance use, health, school and peers; (b) *Loving and Admirable* (alpha = .92), that is, warm, just, intellectually stimulating and socially prestigious; and (c) *Restrictive* (alpha = .92), that is traditional, pressuring and overly directive.

Six of the additional scales refer to observers' assessments of the adolescents' self-esteem, problem behavior, drug use, and sexual acting-out. *Poor Self-Esteem* (alpha = .87) represents the low end of a six item 5-point Likert scale assessing the adolescents' self-esteem in six areas (e.g., peers, parents, school). From the Problem Checklist, three scales were obtained: (a) *General Problem Behavior* (alpha = .93); (b) *Internalizing Problem Behavior* (alpha = .87); and (c) *Externalizing Problem Behavior* (alpha = .88). The latter two scales contain items that correspond to those identified by Achenbach and Edelbrock (1983): Internalizing or overcontrolled behavior involves emotional distress for the individual including social withdrawal, anxiety and depression; externalizing or undercontrolled behavior creates problems for other people, including overactivity, inattentiveness and aggressive behavior. The *Drug Problem* scale is a 4-

point Guttman scale: (1) no use of alcohol or any drug, (2) recreational or habitual use of alcohol but no other drug, (3) recreational or habitual use of alcohol and marijuana, but no other illicit drug, and (4) recreational or habitual use of alcohol, marijuana, and more than one other illicit drug. The *Sexual Acting-Out* scale (alpha = .82) is a two-item 3-point scale: (1) has not had sexual intercourse, (2) has had sexual intercourse, (3) is active sexually with multiple partners.

Six self-report scales completed by the adolescents are included in the Tables. Two self-report measures assess conforming behavior; the Jessor and Jessor Social-Ethical Beliefs, and the Nowicki-Strickland Locus of Control. The *Jessor and Jessor Traditional Beliefs, Religious Beliefs and Attitudes Towards Deviance scales* (1974, 1977) is a frequently used standardized measure that assesses the importance of religion and traditional social-ethical beliefs. Included here are the Traditional Beliefs, and the Attitudes Towards Deviance scales which we combined and refer to as Social-Ethical Beliefs (alpha = .88 for our sample). The *Nowicki-Strickland Locus of Control* (1973) measure is a 40-item scale (alpha = .70 for our sample) that assesses the individual's belief in personal will and action as primary causal agents in determining events central to one's life, by contrast with luck or external agents. The other four self-report scales assess self-image. A 47-item project-designed *Self-esteem Self-Report Inventory* (adapted from schedules by Barron, 1953; Coopersmith, 1967; Fitts, 1965; and Rosenberg, 1965) yielded three subscales and a Self-Devaluation Index: *General Self-Esteem* (alpha = .90) assesses general good feelings about oneself, especially in interpersonal relations; *Academic Self-Esteem* (alpha = .82) assesses positive evaluation of self as a student; and *Low Family-Self-esteem* (alpha = .77), assesses one's sense of not being a valued family member. The *Self-Devaluation* index (alpha = .73), consists of the total number of attributes that one rates as important to one's self-esteem but believes one lacks.

If we accept Cohen's criterion for effect size (Cohen, 1977) then it should be noted that 12 of the 19 additional variables have only a moderate correlation ($r <$ .50 and $>$ .30) with the axes: The six self-report measures; and six of the observer rating scales (adolescents' perception of *each* parent as Loving and Admirable, and as Restrictive; and the ratings of Drug Problem and Sexual Acting-out).

The order in which the variables are listed vertically in Tables 5.2 and 5.3 reflect the circular order of the adolescent variables when graphed along the central axes beginning with the top of the upper left quadrant. The upper left quadrant is defined by high Agency and low Communion. The problem behaviors at the opposite end of the set of adolescent variables circle back to adjoin the normal variables in the upper left quadrant. Thus Sexual Acting-out appears adjacent to Emancipated in the circular order and both are in the upper left quadrant.

TABLE 5.2
Time 3 Correlations Between Daughters and Parents

	Styles of Parental Control (Demandingness)									
	Restrictive				*Assertive*				*Rational*	
	Directive/ Confrontational		*Conforming*		*Monitors*		*Confronts*		*Controls Rationally*	
Adolescent Variables	***Mother***	***Father***	***Mother***	***Father***	***Mother***	***Father***	***Mother***	***Father***	***Mother***	***Father***
Agentic Domain										
Emancipated	-50***	-34*	-44***	-40**	-46***	-18	-24	-07	-23	-01
Explorative	-33**	-14	-30*	-26	-30*	-09	-10	04	-04	09
Socially Conscious	-54***	-47***	-38*	-46***	-05	-00	-03	-02	18	39**
Geregarious	-09	04	06	10	-29*	-09	-01	00	02	-04
General Competence										
Individuated	-36*	-25	-28*	-23	14	06	30*	-01	35**	43***
Optimistic	04	02	01	-01	39**	22	43***	11	47***	45**
Optimum Competence	-14	-02	-10	-02	36**	20	45***	00	53***	48***
Resilient	-18	-04	-21	-01	22	13	45***	-10	46***	33*
General Self-Esteem	-04	03	-06	02	-13	-10	-05	01	00	-04

Communal Domain										
Cognitively Motivated	01	06	03	11	45***	33*	26	08	49***	61***
Self-Regulated	08	14	09	18	54***	30*	50***	01	55***	48***
Achievement Oriented	10	18	06	17	51***	40**	27*	15	41***	53***
Academic Self-esteem	03	20	-01	25	19	22	11	26	20	15
Sees N, as LOV/ADM	-00	-12	10	-00	44***	11	45***	-06	64***	58***
Sees F. as LOV/ADM	21	-08	22	16	54***	19	46***	-01	68***	57***
Socially Responsible	15	12	10	08	51***	27*	55***	02	51***	29*
Sees M. as Eff. Enf.	26	-05	31*	15	59***	08	48***	-12	61***	32*
Sees F. as Eff. Enf.	25	22	26	18	51***	40**	26	17	51***	46***
Conforming										
Social-ethical Beliefs	46***	29*	48***	34*	52***	13	24	-09	15	-13
Sees M. as Restrictive	56***	22	52***	43***	14	-02	13	-02	-06	-29*
Sees F. as Restrictive	30*	43**	38**	33*	-04	-04	-23	22	-33*	-34*
Sex Stereotyped	-09	14	-20	06	-21	22	-06	19	-04	05
External Control Locus	-14	11	-04	-08	-31*	12	-19	25	-52***	-19
Problem Behavior										
Poor Self-esteem	27*	23	11	16	-20	-11	-23	10	-41***	-43***
Self-Devaluation	00	-05	-00	-15	-12	-01	-13	16	-24	-08
Internalizing Problem	05	-10	-07	-08	-22	.+19	-36	03	-35*	-43**
General Problem Behav	-15	-16	-16	-14	-55***	-29*	-53***	00	-59***	-43**
Externalizing Problem	-40**	-17	-14	-07	-63***	-29*	-53***	07	-53***	-33*
Low Family Self-esteem	00	21	-04	13	-25	-20	-24	-11	.-45***	-44**
Drug Problem	-40**	-18	-35**	-30*	-63***	-07	-34**	02	-46***	-13
Sexual Acting Out	-38**	-27*	-20	-17	-45***	-33*	44***	-20	-34**	-21

(continued)

Table 5.2 (*Continued*)

Adolescent Variables	*Psychologically Differentiated*		*Differentiated*		*Responsiveness*					
					Responsive				*Nonintrusive*	
	Agentic/Content		*Influential/Scholarly*		*Considerate*		*Supportive*		*Nonintrusive*	
	Mother	*Father*	*Mother*	*Father*	*Mother*	*Father*	*Mother*	*Father*	*Mother*	*Father*
Agentic Domain										
Emancipated	-09	-07	-06	-06	-02	-11	-17	-04	14	-05
Explorative	00	-02	-03	-17	04	-20	08	10	12	-18
Socially Conscious	18	01	17	21	18	04	20	27*	21	-12
Gregerious	07	-12	-03	-34	21	-08	17	00	34**	-02
General Competence										
Individuated	33**	03	33**	22	28*	21	39**	38**	36**	10
Optimistic	33**	17	30*	13	23	22	53***	42**	22	08
Optimum Competence	37**	02	39**	14	35**	20	56***	40**	35**	10
Resilient	41***	-01	41***	07	27*	24	44***	33*	34**	12
General Self-esteem	-04	-11	01	-08	05	-34*	15	-16	04	-14
Communal Domain										
Cognitively Motivated	31*	25	33**	38**	27*	27*	46***	42**	22	16
Self-regulated	35**	10	36**	21	29*	32*	50***	39**	20	22

Achievement Oriented	21	24	25	35*	19	21	38**	30*	06	13
Academic Self-esteem	08	06	20	09	07	-02	20	-04	04	10
Sees M. as LOV/ADM	53***	10	49***	31*	44***	19	71***	44**	39**	00
Sees F. as LOV/ADM	42***	20	42***	45***	36**	42**	59***	62***	30*	37**
Socially Responsible	37**	-02	36**	05	27*	21	52***	24	24	01
Sees M. as Eff. Enf.	43***	02	36**	28*	34**	17	59***	35*	21	02
Sees F. as Eff. Enf.	19	30*	18	41**	20	23	48***	30*	-00	02
Conforming										
Social-ethical Beliefs	-07	-09	-10	05	10	04	05	-00	-04	10
Sees M. as Restrictive	-14	-08	-22	-02	-04	08	-28*	-13	-04	19
Sees F. as Restrictive	-41**	-02	-44***	-11	-23	-40**	- 26	-48***	-40**	-36**
Sex Stereotyped	01	24	00	-05	-18	14	-11	-05	-02	11
External Control Locus	-29*	09	-39***	-04	-31*	-17	-47***	-34*	-12	-21
Problem Behavior										
Poor Self-esteem	-31*	01	-29*	-01	-32*	-17	-53***	-48***	-33**	-12
Self Devaluation	-07	23	-12	06	-20	-01	-34**	-17	-09	-02
Internalizing Problem	-33*	-05	-19	-05	-34*	-18	-43**	-29*	-36**	-07
General Problem Behavior	-40**	-04	-34**	-08	-38**	-19	-63***	-37**	-31*	-08
Externalizing Problem	-22	14	-29*	01	-18	01	-44**	-29*	-08	05
Low Family Self-esteem	-36**	-17	-39**	-18	-42***	-15	-45***	-50***	-35**	-31*
Drug Problem	-15	05	-17	-15	-31*	-08	-40**	-26	-03	-10
Sexual Acting-out	-21	-20	-23	-19	-14	-08	-24	-12	-16	-05

(Continued)

Table 5.2 (*Continued*)

	Problem Behavior											
	Illicit Drug Usage		*Maladjusted/ Internalizing*		*Exploitive/ Externalizing*		*Alcohol Abuse*		*Family Disorganization*		*Officious*	
Adolescent Variables	*Mother*	*Father*	*Mother*	*Father*	*Mother*	*Father*	*Mother*	*Father*			*Mother*	*Father*
Agentic Domain												
Emancipated	19	17	24	22	30*	31*	07	-03	38**	07	-16	-06
Explorative	13	16	16	25	19	23	-08	-11	21	-06	-18	-01
Socially Conscious	14	11	05	17	04	12	06	-03	00	-11	-35**	-21
Gregarious	24	16	-18	-00	-20	09	12	00	02	-10	-25	08
General Competence												
Individuate	.00	06	-15	09	-04	-18	-09	-25	-21	-19	-43***	-36**
Optimistic	-12	08	-25	-05	-23	-32*	-09	-17	-36**	-30*	-24	-23
Optimum Competence	-02	05	-24	01	-25	-30*	-13	-26	-41***	-18	-41***	-30*
Resilient	11	04	-24	03	-15	-26	-12	-14	-33**	-13	-33**	-27*
General Self-esteem	-02	-00	08	15	06	30*	10	08	14	10	00	19
Communal Domain												
Cognitively Motivated	-05	-01	-27*	-16	-29*	-36**	-18	-23	-39**	-18	-24	21
Self-regulated	-11	-08	-30*	-17	-32*	-45***	-13	-16	-55***	-13	-24	-31*

Achievement Oriented	-12	-03	-20	-21	-25	-37**	-12	-23	-40**	-17	-10	-12
Academic Self-esteem	-08	-13	-03	-16	02	02	13	05	-14	-03	02	09
Sees M. as LOV/ADM	-02	13	-46***	05	-44***	-22	00	-21	-49***	-36**	-48***	-24
Sees F. as LOV/ADM	-23	00	-35**	-15	-41**	-56***	-12	-10	-51***	-31*	-16	-43**
Socially Responsible	-10	-04	-36**	-06	-39**	-31*	-09	-13	-53***	-09	-25	-14
Sees M. as Eff. Enf.	-18	05	-44***	02	-46***	-35*	00	08	-49***	-11	-12	-30*
Sees F. as Eff. Enf.	-16	-09	-22	-24	-34**	-39**	-07	-09	-42**	-19	-09	00
Conforming												
Social-ethical Beliefs	-47***	-27	-18	01	-34**	-35*	-19	-05	-28*	17	07	-07
Sees M. as Restrictive	-41**	-22	-17	-18	-20	-33*	-02	18	-16	.17	32	-02
Sees F. as Restrictive	-18	-24	17	-02	07	25	18	13	09	20	30	41**
Sex Stereotyped	33*	09	-02	-48***	14	-07	18	10	-06	-20	10	15
External Control Locus	02	-26	15	-15	24	21	06	00	20	19	17	22
Problem Behavior												
Poor Self-esteem	01	13	14	-16	23	25	02	12	17	19	39*	34*
Self-Devaluation	03	09	02	-07	21	04	-15	06	20	02	03	-05
Internalizing Problem	-01	01	39**	04	43**	34*	04	26	36**	22	44***	22
General Problem Behavior	13	05	41**	12	54***	46***	02	16	54***	19	36	22
Externalizing Problem	22	10	22	-00	42**	40*	-05	-03	51***	07	05	11
Low Family Self-esteem	-19	-27*	27*	13	29*	21	-04	00	30*	36*	29*	37
Drug Problem	37**	23	19	-02	42***	39**	08	00	-37**	05	04	22
Sexual Acting-out	14	11	43***	23	52***	30*	00	-14	50***	-10	01	-09

Note. * = $p < .05$; ** = $p < .01$; *** = $p < .001$. Underlined correlations indicate that boys and girls differ significantly

TABLE 5.3
Time 3 Correlations Between Sons and Parents

	Styles of Parental Control (Demandingness)									
	Restrictive				*Assertive*				*Rational*	
	Directive/ Confrontational		*Conforming*		*Monitors*		*Confronts*		*Controls Rationally*	
Adolescent Variables	*Mother*	*Father*	*Mother*	*Father*	*Mother*	*Father*	*Mother*	*Father*	*Mother*	*Father*
					Agentic Domain					
Emancipated	-36**	-11	-33**	-15	-32**	-06	-19	-01	03	10
Explorative	-28*	-06	-22	-09	-16	-07	-06	-00	18	12
Socially Conscious	-39**	-18	-23	-09	-02	11	05	-00	40***	37**
Gregarious	-09	-07	-04	-05	-06	-21	05	-07	15	-08
					General Competence					
Individuated	-26	-06	-21	-01	02	14	16	08	46***	45***
Optimistic	-11	10	-08	04	20	16	24	13	49***	28*
Optimum Competence	-17	02	-14	03	10	09	19	10	51***	34**
Resilient	-20	03	-20	01	-01	01	11	08	32**	24
General Self-esteem	-09	-00	-21	-22	06	-03	17	-04	21	00

Communal Domain										
Cognitively Motivated	-06	13	-06	11	24	27*	20	15	51***	39**
Self-regulated	-01	08	-08	02	23	12	17	12	44***	26
Achievement Oriented	08	15	06	19	22	11	30*	23	45***	34**
Academic Self-esteem	-12	00	-16	-19	04	10	03	10	32*	23
Sees M. as LOV/ADM	-14	-05	-16	00	40**	07	23	15	62***	36**
Sees F. as LOV/ADM	-07	-08	07	10	21	10	09	18	37**	58***
Socially Responsible	-02	10	-00	06	21	17	16	08	36**	21
Sees M. as Eff. Enf.	27*	18	16	26	44***	12	48***	23	45***	25
Sees F as Eff. Enf.	21	11	17	19	31*	31*	24	19	35**	33**
Conforming										
Social-ethical Beliefs	61***	31*	44***	38**	37**	06	20	-03	-15	-25
Sees M. as Restricted	61***	29*	68***	46***	35**	04	13	-01	-03	-15
Sees F. as Restricted	55***	50***	42***	54***	36**	10	08	12	00	-18
Sex Stereotyped	14	06	20	09	-08	-23	-15	16	-36**	-32*
External Control Locus	35***	31*	35**	32*	08	21	-16	00	-44***	-13
Problem Behavior										
Poor Self-esteem	16	05	14	02	-09	-07	-21	-06	-54***	40**
Self Devaluation	35**	04	31*	18	10	-05	02	-14	-22	-18
Internalizing Problem	-09	-18	06	04	-08	-19	-07	-07	-09	-06
General Problem Behavior	01	-07	09	01	-18	-14	-24	-08	-39**	-17
Externalizing Problem	-23	-13	-00	-03	-43**	-18	-34*	-04	-32*	-05
Low Family Self-esteem	11	03	17	18	-21	-16	-25	-28*	-46***	-29*
Drug Problem	-43***	-25	-19	-20	-49***	-35**	-33**	-06	-04	-08
Sexual Acting-out	-35**	-20	-08	-11	-22	-17	-23	02	-10	00

(Continued)

Table 5.3 (*Continued*)

	Psychologically Differentiated				*Responsive*		*Nonintrusive*			
	Agentic/ Content		*Influential/ Scholarly*		*Considerate*		*Supportive*		*Nonintrusive*	
Adolescent Variables	*Mother*	*Father*	*Mother*	*Father*	*Mother*	*Father*	*Mother*	*Father*	*Mother*	*Father*
				Agentic Domain						
Emancipated	-01	19	10	21	-12	13	04	17	21	17
Explorative	13	16	19	17	19	18	28*	23	02	12
Socially Conscious	22	14	37**	27*	35**	38**	34**	24	17	39**
Gregarious	26	07	10	00	10	-02	15	12	08	-03
				General Competence						
Individuated	23	27*	36**	36**	22	41**	47***	48***	31*	29*
Optimistic	29*	17	24	21	27*	26	49***	28*	23	25
Optimum Competence	25	23	30*	29*	28*	23	31*	30*	52***	38**
Resilient	21	16	22	22	17	26	33**	24	24	16
General Self-esteem	27*	-03	18	01	01	05	09	02	13	02
				Communal Domain						
Cognitively Motivated	11	16	27*	26	32*	35**	51***	38**	24	22
Self Regulated	18	19	18	22	29*	20	47***	30*	16	13

Achievement Oriented	07	19	19	23	17	24	27*	29*	44***	30*
Academic Self-esteem	16	18	19	28*	11	22	27*	19	14	07
Sees M. as LOV/ADM	40***	12	38**	16	29*	15	41***	27*	59***	41**
Sees F. as LOV/ADM	27*	17	34**	25	18	52***	27*	58***	23	28*
Socially Responsible	20	08	09	11	33**	17	43***	21	10	03
Sees M. as Eff. Enf.	23	-02	16	00	33**	21	39**	21	04	06
Sees F. as Eff. Enf.	13	-09	17	-06	24	20	28*	29*	04	-08
Conforming										
Social-ethical Beliefs	-24	-39**	-30*	-31*	-10	-27*	-19	-29*	-51***	-33**
Sees M. as Restrictive	-10	-20	-20	-10	-17	-28*	-37**	-13	14	-07
Sees F. as Restrictive	-23	-18	-24	-14	-07	-37**	-30*	-20	12	-16
Sex Stereotyped	-29*	-05	-31*	-19	-33**	-33**	-32**	-14	-18	-44***
External Control Locus	-31*	-09	-37**	-16	-40**	-22	-33**	07	-23	02
Problem Behavior										
Poor Self-esteem	-31*	-28*	-34**	-34**	-30*	-35**	-53***	-43***	-32**	-33*
Self Devaluation	-23	-05	-26	-03	-18	-13	-20	-14	-34**	09
Internalizing Problem	-05	-06	02	01	-02	-07	-15	-07	-05	-04
General Problem Behavior	-24	-07	-18	-07	-25	-09	-42***	-24	-12	-01
Externalizing Problem	-08	15	00	05	-27*	12	-34*	-05	10	24
Low Family Self-esteem	-29*	-14	-27*	01	-33**	-19	-47***	-37**	-31*	02
Drug Problem	08	13	14	09	-00	-01	-03	00	10	07
Sexual Acting-out	06	03	-01	04	-03	09	-00	09	11	04

(*Continued*)

Table 5.3 (*Continued*)

Adolescent Variables	Problem Behavior: Illicit Drug Usage		Maladjusted/ Internalizing		Exploitive/ Externalizing		Alcohol Abuse		Family Disorganization		Marital Conflict		Officious	
	Mother	Father	Mother	Father	Mother	Father	Mother	Father	Mother	Father	Mother	Father	Mother	Father
Agentic Domain														
Emancipated	18	08	18	-02	10	-06	02	30*	16	06	-14	-22		
Explorative	17	12	03	-02	-09	-12	08	18	06	03	-29*	-31*		
Socially Conscious	06	-10	-10	-08	-22	-28	23	27*	-15	-26	-26	-19		
Gregarious	15	10	-21	-04	-14	01	13	13	05	01	-22	-14		
General Competence														
Individuated	03	00	-02	-24	-18	-32*	-00	-01	-20	-09	-26	-19		
Optimistic	14	05	-25	-22	-39**	-23	06	-19	-28*	-08	-29*	-18		
Optimum Competence	10	-00	-10	-19	-31*	-22	-03	-14	-20	-06	-28*	-12		
Resilient	11	03	-00	-10	-14	-16	08	09	-04	-05	-18	-08		
General Self-esteem	04	10	-19	-01	07	10	-04	-01	-08	-04	-20	-07		
Communal Domain														
Cognitvely Motivated	-03	-12	-04	-19	-35**	-28*	-08	-25	-29*	-09	-20	-07		
Self-regulated	06	-05	-06	-19	-25	-09	-11	-29*	-19	-02	-17	02		

Achievement Oriented	-08	-20	-10	-33**	-32*	-26	-25	40**	-29*	-16	-18	-04
Academic Self-esteem	20	17	-07	-11	-11	00	09	-11	-14	-30*	-20	05
Sees M. as LOV/ADM	13	04	-34**	-17	-38**	33**	07	-33**	-45***	-24	-36**	-15
Sees F. as LOV /ADM	-15	-00	-02	-15	-12	-43***	01	-26	<u>-19</u>	<u>-44**</u>	-27*	-23
Socially Responsible	08	06	-14	-06	-34**	-10	07	-14	<u>-18</u>	-07	-11	12
Sees M. as Eff. Enf.	-14	-14	-31*	-20	-33**	-34**	-07	-51***	-51**	-25	-13	-03
Sees F. as Eff. Enf.	-13	01	-09	00	-33**	-26	-05	-41***	-27*	-32*	-11	07
					Conforming							
Social-ethical Beliefs	-22	-15	04	26	<u>12</u>	<u>13</u>	-38**	<u>47***</u>	-02	30*	40**	<u>30*</u>
Sees M. as Restrictive	-52***	-32*	-06	04	-08	<u>20</u>	-12	-23	-17	00	37**	18
Sees F. as Restrictive	-33**	-46***	-04	-00	-16	09	-31*	<u>44***</u>	-11	14	22	17
Sex Stereotyped	<u>-03</u>	-02	25	<u>12</u>	23	<u>35**</u>	-11	-12	25	<u>33*</u>	19	07
External Control Locus	-26	-19	13	-10	17	-14	09	03	-03	08	43***	-13
					Problem Behavior							
Poor Self-esteem	-11	-04	15	<u>24</u>	27*	29*	-03	08	25	18	33**	30*
Self Devaluation	-20	-17	11	-03	26	01	13	09	01	-05	33**	-12
Internalizing Problem	-03	-07	<u>00</u>	06	<u>01</u>	01	02	21	06	-04	03	02
General Problem Behavior	-14	-09	<u>10</u>	10	<u>23</u>	13	-07	19	<u>22</u>	00	14	-03
Externalizing Problem	07	06	09	00	21	<u>14</u>	03	29*	35*	-06	-03	-22
Low Family Self-esteem	-12	-22	25	16	33**	25	15	14	22	16	30*	<u>-08</u>
Drug Problem	35**	29*	14	10	<u>02</u>	13	18	<u>47***</u>	24	09	-06	-14
Sexual Acting Out	15	26	<u>05</u>	08	<u>13</u>	04	08	<u>36**</u>	25	-21	-15	-06

Note. * = p < .01; ** = p < .001; *** = p < .001. Underlined correlations indicate that boys and girls differ significantly.

Parent Scales. Six parent behavior scales and four parent attribute scales were obtained from the first order data reduction (principal component analysis). These 10 scales when subjected to a second order principal component analysis yielded two components which were the bases for the *demandingness* and *responsiveness* axes in the parent circumplex. The scales are described in the order in which they appear in the circumplex. The four parent attribute scales are starred.

Directive/Conventional (alpha = .93)—authoritarian control strategies employed to enforce restrictive and traditional values

*Conforming** (alpha = .94)—personal values are traditional

Monitors (alpha = .89)—aware of, and supervises, adolescent's lifestyle, health, friends, school life, and whereabouts

Confronts (alpha = .93)—uses straightforward, overt control strategies and does not avoid conflict over disciplinary issues

Controls Rationally (alpha = .94)—uses reason to modify behavior and encourage internalization of parents' values but remains open to negotiation.

*Agentic/Content** (alpha = .95)—is a socially outgoing, happy, and agentic individual

*Influential/Scholarly** (alpha = .93)—is a successful, productive, independent scholar

*Considerate** (alpha = .94)—is an altruistic, sensitive, nonmanipulative and trustworthy person

Supportive (alpha = .96)—appreciates and enjoys adolescent; shares decision-making and disciplines responsively; encourages adolescent's individuation and enjoyment of life, but also sustains a close and intimate relationship.

Nonintrusive (alpha = .96)—Respects adolescent's privacy and is not enmeshed

In addition to the ten variables that were used to construct the circumplex, seven problem behaviors were graphed onto the circumplex based on their correlations with the axes. Three of these problem variables had only moderate correlations with the axes (Problem Alcohol Use, Illicit Drug Use, and Marital Conflict). Of the seven problem behavior variables, three were derived from a separate Problem Behavior Inventory, two assess substance use, and two assess family disharmony.

The three scales derived from the Parent Problem Behavior Inventory are: (1) *Maladjusted/Internalizing* (alpha = .87), which parallels for adults the internalizing scale for adolescents and assesses neglectful, depressed, unstable, immature, unhappy and somatizing symptoms; (2) *Exploitive/Externalizing* (alpha = .79), which parallels the externalizing scale for adolescents, and assesses competitive, abusive, self-centered and sociopathic behavior, especially as it affects the adolescent; and (3) *Officious* (alpha = .75), which assesses over-controlling, intrusive meddling in the adolescent's ongoing activities.

For each parent, indices of illicit drug use and problem alcohol use were obtained. The *Illicit Drug* scale is a four point scale: No use, Experimental use, Recreational use, and Habitual use. The *Problem Alcohol Use* is a three point scale: No use or Occasional use, Recreational use, and Abuse.

Two scales assess the level of family harmony. The *Family Disorganization* scale (alpha = .57) is a two item scale that assesses the level of disorganization and disequilibrium among family members. The *Marital Conflict* scale (alpha = .90) is a nine-item scale that assesses, disagreement about role responsibilities, lack of support and intimacy between the two adult partners with primary responsibility for the adolescent. (Single parent households, of course, were excluded.)

All parent variables were graphed onto the two-dimensional circumplex model, with Demandingness and Responsiveness the central axes for the parents. The order in which the variables are listed horizontally in Tables 5.2 and 5.3 reflect the circular order of the parent variables when graphed along the central axes beginning with the top of the upper left quadrant. The upper left quadrant is defined by high Demandingness and low Responsiveness. The problem behaviors at the opposite end of the set of parent variables circle back to adjoin the "normal" variables in the upper left quadrant. Thus, Officious appears adjacent to Directive/conventional in the parent circumplex.

Results

The simple linear correlational data presented in Tables 5.2 and 5.3 are the first step in a series of more complex multiple regression and prediction analyses to test specific hypotheses about parent-adolescent relations. (See last section on Future Analyses). The magnitude of these unadorned correlations and their internal consistencies provide a coherent and meaningful framework to guide future developmental analyses, but can in no way substitute for them.

The results are tabled separately for each sex but not for sexes combined. For the sexes combined, the internally consistent and highly significant ($<.01$) results across sex are summarized in text. The significant ($<.05$) results within-sex are tabled but are not summarized. Instead, I summarize the sex-differentiated correlations that are significant ($<.05$).

To facilitate exposition, the adolescent and parent variables are divided into a priori construct domains which correspond to areas on the circumplex. The correlations are summarized within the construct domains which organize the parent and adolescent variables. The adolescent domains are: (a) Agentic, (b) General Competence, (c) Communal, (d) Conforming, and (e) Problem Behavior. The parent domains are: (a) Restrictive Control, (b) Assertive Control, (c) Rational Control, (d) Psychologically Differentiated, (e) Supportive, (f) Nonintrusive, and (g) Problem Behavior. Restrictive Control, Assertive Control, and Rational Control comprise the Demandingness modality; and Psychologically Differentiated, Supportive and Nonintrusive comprise the Responsiveness modality.

Generally speaking, the correlations are much higher and more significant for girls than for boys, and for mothers than for fathers with the important exception of the relation between parents' alcohol use and adolescents' problem behavior where the significant father-son correlations predominate. Before presenting the parent-child correlations, mean sex differences on the parent variables are reviewed.

Sex differences on parent variables. The parent rating scales were compared for mothers versus fathers, and for girls versus boys in two-way analyses of variance. Using the .05 level of significance, the following results were found. For the main effect of sex-of-child, parents of girls were higher on monitors, controls rationally, supportive and nonintrusive. Parents of boys were not higher on any variable. For the main effect of sex-of-parent, mothers were higher on monitors and considerate; and fathers were higher on confronts, influential/scholarly and nonintrusive. None of the interactions were significant. Because both parents were rated by the same observer, it can be assumed that we underestimated the sex-of-parent differences.

Sexes combined. In general, parents who were more demanding had adolescent children with fewer behavior problems. Mothers and fathers who used more *restrictive, assertive,* or *rational* controls had children with lower levels of externalizing behavior problems, including drug use, but each style of parent control was associated with quite different kinds of adolescents. In addition to their relative lack of externalizing behavior problems, children of restrictive parents tended to be conforming and low in agentic traits. Also, children of restrictive mothers had low self-esteem. Children of assertive and rationally controlling parents, unlike those of restrictively controlling parents, tended to be more competent and communal. Furthermore, observer-assessed rational control used by parents was associated with higher agency, nonconformity, and self-esteem in their children. Observer assessments of parental control were matched in part by children's perceptions. Adolescents did not perceive their parents as restrictive when their control was observed to be rational, but they did so strongly when parents' control was evaluated as restrictive.

Children of parents who were more *responsive* tended to be more competent and communal, perceived their mothers as loving and admirable, and had higher self-esteem. *Supportive* parents (in addition to the variables listed under "responsive") tended to have achievement-oriented children with fewer internalizing problems. Similarly, *nonintrusiveness* was associated with optimum competence, low internalizing problem behavior, perception of parents as loving and admirable, and high self-esteem. Unlike the demandingness variables, very few responsiveness variables were associated with presence or absence of externalizing problem behavior in the children.

In the parent problem behavior domain, it was evident that parents who used *illicit drugs* had adolescents who were nonconforming, emancipated, and used drugs themselves; the children, however, were no less competent than children whose parents avoided illicit drugs. The significant impact of parents' *alcohol use* was specific to fathers and sons and is discussed in the next section. Mothers who were more maladjusted (*internalizing*) had children with low optimism, who perceived their mothers as not lovable, admirable, or effective enforcers of rules. From the differential size of the correlations (in many instances significantly so) we can infer that parents', especially fathers', *externalizing* problem behavior had a more negative impact on children's competence than parents' internalizing problem behavior. Children whose parents were more externalizing, and children whose families were *disorganized* were less competent and communal, and tended themselves to have all kinds of behavior problems. Parents' *marital conflict* was associated with low family self-esteem and with perceptions of fathers as not loving or admirable. Parents', especially mothers', *officious,* meddlesome behavior was associated with children's conformity, internalizing but not externalizing problem behavior, poor self-esteem, low optimum competence, and low agency—adolescent problems that were also associated with directive-conventional control. (The two variables are highly correlated.)

In sum, for boys and girls combined, parents' control is associated with low levels of acting-out behavior, but each kind of control has different effects, with assertive control and rational control producing more positive effects on competence and self-esteem. Responsiveness was positively related to competence and self-esteem, but not negatively related to externalizing behavior problems. Child behavior problems were consistently related to measures of adult problems, drug and alcohol abuse, psychological symptoms, family disorganization, marital conflict, and officious, meddlesome behavior.

Sex-differentiated parental correlates. Now let us examine differential connections between parenting and child outcomes in adolescent girls and boys. Parent correlates for girls appear in Table 5.2 and for boys appear in Table 5.3. My task here will not be to describe the many significant correlations in addition to those reported under 'Sexes Combined,' but rather to highlight the patterns of significant gender differences underlying the specific correlations. Sex-differentiated correlates (<.05) are underlined in Table 5.2 and 5.3.

Restrictive control had more negative effects on boys and *assertive control* had more positive effects on girls. For example, the restrictive control variables had larger positive association with adolescent boys' than with girls' external locus of control and self-devaluation. Within the assertive domain for girls relative to boys: Maternal *monitors* had larger associations with communal behaviors, with low general problem behavior and with internal locus of control. Maternal *confronts* had larger positive correlations with girls' resiliency and social responsibility. *Rational control* had strong positive effects on both girls and boys but the associations were somewhat different: For girls compared to boys, maternal rational control had a larger deterrent effect on drug use, and paternal rational control had a larger deterrent effect on internalizing problem behavior.

Fathers' responsiveness appeared to draw girls closer to their fathers' sphere of influence and away from their peers' sphere of influence, but to enhance boys' autonomy and self-determination: Fathers' *influential/scholarly* attributes were associated for girls, but not for boys, with their perceptions of fathers as effective enforcers and with their own nongregariousness; and for boys, but not for girls, with nonconformity and high self-esteem. Further enhancing the interpretation that fathers' responsiveness contributes to boys' autonomy was the finding that fathers' considerateness was associated with greater social consciousness and non-sex stereotyped behavior for boys, but with lower general self-esteem for girls. *Mothers' responsive attributes* had a greater deterrent effect on girls' than on boys' problem behavior: There were more maternal responsive attributes that were negatively associated with girls' than with boys' drug use and internalizing problem behavior. *Parental nonintrusiveness* was associated for boys but not for girls with nonconformity, and perception of mothers as nonrestrictive.

Parents' *problem behaviors* had numerous sex-differentiated effects, particularly for fathers' alcohol use and for both parents' exploitive/externalizing behavior. For boys only, fathers' *alcohol use* was associated with nonconformity, drug usage and sexual acting-out, as well as with perception of both parents as ineffectual. For girls compared to boys, *maternal internalizing problem behavior* was associated with greater general problem behavior, internalizing problem behavior, and sexual acting-out. Both parents' *exploitive/externalizing problem behavior* had much greater negative impact on girls than on boys. For girls only, parents' externalizing problem behaviors were associated: (a) for each parent, with nonconformity, internalizing problem behavior, and general problem behavior; (b) for mothers only, with drug problems and sexual acting out; and (c) for fathers only, with emancipated, explorative, socially conscious and under-controlled behavior. *Family disorganization* was associated more strongly for girls than for boys with low self-regulation and social responsibility and with high general problem behavior. *Officious* parental behavior was correlated more strongly with problem behavior for girls than for boys; officious maternal behavior with internalizing problem behavior, officious paternal behavior with low family self-esteem, and both parents' officious behavior with nonconforming social-ethical beliefs.

Discussion

These correlational data are strong and internally consistent. For purposes of discussion, in the spirit of organizing hypotheses for further test, I treat the parent variables as independent and causal, and the adolescent variables as outcomes, although these linear correlational analyses cannot establish causal direction.

The various parental control variables were grouped on the basis of a priori considerations and their actual location on the two dimensional grid defined by demandingness and responsiveness into three categories—Restrictive control, Assertive control, and Rational control. Each style had some distinctive consequences for adolescent behavior that are of theoretical and practical importance. Adolescents become estranged from restrictive parents even though they accept their conservative values, but identify with, and draw close to, assertive-rational parents. Restrictive control was associated with traditional parent and adolescent social values and deterred externalizing problem behaviors, such as drug use and sexual acting-out. However, restrictive control was also associated with such low competence attributes as an external locus of control, and lack of social assertiveness, individuation, and self-esteem. Also, restrictive control did not generate prosocial behavior.

Although restrictive control was effective in deterring problem behavior, it was not a *necessary* deterrent. Assertive control that includes two processes shown by other investigators to be effective—confronting (see Cooper, Grovtevant & colleagues) and monitoring (see Patterson, 1982; this volume)—had an even greater deterrent effect than restrictive control on externalizing problem behavior, especially for girls. We find that when mutually controlled, assertive control accounts for most of the beneficial effect on drug use of restrictive control. Assertive control had the advantage over restrictive control of being associated with secure attachment to parents, and such high competence attributes as communal behavior, internal locus of control, optimism, and achievement orientation. Rational control, by contrast with restrictive control, did not attenuate social agency and was strongly associated with optimum competence, social responsibility, and respectful love for parents. However, unlike restrictive or assertive control, rational control did not deter boys' drug use.

Responsiveness—that is, encouragement of independence, individuality, and verbal give-and-take together with warmth and support—related highly to all aspects of adolescents' competence, and to secure attachment to parents. But with a few important exceptions (such as maternal support and girls' drug use), responsiveness did not deter externalizing problem behavior. Nonintrusiveness was associated with self-esteem, mental health, autonomy, and gregariousness. Since nonintrusiveness did not have the positive association with drug use that parental neglect often has, we consider it an index of consideration rather than of lack of involvement.

Parents' problem behavior had expectable large associations with children's problem behavior and lack of social responsibility. Fathers' alcohol use was especially pathogenic for boys. Fathers' alcohol use correlated strongly with externalizing problem behavior for boys, including drug problems, sexual-acting out, and perception of both parents as ineffectual and unworthy models. Somewhat surprisingly, however, the only negative effect of parents' illicit drug use was to encourage adolescents' drug use.

These data demonstrate that the dimensions of what parents do or fail to do that I have identified in earlier periods continue to have a substantial impact on adolescent well-being, with the impact of mothers on daughters especially large. New variables assessing parents' own attributes and problem behavior at adolescence are also highly predictive. Whether these personal and problem variables *add* information to that obtained from knowledge of parental demandingness and responsiveness alone will be evaluated using multiple regression methods. The impact of fathers relative to mothers on their adolescents' well-being, although less significant by the indices that we used, was by no means negligible. Fathers' use of rational control, their supportiveness and their social status (influential/scholarly) had particularly large positive effects that were apparent in all domains of child behavior.

Most family factors were less highly associated with adolescent variables for boys than for girls, a common finding in studies of socialization effects during adolescence. This may be due to greater willingness on the part of parents to allow their sons to be influenced by nonfamilial factors, especially the peer group. However, the lesser family influence on boys may also reflect differences in how parents relate to their adolescent sons and daughters. With their daughters, parents monitored more, used more rational control, and were more supportive; and fathers were less intrusive. Mothers attempted to sustain a close bond with their adolescent daughters, resisting the tendency of girls to separate during the *practicing* phase of adolescent individuation. Parents controlled sons with a rather heavy-hand in that their disciplinary methods were less rational and supportive and more intrusive (fathers) than with daughters. When parents were supportively engaged, that is, used rational control and were responsive, the positive impact on communal behavior, self-esteem, and optimum competence was as apparent for boys as for girls. However, this authoritative combination of practices did not deter drug use for boys as it did for girls. An important exception to the lesser impact of family factors on boys was the negative impact on boys, but not on girls, of fathers' alcohol use.

Some parental practices have no negative effects, and others have no positive effects, but most have both. It is evident from the direction of the significant correlations, for example, that restrictive control effectively deters externalizing problem behavior, such as drug use and sexual acting-out, but either fails to have much positive effect on competence, or in some instances has a negative effect. Responsiveness has a powerful positive impact on the development of adolescent optimum competence, self-esteem, and harmony in the home but, especially for boys, fails to deter drug use. Assertive control, however, both deters problem behavior, and generates competence, especially in girls. By contrast with most normative parenting practices (i.e., demandingness and responsiveness), where some tradeoff between promoting optimum competence and deterring externalizing problem behavior was noted, many parent problem behaviors both generated adolescent problem behavior and attenuated their level of competence. Mothers' and fathers' exploitive/externalizing behaviors were associated with low communal behavior, lack of competence, low self-esteem, and internalizing and externalizing problem behavior. Fathers' alcohol use attenuated communal behavior and increased problem behavior for boys. Meddlesome, officious interference failed to deter externalizing problem behavior and instead attenuated children's optimum competence and estranged adolescents from their parents. Family disorganization resulted in negative attitudes towards parents, low communal behavior and high problem behavior.

TOWARDS FUTURE ANALYSES OF THE ADOLESCENT DATA

These analyses attempt to untangle and clarify some of the antecedent-consequent relations that may exist in developmental studies of parental influences and adolescent behavior. Parental influences refer to parenting practices that have significant correlations with adolescent behaviors.

Parental influences in our analyses refer to both parents. The contributions of each are examined separately, just as boys and girls are examined separately. At the level of correlational analyses, it would appear that maternal effects greatly predominate. In a separate analysis of level of involvement, we found that mothers were much more highly involved than fathers, particularly in the day-to-day supervision of their adolescents. However, even with level of involvement controlled, the number of significant maternal-adolescent correlates greatly exceeded those of fathers. We do not conclude from this that fathers are unimportant, but rather that more complex analyses are required to uncover the nature of their effects which may be indirect (e.g., as moderators of mothers' effects), or nonlinear. We plan to examine the effects of father-absent homes and expect to find that these are more negative for boys than for girls (e.g., see Hetherington, this volume), although in our sample we know already that some of the boys' problems preceeded divorce, and may indeed have helped to precipitate it. Family disorganization and a chaotic environment adversely affect adolescents, and this may be in part by undermining parental authority and support. As the power of adolescents increase, it may well take two mutually supportive adults to influence them in positive ways. Although it is usually the mother who is most involved in the family, we have yet to examine whether the sex of the parent who provides most of the supervision or support makes a difference. We also plan to look at combinations of parents in typological analyses, in addition to the Traditional family type in which mother is more responsive and father is more demanding, to see for example, whether both parents need to be authoritative or only one suffices. My hunch is that one adult who clearly is engaged and in charge suffices to prevent serious problem behavior provided that the other parent is supportive of the parent who is in charge. We plan to address these issues with information available on role division in the family and the satisfaction of each parent with the extent and nature of the other parent's participation.

Proposed analyses will focus on two primary topics: (1) the developmental precursors of adolescent problem behaviors and competencies of parental influences, and (2) the effect of child and adolescent behaviors on T3 parental influences.

Developmental Precursors

The T1 and T2 precursors (parent-to-adolescent and child-to-adolescent) of adolescent behaviors will be examined using the prospective data obtained from the children and their parents when the children were ages four and nine. Certain early personality attributes (such as interpersonal dominance and independence-seeking), and certain parenting styles (such as nonconformity) which are in no sense pathological, may, nevertheless, predispose some, but not all, children to engage in risky explorative behavior during adolescence. We will attempt to identify the protective family factors that deter the development during adolescence of externalizing problem behavior in nontraditional families, and in children who were socially agentic. Likely candidates for protective family factors include monitoring, and parents' nonuse of drugs.

In examining precursors, it should be noted that we will not limit the analyses to the correlation of measures of the same construct from different time periods. Instead, we will look at how variables from one time period *predict* a variable at a later time period, thus allowing for parent predictors of adolescent behavior that differ across the three time periods. Note that the proposed analyses do not necessarily imply continuity or stability since the predictive T2 parent variables may be quite different from the T3 variables being predicted. For example, imagine that T3 Supportive predicts some adolescent behavior, but that Supportive at T3 is not related to Supportive at T2, but rather to high Firm. Such a result may reflect a developmental transformation (Wohlwill, 1973) or a heterotypic continuity (Kagan, 1971) in the expression of parental commitment. In addition, the relation between T2 and T3 parenting is not necessarily causal: The common variance does not mean that T3 parenting is caused by T2 parenting, any more than that the correlation between height at 15 and 21 years means that height at 21 is caused by height at 15. Rather it means that some common process is active across these time periods.

In order to determine which predictors of adolescent behaviors are stable across time and which change, the predictors (parent-to-adolescent and child-to-adolescent) from T1 and T2 of a given adolescent behavior will be compared to each other and to the T3 predictors of the same adolescent behavior. Further, the predictors that do change, can themselves be a topic of investigation of developmental discontinuity.

We are particularly interested in explaining developmental discontinuities that appear at T3 as functional decrements or suboptimal performance. *Functional decrement* is a sharp break in the developmental trajectory, due to some event, (e.g., drug or stress) and can be investigated by whether certain variables act as suppressor variables on continuity, that is on the correlations between measures of the same dimension of competence across time periods. *Amotivational syndrome* is a typical example of functional decrement that can occur as a result of drug use in adolescence. *Suboptimal performance* is a discrepancy between performance and capacity (what would be expected on the basis of other information about the individual). For example, a child who exhibits normal behavior in school but whose intellectual level indicates the potential for superior performance, or one who is socially skilled but withdrawn, or who is in physically poor condition without any apparent physical reason, demonstrates suboptimal performance. The histories of adolescents who exhibit suboptimal functioning will be examined for factors that may produce these discrepancies, as for example maternal depression, or family conflict. Suboptimal functioning may occur in only a particular social or intellectual domain whereas the expression of a functional decrement will be more pervasive. In addition, unlike functional decrements the existence of suboptimal functioning can be determined from concurrent information (e.g., a discrepancy between intelligence and academic performance), but like functional decrement can only be understood in a developmental context.

The causes of a functional decrement may be based on individual variation (e.g., stressors, drugs), or upon universal factors that differ only in timing, such as puberty. The advent and timing of puberty are known to affect the way parents interact with their children, and to mediate the impact of parenting variables on adolescent behavior. Therefore, the direct and mediating effects of (a) pubertal stage, and (b) timing of puberty (early, on-target, late) on consistency of parent and adolescent behaviors will be examined using the several pubertal indices available in this study.

In the same vein, whereas some variables may disrupt consistency over time, other variables such as SES and intelligence may promote consistency by enabling individuals to handle disruptions that would otherwise result in functional decrements. Accordingly, although the population from which our sample was drawn is relatively homogenous, such factors extrinsic to our core variables as SES and intelligence will be controlled in subsequent multiple regression analyses predicting adolescents' communion, optimum competence, and problem behavior from the parents' practices and attributes.

In addition to trying to predict adolescent behaviors from antecedent parenting variables, we are also interested in the presence of parent-to-adolescent effects that are unique to that time period. Specifically, for critical adolescent variables we will examine how much of the common variance between adolescent and parent variables cannot be predicted (in a multiple regression) from T1 and T2 parenting behavior.

In attempting to understand the predictors of adolescent behavior, both from the same and preceding time periods, we will consider nonlinear as well as linear relationships. As Roberts (1986) argued convincingly, many important developmental phenomena are nonlinear in nature. Some systems with strong maturational components exhibit threshold effects so that after a *good enough* level is reached, further increase in enabling environmental factors, (for example, warmth and autonomy,) is followed by a plateau in children's competence. During adolescence, intense peer attachment is a behavioral system with strong maturational components of the kind that Roberts suggests should exhibit threshold effects. For example, too low levels of family factors that are associated with normal peer involvement, such as warmth, should result in suboptimal peer attachment. But after the minimal environmental threshold is passed that allows for normal development, warmth may have minimal effects, and indeed may reverse its effects, drawing the child too close to the parent. From analyses at earlier time periods we found that both warmth and control had inverted-U relations with child competencies suggesting that there is an optimal middle-ground for both (Baumrind, 1971; under review).

Child effects on Parenting Behavior

Prior to adolescence, the focus of this study was clearly on parent-to-child effects. In contrast to earlier time periods, I believe that child effects during adolescence are probable and theoretically important. Adolescents can disequilibrate parents in important ways as the relative power in the family system becomes more symmetrical. Adolescents may become actively involved in efforts to change their parents' behavior toward them and may even try to change their parents' personal views and attributes. Therefore, we will want to evaluate hypotheses pertaining to specific adolescent-to-parent effects.

In these analysis we will address the extent to which certain T3 parenting behaviors are a response to antecedent child behaviors as well as to concurrent adolescent behavior. The goal of these analyses is to identify a developmental process in parent-child relations and not to announce a "causal winner" (Rogosa, 1979) between child and parent effects.

First we will focus on the effect upon T3 parenting behavior of child behavior *prior* to T3. Specifically, we will assess how much of the common variance between T3 parenting practices and a particular adolescent behavior can be explained by earlier child behaviors. If any of the T3 parent–adolescent relations can be reduced in this manner, then a child-to-parent effect can be concluded.

The variance unique to T3 may also be attributable to a T3 adolescent effect on the T3 parenting behavior. This possibility is investigated in the next proposed analysis. While the T2 and T1 child to T3 parenting analysis is based on the simple principle that events preceding in time may be a cause of later events, the T3 adolescent to parent analysis cannot be based on this widely accepted principle. Rather the argument for the T3 adolescent-to-parent analysis is based on the following:

T3 parent behavior may be a product of enduring characteristics of the parents such as personality and parenting practices carried over from earlier ages, or T3 parent behavior practices may be a response to the unique aspects of adolescence such as changes in the child resulting from puberty, changing social demands, and new opportunities (e.g., substance abuse, increased freedom of choice in school), which in turn may provoke changes in adult behavior. If T3 adolescent behavior explains a substantial amount of variance in a T3 parent behavior after other parent characteristics are considered, then it seems likely that there are adolescent-to-parent effects for that parent behavior. Adolescent drug use is an example of an adolescent variable expected to account for substantial variance in otherwise stable characteristics of parents, such as supportiveness and intrusiveness. However, if the T3 parent behavior (e.g., supportiveness) can be predicted solely from other parent characteristics, and T3 adolescent behaviors (e.g., drug use) have little additional effect upon the T3 parenting behavior, then it would seem unlikely that there is an adolescent-to-parent effect for that behavior.

Even when the preceding analyses do not show child effects on their parents, we cannot rule out such effects. The preceding analyses do not say anything about how the child's cognitive or affective system may act as an intervening variable. That is, the manner in which the child encodes or represents the parenting behavior may change the effects of the parenting behavior on adolescents, without directly affecting parenting behaviors. Thus depending upon how the parents' behavior is construed by the child, the same parenting behavior could have different effects due to the cognitive activity of the child. Therefore, we are especially interested in how adolescents' perceive their parents. We asked the adolescents to evaluate their mother and their father using a 35-item forced choice distribution Q-Sort to describe the relationship. The possible effect of the adolescents' perceptions in moderating the effect of parenting practices will be examined in the same way as functional decrements previously described. In addition adolescents' perceptions will be related to the (a) adolescent measures in order to assess how the adolescents' perceptions of their parents predict their own competence and problem behavior; and (b) parent measures in order to evaluate the correspondence between the adolescents' and the observers' perceptions of their parents as conforming, nurturing, and rational.

Our previous discussion of functional decrements also bears on the issue of child effects on parents. Just as some events may disrupt the developmental trajectory of the child, other events may upset the stability and trajectory of the parenting behavior. For example, parenting may change with the advent of normative events such as puberty or with the onset of nonnormative events, such as drug abuse or underachievement. The potential impact of these events on parenting will be investigated, both in terms of precursors and direction of effects.

The last topic we will address in the child-to-parent effect is how enduring characteristics of the child affects parenting practices. The primary characteristic we will examine is the gender of the child. During childhood (T2) we found significant sex-differentiated effects. We expect these to occur in adolescence as well. In all analyses, we will examine whether parenting behavior is significantly more common with one sex than with the other, and whether the impact of the same behavior has significantly different effects on boys and girls. Other child characteristics whose effects on parents we may wish to consider include intelligence and school achievement.

To conclude: The process of adolescent individuation, entailing as it does rebellious, oppositional, and resistive strivings is inherently risky. During adolescence, developmentally normative and healthy features such as establishing a friendship network that excludes parents as part of exploring the world outside the home, coexist with problematic, experimental risk-taking behavior such as substance use. Experimental risk-taking during adolescence is problematic and may even be pathogenic, but it is not per se pathological. That is, during adolescence perhaps more so than at any other developmental stage, an individual may be competent in the sense of *becoming autonomous,* but as a result also engage in potentially self-destructive exploratory behavior. For this reason also the familial antecedents of competence and of experimental risk-taking behavior are not mutually exclusive. At the extremes, parents' traditionality and nontraditionality each has costs as well as benefits. The prevention of problem behavior during adolescence will be uppermost in the minds of some, and the generation of optimal competence, including individuation and early emancipation, will take precedence for others. Whatever their values, parents and policy makers will want to be informed about the costs and the benefits of the strategy they favor for dealing with the process of adolescent development. Our future research, together with that of other investigators, should provide such information.

ACKNOWLEDGMENTS

During the preparation of this paper, the author was supported by a Research Scientist Award (#1-K05-MH00485-01) and a research grant (#-R01-MH38343-01) from the National Institute of Mental Health. During the adolescent phase of the research, the project was supported by a research grant (#1-R01-DA01919) from the National Institute on Drug Abuse, and by one from the John D. and Catherine T. MacArthur Foundation. The William T. Grant Foundation has provided consistent and generous support of this longitudinal program of research including the present phase of analysis of the early adolescent data (supported by grant #84044973).

REFERENCES

Achenbach, T. M., & Edelbrock, C. S. (1983). *Manual for child behavior checklist and revised child behavior profile*. Burlington, VT: Department of Psychiatry.

Bachman, J. G., Green, S., & Wirtanen, I. (1971). Dropping out—problem or symptom? *Youth in Transition, 3*. Ann Arbor, MI: Institute for Social Research.

Bakan, D. (1966). *The duality of existence: Isolation and communion in western man*. Boston: Beacon Press.

Barron, F. (1953). An ego-strength scale which predicts response to psychotherapy. *Journal of Consulting and Clinical Psychology, 17,* 327–333.

Baumrind, D. (1967). Child care practices anteceding three patterns of preschool behavior. *Genetic Psychology Monographs, 75,* 43–88.

Baumrind, D. (1971). Current patterns of parental authority. *Developmental Psychology Monographs, 4*(1), Part 2.

Baumrind, D. (1987). A developmental perspective on adolescent risk-taking in contemporary America. In C. Irwin (Ed.), *New Directions for Child Development, 37,* 93–126. San Francisco: Jossey-Bass.

Baumrind, D., & Black, A. E. (1967). Socialization practices associated with dimensions of competence in preschool boys and girls. *Child Development, 38,* 291–327.

Baumrind, D., & Moselle, K. A. (1985). A developmental perspective on adolescent drug abuse. *Advances in Alcohol and Substance Abuse. 4*(3/4), 41–67.

Beiser, H. R. (1980). Ages 11 to 14. In S. Greenspan & G. Pollock (Eds.), *The course of life: Psychoanalytic contributions toward understanding personality development, Vol. 2: Latency, adolescence and youth* (DHHS Pub. No. [ADM]80-999, pp. 293–308). Washington, DC: Government Printing Office.

Bell, N. J., Avery, A. W., Jenkins, D., Feld, J., & Schoenrock, C. J. (1985). Family relationships and social competence during late adolescence. *Journal of Youth and Adolescence, 14,* 109–119.

Bellah, R. N., Madsen, R., Sullivan, W. M., Swidler, A., & Tipton, S. M. (1985). *Habits of the heart: Individualism and commitment in American life*. Berkeley: University of California Press.

Bloom, M. V. (1980). *Adolescent-parental separation*. New York: Gardner Press.

Blos, P. (1962). *On adolescence*. New York: The Free Press.

Blos, P. (1979). The second individuation process. In P. Blos (Ed.), *The adolescent passage: Developmental issues of adolescence* (pp. 141–170). New York: International University Press.

Brittain, C. V. (1968). A comparison of urban and rural adolescence with respect to peer versus parent compliance. *Adolescence, 2,* 445–458.

Bronfenbrenner, U. (1985). Freedom and discipline across the decades. In G. Becker, H. Becker, & L. Huber (Eds.), *Ordnung und Unordnung* (pp. 326–339). Berlin: Beltz.

Brown, S. S. (1979). The health needs of adolescents. In U.S. Department of Health, Education and Welfare, *Healthy people: The surgeon general's report on health promotion and disease prevention* (DHEW Publication No. 79-55071). Washington, DC: U.S. Government Printing Office.

Cattell, R. (1966). The meaning and strategic use of factor analyses. In R. B. Cattell (Ed.), *Handbook of multivariate experimental psychology*. Chicago: Rand McNally.

Chodorow, N. (1978). *The reproduction of mothering: Psychoanalysis and sociology of gender*. Berkeley: University of California Press.

Clark, R. (1983). *Family life and school achievement: Why poor black children succeed or fail.* Chicago: University of Chicago Press.

Cohen, J. (1977). *Statistical power analysis for the behavioral sciences.* New York: Academic Press.

Coleman, J. S. (1978). Current contradictions in adolescent theory. *Journal of Youth and Adolescence, 7,* 1–11.

Cooper, C. R., Grotevant, H. D., & Condon, S. M. (1982). Methodological challenges of selectivity in family interaction: Addressing temporal patterns of individuation. *Journal of Marriage and the Family, 44,* 749–754.

Cooper, C. R., Grotevant, H. D., & Condon, S. M. (1983). Individuality and connectedness in the family as a context for adolescent identity formation and role-taking skill. In H. D. Grotevant & C. R. Cooper (Eds.), *New directions for child development, 22: Adolescent development in the family.* (pp. 43–59). San Francisco: Jossey-Bass.

Coopersmith, S. (1967). *The antecedents of self-esteem.* San Francisco: W. H. Freeman.

Crandall, V., Crandall, V. J., & Katkovsky, W. (1965). A children's social desirability questionnaire. *Journal of Consulting Psychiatry, 29,* 27–36.

Davies, M., & Kandel, D. B. (1981). Parental and peer influences on adolescent's educational plans: Some further evidence. *American Journal of Sociology, 87*(2), 363–387.

Dinnerstein, D. (1977). *The mermaid and the minotaur: Sexual arrangements and human malaise.* New York: Harper & Row.

Dornbusch, S. M., Ritter, P. L., Leiderman, P. H., Roberts, D. F., & Fraleigh, M. J. (1987). The relation of parenting style to adolescent performance. *Child Development, 58,* 1244–1257.

Douvan, E., & Adelson, J. (1966). *The adolescent experience.* New York: Wiley.

Dubin, E. R., & Dubin, R. (1963). The authority inception period in socialization. *Child Development, 34,* 885–898.

Erikson, E. H. (1959). Identity and the life cycle: Selected papers. *Psychological Issues, 1*(1).

Feather, N. (1980). Values in adolescence. In J. Adelson (Ed.), *Handbook of adolescent psychology* (pp. 247–294). New York: Wiley.

Fitts, W. (1965). *Tennesses self-concept manual.* Nashville, TN: Counselor Recordings and Tests.

Freud, A. (1969). Adolescence as a developmental disturbance. In G. Kaplan & S. Lebovici (Eds.), *Adolescence: Psychosocial perspectives* (pp. 5–10). New York: Basic Books.

Friedenberg, E. Z. (1971). *The anti-American generation.* New Brunswick, NJ: Transaction.

Furstenberg, F. F., Jr. (1981). The Social Consequences of Teenage Parenthood. In F. F. Furstenberg, Jr., R. Lincoln, & J. Menken (Eds.), *Teenage sexuality, pregnancy, and childbearing* (pp. 184–210). Philadelphia: University of Pennsylvania Press.

Gilligan, C. (1982). *In a different voice: Psychological theory and women's development.* Cambridge, MA: Harvard University Press.

Gilligan, C., & Wiggins, G. (1987). The origins of morality in early childhood relationships. In J. Kagan & S. Lamb (Eds.), *The emergence of morality in young children.* Chicago: University of Chicago Press.

Goodman, P. (1964). *Compulsory mis-education.* New York: Horizon.

Gordon, C. (1972). *Looking ahead: Self-conceptions, race and family as determinants of adolescent orientation to achievement.* Washington, D.C.: American Sociological Association.

Gorsuch, R. L. (1974). *Factor analysis.* Philadelphia: W. B. Saunders.

Greenberger, E. (1984). Defining psychosocial maturity in adolescence. In P. Karoly & J. J. Steffen (Eds.), *Adolescent behavior disorders: Foundations and contemporary concerns* (pp. 3–39). Lexington, MA: D. C. Heath. (Revision).

Haley, J. (1980). *Leaving home.* New York: McGraw-Hill.

Hamburg, B. A. (1974). Coping in early adolescence: The special challenges of the junior high school period. In S. Arieti (Ed.), *American handbook of psychiatry, Vol. 2: Child and adolescent psychiatry, sociocultural and community psychiatry* (Gerald Caplan, Vol. editor) (2nd edition, pp. 385–397). New York: Basic Books.

Hartup, W. W. (1979). The social worlds of childhood. *American Psychologist, 34,* 944–950.

Hawkins, J. D., Lishner, D. M., & Catalano, R. F., Jr. (1985). Childhood predictors and the prevention of adolescent substance abuse. In C. L. Jones & R. J. Battjes (Eds.), *Etiology of drug abuse: Implications for prevention* (NIDA Research Monograph No. 56; DHHS Publication No. ADM 85-1335, pp. 75–126). Rockville, MD: National Institute on Drug Abuse.

Hill, J. P. (1980). The early adolescent and the family. In M. Johnson (Eds.), *The seventy-ninth yearbook of the National Society for the Study of Education* (pp. 32–55). Chicago: University of Chicago Press.

Hill, J. P., & Holmbeck, G. N. (1986). Attachment and autonomy during adolescence. In G. Whitehurst (Ed.), *Annals of Child Development* (Vol. 3, pp. 145–189). Greenwich, CT: JAI Press.

Holt, J. (1974). *Escape from childhood: The needs and rights of children.* New York: E. P. Dutton.

Jessor, R., & Jessor, S. L. (1977). *Problem behavior and psychosocial development: A longitudinal study of youth.* New York: Academic Press.

Jessor, R., & Jessor, S. L. (1978). Theory testing in longitudinal research on marihuana use. In D. B. Kandel (Ed.), *Longitudinal research on drug use: Empirical findings and methodological issues* (pp. 41–71). Washington, DC: Hemisphere.

Jessor, S. L., & Jessor, R. (1974). Maternal ideology and adolescent problem behavior. *Developmental Psychology, 10,* 246–254.

Johnston, L. D., Bachman, J. G., & O'Malley, P. M. (1980). *Student drug use in America, 1975–1980* (National Institute on Drug Abuse). Rockville, MD: U.S. Government Printing Office.

Jorgensen, E. C., & Howell, R. J. (1969). Changes in self, ideal-self correlations from ages 3 through 18. *Journal of Social Psychology, 79,* 63–67.

Josselson, R. L. (1973). Psychodynamic aspects of identity formation in college women. *Journal of Youth and Adolescence, 2,* 3–52.

Kagan, J. (1971). *Changes and continuity in infancy.* New York: Wiley.

Kandel, D. B., & Lesser, G. S. (1972). *Youth in two worlds.* San Francisco: Jossey-Bass.

Kaplan, H. B. (1980). Deviant behavior in defense of self. New York: Academic Press.

Kenny, M. E. (1987). The extent and function of parental attachment among first-year college students. *Journal of Youth and Adolescence, 16*(1), 17–29.

Langner, T. S., Gersten, J. C., Wills, T. A., & Simcha-Fagan, O. (1983). The relative roles of early environment and early behavior as predictors of later child behavior. In D. F. Ricks & B. S. Dohrenwend (Eds.), *Origins of psychopathology: Problems in research and public policy* (pp. 43–70). New York: Cambridge University Press.

Lasch, C. (1979). *The culture of narcissism.* New York: W. W. Norton.

Leary, T. (1957). *Interpersonal diagnosis of personality: A functional theory and methodology for personality evaluation.* New York: Ronald Press.

Lonner, W. J. (1980). The search for psychological universals. In H. C. Triandis & w. W. Lambert (Eds.), *Handbook of cross-cultural psychology. Vol. 1* (pp. 143–204). Boston: Allyn & Bacon.

Marcia, J. E. (1980). Identity in adolescence. In J. Adelson (Eds.), *Handbook of adolescent psychology* (pp. 159–187). New York: Wiley.

Maslow, A. H. (1954). *Motivation and personality.* New York: Harper.

Moore, D. (1987). Parent-adolescent separation: The construction of adulthood by late adolescents. *Developmental Psychology, 23*(2), 298–307.

Neill, A. S. (1964). *Summerhill.* New York: Hart.

Nickols, J. E., Jr. (1963). Changes in self-awareness during the high school years: A study of mental health using paper-and-pencil tests. *Journal of Educational Research, 56,* 403–409.

Nowicki, S., & Strickland, B. R. (1973). A locus of control scale for children. *Journal of Consulting and Clinical Psychology, 40,* 146–152.

Papini, D., & Sebby, R. (1985, April). *Multivariate assessment of adolescent physical maturation as a source of change in family relations.* Paper presented at the biennial meetings of the Society for Research in Child Development, Toronto, Ontario, Canada.

Patterson, G. R. (1982). *Coercive family process.* Eugene, OR: Castalia Press.

Piaget, J. (1965). *Moral judgment of the child.* New York: Free Press. (Original work published 1932).

Powers, S. I., Hauser, S. T., Schwartz, J. M., Noam, G. G., & Jacobson, A. M. (1983). Adolescent ego development and family interaction: A structural-developmental perspective. In H. D. Grotevant & C. R. Cooper (Eds.), *Adolescent development in the family* (pp. 5–26). San Francisco: Jossey-Bass.

Rawls, J. (1972). *A theory of justice.* Cambridge, MA: Harvard University Press.

Robert, W. L. (1986). Nonlinear models of development: An example from the socialization of competence. *Child Development, 57*(5), 1166–1178.

Rogers, C. R. (1960). A therapist's view of personal goals. *Pendle Hill Pamphlet 108.* Wallingford, PA: Pendle Hill.

Rogosa, D. (1979). Causal models in longitudinal research: Rationale, formulation, and interpretation. In J. R. Nesselroade & P. B. Baltes (Eds.), *Longitudinal research in the study of behavior and development* (pp. 263–302). New York: Academic Press.

Rosenberg, M. (1965). *Society and the adolescent self-image.* New Jersey: Princeton University Press.

Schaefer, E. S. (1959). A circumplex model for maternal behavior. *Journal of Abnormal and Social Psychology, 59,* 226–235.

Shafer, M. A., & Irwin, C. E. (1983). Sexually transmitted diseases in adolescents. In M. Green & R. J. Haggerty (Eds.), *Ambulatory pediatrics, III* (pp. 214–233). Philadelphia: W. B. Saunders.

Spence, J. T., & Helmreich, R. L. (1978). *Masculinity and femininity: Their psychological dimensions, correlates, and antecedents.* Austin: University of Texas Press.

Spotts, J. V., & Shontz, F. C. (1985). A theory of adolescent substance abuse. *Advances in Alcohol and Substance Abuse, 4*(3/4), 117–138.

Steinberg, L. (1981). Transformations in family relations at puberty. *Developmental Psychology, 17,* 833–840.

Steinberg, L. (1985). Adolescence. New York: Knopf.

Steinberg, L. (1987). Impact of puberty on family relations: Effects of pubertal status and pubertal timing. *Developmental Psychology, 23*(3), 451–460.

Steinberg, L., & Silverberg, S. B. (1986). The vicissitudes of autonomy in early adolescence. *Child Development, 57*(4), 841–851.

Stierlin, H. (1981). *Separating parents and adolescents.* New York: Jason Aronson.

Turiel, E. (1978). Social regulations and domains of social concepts. In W. Damon (Ed.), *Directions for child development: Social cognition* (pp. 45–74). San Francisco: Jossey-Bass.

U. S. Department of Health, Education, and Welfare. (1979). Background papers for *Healthy people: The surgeon general's report on health promotion and disease prevention* (DHEW Publication No. 79-55072). Washington, DC: U.S. Government Printing Office.

Warner, K. (1978). Possible increases in the underreporting of cigarette consumption. *Journal of the American Statistical Associates, 73,* 314–318.

Wiggins, J. S. (1979). A psychological taxonomy of trait-descriptive terms: The interpersonal domain. *Journal of Personality and Social Psychology, 37,* 395–412.

Wiggins, J. S. (1980). Circumplex models of interpersonal behavior. In L. Wheller (Ed.), *Review of personality and social psychology. Vol. 1* (pp. 265–294). Beverly Hills: Sage.

Wohlwill, J. F. (1973). *The study of behavioral development.* New York: Academic Press.

Worsfold, V. L. (1974). A philosophical justification for children's rights. In *The rights of children* (pp. 29–44). Cambridge, MA: Harvard Educational Review.

Yamemoto, K., Thomas, E. C., & Karns, E. A. (1969). School-related attitudes in middle school-age students. *American Educational Research Journal, 6,* 191–206.

Zahaykevich, M., Sirey, J. A., & Lortie, M. (1987, April). An object relations view of adolescent gender formation in maternal discourse. In M. Zahaykevich (Chair), *Adolescent gender formation and individuation in family discourse*. Symposium conducted at the biennial meeting of the Society for Research in Child Development, Baltimore.

Zahaykevich, M., Sirey, J., & Sprik, M. (1987). *The construction of consensus in mother-daughter discourse*. Unpublished manuscript, University of Rochester.

6 The Role of Individual Differences and Family Relationships in Children's Coping with Divorce and Remarriage[1]

E. Mavis Hetherington
University of Virginia

In the past decade there has been an increasing concern with the study of stress and coping in children (Garmezy, 1983; Hetherington & Clingempeel, 1989; Rutter, 1987; Werner, 1988). Although some children appear to be vulnerable and to develop serious or sustained problems in response to adversity, others appear resilient in the face of stressful experiences and develop into competent, fulfilled individuals. Both attributes of the child and family factors have been found to be salient in modifying children's responses to stressful life events such as their parents marital transitions.

In this chapter data from the 6-year follow-up of the Virginia Longitudinal Study of Divorce and Remarriage are used to explore some of the attributes of the child, specifically temperament and sex, and characteristics of the family environment that contribute to children's long-term vulnerability or resiliency in coping with their parents' divorce and remarriage. Since this study involves divorced families with custodial mothers and remarried families with a divorced custodial mother and a stepfather, these families for the most part are the focus of the following literature review.

TEMPERAMENT

It has frequently been noted that individual characteristics of children such as age, sex, intelligence, temperament, personality and psychopathology buffer or put children at risk when they confront stressful life events (Garmezy, 1983;

[1]Parts of this paper have appeared in Hetherington 1987, 1988, 1989, in press).

Rutter, 1983, 1987; Werner, 1988; Wallerstein & Kelly, 1980; Werner & Smith, 1982; Zill, 1988). Children who already have vulnerabilities such as poor cognitive competence, behavior problems or a difficult temperament are likely to have these difficulties exacerbated or amplified by stress (Elder, Caspi, Van Ngwyen, in press; Patterson & Dishion, 1988). In contrast, cognitively and socially competent children, or children with easy temperaments, are more able to cope with adverse life experiences and it has even been suggested that such children with some supports available, may be enhanced by dealing with challenging situations (Werner, 1988; Rutter, 1987). Thus under conditions of stress the psychologically poor get poorer and the psychologically rich may sometimes get richer.

This to some extent may be because during or following stressful events or transitions children who already have personal problems in contrast to less vulnerable children are more likely to encounter multiple aversive experiences in interpersonal relations (Block, Block, & Gjerde, 1986; Stoneman, Brody, & Burke, in press; Crockenberg, 1981; Crockenberg & McCluskey, 1986; Hetherington, Cox, & Cox, 1985; Werner, 1988; Werner & Smith, 1982). Rutter (1987) has proposed that children with difficult temperaments are more likely to be both the elicitors and the targets of aversive responses by parents, while in times of stress the temperamentally easy child is not only less likely to be the recipient of criticism and displaced anger and anxiety, but also is more able to cope with adversity when it hits. In addition, temperamentally difficult children may be less able to attract support in times of stress and less able to utilize it when it is available. Although there is little available research on the role of temperament in the adjustment of children to their parents marital transitions, Rutter's model seems a most appropriate one to test in examining children's responses to divorce and remarriage.

The modest or insignificant relations found between preschool measures of temperament and later school aged measures of adjustment suggest that early assessments of temperament alone are insufficient predictors of subsequent problem behaviors (Garrison, Earls, & Kindlon, 1984; Graham, Rutter, & George, 1973; Thomas & Chess, 1984). Research findings indicate that this relation is modified by stressful life experiences and by supports and resources, particularly those involving positive family relations, which are available to children (Buss, 1981; Cutrona & Troutman, 1986; Goldberg & Easterbrooks, 1984; Wilkie & Ames, 1986).

Sex differences in the predisposing role of difficulties of temperament in relation to family functioning or family adversity have been inconsistently obtained. Earls, Beardslee, and Garrison (1987) report that this relation is much clearer in males than in females, whereas Stoneman, Brody, and Burke (in press) suggest that it is most marked in girls. The interaction between gender and child temperament may vary with the age of the child. With infants and younger children, males are generally recognized to have the most difficult temperament (Cameron, 1978; Moss, 1967; Thomas & Chess, 1977) and their difficult temperament seems to have a greater negative impact on family functioning (Abbott & Brody, 1985). With school aged children, however, the dimensions of activity and negative affect which are central in most definitions of difficultness of temperament are viewed as more gender appropriate for boys than for girls. These sex typed expectations for behavior may contribute to findings of a more marked association between temperament and aversive or disrupted family relations with older girls than older boys (Stoneman, Brody, & Burke, in press).

SEX OF CHILD

In contrast to the paucity of research on the role of temperament in children's adjustment to their parents' marital transitions the role of sex differences has been extensively studied (For more comprehensive reviews of this topic see Hetherington, Stanley-Hagan, & Anderson, 1989; Zaslow, 1987).

DIVORCE

Following divorce about 90% of children reside with a custodial mother. The deleterious effects of marital discord, divorce, and life in a single parent mother-custody family are more pervasive for boys than for girls (Hetherington, Cox, & Cox, 1982, 1985; Porter & O'Leary, 1980; Rutter, 1981). Boys, in contrast to girls in single-mother homes and to children in nondivorced homes, show a higher rate of behavior disorders and problems in interpersonal relations both in the home and in the school with teachers and peers. Boys also are more likely to show more sustained noncompliant, aggressive behavior even 2- to 3-years after divorce (Hetherington et al., 1982, 1985; Hetherington & Clingempeel, 1989). However, while the disturbances in social and emotional adjustment in girls living with their mothers have largely disappeared by 2 years after divorce, problems may reemerge at adolescence in the form of parent-child conflict and disruptions in heterosexual relations (Hetherington, 1972; Wallerstein, Corbin, & Lewis, 1988; Hetherington & Clingempeel, 1989).

There is some evidence that children adapt better in the custody of a parent of the same sex (Camara & Resnick, 1988; Zill, 1988). Boys in father custody homes are more mature, social and independent, are less demanding, and have higher self-esteem than do girls in father custody homes (Santrock & Warshak, 1979). However, sons in father-custody homes are also less communicative and less overtly affectionate perhaps as a result of less exposure to female expressiveness. Girls in father-custody homes show higher levels of aggression and behavioral problems and fewer incidences of prosocial behavior than do girls in mother-custody homes (Furstenberg, 1988). It should be noted, however, that research on children's adjustment in father-custody homes is scant and most studies on father custody involve school aged children. Furthermore, there is evidence that the quality of the custodial father-child relationship is related to whether or not the father actively sought custody or was awarded custody because of his ex-wife's inability to take custody (Hetherington & Stanley-Hagan, 1986).

Boys in both mother-custody and father-custody homes show more acting out behaviors than do girls (Furstenberg & Allison, 1985; Hetherington et al., 1982; Hetherington & Camara, 1984; Zeiss, Zeiss, & Johnson, 1980). This in part may be attributable to the fact that family conflict and children's externalizing behavior are correlated. Boys seem to be particularly vulnerable to the effects of conflict. Why should this be? The period surrounding divorce is a time of high rates of parental acrimony and boys are more likely than girls to be exposed to parental conflict. Parents fight more and their fights are longer in the presence of sons than daughters (Hetherington et al., 1982). Moreover, a recent study (Morgan, Lye, & Condron, 1988) reports that families with sons are 9% less likely to divorce than are those with daughters. This may be because of greater involvement and attachment of fathers to sons or to the reluctance of mothers to attempt raising sons alone. Whatever the reason it seems likely that parents of sons may remain together longer even in a contentious marriage. Thus sons may be exposed to more conflict both before and after divorce. It is not surprising therefore that boys interpret family disagreements less positively than do girls (Epstein, Finnegan, & Gythell, 1979). Furthermore, since boys are more likely than girls to respond to stress with externalizing, noncompliant, antisocial behaviors, firm consistent authoritative control may be more essential in the parenting of boys than girls. During and following divorce, however, the discipline of custodial mothers often becomes erratic, inconsistent, peremptory, and punitive especially with sons. Finally, in times of family stress males are less able than females to disclose their feelings and to solicit and obtain support from parents, other adults, and peers (Hetherington, 1989). Thus in times of family conflict or divorce boys may experience more stress than girls and may have fewer resources available to them in dealing with their turbulent family environments.

There are some reports that marital discord is associated with anxiety and depression in girls (Emery, 1982; Emery & O'Leary, 1982; Rutter, 1971; Wallerstein et al., 1988). However, while internalizing behaviors are sometimes found in girls following divorce, girls demonstrate such behaviors less frequently than they do conduct disorders (Furstenberg & Seltzer, 1983; Garbarino, Sebes, & Schellenbach, 1984; Hetherington et al., 1985; Jacobson, 1984; Zill & Peterson, 1983). Thus in both boys and girls acting out disorders are the most common response to divorce.

REMARRIAGE

Following the remarriage of the custodial parent, there often is a re-emergence of emotional and behavioral problems in girls and an intensification of problems in boys (Bray, 1988; Hetherington et al., 1985; Santrock & Warshak, 1979;

Santrock, Warshak, Lindbergh, & Meadows, 1982; Zill & Peterson, 1983). While boys experience more pervasive problems in postdivorce adjustment, some studies report that girls have more problems adjusting to remarriage (Brand, Clingempeel, Bowen-Woodward, 1988). Sons who are often involved in conflictual, coercive relations with their custodial mothers may have little to lose and much to gain by the introduction of a warm, involved stepfather. In contrast, daughters who often have a close relationship with their custodial mothers and considerable independence may find a stepfather disruptive and constraining.

Sex differences in response to remarriage however are less consistently found in adolescents (Wallerstein et al., 1988). A recent study reports that there is an extremely high level of behavior disorders in both boys and girls when custodial mothers marry when the children are early adolescents. This disorder did not decline in either girls or boys over the 2½ years following the remarriage as it does in younger children (Hetherington & Clingempeel, 1989). Early adolescence seems to be a period in which children are particularly vulnerable to the adverse effects of remarriage. Since two of the tasks early adolescents confront are dealing with their own developing sexuality and gaining autonomy, the presence of a stepparent may be particularly disruptive in the attainment of these goals.

It seems likely that the effects of sex differences in the response to a wide range of stressors may interact with age. Werner and Smith (1982) have suggested that the normative developmental challenges encountered in preadolescence are more stressful for boys whereas those in adolescence are more stressful for girls. Non normative stresses such as divorce and remarriage may compound these normative stresses. It is essential to consider the age of the child in appraising sex differences in coping with parents' marital transitions.

FAMILY RELATIONS

The quality of family relations is an important mediator of children's responses to their parents' divorce or remarriage (See Hetherington, Arnett, & Hollier, 1988; Hetherington, Stanley-Hagan, & Anderson, 1989 for more detailed reviews). A period of disrupted or diminished parenting is often found following divorce and remarriage (Bray, 1988; Brand et al., 1988; Hetherington & Clingempeel, 1989; Hetherington et al., 1982). In the early period of transition a preoccupied or emotionally disturbed parent and a distressed, demanding child may have difficulty giving each other support or solace. They may exacerbate each others problems. Both custodial divorced mothers and remarried mothers initially become less authoritative in their parenting practices. It is in problems in control and in monitoring their children's behavior that these mothers differ most from mothers in nondivorced families. They also, however, frequently become erratic, uncommunicative, nonsupportive and inconsistently punitive in dealing with their children. This behavior is more marked and sustained with mothers of boys than with mothers of girls. Most divorced custodial mothers and remarried mothers become more authoritative by 2 years after a marital transition; however many mothers and sons continue to be involved in coercive interchanges. In contrast to their relationship with sons, divorced mothers and their preadolescent daughters often form close congenial relationships, but these relationships especially with early maturing girls may become disrupted and conflictual in early adolescence, especially if the mother remarries.

Stepfathers take a considerably less active role in parenting than do custodial parents (Bray, 1988; Hetherington et al., 1985; Hetherington & Clingempeel, 1989; Santrock & Sitterle, 1987). Even 2 years following remarriage disengagement from childrearing is more commonly found in stepfathers than residential biological fathers (Bray, 1988; Hetherington, 1988; Hetherington & Clingempeel, 1989). Stepfathers tend to be particularly ineffective in control and monitoring of their stepchildren's activities.

Although immediately following the remarriage both mothers and stepfathers have more problems with sons, in the long run stepfathers have more difficulty in their relationship with stepdaughters, particularly adolescent stepdaughters. Stepfathers who initially spend time establishing warm involved relations with their step children and who do not use punitive controls may eventually be accepted and play a positive role in the adjustment of boys (Hetherington, 1987; Hetherington & Clingempeel, 1989). Research suggests that if stepfathers persist with authoritative parenting, eventually this will lead to positive outcomes for children (Bray, 1988; Brand et al., 1988; Hetherington & Clingempeel, 1989), although again this result is less consistently found for girls especially adolescent girls, than for boys.

THE VIRGINIA LONGITUDINAL STUDY OF DIVORCE AND REMARRIAGE

In order to examine the role of sex, temperament, and family factors that contribute to children's long-term adjustment to divorce and remarriage some of the results of a 6-year follow-up study of divorce and remarriage that I began in collaboration with Martha and Roger Cox (Hetherington et al., 1982) are presented. The sample in the original study (Hetherington et al., 1982) was composed of 144 well educated middle-class White parents and their children. Half of the children were from divorced, mother-custody families, and the other half were from nondivorced families. Within each group, half were boys and half were girls. The target child who was 4 years-of-age at the beginning of the study and his or her parents were studied at 2-months, 1 year, 2 years, and 6 years following divorce.

In the 6-year follow-up the subjects were residential parents and children in 124 of the original 144 families who were available and willing to continue to participate in the study. A new group of families matched on demographic characteristics with the original sample was added to the group of participating original families in order to expand the size of the groups to 30 sons and 30 daughters in each of three groups—a remarried mother/stepfather group, a nonremarried, mother-custody group, and a nondivorced group—for a total of 180 families. For some analyses, the remarried group was divided into those remarried less than 2 years and those remarried longer than 2 years. The cross sectional analyses of families 6 years after divorce for the most part used the expanded sample, the longitudinal analyses used the original sample.

ADJUSTMENT IN THE TWO YEARS FOLLOWING DIVORCE

In this study it was found that during the first 2 years following divorce most children and many parents experienced emotional distress, psychological, health and behavior problems, disruptions in family functioning, and problems in adjusting to new roles, relationships and life changes associated with their altered family situation. However, as is reported in other studies, by 2 years following divorce the majority of parents and children were adapting reasonably well and certainly were showing great improvement since the time of the divorce. In the 2-year assessment period in this study some continuing problems were found in the adjustment of boys and in relations between divorced custodial mothers and their sons. These boys from divorced families in comparison to boys in nondivorced families showed more antisocial, acting out, coercive, noncompliant behaviors in the home and in the school and exhibited difficulties in peer relations and school achievement. In contrast, girls from divorced families in which remarriages had not occurred were functioning well and had positive relations with their custodial mothers.

In considering these results two things must be kept in mind, the first is that this study involves families with a custodial mother and as has been noted there is evidence that children adjust better in the custody of a parent of the same sex (Camara & Resnick, 1987; Santrock & Warshak, 1987; Zill, 1988). The second is, as was previously discussed, age of the child may be an important factor in sex differences in children's responses to divorce and remarriage. In this study children were an average age of 4 at the beginning of the study, 5 at the second assessment, 6 at the third assessment, and 10 at the time of the 6-year follow-up. Reports of more severe and long lasting disruption of behavior in boys than girls following their parents divorce have tended to come from studies of preadolescent children. However, our children were just entering adolescence at the time of the 6-year follow-up and this is a time when problems in girls' behavior, and in parent-child relations in divorced mother custody families may emerge (Hetherington, 1972; Hetherington & Clingempeel, 1989; Wallerstein, Corbin, & Lewis, 1988).

The 6-year follow-up had not been planned, however, we were concerned that at 2 years after divorce, we had not followed these families long enough to see a restabilizing in the mother-son relationship and a final readjustment of the sons in divorced families. Moreover it was apparent that the effects of divorce alone could not be considered in appraising the long-term adjustment of the children since remarriages were presenting new adaptive challenges to many of our parents and children.

Let us turn now to an examination of how temperament, sex of the child and family factors interact to protect the child and enhance the development of competence or put the child at risk for long term adverse consequences following their parents' marital transitions.

PROCEDURE AND ANALYSIS

Only the procedures involved in data to be included in this paper are presented. Most methods used in the first 2 years of data collection are presented in Hetherington et al. (1982). Only the temperament measures from the first 2 years are presented in any detail. More details on the methods and measures in the 6-year follow-up can be obtained from Hetherington et al. (1985) for child adjustment measures and Hetherington (1987) for family relations measures.

As in the first three waves of data collection, in the fourth wave multiple measures of family relations, stresses and support systems, and parent and child characteristics and behavior were obtained from the child and residential parents, from the nonresidential parent when available, and from the sibling closest in age when appraising sibling relations. These measures involved standardized tests, interviews, 24-hour behavior checklists and observations of the family in family problem solving sessions and in naturalistic unstructured interactions in the home. In addition, as a measure of marital satisfaction, both spouses filled out the Dyadic Adjustment Scale (Spanier, 1976). The parent personality measures to be included in the analyses in this paper were the Speilberger State Trait Anxiety Scale (Speilberger, Gorsuch, & Lushane, 1970) and the Beck Depression Inventory (Beck, 1979) and the Substance Abuse Scale, a scale developed for this study. In addition observer ratings of depression, and irritability were available.

Child adjustment measures were obtained from parents, teachers, peers, and the children. These measures were selected or constructed to measure internalizing, externalizing and social competence in children. Details on these measures are available in Hetherington et al. (1985). The measures included parents' and teachers' reports on the Child Behavior Checklist (Achenbach & Edelbrock, 1983) and on modifications of scales used in the three initial waves of the study, a peer nomination and self nomination measure based on a modification and extension of the Pupil Evaluation Inventory (Pekarik et al., 1976), parents' and teachers' ratings of temperament, 24-hour behavior checklists by the residential parents and child, and parent, teacher and child ratings on the Harter Perceived Competence Scale (1982). In addition, measures of temperament, externalizing, internalizing and social competence were obtained from observations using both 5-point rating scales and a molecular sequential coding of family interactions and of the child's interactions at school.

Finally measures of Life Events and of Support systems were administered to parents and children. The adult life events measure was adapted from Sarason, Johnson, and Siegal (1978). The Family Life Events Checklist was based on the work of Coddington (1972), Yamamoto (1970) and McCubbin, Patterson, and Harris, (1980). A Support Inventory to measure frequency, source and satisfaction with social emotional, economic and pragmatic (including child rearing) support was developed for adults and children.

COMPOSITE MEASURES

In many of the analyses that follow composite measures were used. Composites were developed by transforming measures to Z scores and averaging these measures. An average rather than a sum was used since residential father reports were not available in the divorced one parent households. In general, compositing across reports of informants in different situations (e.g., home and school) or across different types of measures (e.g., interview and observation) led to less internal consistency in the composite measures that were obtained for composites within situations or within one type of measure. In addition, children's reports were less congruent with adults' reports than the adults' reports were with each other. Some behaviors which might be considered more subtle or difficult to detect, such as internalizing, had lower Chronbachs alphas than more overt behaviors such as externalizing or social competence. Furthermore we expected higher internal consistency on some measures such as those of child adjustment than we did for such composite measures as the children's index of family stressors where a heterogeneous set of behaviors such as parental alcoholism, parental depression, sibling conflict, etc. were being combined.

COMPOSITE MEASURE OF TEMPERAMENT

The composite measure of temperament was based on mothers, fathers, and teachers ratings of the child's temperament plus ratings of the child's temperament based on observations in the home and the school. The temperament scales used were developed for this study and show satisfactory psychometric properties. The individual scales had an average test retest reliability of .65 when assessments were made 1 year apart and the average Chronbachs alphas for the scales was .72. The items focused on affective/reactive aspects of the child's behavior. The scales were based on the work of Thomas and Chess (1977), Buss and Plomin (1975), and Diamond (1957). Four factors that were present at all ages, and which have been associated with difficult temperaments and problem behavior in other studies were combined to form an index of difficultness of temperament. These were negative mood, activity, distractibility, and adaptability. Negative mood involved intense, easily elicited, and sustained expression of negative emotion. Activity involved fidgeting and vigorous motoric activity especially in inappropriate settings such as the classroom or school. Distractibility involved short attention span, an inability to sustain attention or focus on tasks and a tendency to be distracted by low level stimuli. Adaptability measured the ease and flexibility with which the child made positive adjustments to social and learning situations. In addition to current ratings of temperament fathers and mothers made retrospective ratings of children's temperament in the first 3 years of life. An attempt to validate these measures was made using nurses' ratings of the child's behavior during well baby visits on a subset of children on whom detailed records were available from behaviorally oriented pediatricians. The limitations in the information in the well baby records led to a rather simple rating scheme for nurses involving items related to irregularity and difficulties in habit training, irritability, soothability, sociability, and fearfulness as well as a single rating scale going from easy to difficult temperament. The correlations between mothers' retrospective ratings of difficultness of infant temperament and those of nurses' ratings of well baby records after the age of 6 months was $r = .38$ $p < .05$, offering some validation for mothers' retrospective reports. Nurses' ratings before the infant reached the age of 6 months did not correlate with their own ratings after 6 months or with mothers' ratings and were not used in any additional analyses. Fathers' retrospective reports did not correlate with either those of mothers or nurses and were dropped from the study. Correlations between parents' concurrent ratings of temperament however averaged .48 and ranged from .28 to .75.

RESULTS

Child Temperament and Later Divorce

The analyses described in this section were performed in order to explore the following questions:

Are there early temperamental differences in children whose parents are later likely to divorce or not to divorce?

Do parents behave differently toward difficult and easy boys and girls in nondivorced, divorced and remarried families?

How do characteristics of the parent, stress and support systems interact to modify the responses of parents to temperamentally easy and difficult children?

Do difficult and easy boys and girls behave differently toward their parents in nondivorced, divorced and remarried families?

How do early temperamental differences moderate children's responses to family risk and family protective factors in the development of later externalizing disorders and social competence?

Block, Block, and Gjerde (1986) found that children with behavior problems had parents who were later likely to divorce. Many of the descriptions of those children such as emotional, restless and fidgety, and anxious in unpredictable environments might be considered temperamental characteristics and are included in the temperament scales used in this study.

In an attempt to replicate Block et al.'s findings, point-biserial correlations were calculated between parental marital status and the child's temperament before the divorce. First the mothers' retrospective ratings of infant temperament and their mothers' marital status at the beginning of the study were correlated for all 144 families in the study r = .22 $p < .01$. Divorced mothers were more likely to report their children as having been difficult infants. Moreover when analyses were done separately for boys and girls these effects were more marked for boys than girls. These results have to be viewed with caution as they involve retrospective reports, however on the subset of children on whom nurses' ratings in the first 3 years of life were available, a significant correlation was also obtained (r = .31 $p < .05$).

Eleven of the 64 families in the nondivorced comparison group who continued in the study at the wave 4 follow-up were now divorced. A point biserial correlation was performed between the composite measure of temperament in the time immediately preceding the divorce and divorce status at age 10 (ever divorced, never divorced). Again children with difficult temperaments were found to have parents who were more likely to later divorce (r = .42 $p < .05$). An analysis for sex of child could not be performed because of sample size.

These findings are open to several interpretations. First, that difficult children promote stress in marriages that may eventually lead to divorce. Other studies have found a significant relation between simultaneous measures of marital satisfaction and child temperament (Stoneman, Brody, & Burke, in press). Second, that problems in family relations which precede, sometimes by a prolonged period, an eventual divorce also produce in children temperamental difficulties. Although temperamental factors are thought to be biologically based they are also influenced by experience. We will turn now to see how family dynamics are moderated by the temperament of the child by examining Rutter's hypotheses about parent child relations with temperamentally easy and temperamentally difficult children.

THE ROLE OF SEX AND TEMPERAMENT OF THE CHILD IN FAMILY RELATIONS

The Behavior of Parents with Difficult and Easy Boys and Girls in Nondivorced, Divorced and Remarried Families

Rutter's first proposition is that the difficult child especially in times of parental stress is more likely to be both the target and elicitor of aversive responses by the parents. On the basis of past research we expected that there would be more stress, and hence greater parental reactivity to children's temperament in the first 2 years of remarriage when family members were adjusting to their new life situation than in longer term remarriages or in first marriages. Our divorced mother custody families are what we might call stabilized divorced families since they have been divorced for an average of 6 years and are well beyond the initial crisis period of divorce. However on the basis of past research (Colletta, 1981; Hetherington et al., 1982; Stohlberg & Anker, 1983) we expected that mothers in one parent families, especially those raising sons, would experience more stress and be likely to be more responsive to temperamental differences in their children than those in nondivorced families.

We will address Rutter's hypothesis in the larger framework of examining how temperament and sex of the child affects not only aversive responses but also a wider range of parenting behaviors in nondivorced, divorced, and remarriage families.

MANOVAS involving temperament (with a median split), sex of child and family type (divorced, nondivorced, remarried less than 2 years, remarried more than 2 years) were performed on individual scales and on composite measures of mothers' or fathers' warmth/involvement, coerciveness/punitiveness, control and monitoring based on interview and observational ratings. Similar MANOVAS were conducted on probabilities of parents' observed negative startups, counterattacks and continuance of negative behavior based on sequential molecular coding of behavior. This sequence of behaviors has been called the fight cycle by Patterson (1982). One fight cycle would be one where the parent initiates a conflict by showing aversive behavior toward a child who is behaving in a neutral or positive fashion, the child counterattacks, and the parent continues the negative behavior. Another fight cycle would be where the child begins with a negative startup, the parent counterattacks and the child continues with his aversive behavior. Measures of parents' negative startups, counterattacks and negative continuance all seem directly relevant to Rutter's hypothesis. The probabilities of mothers' and children's behaviors in the fight cycle are presented in Table 6.1; probabilities for fathers and children are presented in Table 6.2. The analyses reported in this section include only wave 4 data on the expanded sample of 180 families. Thus the measures are contemporaneous. All differences that are discussed were significant at least at $p < .05$.

The analyses on the composite measures and on the fight cycle data indicate that effects of child temperament on parents' behavior are found mainly in measures related to coercive, punitive behavior, and control. In contrast, although effects for family type and sex of child also often are found in measures of coercive discipline and control, they also emerge in monitoring and less frequently in warmth, supportive behavior. In most analyses however main effects are modified by higher order interactions.

The findings in our study indicate that the effects on parental behavior of a child's difficult temperament are more likely to be manifested in families that have undergone marital transitions and are more likely to occur with male than female children. An exception to this is in remarried families where parents are equally likely to exhibit aversive behavior toward temperamentally difficult boys and girls.

Mother/son relations in the divorced nonremarried families and parent child relations in the early remarried families particularly with stepdaughters were problematic. The problems of divorced mothers and their sons and of remarried parents with their children were exacerbated by a difficult temperament in the child. Divorced nonremarried mothers were continuing to exhibit many of the behaviors with their sons 6 years after divorce that were seen 2 years after divorce.

Divorced Mothers. It was more differences in control attempts and in punitive, coercive behaviors than in warmth and affection that distinguished divorced mothers from mothers in the other family types. Divorced mothers were ineffectual in their control attempts and gave many instructions with little follow through. They tended to nag, natter, and complain and more often were involved in angry, escalating coercive cycles with their sons. As can be seen in Table 6.1, in all three stages of the fight cycle, divorced mothers were more likely than mothers in nondivorced families to behave in a hostile coercive fashion with their sons, especially if the sons had difficult temperaments. Spontaneous negative start-ups, were more than twice as likely to occur with mothers and sons in divorced families as with those in nondivorced families. Moreover if boys were behaving in an aversive fashion divorced mothers were more likely than nondivorced to counterattack. Once these negative interchanges between divorced mothers and sons occurred they were likely to continue significantly longer than in any other dyad in any family type. The probability of continuance of a negative response was higher in the divorced mother-difficult son dyad than in any other parent-child dyad. In spite of the conflict between custodial mothers and their early adolescent sons it might be best to view this relationship in early adolescence as intense and ambivalent rather than as purely hostile and rejecting, since there also were warm feelings expressed in many of these dyads.

Both sons and daughters in divorced families were allowed more responsibility, independence, and power in decision making than were children in non-

TABLE 6.1
Three Fight Cycle Variables for Easy and Difficult Children and Mothers

	Nondivorced				*Divorced*				*Remarried Less than 2 Years*				*Remarried More than 2 Years*			
	Difficult		*Easy*		*Difficult*		*Easy*		*Difficult*		*Easy*		*Difficult*		*Easy*	
	Male (N=12)	*Female (N=11)*	*Male (N=18)*	*Female (N=19)*	*Male (N=18)*	*Female (N=16)*	*Male (N=12)*	*Female (N=14)*	*Male (N=9)*	*Female (N=9)*	*Male (N=6)*	*Female (N=7)*	*Male (N=8)*	*Female (N=7)*	*Male (N=7)*	*Female (N=7)*
Start up																
Mother to Child	.046	.023	.037	.019	.089	.031	.052	.029	.067	.071	.040	.053	.052	.041	.029	.033
Child to Mother	.046	.019	.011	.016	.078	.034	.032	.016	.052	.055	.033	.037	.049	.041	.036	.031
Counter Attack																
Mother to Child	.184	.146	.132	.118	.267	.154	.183	.129	.192	.204	.161	.167	.163	.160	.140	.142
Child to Mother	.115	.072	.086	.069	.316	.082	.222	.059	.281	.259	.190	.219	.126	.098	.077	.065
Continuance																
Mother to Child	.143	.096	.072	.080	.336	.094	.204	.089	.249	.225	.118	.137	.166	.139	.155	.147
Child to Mother	.155	.101	.069	.120	.368	.114	.293	.096	.240	.221	.179	.165	.198	.212	.126	.158

divorced families. They did in the words of Robert Weiss (1979) "grow up faster." They successfully interrupted their divorced mother and their mother yielded to their demands more often than in the other family types. In some cases this greater power and independence resulted in an egalitarian mutually supportive relationship. In other cases, where the emotional demands or responsibilities required by the mother were inappropriate, were beyond the capabilities of the child or interfered with normal activities of the child such as in peer relations or school activities, resentment, rebellion or behavior problems often followed.

Finally, divorced mothers monitored their children's behavior less closely than did mothers in nondivorced families. They knew less about where their children were, who they were with, and what they were doing than did mothers in two parent households. Although divorced mothers were equal in their monitoring attempts with temperamentally difficult and easy children both their attempts at monitoring and control were less successful with the temperamentally difficult sons. Discrepancies between the children's activities reported on 24-hour checklists by divorced mothers and their temperamentally difficult children were marked.

In addition, children in the one-parent households were less likely than those in the two-parent households to have adult supervision in their parents absence. Both Robert Weiss (1979) and Wallerstein and Kelly (1980) report that one way that children may cope with their parents' divorce is by becoming disengaged from the family. In this study boys from divorced families were spending significantly less time in the home with their parents or with other adults and more time alone or with peers than were any of the other groups of children. However stepsons also were significantly more disengaged than were sons in nondivorced families.

In contrast to divorced mothers and sons, there are few differences in the relationship between divorced mothers and daughters and that of mothers and daughters in nondivorced families and no effects of daughters' temperament. Mothers and daughters in mother headed families 6 years after divorce express considerable satisfaction with their relationship. However there is an exception to this happy picture and this is found in divorced others with early maturing daughters. Family conflict was higher in all three family types for these early maturing girls versus late maturing girls, however it was most marked between mothers and daughters in the single parent households. Early maturity in girls was associated with a premature weakening of the mother child bonds, increased parent-child conflict, and greater involvement in activities with older peers. Past research suggests that divorced mothers and daughters may experience problems as daughters become pubescent and involved in heterosexual activities (Hetherington, 1972; McLanahan & Bumpass, in press). The difficulties in interactions between these early maturing girls and their divorced mothers may be precursors of more intense problems yet to come.

Remarried Mothers. In looking at stepfamilies it is important to distinguished between those families in the early stages of remarriage, when they are still adapting to their new situation, and those in the later stage of remarriage, when family roles and relationships should have been worked through and established. Although we are mainly using composite measures in this report it should be noted that there are more discrepancies among reports of families members in stepfamilies than in other families.

Thus it is often important in discussing stepfamilies to consider which family members' perspective is being discussed. For instance, family members agree that mothers in remarried families are as warm to their children as mothers in other types of families. However, children and stepfathers rate remarried mothers as having less control and poorer monitoring of their children's behavior than these mothers rate themselves as having. Both interview and observational data indicate that remarried mothers have greater control over their sons than do single divorced mothers, but less control over their daughters than do mothers in either of the other two family types. Control over both daughters and sons, is greater for mothers who have been remarried more than 2 years. In the first 2 years following remarriage, conflict involving frequent initiations and exchanges of negative behavior between mothers and daughters is high. This declines over time. Mothers in step families have less control and show more negativity to difficult than to easy sons and daughters in the first 2 years following remarriage. An effect of children's temperament on mothers' behavior is not found in the families remarried for over 2 years.

Stepfathers. In the first 2 years following remarriage stepfathers reported themselves to be low on felt or expressed affection for their stepchildren although they spent time with them attempting to establish a relationship. They expressed less strong positive affect and showed fewer negative, critical responses than did the nondivorced fathers. Biological fathers were freer in expressing affection and in criticizing their children for poor personal grooming, for not doing their homework, not cleaning up their rooms, or for fighting with their siblings. However, they also were more involved and interested in the activities of their children. Initially, stepfathers were less supportive and showed more negative behavior toward stepsons than to stepdaughters. In the interactions in the fist 2 years of the remarriage the stepfathers' behavior was almost that of a stranger who was attempting to be ingratiating, was seeking information, and was polite but emotionally disengaged. These stepfathers were remaining relatively pleasant in spite of the aversive behavior they encountered with their stepdaughters. By 2 years after remarriage stepfathers are more impatient. Although they try to remain disengaged as can be seen in Table 6.2, they occasionally get into extremely angry interchanges with their stepdaughters and their negativity tends to increase rather than decrease over time. These conflicts tend to focus on issues of parental authority and respect for the mother. Stepdaughters view their step-

TABLE 6.2
Three Fight Cycle Variables for Easy and Difficult Children and Fathers/Stepfathers

	Nondivorced				*Remarried Less than 2 Years*				*Remarried More than 2 years*			
	Difficult		*Easy*		*Difficult*		*Easy*		*Difficlut*		*Easy*	
	Male (N=12)	Female (N=11)	Male (N=18)	Female (N=19)	Male (N=9)	Female (N=9)	Male (N=6)	Female (N=7)	Male (N=8)	Female (N=7)	Male (N=7)	Female (N=7)
Start Up												
Father to Child	.042	.031	.030	.027	.020	.017	.016	.019	.072	.081	.043	.052
Child to Father	.010	.003	.006	.004	.031	.093	.078	.085	.020	.083	.003	.079
Counter Attack												
Father to Child	.095	.052	.074	.049	.046	.052	.061	.049	.213	.209	.122	.141
Child to Father	.103	.062	.097	.067	.150	.172	.217	.183	.154	.153	.120	.101
Continuance												
Father to Child	.120	.054	.099	.056	.084	.034	.076	.042	.169	.183	.127	.157
Child to Father	.041	.022	.034	.025	.061	.313	.159	.294	.101	.233	.050	.135

fathers as hostile, punitive, and unreasonable on mattes of discipline. The interchanges between stepfathers and stepdaughters and the conflicts between divorced mothers and sons are rated as the highest on hostility of any dyad. Stepfathers make significantly fewer control attempts and are less successful in gaining control with both sons and daughters than are nondivorced fathers. Their control of stepsons but not stepdaughters is better in longer remarriages.

The effects of the child's temperament on stepfathers' behavior differ from the effects on mothers in remarried families. Initially there is no difference in the behavior of stepfathers toward temperamentally easy and temperamentally difficult stepchildren however greater negativity toward difficult children emerges after the first 2 years of remarriage. In the initial honeymoon period of the remarriage many new stepfathers are trying to establish a positive relationship with their stepchildren in spite of their stepchildren's difficult behavior, however over time disengagement becomes a more common pattern of stepfathers with stepchildren. They give up on establishing a relationship and try to remain detached from or avoid contact with their stepchildren. Disengagement from a demanding, irascible difficult child may be hard to sustain. This maybe especially true in the family problem solving situation which is one of enforced togetherness. It can be seen in Table 6.2 that the effects of temperament in observed interactions are more marked in counterattacks and continuations than in initiations, although the temperament effect is also significant for initiations.

The Effects of Stress, Parental Adjustment, Support, and Child Temperament on Parents' Behavior

Although the analyses thus far demonstrate complicated interactions between effects of family type, sex of child and temperament on parents' behavior, past research also suggests that other factors such as parents' personality problems, stresses and available supports will affect parents' responses to difficult and easy children (Cutrona & Troutman, 1986; Engfer, 1988; Meyer, 1988). MANOVAS were run separately for mothers and fathers involving child temperament (a median split easy/difficult), personality problems of the parent (a median split on a composite index of depression and anxiety), parental stress (a median split on a composite of negative life events occurring in the past year and daily hassles recorded six times in the last month) and support systems (a median split on a composite of economic, emotional, social and pragmatic support). The dependent measures were parents' positivity and negativity toward the child. It was not possible to include family type and sex of the child in this analyses because of the sample size.

Again, more differences were obtained for parents' negative than positive behavior toward children. The only significant effects of the independent variables on mothers' positive behavior was a main effect for personality problems in mothers. Mothers who are poorly adjusted exhibit less positive behavior toward their children.

The findings for negative parental behavior were almost always associated with higher order interactions. Under conditions of low levels of psychopathology in the mother and low stress there were no differences in the negative responses of mothers toward difficult or easy children. Thus, unless difficultness of temperament was compounded by other risk or vulnerability factors there was no difference in aversive maternal responding. However the presence of either personality problems such as depression or anxiety in the mother or of high levels of stress in combination with a difficult child increased the level of negative behaviors in mothers. Furthermore the co-occurrence of these risk factors significantly increased maternal aversive responses to difficult children over the level found with either stress or personality problems alone. In addition, these effects were moderated in a somewhat unexpected way by the availability of supports, which suggest that social supports are protective only within a limited range of risk. Under conditions of low stress and a low level of personality problems the availability of supports had no effect on the aversive behaviors of mothers in dealing with either easy or difficult children. However surprisingly the availability of supports also had no effects under the most stressful situation involving a combination of high levels of maternal personality problems, high stress, and a difficult child. In the former instance there were not enough deleterious factors to need support. In the latter the compounding of deleterious factors was so great that it overwhelmed the effects of resources. Furthermore, under such conditions even when supports were available these multiply stressed mothers did not use them effectively. Supportive resources had their greatest effect in moderating maternal responses toward difficult children when only maternal personality problems or only life stresses were present. Although the effects discussed were significant for the composite measures they were most marked in the observational measures which might be viewed as more objective than those involving parent reports. The ratings of observed maternal negative behaviors with temperamentally difficult children under high and low support are shown in Fig. 6.1.

The effects of personality problems and/or stress in the responses of fathers/stepfathers to difficult and easy children was similar to the pattern found in others but not as marked. It was in the role of supports that the pattern of results differed for mothers and fathers. Fathers were not able to use extrafamilial supports to moderate their aversive responses when they were under duress. This inability of fathers in contrast to mothers to solicit or utilize emotional support from friends and family was frequently found in this study. For many men their wives were the only person to whom they would disclose their feelings or turn for solace. When there was an alienated or discordant marriage or a divorce their one source of support was gone. In contrast, mothers sought emotional support and confided in a wide network of friends and family. Moreover, we found similar

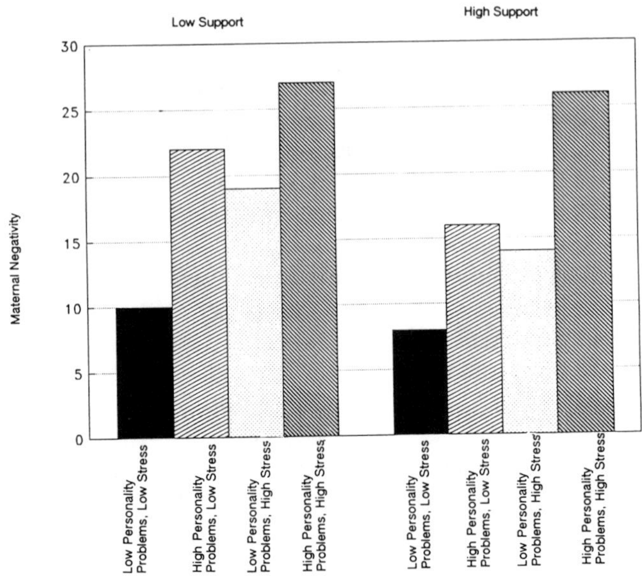

FIG. 6.1. Ratings of observed maternal negativity with temperamentally difficult children under high and low support.

sex differences in the ability to self disclose and to obtain emotional support in boys and girls and these differences increased with age.

We have responded to the first part of Rutter's proposal that temperamentally difficult children are most likely to be the target of their parents' aversive responses and have identified some of the conditions under which this occurs. Most parents can deal with the single stress of raising a temperamentally difficult child, however if this challenge is compounded by personal vulnerabilities such as personality problems or stressful life experiences including marital transitions, parents are more likely to respond in a negative, coercive fashion with their children. Social supports can moderate these responses within a restricted range of risks however, the effect of social supports differ for men and women. A close marital relationship plays an important role in enhancing the parenting of both mothers and fathers with difficult children. Fathers are less willing or able than mothers to utilize resources outside of the family to support them in dealing with a difficult child.

Let us turn now to Rutter's second proposal that temperamentally difficult children are more likely to behave in a way that will elicit negative responses from parents and are less able than temperamentally easy children to copy with this abusive behavior from parents when it occurs. First, we examine difficult and easy children's behavior in interactions with their parents. Then, we study the relation between early temperament, an index of family stresses, a composite index of protective factors and social competence and externalizing behavior at age 10.

The Behavior of Difficult and Easy Boys and Girls in Nondivorced, Divorced and Remarried Families

Although the long-term adjustment of easy and difficult children partially may be shaped by differences in their treatment by parents, the children exhibit behaviors that may elicit differential parental treatment. The composite of children's negativity and positivity in these analyses are based both on parent and child reports and on observed ratings of negativity or positivity of behavior directed toward either the mother or the father. In addition the likelihood of negative start ups, counterattacks, and continuations of aversive behavior in interactions with mothers and fathers included in Tables 6.1 and 6.2 are discussed. Again it is found that differences associated with family type or temperament are found most often in negative and rarely in positive behaviors.

Boys with divorced nonremarried mothers show more negativity toward their mothers than do boys in nondivorced families or boys whose mothers have been remarried for more than 2 years. They are more likely to initiate, counterattack, and continue in acrimonious exchanges. These differences are more marked in boys with difficult than easy temperaments. Girls in divorced families show no differences in either positive or negative behavior from those in nondivorced families. However, girls with difficult temperaments do exhibit more negative behaviors than those with easy temperaments toward their mothers in both divorced and remarried families.

In the first 2 years following remarriage daughters exhibit more hostility, coercion, and negativity and less warmth toward both parents than do girls in nondivorced or divorced families. They are more likely to initiate and reciprocate hostility and continue in aversive exchanges. Their behavior improves over the course of remarriage, however, even 2 years after remarriage these girls are still more antagonistic and disruptive with their parents than are girls in the other two family types. This noxious behavior is affirmed in the reports of both parents and children and in observational measures of family interaction.

The behavior of stepsons with their mother and stepfather is very different than that of stepdaughters. Although mothers and stepfathers viewed sons as initially being extremely difficult, and the sons exhibited high rates of aversive behavior, their behavior improved over time. Boys whose mothers had been remarried for over 2 years show no more negative behaviors toward their parents than do boys in nondivorced families (Hetherington et al., 1985). Although stepfathers continue to view stepchildren, especially stepdaughters, as being more hostile and resistant to them than do nondivorced fathers, they report improvement in the stepson's behavior and exhibit greater warmth and involvement with them than with the stepdaughters. The stepsons in the longer remarried families frequently report being close to their stepfathers, enjoying his company and seeking his advice and support. An unexpected effect occurs for temperament in children in remarried families. In the early stage of the remarriage in relations with their mother as might be predicted, it is the temperamentally difficult child who shows the most negative behavior. In relations with the stepfather however it is the temperamentally easy stepson who is most resistant, acrimonious, and negative initially but this relationship reversed itself after 2 years of remarriage when negativity toward stepfathers by sons with difficult temperaments is greater. There is no effect for temperament in the response of stepdaughters to stepfathers in families remarried for less than 2 years. When the stepfather first enters the family both easy and difficult girls behave in an agonistic, resistant fashion.

What might explain these differences in responses to their mother's remarriage by sons and daughters and by children with differing temperaments? Some suggested answers are found in the different patterns of correlations between marital satisfaction and children's responses in non divorced and remarried families. In nondivorced couples a close marital relationship, and support by the spouse for participation in child rearing were related to parental warmth and involvement and to low parent-child conflict. However, in the stepfamilies there occurred what might appear to be an anomalous finding. As has been found in other studies (Brand et al., 1988; Bray, 1987), in remarried families in contrast to nondivorced families a close marital relationship and active involvement in parenting by the stepfather was associated with high levels of conflict and negativity between the child and both the mother and the stepfather and with high rates of children's behavior problems especially when the stepchild was a girl. For sons this relationship was significant in the early but not in the later stages of remarriage. How can we explain these unexpected results? It seems likely that in the early stages of remarriage the new stepfather was viewed as an intruder or a competitor for the mothers affection. Since boys in divorced families often have been involved in coercive or ambivalent relations with their mothers, in the long run they may have little to lose and something to gain from the remarriage. The temperamentally easy boy may be less fearful and more capable than the temperamentally difficult boy in his initial interactional assaults on the stepfather, but eventually is more adaptive and able to realize the benefits of a new relationship with an adult male. Some evidence for better adapted less psychologically vulnerable boys being more resistant to the intrusion of the stepfather is found in a significant positive correlation of both self-esteem and internal locus of control in boys with negativity toward the stepfather in the first 2 years of the remarriage. These correlations become negative after 2 years of remarriage.

In contrast to boys, daughters in one-parent families have played more responsible, powerful roles than girls in nondivorced families and have had more positive relations with their divorced mothers than have sons. They may see both their independence and their relationship with the mother threatened by the introduction of the stepfather and therefore be even more apprehensive about the mother remarrying than are boys. The trauma of their mother's remarriage may be greater for girls than for boys and may suppress any possible effects of temperament.

THE RELATION BETWEEN SEX, TEMPERAMENT, FAMILY STRESS, PROTECTIVE FACTORS AND SOCIAL COMPETENCE AND EXTERNALIZING BEHAVIOR AT AGE TEN

In this section we examine Rutter's last proposition, i.e., that when adversity occurs in the family the temperamentally difficult child is less able to deal with it and suffers more deleterious effects than does the temperamentally easy child. In the analyses, we explored the conditions under which early temperamental characteristics will predispose children to develop later social competence or psychopathology.

MANOVAS examined the relation of temperament, sex of the child, family stress, and family protective factors to social competence and externalizing at age 10. These analyses were performed once using concurrent measures of temperament and the full crossectional sample of 180 families when the child was age 10, and a second time using only the 124 families from the original study who remained in the study at Wave 4 and a measure of early temperament, which was a composite of assessments of temperament in Waves 1, 2, and 3. The pattern of findings for the two sets of analyses were remarkably similar with significance levels for differences involving temperament being greater for the analyses using contemporaneous rather than antecedent measures of temperament. The family stress index in both sets of analyses included contemporaneous measure when the child was aged 10 of a low income to needs ratios, parental alcohol use one standard deviation above the mean, parental depression one standard deviation above the mean, parental anxiety one standard deviation above the mean, family conflict one standard deviation above the mean, parent negativity one standard deviation above the mean, sibling negativity one standard deviation above the mean, divorce, remarriage, second divorce, second remarriage, negative relation with significant family member outside of the home. As can be seen in the foregoing description, because of sample size, we could not include family type as an additional independent variable, family transitions were incorporated within the family stress index. The family protective factors index included concurrent measures parent score on CPI Socialization Scale one standard deviation above the mean, parent self esteem one standard deviation above the mean, parent positivity one standard deviation above the mean, sibling positivity one standard deviation above the mean, parent control one standard deviation above the mean, parent monitoring one standard deviation above the mean, positive relation with significant family member outside of the home, parent education beyond high school. It should be noted that these are family stressors and family protective factors and are very different from the stressors and support system measures used in the analyses previously discussed on parents' behaviors toward children. Figure 6.2 presents the findings involving measures all obtained at Wave 4 with 180 families. The discussion that follows would be equally appropriate for analyses using antecedent measures of temperament.

As seen in Fig. 6.2 no differences in the social competence of easy and difficult children were observed under conditions of low stress and high protective factors. Under conditions in which there was low availability of protective factors an increased frequency of family stressors led to less socially competent behavior at age ten in both temperamentally easy and difficult children although easy children were more adaptable and competent than difficult children. However under conditions of high availability of protective factors a very different pattern emerged. Although a linear relationship between stress and social competence for difficult children was obtained with increased stress being associated with less competence, a curvilinear relationship for the temperamentally easy girls emerged. Under supportive conditions, these temperamentally easy girls actually developed more social competence and adaptive skills in response to moderate levels of stress than in response to extremely low or high levels of

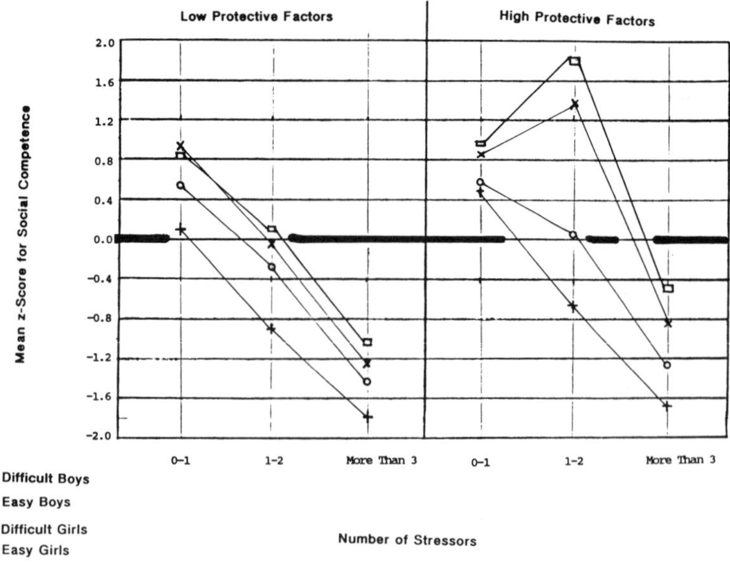

FIG. 6.2. Social competence of easy and difficult children under high and low stress and high and low protective factors.

stress. This effect, however, was only found for girls not for boys. For temperamentally easy girls some practice in solving stressful problems under supportive conditions enhanced their later ability to be responsive, sensitive in dealing with others. Other analyses indicated that if stresses did not occur simultaneously but were distributed across time, children could cope with them more easily. It was the simultaneous occurrence of multiple stressors or a series of unresolved stresses with no available protective resources that had the most deleterious outcomes for children's long term adjustment. As Rutter (1987) has stated, "Inoculation against stress may be best provided by controlled exposure to stress in circumstances favorable to successful coping or adaptation" (p. 326). This seemed to be true for the development of social competence for girls but not for externalizing in either boys or girls.

As can be seen in Fig. 6.3, there were greater effects of stress and temperament for externalizing behavior in boys and stronger effects of support for externalizing behavior in girls. Greater stress was associated with more externalizing behavior especially in temperamentally difficult boys under conditions of very low stress the protective factors associated with good family relations did however lead to no differences between externalizing behavior of difficult and easy boys. When there are no positive protective family relationships even under low levels of stress, temperamentally difficult boys exhibit more acting out behavior than do temperamentally easy boys. The steeling or inoculation effect associated with moderate stress under supportive conditions did not occur in externalizing

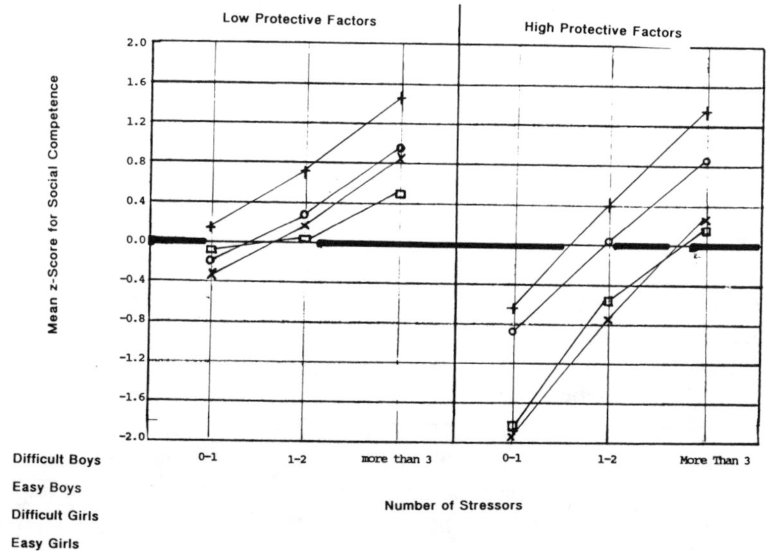

FIG. 6.3. Externalizing of easy and difficult children under high and low stress and high and low protective factors.

for either temperamentally easy or difficult boys or girls. Moreover, there were few effects of temperament on externalizing for girls. Only under the most adverse conditions of high stress and low protective factors did differences associated with early temperament emerge for females. When stressful life events outweigh available protective factors even the most resilient child can develop problems (Werner, 1988).

SUMMARY AND CAUTIONARY NOTE

The responses to divorce and remarriage involve pervasive changes in family functioning and in the adaptation of family members. These changes may be particularly adverse for temperamentally difficult boys. As Rutter has suggested differences in parent-child relations with easy and difficult children are exacerbated when families are undergoing stressful marital transitions and seem to mediate the subsequent adjustment of children. When parents are sensitive to the needs of their temperamentally difficult children and able to maintain authoritative parenting they can to some extent diminish the adverse outcomes for these vulnerable children. During marital transitions, however, parents may become involved in the new challenges they face and their own emotional needs to the long-term detriment of temperamentally difficult boys.

The findings of this study should be viewed as hypotheses generating rather than conclusive. Although the sample size is large in comparison to most longitudinal family studies which use an extensive array of multiple method including observational methods, it is not large enough to simultaneously examine the multiple factors that interact with children's temperamental predispositions to produce later psychopathology or social competence. The effects of personal vulnerabilities such as a difficult temperament are moderated by their interactions with other risk and protective factors.

Furthermore, this study involved middle class, White, divorced, mother custody and stepfather families. The findings may not generalize to other social class or racial groups or to other types of divorced and remarried families. In particular, the behavior and adjustment of boys and girls may vary with custodial arrangements and whether the remarriage involves the addition of a stepfather or stepmother to the home.

Finally, this paper focuses on parent child relations within the home. We know that other relationships with siblings, grandparents, the noncustodial parent, peers, and teachers influence the adjustment of children and play an important role in children's coping with their parents' marital transitions (Hetherington, 1988, 1989). They seem likely also to moderate the effects of gender and temperament on children's long-term adjustment. A broader ecological perspective would be likely to contribute to the understanding of the interaction among these factors.

REFERENCES

Abbott, D. A., & Brody, G. H. (1985). The relation of child age, gender, and number of children to the marital adjustment of wives. *Journal of Marriage and the Family, 47,* 77–84.

Achenbach, T. M., & Edelbrock, C. (1983). *Manual for the Child Behavior Checklist.* New York: Queen City Printers.

Beck, A. T. (1979). *Depression: Causes and treatment.* Philadelphia: University of Pennsylvania Press.

Block, J. H., Block, J., & Gjerde, P. F. (1986). The personality of children prior to divorce: A prospective study. *Child Development, 57,* 827–840.

Brand, E., Clingempeel, W. E., & Bowen-Woodward, K. (1988). Family relationships and children's psychological adjustment in stepmother and stepfather families: Findings and conclusions from the Philadelphia Stepfamily Research Project. In E. M. Hetherington & J. D. Arasteh (Eds.), *Impact of divorce, single parenting, stepparenting in children* (pp. 299–324). Hillsdale, NJ: Lawrence Erlbaum Associates.

Bray, J. H. (1987, August). *Becoming a stepfamily.* Symposium presented at the meeting of American Psychological Association, New York.

Bray, J. H. (1988). Children's development during early remarriage. In E. M. Hetherington & J. Arasteh (Eds.), *Impact of divorce, single parenting and stepparenting on children* (pp. 279–298). Hillsdale, NJ: Lawrence Erlbaum Associates.

Buss, A. H., & Plomin, R. (1975). *A temperament theory of personality development.* New York: Wiley.

Buss, A. H., & Plomin, R. (1984). *Early developing personality traits.* Hillsdale, NJ: Lawrence Erlbaum Associates.

Camara, K. A., & Resnick, G. (1987). Marital and parental subsystems in mother-custody, father-custody, and two-parent households: Effects on children's social development. In J. Vincent (Ed.), *Advances in family intervention, assessment, and theory* (Vol. 4, pp. 165–196). Greenwich, CT: J.A.I. Press.

Camara, K. A., & Resnick, G. (1988). Interparental conflict and cooperation: Factors moderating children's post-divorce adjustment. In E. M. Hetherington & J. D. Arasteh (Eds.), *Impact of divorce, single parenting, and stepparenting on children* (pp. 169=195). Hillsdale, NJ: Lawrence Erlbaum Associates.

Cameron, J. (1977). Parental treatment, children's temperament and the risk of childhood behavior problems. *American Journal of Orthopsychiatry, 47,*568–575.

Coddington, R. D. (1972). The significance of life events as etiological factors in the diseases of children: A survey of professional workers. *Journal of Psychosomatic Research, 16,* 7–18.

Colletta, N. D. (1981). Social support and risk of maternal rejection by adolescent mothers. *Journal of Psychology, 109,* 191–197.

Crockenberg, S. B. (1981). Infant irritability, mother responsiveness, and social support: Influences on the security of infant-mother attachment. *Child Development, 52,* 857–865.

Crockenberg, S. B., & McCluskey, K. C. (1986). Change in maternal behavior during the baby's first year of life. *Child Development, 57,* 746–753.

Cutrona, C. E., & Troutman, B. R. (1986). Social support, infant temperament and parenting self-efficacy. A mediational model of postpartum depression. *Child Development, 57,* 1507–1518.

Earls, F., Beardslee, & Garrison, ■. (1987). Correlates and predictors of competence in young children. In E. J. Anthony & B. J. Cohler (Eds.), *The invulnerable child.* New York: Guilford Press.

Elder, G. H. Jr., Caspi, A., & Nguyen, T. V. (in press). Resourceful and vulnerable children: Family influences in stressful times. In R. K. Silbereisen & K. Eyferth (Eds.), *Development in context: Integrative perspectives on youth development.* New York: Springer.

Emery, R. E. (1982). Interparental conflict and the children of discord and divorce. *Psychological Bulletin, 92,* 310–330.

Emery, R., & O'Leary, K. (1982). Children's perceptions of marital discord and behavior problems of boys and girls. *Journal of Abnormal Child Psychology, 10,* 11–24.

Engfer, A. (1988). The interrelatedness of marriage and the mother-child relationship. In R. A. Hinde & J. Stevenson-Hinde (Eds.), *Relationships within families* (pp. 104–118). London: Clarendon Press.

Epstein, N., Finnegan, D., & Gythell, D. (1979). Irrational beliefs and perceptions of marital conflict. *Journal of Consulting and Clinical Psychology, 67,* 608–609.

Furstenberg, F. F. (1988). Child care after divorce and remarriage. In E. M. Hetherington & J. D. Arasteh (Eds.), *Impact on divorce, single parenting, and stepparenting on children* (pp. 245–261). Hillsdale, NJ: Lawrence Erlbaum Associates.

Furstenberg, F. F., & Allison, P. D. (1985). *How marital dissolution affects children: Variations by age and sex.* Unpublished manuscript.

Furstenberg, F. F., & Seltzer, J. A. (1983, August). *Encountering divorce: Children's responses to family dissolution and reconstitution.* Paper presented at the meeting of the American Psychological Association, Detroit, MI.

Garbino, J., Sebes, L., & Schellenbach, C. (1984). Families at risk for destructive parent-child relations in adolescence. *Child Development, 55*(1), 174–183.

Garmezy, N. (1983). Stressors of childhood. In N. Garmezy & M. Rutter (Eds.), *Stress, coping, and development in children* (pp. 43–84). New York: McGraw-Hill.

Garrison, W. & Earls, F. (1983). The social context of early human experience. In M. Schmidt & H. Remschmidt (Eds.), *Epidemiology and child psychiatry (Vol. 2).* New York: Thieme-Stratton.

Goldberg, W. A., & Easterbrooks, M. A. (1984). Role of marital quality in toddler development. *Developmental Psychology, 20,* 504–514.

Graham, P., Rutter, M., & George, S. (1973). Temperamental characteristics as predictors of behavior disorders in children. *American Journal of Orthopsychiatry, 43,* 328–339.

Harter, S. (1982). The Perceived Competence Scale for Children. *Child Development, 53,* 87–97.

Hetherington, E. M. (1982). Effects of fathers' absence on personality development in adolescent daughters. *Developmental Psychology, 7,* 313–326.

Hetherington, E. M. (1987). Family relations six years after divorce. In K. Pasley & M. Ihinger-Tallman (Eds.), *Remarriage and stepparenting today: Current research and theory* (pp. 185–205). New York: Guilford Press.

Hetherington, E. M. (1988). Parents, children and siblings six years after divorce. In R. Hinde & J. Stevenson-Hinde (Eds.), *Relationships within families.* London: Clarendon Press.

Hetherington, E. M. (1989). Coping with family transitions: Winners, losers and survivors. *Child Development, 60,* 1–14.

Hetherington, E. M., & Anderson, E. R. (1987). The effects of divorce and remarriage on early adolescents and their families. In M. D. Levine & E. R. McAnarney (Eds.), *Early adolescent transitions* (pp. 49–67). Lexington, MA: D. C. Heath.

Hetherington, E. M., Arnett, J., & Hollier, E. A. (1988). Adjustment of parents and children to remarriage. In S. Wolchik & P. Karoly (Eds.), *Children of divorce: Perspectives on adjustment.* New York: Gardner Press.

Hetherington, E. M., & Camara, K. A. (1984). Families in transition: The process of dissolution and reconstitution. In R. Parke (Ed.), *Review of child development research* (Vol. 4, pp. 398–439). Chicago: University of Chicago Press.

Hetherington, E. M., Cox, M., & Cox, R. (1982). Effects of divorce on parents and children. In M. Lamb (Ed.), *Nontraditional families* (pp. 233–288). Hillsdale, NJ: Lawrence Erlbaum Associates.

Hetherington, E. M., Cox, M., & Cox, R. (1985). Long-term effects of divorce and remarriage on the adjustment of children. *Journal of American Academy of Psychiatry, 24*(5), 518–830.

Hetherington, E. M., & Clingempeel, G. (submitted, 1989). The formation of stepfamilies: Family process and children's adjustment.

Hetherington, E. M., & Stanley-Hagan, M. (1986). Divorced fathers: Stress, coping, and adjustment. In M. Lamb (Ed.), *The father's role: Applied perspectives* (pp. 103–134). New York: Wiley.

Hetherington, E. M., Stanley-Hagan, M., & Anderson, E. R. (1989). Marital transitions: A child's perspective. *American Psychologist, 44,* 303–312.

Jacobson, D. S. (1984). *Factors associated with healthy family functioning in stepfathers.* Paper presented at the meeting of the Society for Research in Child Development, Lexington, KY.

McCubbin, H. I., Patterson, J. M., Harris, L. H., & Bauman, E. (1980). *Adolescent family inventory of life events and changes.* Family Health Program, University of Minnesota, Saint Paul.

McLanahan, S., & Bumpass, L. (in press). Intergenerational consequences of marital disruption. *American Journal of Sociology.*

Meyer, H. J. (1988). Marital and mother-child relationships: developmental history parent personality and child difficultness. In R. A. Hinde & J. Stevenson-Hinde (Eds.), *Relationships within families* (pp. 119–142). London: Clarendon Press.

Morgan, P. S., Lye, D. N., & Condron, G. A. (in press). Sons, daughters, and divorce: Does the sex of children affect the risk of marital disruption? *American Journal of Psychology.*

Moss, H. A. (1967). Sex, age and state of determinants of mother-infant interaction. *Merrill-Palmer Quarterly, 13,* 19–36.

Patterson, G. R. (1982). *Coercive family processes: A social learning approach.* (Vol. 3). Eugene, OR: Castalia.

Patterson, G. R., & Dishion, T. J. (1988). Multilevel family process models: Traits, interactions and relationships. In. R. A. Hinde & J. Stevenson-Hinde (Eds.), *Relationships within families* (pp. 283–310). London: Clarendon Press.

Pekarik, E. G., Prinz, R. J., Liebert, D. E., Weintraub, S., & Neale, J. M. (1976). The Pupil Evaluation Inventory. *Journal of Abnormal Child Psychology, 4,* 83–97.

Porter, B., & O'Leary, K. D. (1980). Marital discord and childhood behavior problems. *Journal of Abnormal Child Psychology, 8,* 287–295.

Rutter, M. (1971). Parent-child separation: Psychological effects on the children. *Journal of Child Psychology and Psychiatry, 12,* 233–260.

Rutter, M. (1981). Parent-child separation: Psychological effects on the children. *Journal of Child Psychology and Psychiatry, 12,* 233–260.

Rutter, M. (1983). Stress, coping, and development: Some issues and some questions. In N. Garmezy & M. Rutter (Eds.), *Stress, coping, and development in children* (pp. 1–43). New York: McGraw-Hill.

Rutter, M. (1987). Psychosocial resilience and protective mechanisms. *American Journal of Orthopsychiatry, 57,* 316–331.

Santrock, J. W., & Sitterle, K. A. (1987). Parent-child relationships in stepmother families. In K. Pasley & M. Ihinger-Tallman (Eds.), *Remarriage and stepparenting: Current theory and research* (pp. 273–299). New York: Guilford.

Santrock, J. W., & Warshak, R. A. (1979). Father custody and social development in boys and girls. *Journal of Social Issues, 35*(4), 112–125.

Santrock, J. W., & Warshak, R. A. (1987). Development of father custody relationships and legal/clinical considerations in father-custody families. In M. E. Lamb (Ed.), *The father's role: Applied perspectives* (pp. 135–166). New York: Wiley.

Santrock, J. W., Warshak, R., Lindbergh, C., & Meadows, L. (1982). Children's and parents' observed social behavior in stepfather families. *Child Development, 53,* 472–480.

Sarason, I. G., Johnson, J., & Siegel, J. (1978). Assessing the impact of life changes: Development of the life experiences survey. *Journal of Consulting and Clinical Psychology, 46,* 932–946.

Spanier, K. (1976). Dyadic adjustment scale. *Journal of Marriage and the Family, 38,* 27–37.

Speilberger, C. D., Gorsuch, R. L., & Lushane, R. (1970). *State-Trait Anxiety Inventory.* Palo Alto, CA: Consulting Psychologist Press.

Stolberg, A. L., & Anker, J. M. (1983). Cognitive and behavioral changes in children resulting from parental divorce and consequent environmental changes. *Journal of Divorce, 7,* 23–41.

Stoneman, Z., Brody, G. H., & Burke, M. (in press). Sibling temperaments and maternal and paternal perceptions of marital, family and personal functioning. *Journal of Marriage and the Family.*

Thomas, A., & Chess, S. (1977). *Temperament and development.* New York: Brunner/Mazel.

Thomas, A., & Chess, S. (1984). Genesis and evolution of behavior disorder. *American Journal of Psychiatry, 41,* 1–9.

Wallerstein, J. S., Corbin, S. B., & Lewis, J. M. (1988). Children of divorce: A ten-year study. In E. M. Hetherington & J. Arasteh (Eds.), *Impact of divorce, single parenting, and stepparenting on children* (pp. 198–214). Hilisdale, NJ: Lawrence Erlbaum Associates.

Wallerstein, J. S., & Kelly, J. B. (1980). *Surviving the breakup: How children and parents cope with divorce.* New York: Basic.

Weiss, R. S. (1979). Growing up a little faster: The experience of growing up in a single-parent household. *Journal of Social Issues, 35,* 97–111.

Werner, E. E. (1988). Individual differences, universal needs: A 30-year study of resilient high risk infants. *Zero to Three Bulletin of National Center for Clinical Infant Programs, 8,* 1–5.

Werner, E. E., & Smith, S. S. (1982). *Vulnerable but invincible: A longitudinal study of resilient children and youth.* New York: NcGraw-Hill.

Wilkie, C. F., & Ames, E. W. (1986). The relationship of infant crying to parental stress in the transition to parenthood. *Journal of Marriage and the Family, 48,* 545–550.

Yamamoto, K. (1979). Children's ratings of the stressfulness of experiences. *Developmental Psychology, 15,* 581–582.

Zaslow, M. J. (1987). Sex differences in children's response to divorce. *Committee on Child Development Research and Public Policy.* National Research Council.

Zeiss, A., Zeiss, R. A., & Johnson, S. W. (1980). Sex differences in initiation of and adjustment to divorce. *Journal of Divorce, 4,* 21–33.

Zill, N. (1988). Behavior, achievement, and health problems among children in stepfamilies: Findings from a national survey of child health. In E. M. Hetherington & J. D. Arasteh (Eds.), *Impact of divorce, single parenting and stepparenting on children* (pp. 325–368). Hillsdale, NJ: Lawrence Erlbaum Associates.

Zill, N., & Peterson, J. L. (1983, April). *Marital disruption, parent-child relationships, and behavior problems in children.* Paper presented at the meeting of the Society for Research in Child Development, Detroit MI.

7 Antisocial Parents: Unskilled and Vulnerable

G. R. Patterson
D. M. Capaldi
Oregon Social Learning Center, Eugene, Oregon

This report explores the question of why some families seem more vulnerable than others. Based on findings from their longitudinal studies, both Furstenberg (1988) and Hetherington, Cox, and Cox (1985) assert that the majority of children of divorced families do not seem to have significant adjustment problems. Our general thesis is that antisocial parents are at significantly greater risk for a variety of problems, such as unskilled parenting practices and stressful life events (e.g., marital transitions and unemployment). In keeping with the perspective provided by the coercion model (Patterson, 1982), the disrupting effects of negative life events may exacerbate the poor parenting practices. The nature of this vulnerability is explored utilizing both cross-sectional and longitudinal data.

In the present report, the literature pertaining to the issue of whether parenting practices are causally related to child antisocial behavior is reviewed. Evidence of across-generation consistency in antisocial behavior is then discussed. This hypothesis is tested with structural equation models relating grandparental antisocial behavior to parental antisocial behavior in the Oregon Youth Study (OYS) sample.

The general hypothesis that socially disadvantaged and antisocial parents both make significant and unique contributions to poor parenting practices is presented first. Models are tested for discipline and monitoring practices, separately for mothers and fathers, again from the OYS data.

The contribution of the antisocial parent to stress and disequilibrium in the family is considered, especially the hypothesis that antisocial behavior places the parent at risk for relationship transitions (e.g., divorce, short-lived relationships). Structural equation models based on cross-sectional data were used to predict which parenting practices would be disrupted following the transition, and longitudinal data were used to test the prediction. Finally, the effect of stress resulting from the transition on the mother herself in causing depression is examined.

We believe that the evidence that is presented for the relation between parental antisocial behavior, unskilled parenting practices, and family transitions can illuminate the relation between transitions such as divorce and child antisocial behavior.

Sample and Procedures

Subjects. The hypothesis was tested with a sample of boys in Grade 4 (N = 206) and their parents. Two successive birth cohorts of boys were selected from schools in the higher crime areas of a medium-sized metropolitan area in the Pacific Northwest; thus, the boys had a higher chance of involvement in delinquency than was average for the area. Three-quarters of the families invited to be in the study agreed to participate. The two cohorts look very similar on all major variables and were combined for these analyses. A more detailed description of the sample and of selection and recruitment procedures can be found in Capaldi and Patterson (1987). Comparisons of teachers' ratings of the boys' academic skills and psychopathological behaviors showed that those who declined participation in the study were slightly less problematic than the participants on all measures. The sample was predominantly lower and working class (Hollingshead, 1975); one third received welfare. Only 39% of the boys lived with two biological parents. Of those fathers in the home, 27% had an adult arrest record.

The data reported here were collected at Grades 4 and 6. Each construct used in the models was defined by indicators assessed by multiple methods and agents. Assessment procedures included interviews, home observations, questionnaires, school data, and records data (Patterson, Reid, & Dishion, 1989).

Measures

The general strategy for building constructs in this study has been described in Patterson and Bank (1986, 1987) and in Patterson et al. (1989). The indicators for each construct had to survive a 3-stage process. First, they had to show internal consistency (alpha .6 or higher, item-total correlations of .2 or higher) with the first cohort. Second, they had to converge with the other indicators designed to assess the construct (the factor loading for the forced one-factor solution had to be .3 or higher). Finally, the indicators had to replicate in a similar fashion on the second cohort.

The details of the itemetric and factor analyses for each of the constructs are available in Capaldi and Patterson (1989). In that report, data are presented for the reliability of each indicator and the distributional characteristics of the composite score for the construct itself. Each section summarizes data separately and combined for the two cohorts. Each construct is defined by at least two indicators. To form the indicators, items were first standardized and the mean was then calculated. For the parent report indicators, scales were calculated separately for mothers and fathers, and the means of the scales were then taken for two-parent families.

Causal Models

Cross-sectional data were used to model the assumed relation between parental social disadvantage, parental antisocial behavior, and parenting practices. In our clinical experience, the socially disadvantaged parents (especially those who were also antisocial) seemed to have particular difficulty in discipline confrontations. They scolded and threatened, but tended not to follow through; they were also periodically physically abusive (Patterson, 1982). Many of these parents seemed to be uninvolved in the task of supervising or monitoring their sons' activities. When considering the child's current level of antisocial behavior, it was our clinical impression that the primary determinant was parental skill in discipline and monitoring. It was this conviction that led to an early emphasis on teaching more effective parenting skills to families referred for treatment because of their extremely antisocial children (Patterson, 1985).

We believe it is important to retain the clinical impression that changes in parenting practices bring about changes in child behavior. It is also important to retain the idea that the antisocial parents' behavior places them at risk for stressful life events, including relationship transitions, and that these transitions cause certain disruptions in parenting practices. The general strategy for testing for the causal status of such clinical variables is considered in detail in Forgatch (1989) and Patterson et al. (1989). Briefly, the first step requires the development of multiagent, multimethod indicators to define the dependent and independent constructs. Structural equation modeling (SEM) is useful in identifying those covariations that are consistent with the causal hypothesis and therefore worthy of more rigorous study (i.e., correlational models flag relations that are worth experimental manipulations). A third step, and one used in the present study, is to demonstrate that a variable thought to be a determinant can be used to predict a future event in a longitudinal design. Data from the present report and from Patterson and Bank (1989) illustrate such an approach. Even though the across-time prediction accurately reflects what would be expected from a cause and effect relationship, only a series of experimental manipulations can rule out the possibility that both effects are the result of some third, unknown variable.

It is proposed that random assignment designs, in conjunction with clinical interventions of demonstrated effectiveness, can serve as experimental manipulations to test causal status of variable such as the ones presented here. Forgatch

(1989) provided the first experimental test for the hypothesis that changes in parental monitoring and discipline bring about the predicted changes in child antisocial behavior.

MONITORING AND DISCIPLINE PRACTICES AS DETERMINANTS

The underlying assumption of much of the work reported here is that ineffective discipline and monitoring practices are prime determinants for younger childrens' antisocial behavior. This section provides a brief review of the evidence that relates to this assumption.

From a social interactional perspective, child behaviors are thought to be direct outgrowths of the thousands of social exchanges that occur on a daily basis among family members. The positive and negative reinforcing contingencies that strengthened social behaviors and the punishing contingencies that weaken them occur in this context. The function of parenting practices such as discipline, monitoring, and other family-management skills is to *control the microsocial exchanges* (Patterson, 1982; Patterson et al., 1989).

From this perspective, skillful employment of family-management procedures plays a key role in the socialization process. The presence of deviant child behavior implies ineffective parenting skill in one or more family management areas (i.e., monitoring, discipline, problem solving, positive reinforcement, involvement).

In their careful review of the empirical literature, Loeber and Dishion (1983) provided strong support for the assumption that parenting practices covary with antisocial and delinquent behavior. For example, they concluded that variables such as supervision and discipline practices account for the most variance in predicting concurrent and future delinquent behaviors.

Forgatch (1989) reviewed the findings from three different samples that used multimethod, multiagent definitions of parental discipline and monitoring practices. She showed consistent correlations of both monitoring and discipline with antisocial child behavior. The discipline and monitoring model accounted for 30% of the variance in antisocial behavior for the OYS sample of boys in Grade 4. The comparable figure for boys aged 9 to 12 in a recently divorced sample was 52%; for a clinical sample of boys and girls aged 6 to 12, it was 30%. It seems reasonable to conclude that a careful assessment of parenting practices and child adjustment behaviors generates a correlational model that is replicable across a range of samples. Our colleague, Beverly Fagot, has recently been successful in demonstrating an acceptable fit for a variant of this model for preschool samples of both boys and girls.

Obviously, replicated correlational models cannot be considered a sufficient basis for concluding that parenting practices determine child outcomes. The analyses of the longitudinal data set by Patterson and Bank (1987) provided a stronger basis for such a conclusion. Over a 2-year interval, those boys whose parents' discipline or monitoring practices worsened showed significant increases in antisocial behavior. When parenting practices improved or stayed the same, the sons' antisocial behavior decreased. While the findings are consistent with the idea that parenting practices determine child behaviors, they also support the hypothesis that the child behaviors changed the parenting practices.

A more powerful test of the hypothesis would require an experimental manipulation. A quasi-experimental study described by Forgatch (1989) represents our first effort to directly manipulate parenting practices as a test for causal status. In a clinical sample of antisocial children referred for treatment, those children whose parents improved their monitoring and discipline practices showed a reduction in antisocial behavior. In contrast, those children whose parents were unable or unwilling to change their parenting practices showed either no improvement or an increase in antisocial behaviors. Our colleague, Tom Dishion, has extended this work by adding a random assignment component to a replication study of children at risk for substance abuse.

Even if the replication studies are consistent with the hypothesis that parenting practices determine child outcomes, there may be some unknown variable that determines the changes in both parenting practices and child behavior. For example, it might be that the relationship with the therapist leads to greater parental warmth in interacting with the problem child and it is this variable, not changes in parenting practices, that produces the changes. The next step will be to introduce a series of single-subject studies using multiple-baseline designs and time-series analyses. It will then be possible to directly test for the contribution of alternative variables (e.g., changes in parental warmth).

The correlational, longitudinal, and quasi-experimental manipulation studies are all consistent with the idea that parental monitoring and discipline are causally related to child antisocial behaviors. Obviously, the issue is not closed. Much more experimentation must be done before we can accept this crucial hypothesis with any degree of comfort. For now, we must be content with the knowledge that part of the parental discipline and monitoring model has *some* empirical basis. The replicated correlational findings are consistent with the model. The findings from our first quasi-experimental study also support the hypothesis.

In the sense of Popper's (1972) position, either set of studies could have falsified the hypothesis. In light of the fact that it is the next generation of single-subject design studies that will place the hypothesis at even greater risk for falsification, the reader may be well advised to withhold judgment about the causal status of parenting practices. The point of this discussion is not to attempt to convince the reader about established causal status for these variables, but to outline a strategy by which developmental psychologists can move from correlations to experimental manipulations.

ANTISOCIAL TRAITS ACROSS GENERATIONS

The material reviewed in this section relates to the hypothesis that antisocial behavior is a trait that is passed from one generation to another. The mediating mechanism for this transmission is very likely ineffective parental discipline. The specific hypothesis examined here is that there is a significant correlation between an account of the grandparents' discipline practices and the parental antisocial trait. The SEM also examines the relation between parental antisocial traits and their classification as socially disadvantaged. The antisocial trait may be associated with a downward drift toward lower socioeconomic status.

From the perspective of the coercion formulation, the concept of trait is a useful one. The findings reviewed in Patterson et al. (1989) demonstrated acceptable correlations (above .6) for the stability of measures of aggression across both time *and* settings. In that measures of aggression in children are generalizable across time and settings, Allport's (1937) criteria for the definition of the trait concept have been met. Mischel (1968) noted that earlier studies failed to meet these dual requirements and quite properly called into question the use of the trait concept. Later studies using more carefully designed assessment strategies have repeatedly shown that measures of child antisocial behavior are stable across time and settings. For example, Ramsey, Patterson, and Walker (1989) used a multimethod, multiagent assessment for antisocial behaviors in the homes of 4th-grade boys and a comparable assessment a year later based on data from the school. The path coefficient of .73 demonstrated a high level of stability across time and settings.

The definition of the antisocial trait for mothers and fathers used in the present report is in keeping with the position that multimethod, multiagent indicators will provide a more generalizable construct. The indicators used included state records of arrests, subjects' self-reported deviance as assessed by the hypomania and psychopathic deviance scores on the Minnesota Multiphasic Personality Inventory (MMPI) (Hathaway & McKinley, 1967), state records of driver's license suspensions, and subjects' self-reported substance use.

There is now evidence from several longitudinal studies that various measures of the antisocial trait are moderately stable across generations (Caspi, Elder, & Bem, 1987; Huesmann, Eron, Lefkowitz, & Walder, 1984). In keeping with these findings Robins, West, and Herjanic's (1975) study of Black families showed that having an antisocial grandparent places children at significant risk for delinquency. Patterson and Dishion (1988) used multimethod, multiagent definitions for the antisocial trait to show that measures of the trait in one generation correlate significantly with measures of antisocial traits for the next generation. The correlation between measures for mothers and sons was .34 ($p < .001$); for fathers and sons, it was .39 ($p < .001$).

Patterson and Dishion (1988) hypothesized that faulty discipline may be the mediating link between antisocial behavior in one generation and the next. Presumably, antisocial parents are at risk for using ineffective discipline in rearing their children; in so doing, they produce an antisocial child. The hypothesis itself was based on earlier findings from two longitudinal studies. Huesmann et al. (1984) were the first to show that discipline practices may be the mediating link between antisocial traits in one generation and antisocial traits several generations later. They found significant correlations between grandparental discipline practices and antisocial behavior in the grandsons. A comparable set of findings was presented by Elder, Liker, and Cross (1984). They demonstrated that irritable parents tended to use explosive discipline practices. This in turn was associated with antisocial behavior in the sons. The retrospective ratings of grandparental explosive discipline practices were then shown to covary significantly with measures of parental traits such as irritability.

In the present report, an effort has been made to replicate part of these earlier findings. Parents' retrospective accounts of grandparental discipline practices are related to multimethod, multiagent measures of parental trait for antisocial behavior and to the parents' current monitoring and discipline practices. The effects are modeled separately for mothers and for fathers. The mothers' and fathers' retrospective ratings of grandparental practices were obtained from the *Assessing Environments* questionnaire (Knutson, 1985). Three a priori scales were constructed from the item pool to measure abusive and explosive discipline and negative atmosphere; the data from the OYS sample showed that these three scales converged sufficiently to define a construct for grandparental discipline.

The secondary hypothesis we examine concerns the relation between the adult trait for antisocial behavior and their social disadvantage. Presumably, grandparental discipline practices contribute directly to parental antisocial behavior, but only indirectly to parental social disadvantage. It must be said that this particular hypothesis is not "theory driven" in any real sense of the word. It is something that follows not from a careful reading of the coercion model, but rather from a review of the literature on antisocial adults. For example, literature reviews generally show that lower social status is significantly related to a higher incidence of serious criminal and delinquent offenses (Elliott, Ageton, Huizinga, Knowles, & Canter, 1983). However, the possible causal contribution of the antisocial trait to downward drift was strongly suggested in the analysis of longitudinal data (Caspi et al., 1987). Their findings showed that by midlife, men who had been ill tempered as children were characterized by an erratic work history. They achieved a lower-status occupation than their own fathers. The relation between early temper tantrums and downward mobility held even after IQ was partialed out. These findings are in close accord with our own clinical experience in trying to intervene with antisocial parents. The core problem for them, as well as for their problem children, is noncompliance. The inability to follow either implicit or explicit rules is learned in the home and generalizes to the classroom and, later still, to the work place. Refusal to accept criticism or authority in the workplace results in the antisocial person being fired from one job after another. Each failure is followed by a lower paying job.

Although we suspect that more careful attention to this problem will demonstrate that the relation between adult antisocial behavior and social disadvantage is a bidirectional one, it does not interfere with our current interest in determining whether the relation between grandparental discipline practices and later parental social disadvantage is direct or indirect. In keeping with the Hollingshead (1975) approach to defining social status, the Social Disadvantage construct was defined by an indicator that combined occupation and education data. We added to this the measure of intelligence based on the vocabulary section of the Wechsler Adult Intelligence Scale (WAIS) (Wechsler, 1955). The resulting convergence was excellent for fathers (.50) and certainly within acceptable limits for mothers (.27). This definition for social disadvantage gives substantial weight to cognitive factors; using education, occupation, and intelligence as three separate indicators might evoke a somewhat different picture.

The intercorrelations among the indicators that define the models are summarized for fathers in Table 7.1 and for mothers in Table 7.2. It can be seen from the intercorrelations that the three scales from the Knutson (1985) questionnaire on grandparental discipline showed strong convergence in defining grandparental practices. The median correlation was .598 for fathers and .593 for mothers.

On the other hand, the convergence in defining the antisocial trait for the two parents was rather modest. The median convergence correlation was .26 for mothers and .21 for fathers; the findings only barely satisfy our requirements for a successful definition. Notice, too, that the Social Disadvantage construct is more strongly defined for fathers than for mothers. An inspection of the magnitude of the discriminant correlations suggests no particular problems for modeling these data.

The SEM was carried out separately for mothers and for fathers. The results are summarized in Fig. 7.1. Three hypotheses were examined. The first was that the path from grandparental Discipline to the parental Antisocial Behavior constructs would be significant. The second hypothesis was that parental Antisocial Behavior and Social Disadvantage would be significantly related. The third hypothesis was that there would be no significant direct path from grandparental Discipline to parental Social Disadvantage.

The nonsignificant chi-square values showed that the overall fit was acceptable for both models. The data from the fathers provide solid support for the first two hypotheses: The path from grandparental Discipline to the parental trait score was significant, but only a very modest 14% of the variance in discipline practices was accounted for. The path from paternal Antisocial Behavior to Social Disadvantage was also significant, with Antisocial Behavior accounting for 26% of the variance in the measure of Social Disadvantage. The comparable relation for the mothers' model was of borderline significance; the magnitude of

TABLE 7.1
Convergent and Discriminant Correlation Matrices for Grandparental Model for Father

	Grandparental Discipline			*Parental Antisocial Trait*			*Social Disadvantage*	
	Paternal Abuse Cluster	*Paternal Explosive Discipline*	*Paternal Negative Atmosphere*	*Driver's License Suspension*	*Paternal MMPI*	*Paternal Drug Use*	*Socio-Economic Status*	*WAIS Vocabulary Test*
Abuse cluster	1.00							
Explosive discipline	.598	1.00						
Negative atmosphere	.449	.673	1.00					
Driver's License suspension	.347	.167	.095	1.00				
Paternal MMPI	.247	.135	.050	.520	1.00			
Drug use	.168	.213	.094	.211	.207	1.00		
Socioeconomic status	.163	.090	.092	.280	.195	.257	.1.00	
WAIS vocabulary	.133	.020	.074	.345	.169	.000	.495	1.00

TABLE 7.2
Convergent and Discriminant Correlation Matrices for Grandparental Model for Mothers

	Grandparental Discipline			*Pareental Antisocial Trait*			*Social Disadvantage*	
	Maternal Abuse Cluster	*Maternal Explosive Discipline*	*Maternal Negative Atmosphere*	*Driver's License Suspension*	*Maternal MMPI*	*Maternal Drug Use*	*Socio-economic Status*	*WAIS Vocabulary Test*
Abuse cluster	1.00							
Explosive discipline	.593	1.00						
Negative atmosphere	.622	.708	1.00					
Driver's license suspension	.020	-.115	-.016	1.00				
Paternal MMPI	.158	.177	.291	.201	1.00			
Drug use	.066	.086	.142	.314	.268	1.00		
Socioeconomic status	.061	.014	.113	.099	.139	.094	1.00	
WAIS vocabulary	-.018	-.021	.025	.153	.158	-.016	.267	1.00

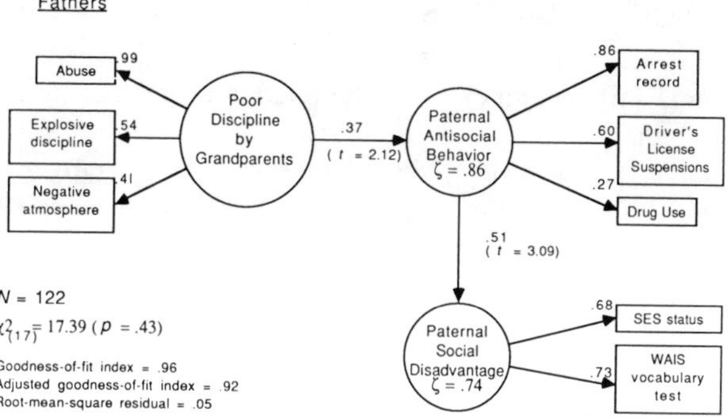

Error terms allowed to covary: Negative Atmosphere and Explosive Discipline (.45)

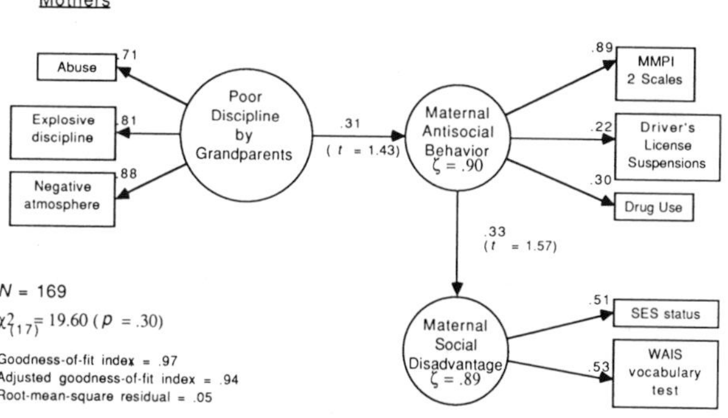

Error terms allowed to covary: Drug Use and Driver's License Suspensions (.25)

FIG. 7.1. Grandparental discipline: The first step.

variance accounted for was even smaller. Obviously, there are important variables other than those specified in the model that account for variance in parenting practices and social disadvantage.

The third hypothesis was tested by examining alternative models, including a direct path from grandparental practices to Social Disadvantage. Adding this path did not improve the fit for either parent model. For both the mothers and the fathers, the coefficients for the new path were nonsignificant (.16 for fathers and .08 for mothers). An effort was also made to demonstrate that the effect of grandparental Discipline on the parental antisocial trait was mediated through parental Social Disadvantage. The models for both mothers and fathers failed to provide a fit to the data.

It seems reasonable to conclude that these data support earlier findings from longitudinal studies that a covariation exists between grandparental discipline practices and parental antisocial behavior.

ANTISOCIAL PARENTS AND PARENTING PRACTICES

The discussion in this section explores the relation of monitoring and discipline practices to both the parental antisocial trait and their status as socially disadvantaged. Within the coercion model, the assumption is that the effects of contextual variables such as stress, socioeconomic status, divorce, or parental depressive and antisocial traits on child adjustment would all be mediated through their disrupting impact on family-management practices (Patterson et al., 1989). Both social disadvantage and antisocial behavior may be associated with a lack of social skill and less skilled parenting practices. Social disadvantage and parental antisocial behavior covary, and it is important to ask whether a measure of parental antisocial behavior adds some unique information to our understanding of discipline practices beyond what is already communicated by social disadvantage. In the present report, the specific hypothesis is that both parental social disadvantage and antisocial trait scores would covary significantly with both discipline and monitoring practices. Again, the effects were analyzed separately for mothers and fathers.

Some of the strongest support for the idea that the effect of social status and other contextual variables on child adjustment may be mediated through parenting practices was recently supplied by a reanalysis of the Gluecks' data set (e.g., Glueck & Glueck, 1968). Laub and Sampson (1988) regressed parental discipline practices on parental drunkenness and criminality combined and on economic dependence. Both betas were significant, and the effect was significant for the separate analyses of mothers and fathers. This means that either measure (parental antisocial personality or economic status) correlated with discipline practices even after the contribution of the other had been partialed out. The two variables also correlated significantly with poor monitoring.

It was thought that the strongest test of the contribution of parental trait and social status to parenting practices would be to embed the model in a longitudinal data set. Therefore, the measures of the parental traits and status were collected when the boys were in Grade 4 and the measures of monitoring and discipline practices (modeled separately) were each based on data collected at Grade 6. The data for mothers and fathers were modeled separately.

The Discipline construct was assessed using measures from the parent interview, parent interviewer impressions, and the microsocial variable of parental nattering from the home observations. The Monitoring construct was assessed using four measures: mother report of rules from the interview, child report of rules, interviewer impressions (a mean of mother, father, and child), and parent telephone interview. The details of the psychometric analyses for both of these constructs are summarized in Capaldi and Patterson (1989).

The correlations among the indicators for the maternal and paternal discipline models are summarized in Tables 7.3 and 7.4 respectively. The convergence among the indicators for the Discipline construct meet our arbitrary requirements

TABLE 7.3
Convergent and Discriminant Correlation Matrices for Maternal Discipline Model

	Maternal Antisocial Trait			*Social Disadvantage*		*Parental Discipline*		
	Maternal Drug Use	*Driver's Licence Suspension*	*Maternal MMPI*	*Socio-economic Status*	*WAIS Vocabulary Test*	*Interviewer Impressions*	*Parent Interview: Discipline*	*Nattering*
Maternal drug use	1.00							
Driver's license suspension	.280	1.00						
Maternal MMPI	.291	.196	1.00					
Socioeconomic status	.076	.075	.154	1.00				
WAIS vocabulary test	-.011	.166	.164	.275	1.00			
Interviewer impressions	-.164	-.123	-.123	-.135	-.254	1.00		
Parent interview: discipline	-.108	-.023	-.087	-.070	-.143	.527	1.00	
Nattering	-.088	-.048	-.271	-.248	-.233	.312	.354	1.00

TABLE 7.4
Convergent and Discriminant Correlation Matrices for the Paternal Discipline Model

	Paternal Antisocial Trait			*Social Disadvantage*		*Parental Discipline*		
	Paternal Drug Use	*Paternal MMPI*	*Driver's License Suspensions*	*Socio-economic Status*	*WAIS Vocabulary Test*	*Interviewer Impressions*	*Parent Interview: Discipline*	*Nattering*
Paternal drug use	1.00							
Driver's license suspension	.200	1.00						
Paternal MMPI	.220	.504	1.00					
Socioeconomic status	.257	.194	.249	1.00				
WAIS vocabulary test	.019	.180	.371	.512	1.00			
Interviewer impressions	-.188	-.125	-.206	-.371	-.347	1.00		
Parent interview: discipline	-.048	.037	.002	-.232	-.214	.615	1.00	
Nattering	.039	-.186	-.275	-.160	-.152	.295	.316	1.00

(.20 or better) for satisfactory convergence. The median was .354 for the sample of mothers and .316 for fathers. The correlation matrices for the monitoring models are not included due to lack of space.

The SEM in Fig. 7.2a examines the relations between the maternal Discipline construct and the Social Disadvantage and Antisocial Behavior constructs. Modifications made to fit the model are reported at the bottom of the figure. In this case the residual, or error, terms for the nattering and MMPI indicators were allowed to covary. The nonsignificant chi-square value showed an acceptable fit between the a priori model and the data set, but of the three structural relations, only the path from maternal Social Disadvantage to Discipline was significant. Earlier analyses by Patterson and Dishion (1988) had shown a significant path between maternal Antisocial Behavior and Discipline (path coefficient .27). It is clear, however, that when the effects of maternal Social Disadvantage are par-

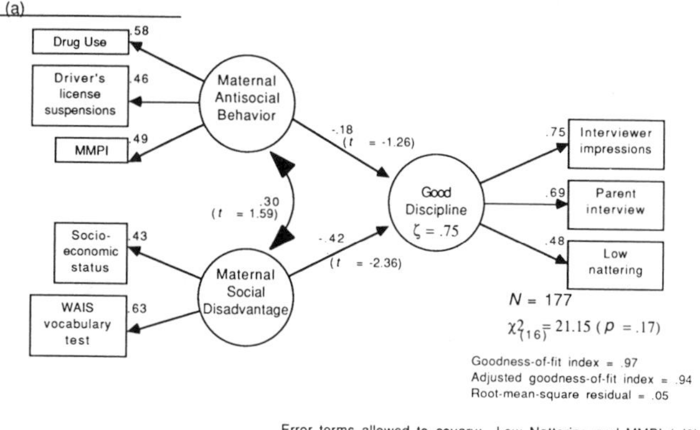

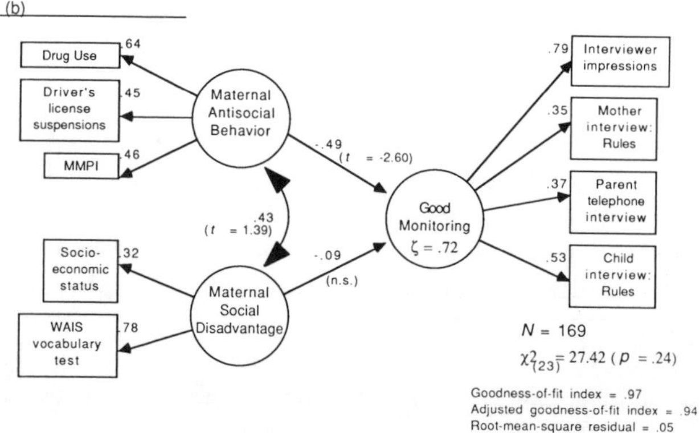

FIG. 7.2. The effects of maternal social disadvantage and antisocial behavior.

tialed out, the contribution of Antisocial Behavior to Discipline is reduced. The two maternal constructs accounted for 25% of the variance in parental discipline practices.

As shown in Fig. 7.2b, the maternal model for monitoring also showed an acceptable fit of the a priori model to the data set ($p = .24$). This time, however, the only significant structural relation was the path from maternal Antisocial Behavior to parental Monitoring (path coefficient −.49). The more antisocial mothers provide less supervision for their children.

The differences between the discipline and monitoring models emphasize the fact that social disadvantage places the mother at risk for poor discipline, while maternal antisocial behavior seems to place her at risk for inadequate monitoring. Note that this selective effect holds even after controlling for the effect of one maternal disposition on the other.

The findings from the SEM for the paternal data sets are summarized in Figs. 7.3a and 7.3b. As shown there, the relation between the paternal Social Disadvantage and Antisocial Behavior constructs was substantial (.48). Furthermore, when the contribution of Social Disadvantages was controlled, the effect of the antisocial trait was nonsignificant for both Discipline and Monitoring.

Overall, the findings from the four models emphasize the relation between antisocial behavior and social disadvantage. Knowing that the mother or the father is socially disadvantaged provides a substantial basis for predicting that his or her discipline practices will be ineffective. Adding information about the parents' antisocial personality adds very little to our ability to predict this. The antisocial trait makes a unique contribution to inadequate monitoring for mothers, but not for fathers.

THE DISEQUILIBRATING FUNCTION OF THE ANTISOCIAL PARENT

Parental levels of stress and distress seem to be highly related phenomena. Parents who are antisocial, depressed, or alcoholic report high levels of stressful life events and daily hassles. In this section, we examine the possibility that antisocial mothers may actually contribute not only to their own personal levels of stress, but also to disrupted family processes. The specific hypotheses tested were as follows:

1. Antisocial men and women experience a greater number of stressful events, both major life events and minor day-to-day incidents.

2. Distressed and antisocial women are more likely to have a higher incidence of transitions (e.g., from intact to divorce, from divorce to remarriage, and from remarriage to divorce).

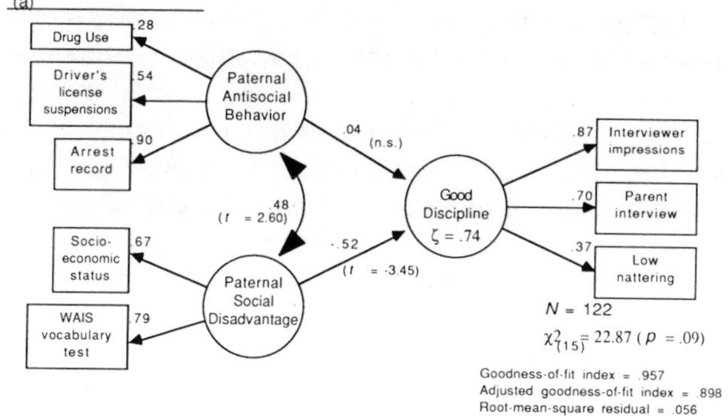

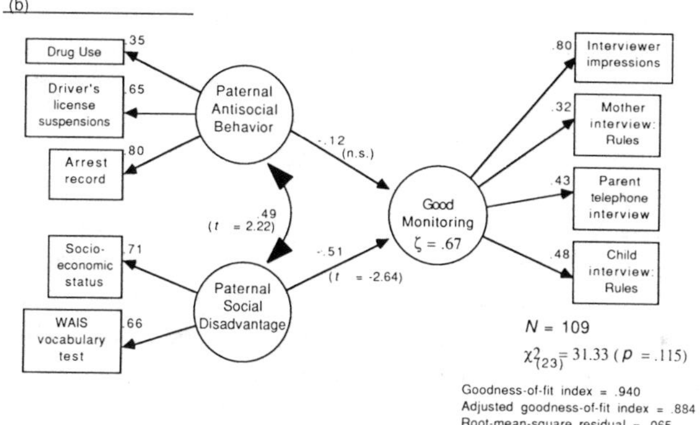

FIG. 7.3. The effects of paternal social disadvantage and antisocial behavior.

3. Following a transition, there is increased risk for disruptions in single mothers' monitoring.

4. Following a transition, there is a significant increase in maternal depression.

Fathers were tested only on the first hypothesis due to the inadequate sample size for single fathers.

Distress and Stress

There is a growing body of literature suggesting that some individuals are more likely to be chronically distressed than others. Some reviewers of this literature suggest that up to 25% of the community might well be characterized as chronically distressed (Depue & Monroe, 1986). Depue and Monroe underscore the intricate relationship between chronic distress and stress. For example, the majority of psychiatric patients report themselves to be severely stressed. As they point out, a distressed individual's behavior often produces an increase in stress.

It is hypothesized that an important function of the antisocial trait lies in its contribution to maintaining high levels of stress. Our clinical work with antisocial parents suggests that their general negligence is such that bills go unpaid, agreements are not kept, and responsibilities are regularly set aside. This lifestyle has been detailed in the studies of violent men by Toch (1969). Such an orientation is thought to contribute to continued high levels of daily hassles. Their irritable reactions to criticism or to demands for conformity, inability to plan effectively, and disregard for their own health are all associated with increased risk for such major life events as high rates of accidents, recurring unemployment, and increasingly poor health. Their antisocial behavior places them at continued risk for arrest and incarceration, both of which contribute to further stress. In the present context, it is hypothesized that this trait also places them at risk for separation and divorce.

The data are generally consistent with these hypotheses. The OYS data from Grade 4 were used to regress the stress scores against the measures of parental antisocial trait scores and the measure of social disadvantage. For both mothers and fathers, the main contribution was made by the measure of parental antisocial behavior; the contribution of social disadvantage was not significant. The multiple R was .4 for mothers and .38 for fathers. The SEM analyses of data collected for the OYS at Grade 4 also showed strong associations between measures of parental stress and antisocial behavior for both mothers and fathers (Patterson & Dishion, 1988). The path coefficient was .62 for fathers and .59 for mothers. In keeping with the hypothesis, measures of parental stress and antisocial behavior are highly correlated.

Antisocial Parents and Risk for Future Transitions

The hypothesis examined here is that antisocial parents are at increased risk for future transitions in family structure. Presumably, it is the antisocial parent who is more likely to separate, to remarry, and to separate again.

The hypothesis is suggested by the findings from Capaldi (1989), who showed a linear relation between the number of past family transitions and a general risk score for parental pathology that included measures of depression, driver's license suspensions, arrests, drug use, and stress. She showed that the general measure of parental distress (depression + drug use + stress + driver's license suspensions + arrests) correlated .35 with fathers' history of transitions and .48 with mothers' history of transitions. Of course, it was not clear whether parental distress caused the long history of transitions or whether the stress engendered by these transitions led to parental distress.

Longitudinal data collected for the families in the OYS at Grades 4 and 6 were used to test the hypothesis. Shifts from intact to single-parent, single-parent to step-, or step- to single-parent family were all classified as transitions. In the 2-year interval, 24 intact and/or single-mother families were involved in one or more transitions. The sample also contained five single fathers, but they were not included in the analyses. The data showed that 71% of the transitional mothers were above the median score for the whole sample on the antisocial trait. The results of the two-tailed and one-tailed t tests were 1.83 and .041, respectively. This finding is consistent with our hypothesis; it is also consistent with the findings from Lahey et al. (1988), who found a higher incidence of antisocial traits among single mothers in their clinical sample than among mothers from intact families. Furthermore, they emphasized the relation between antisocial single mothers' poor discipline and their sons' antisocial behavior.

These findings raise several important questions. Once the transition has occurred, are parenting practices worse than they had been prior to the transition? What is the effect of the transition on the mother? Does she become more depressed than she had previously been?

The Effect of Transitions on Parenting Practices

As described in the coercion model, the effects of contextual variables on child adjustment are mediated through their impact on one or more family management practices (Patterson et al., 1989). Presumably, the effects of contextual variables such as social class, parental intelligence, stress, or family transitions are mediated in the same way. In the present context, it would be assumed that single-mother families in transition are at significant risk for disrupted monitoring or discipline practices. The SEM analyses in the preceding sections suggest that it might be the monitoring practices that are particularly vulnerable to disruptions for this sample.

The data used to test these hypotheses were based on assessments of OYS families at Grades 4 and 6. The 24 families who had made a transition during the interval comprised one group, and the 173 who had not experienced a transition comprised the comparison group. The findings summarized in Table 7.5 showed that those families who later experienced a transition *initially* showed poor discipline practices. The F-value for the group comparison was 14.01 ($p < .001$), but neither of the values for trials or interactions was significant. The findings suggest that being involved in the transition did not worsen an already bad situation. There was no change in the level of discipline practices for the comparison group.

The data for monitoring practices showed a rather different effect. The significant F value of 5.94 ($p = .016$) for the interactive effect indicates that the relationship transition disrupts the mothers' monitoring practices.

The findings suggest that the effect of a transition may be selective. Those

TABLE 7.5
The Effect of Transitions on Parenting Practices

		Mean Family Management Score	
Parenting Practice	*N*	*Grade 4*	*Grade 6*
Discipline			
In transition	24	-.46	-.35
No transition	173	.06	.06
Monitoring			
In transition	24	-.06	-.37
No transition	173	.02	.05

families at risk for becoming involved in a transition are more likely to demonstrate poor discipline, but not poor monitoring. Following the transition, the families show disrupted monitoring as well as poor discipline practices. This finding is important because the analyses of longitudinal data by Dishion, Patterson, and Skinner (1989) have shown that poor monitoring is significantly related to a drift into the deviant peer group.

The Effect of Transitions on Parental Depression

In this section, we explore the hypothesis that parents involved in transitions would be at increased risk for depression. The process model developed for maternal depression showed that it was most likely the loss of support and increased stress that determined the level of depression (Patterson & Forgatch, 1989). It would follow that those mothers whose recent transitions resulted in the loss of social support (i.e., spouse or partner) would show increases in self-reported depression, and those who had gained a partner would report a reduction in depression.

The findings are summarized in Table 7.6. Both sets of data are consistent with the hypotheses; given the small sample sizes, however, the findings are only marginally significant. The critical finding here is the interaction term. The F value of 2.85 (p = .11) summarizes two important shifts in maternal depression.

TABLE 7.6
The Effects of Transitions on Single Mothers' Depression

		Mean Family Depression Score	
	N	*Grade 4*	*Grade 6*
Gained support	11	.36	.04
Lost support	12	.00	.53

Those mothers who *lost* a partner during the transition reported themselves to be more depressed; those who *gained* a partner reported themselves to be less depressed.

In a retrospective study of adult males and females, Robins (1984) noted that women who reported themselves to have antisocial adolescents also reported themselves to be currently at greater risk for problems with depression, phobias, alcohol, etc. The present findings suggest that one of the reasons for the covariation between antisocial behaviors and depressed behaviors for single mothers might be in the loss of support they have experienced.

IMPLICATIONS

The pattern of findings is consistent with the idea that certain parental traits place the family at risk for change. Although some effects are direct and some are indirect, most of these changes are negative ones.

The general findings reviewed and presented support the idea of an across-generation linkage for antisocial behavior. Parents who are antisocial are at significant risk of producing boys who are antisocial. There is even limited longitudinal evidence for such a linkage across three generations. The findings are also consistent with the idea that the antisocial parent is more likely to employ ineffective discipline and monitoring practices. This suggests that ineffective discipline may be the mediating factor that explains the linkage in the antisocial trait across generations.

There is also a consistent set of correlations between antisocial behavior and social disadvantage. Antisocial parents seem to be less educated, have lower-status occupations, and score lower on tests of intelligence. We have explored the relation between parenting practices and parental antisocial traits and social disadvantage. For fathers, both social disadvantage and antisocial trait scores covaried significantly with their monitoring and discipline practices. When social advantage was partialed out, however, father antisocial behavior no longer made a significant contribution to either parenting practice. Social disadvantage also accounted for most of the variance in maternal discipline practices, but antisocial behavior (rather than social disadvantage) was significantly associated with monitoring in the model for mothers. Antisocial mothers were significantly less effective in their monitoring than nonantisocial mothers; this relation held even when social disadvantage was partialed out.

One of the most interesting findings was that maternal antisocial behavior may place families at risk for future change and stress. (The relation between paternal antisocial behavior and transitions was not tested.) The antisocial mother was shown to be at significant risk for transitions during the ensuing 2-year interval.

We believe that parental social disadvantage and antisocial behavior may help explain why some divorced families produce antisocial boys but most do not.

Roughly half of all current marriages will end in separation and/or divorce; presumably, a small subset of single mothers will be antisocial. The present findings suggest that the children will be most at risk when the single mother is *both* antisocial and socially disadvantaged. Being socially disadvantaged would place the single mother at risk for poor discipline practices. This would imply that the family interaction itself provides a basis for the boys' learning to perform coercive behaviors. If she is also antisocial, she may be doubly at risk in that her monitoring may be disrupted after the divorce. Disrupted monitoring would suggest that during early adolescence the boys are at risk for involvement in the deviant peer group (Dishion et al., 1989).

This may result in *experimenting* or even heavier involvement in delinquency. A boy who becomes involved in delinquency during adolescence due to disrupted monitoring at home, but who was not antisocial in earlier childhood should be a less serious delinquent who drops out of the process early.

The other outcome of the mothers' transitions and stress was increased depression. One of the primary characteristics of the depressed adult is the recurrent nature of the depression. The link between the antisocial trait and recurrent transitions that disrupt social support and increase stressors suggests one potential mechanism for the chronic status of depression in some adults. Our future studies will focus on the outcomes of the increased depression that accompany transitions. Does the depression that accompanies the shift from intact to single-parent status place the mother at greater risk for substance abuse?

The overall pattern of findings emphasizes the dynamic alterations in family life that can be set in motion by seemingly small differences in parental traits. Not all of the mothers over the median on antisocial behavior scores were involved in transitions. Only 12% of mothers with high antisocial scores actually made the change in the 2-year interval. Once the transition occurred, however, it introduced still further changes in parenting practices and maternal mood. These changes in turn introduce further changes in the family. A transitional shift is, of course, a dramatic alteration, perhaps analogous to Elder's studies (e.g., Elder et al., 1984) of the effects of a 40% loss in income associated with the Great Depression. Given its dramatic nature, what seems to disrupt the family are the accompanying shifts in family-management practices. If these shifts persist, there are likely to be long-term increases in child adjustment problems, both at home and at school, accompanied by fundamental shifts in roles within the family.

ACKNOWLEDGMENTS

Support for the research presented in this chapter was provided by Grant Nos. MH 37940 and MH 17126, Center for Studies of Antisocial and Violent Behavior, NIMH, U.S. PHS; Grant No. MH 38318, Mood, Anxiety, and Personality

Disorders Research Branch, Division of Clinical Research, NIMH, U.S. PHS; Grant No. HD 22679, Center for Research for Mothers and Children, NICHD, U.S. PHS; and Grant No. DA 05304, National Institute of Drug Abuse, U.S. PHS.

The writers particularly wish to thank Lew Bank and Mike Stoolmiller for their contributions to the analyses of the data sets and our colleagues John Reid, Tom Dishion, and Marion Forgatch for their insightful comments about the material itself.

REFERENCES

Allport, G. W. (1937). *Personality: A psychological interpretation*. New York: Holt.

Capaldi, D. M. (1989). *The relation between parent antisocial behavior, depression, and marital transitions*. Unpublished manuscript, Oregon Social Learning Center, Eugene.

Capaldi, D. M., & Patterson, G. R. (1987). An approach to the problem of recruitment and retention rates for longitudinal research. *Behavioral Assessment, 9*, 169–177.

Capaldi, D. M., & Patterson, G. R. (1989). *Psychometric properties of fourteen latent constructs from the Oregon Youth Study*. New York: Springer-Verlag.

Caspi, A., Elder, G. H., & Bem, D. J. (1987). Moving against the world: Life-course patterns of explosive children. *Developmental Psychology, 23*, 308–313.

Depue, R. A., & Monroe, S. M. (1986). Conceptualization and measurement of human disorder in life stress research: The Problem of chronic disturbance. *Psychological Bulletin, 99*, 36–51.

Dishion, T. J., Patterson, G. R., & Skinner, M. L. (1989). *Parent monitoring and peer relations in the drift to deviant peers: From middle childhood to early adolescence*. Manuscript submitted for publication.

Elder, G. H., Liker, J. K., & Cross, C. E. (1984). Parent-child behavior in the Great Depression: Life course and intergenerational influences. In P. B. Baltes & O. G. Brim (Eds.), *Life span development and behavior* (Vol. 6, pp. 109–158). New York: Academic.

Elliott, D. S., Ageton, S. S., Huizinga, D., Knowles, B. A., & Canter, R. J. (1983). *The prevalence and incidence of delinquent behavior: 1976–1980. National estimates of delinquent behavior by sex, race, social class, and other selected variables* (National Youth Survey Report No. 26). Boulder, CO: Behavioral Research Institute.

Forgatch, M. S. (1989). The clinical science vortex: Developing a theory for antisocial behavior. In D. Pepler & K. H. Rubin (Eds.), *The development and treatment of childhood aggression*. Hillsdale, NJ: Lawrence Erlbaum Associates.

Furstenberg, F. F. (1988). Childcare after divorce and remarriage. In M. E. Hetherington & J. D. Arasteh (Eds.), *Impact of divorce, single parenting, and stepparenting on children* (pp. 245–261). Hillsdale, NJ: Lawrence Erlbaum Associates.

Glueck, S., & Glueck, E. (1968). *Delinquents and nondelinquents in perspective*. Cambridge, MA: Harvard University Press.

Hathaway, S. R., & McKinley, J. C. (1967). *Minnesota Multiphasic Personality Inventory*. New York: The Psychological Corporation.

Hetherington, E. M., Cox, M., & Cox, R. (1978). The aftermath of divorce. In J. H. Stevens, Jr., & M. Matthews (Eds.), *Mother-child, father-child relations* (pp. 110–155). Washington, DC: National Association for the Education of Young Children.

Hetherington, E. M., Cox, M., & Cox, R. (1985). Long-term effects of divorce and remarriage on the adjustment of children. *Journal of the American Academy of Child Psychiatry, 24*, 518–530.

Hollingshead, A. B. (1975). *Four-factor index of social status.* Unpublished manuscript, Yale University, Department of Sociology, New Haven, CT.

Huesmann, L. R., Eron, L. D., Lefkowitz, M. M., & Walder, L. O. (1984). Stability of aggression over time and generations. *Developmental Psychology, 20,* 1120–1134.

Knutson, J. F. (1985). *Assessing environments.* Unpublished manuscript, University of Iowa, Department of Psychology, Iowa City.

Lahey, B. B., Hartdagen, S. E., Frick, P. J., McBurnett, K., Connor, R., & Hynd, G. W. (1988). Conduct disorder: Parsing the confounded relation to parental divorce and antisocial personality. *Journal of Abnormal Psychology, 97,* 334–337.

Laub, J. H., & Sampson, R. J. (1988). Unraveling families and delinquency: A reanalysis of the Gluecks' data. *Criminology, 26,* 355–379.

Loeber, R., & Dishion, T. J. (1983). Early predictors of male delinquency: A review. *Psychological Bulletin, 94,* 68–99.

Mischel, W. (1968). *Personality and assessment.* New York: Wiley.

Patterson, G. R. (1982). *A social learning approach to family intervention: III. Coercive family process.* Eugene, OR: Castalia.

Patterson, G. R. (1985). Beyond technology: The next stage in developing an empirical base for parent training. In L. L'Abate (Ed.), *Handbook of family psychology and therapy* (Vol. 2, pp. 1344–1379). Homewood, IL: Dorsey.

Patterson, G. R., & Bank, L. (1986). Bootstrapping your way in the nomological thicket. *Behavioral Assessment, 8,* 49–73.

Patterson, G. R., & Bank, L. (1987). When is a nomological network a construct? In D. R. Peterson & D. B. Fishman (Eds.), *Assessment for decision* (pp. 249–279). New Brunswick, NJ: Rutgers University Press.

Patterson, G. R., & Bank, L. (1989). Some amplifying mechanisms for pathologic processes in families. In M. R. Gunnar & E. Thelen (Eds.), *Systems and development: The Minnesota symposia on child psychology* (Vol. 22, pp. 167–209). Hillsdale, NJ: Lawrence Erlbaum Associates.

Patterson, G. R., & Dishion, T. J. (1988). Multilevel family process models: Traits, interactions, and relationships. In R. Hinde & J. Stevenson-Hinde (Eds.), *Relationships within families: Mutual influences* (pp. 283–310). Oxford: Clarendon Press.

Patterson, G. R., & Forgatch, M. S. (1989). Initiation and maintenance of processes disrupting single-mother families. In G. R. Patterson (Ed.), *Depression and aggression in family interaction* (pp. 209–245). Hillsdale, NJ: Lawrence Erlbaum Associates.

Patterson, G. R., Reid, J. B., & Dishion, T. J. (1989). *Antisocial boys.* Manuscript submitted for publication.

Popper, K. R. (1972). *Objective knowledge: An evolutionary approach.* Oxford: Clarendon.

Ramsey, E., Patterson, G. R., & Walker, H. M. (1989). *Generalization of antisocial behavior in boys from home to school settings.* Manuscript submitted for publication.

Robins. L. N. (1984). *Conduct disorder in adult psychiatric diagnosis.* Unpublished manuscript.

Robins, L. N., West, P. A., & Herjanic, B. L. (1975). Arrests and delinquency in two generations: A study of black urban families and their children. *Journal of Child Psychology and Psychiatry, 16,* 125–140.

Toch, H. (1969). *Violent men.* New York: Aldine.

Wechsler, D. (1955). *The Wechsler Adult Intelligence Scale.* New York: The Psychological Corporation.

8 Effective Communication: Enabling Multiproblem Families to Change

Elaine A. Blechman
University of Colorado, Boulder

This chapter is about multiproblem families, their communication deficits, and their difficulties with normative and nonnormative transitions. It is also about a promising method of enabling multiproblem families to change.

MULTIPROBLEM FAMILIES AND TRANSITIONS

Consider Maria, a 27-year-old, bilingual, Hispanic mother and her two daughters, Juanita, aged 7 and Dolores, 3. Dolores' father, a drug addict, drifts in and out of the household. Violent arguments between the parents are frequent when he is at home. Maria did not finish high school and has never been employed. As a teenager she made several suicide attempts following episodes of sexual abuse by her father. She suffers from Type 1 diabetes and has been hospitalized at least yearly with episodes of major depressive disorder since age 20. Juanita has diabetes and spina bifida and moves around with the help of a walker. She has been subject to physical and sexual abuse and neglect by her mother and stepfather and isolated from contact with peers. She has a sweet, sunny manner and wants very much to please adults. Despite her obvious desire to please her teacher, her academic achievement is considerably below her capabilities. Dolores is a healthy, boisterous child who shows signs of language delay.

The family is supported by public assistance. For the last year, they have lived in a new apartment for the handicapped. A van for the handicapped transports Juanita to school and the whole family to the hospital for clinical visits. A homemaker assists the mother on week-days, but funding for her services is unlikely to continue. As a condition for retaining custody of her children, after she threatened to kill herself and her daughters, Maria was required to seek help from our clinic. Maria cancels about 3 of 4 appointments she makes for regular clinic visits. When she does come, she is anxious, overwhelmed, and angry about a crisis. The crisis might involve her husband's behavior, a neighbor's threat to report her to the police, or a misplaced welfare check. As she describes her most recent crisis, and her children play together on the floor, Maria punctuates her comments to the clinician with angry rebukes which quickly quiet the children.

This family certainly fits the definition of multiproblem families that I provide below. At the same time, given her meager resources and terrible childhood, Maria has coped far better than many others do. She knows how to get the most out of the public-assistance bureaucracy (apartment, transportation, and homemaker). She comes to the hospital and uses its services when she feels the need. She has not succumbed to drug or alcohol addiction, prostitution, or HIV infection. She has kept her family together. Her children are well-nourished, clean, and well-dressed. She often says that she wants to make a better life for her children than her own. She also says, she does not know how.

What is a Multiproblem Family?

In the absence of a standard definition of the multiproblem family, consider this one. A multiproblem family has at least three current psychosocial problems that have persisted for a year or more and are serious as judged by relevant population statistics. Current problems might include: in the family, poverty-level income; in the couple, marital dissatisfaction; among adult family members, chronic unemployment; in any family member, depression or other DSM-IIIR diagnosable psychopathology, incarceration, involuntary institutionalization, drug or alcohol addiction. A common profile of a multiproblem two-parent family involves significant marital conflict, maternal depression, and child antisocial behavior (Bond & McMahon, 1984; Christensen, Phillips, Glasgow & Johnson, 1983; Emery, 1982; Emery, Weintraub, & Neale, 1982; Ghodsian, Zajicek, & Wolkind, 1984; Jones & Demaree, 1975; McLean, 1976; O'Leary, 1984; Oltmanns, Broderick, & O'Leary, 1977; Weissman & Paykel, 1974).

This operational definition of the multiproblem family recognizes that a multitude of unresolved psychosocial problems rather than a specific type of problem (such as poverty or parental psychopathology or single parenthood) exposes children to developmental risk (Belsky, 1981; Blechman, 1982; Blechman, Berberian, & Thompson, 1977; Blechman & Manning, 1976; Breitmayer & Ramey, 1986; Holahan & Moos, 1987; Kauffman, Grunebaum, Cohler, & Gamer, 1979; Kohn, 1973; Lewis, 1966).

Chance or Skill? Multiproblem families differ in the chronicity of their status from families who spend a relatively brief time (perhaps only a year) burdened with multiple problems to families who perpetually suffer from multiple problems. Bad luck and a difficult environment can conspire against any family, for a brief time. But skill deficits combined with a nonsupportive environment may well account for how families become permanent members of the underclass.

The role that skill deficits play in perpetuating a family's psychosocial problems is illustrated by mounting evidence about multiproblem families whose children evidence behavior problems. Behavioral parent training has proved a great success with the broad range of child behavior problems. Nevertheless, multiproblem families are difficult to engage and help via this approach (Bernal, Klinnert, & Schultz, 1980; Bijou, 1984; Blechman, Tryon, Ruff, & McEnroe, 1989; Fleischmann & Szykula, 1981; Forehand, Griest, Wells, & McMahon, 1982; Forehand, Middlebrook, Rogers, & Steffe, 1983; Forehand & Wells, 1977; Griest & Forehand, 1982; Hargis & Blechman, 1979; Harris, 1986; Horne & van Dyke, 1983; Lindsley, 1970; Lutzker, McGimsey, McRae, & Campbell, 1983; McMahon, Forehand, Griest, & Wells, 1981; McMahon, Tiedemann, Forehand, & Griest, 1984; Patterson & Fleischman, 1979; Reppucci & Saunders, 1974; Sanders & James, 1983; Stuart, 1971; Stuart & Tripodi, 1973; Szykula & Fleischmann, 1980; Weathers & Liberman, 1975). Although the multiproblem family is surely not the sole cause of their children's behavior problems, the manner in which the family interacts (or fails to interact) with mental-health professionals, at the very least, perpetuates these problems.

By definition, multiproblem families are not distinguished by poverty, or single parenthood, or parental psychopathology, or by any other single structural or demographic or environmental feature. By definition, the multiproblem family is distinguished by an accumulation of long unresolved psychosocial problems. I suspect that the multiproblem family, so defined, is also distinguished by its singular inability to cope with the usual and unusual problems with which it (like many other families) is faced. In my opinion, a family accumulates multiple, unresolved problems not because of lower SES, or minority status, but because it lacks the skills to master the harsh world in which all (not just multiproblem) lower SES and minority families live. A family confronted with a harsh environment and bad luck yet equipped with very good communication skills (including information exchange, behavior management, and problem solving skills defined below) has a decent chance of avoiding downward mobility. A family confronted with the same harsh environment but seriously deficient in communication has little or no chance of avoiding permanent membership in the underclass. In short, I view communication skill as the external, observable manifestation of coping and the psychological salvation of families in high-risk environs. I believe that we will eventually demonstrate a dose-response relationship between communication skill and openness to change. As the family's communication skill increases, so does the group's permeability to change.

Maria provides a concrete illustration of the importance of communication skill. Maria is relatively good at the information-exchange component of communication (sending and receiving messages accurately). She knows how to get the information she needs and how to let people know when she is in trouble. This seems to be the key to her success with institutional bureaucracies. Single mothers who are completely unskilled at information exchange have no hope of coping with the demands of multiple bureaucracies (welfare, medical, legal) or of making use of the help they offer (no matter how limited). As a result, these women are often depressed and their families face an ever-increasing burden of chronic, unresolved problems (Blechman & Tryon, in press-b).

Problems. The definition of the multiproblem family offered earlier uses expert social consensus to nominate serious psychosocial problems such as psychopathology. These chronic unresolved problems appear to emerge in two ways. On the one hand, the communication deficits of multiproblem families appear to prevent them from routine recognition and informal resolution of small, malleable problems. For example, Maria's attempt to give Juanita her insulin injection provokes a temper tantrum which escalates into an argument and culminates in physical abuse. On the other hand, the communication deficits of multiproblem families appear to prevent them from recognizing and formally resolving large problems with outside help. For example, when Maria brings Juanita to the emergency room in diabetic ketoacidosis, she doesn't admit that Juanita hasn't been getting her injections regularly and so the advice she gets is of little help to her.

In the example of Maria, because I've applied the word problem to big and small concerns, and to circumstances about which outsiders may see things differently from Maria, a definition of the word problem is needed. A problem can be defined by its impact: A discriminable change in circumstances—biological, intrapersonal, interpersonal, societal—represents a problem when application of available skills and habits yields a less desirable outcome than usual. Cowan's quote (this volume) from Alice in Wonderland provides an apt illustration of this definition of "a problem."

> "Who are you?" said the Caterpillar. "I-I hardly know, Sir, just at present," Alice replied rather shyly. "At least I know who I was when I got up this morning, but I think I must have changed several times since then."

Alice's physical nature has changed several times since morning. Her habitual, automatic ways of recognizing who she is and identifying herself to strangers no longer works. And so she fails the caterpillar's mental-status exam. Alice's changed self is a problem for her only because she used to be able to recognize herself and tell others (her usual desirable outcome). Her changed self is a problem for the caterpillar, regardless of Alice's view of the situation, because all the other strangers he meets immediately answer his question (his usual desirable outcome).

This functional definition of a problem emphasizes the impact of changed circumstances (Alice's altered body) on usual outcomes (self-recognition, self-introduction to caterpillars) from multiple vantage points (Alice, the caterpillar). If Alice never could recognize herself, she would not consider her recent bodily alterations to be either a substantial change or a problem. If the caterpillar was universally shunned, he would not consider her failure to answer to be a problem. If Alice never could recognize herself, but the caterpillar was used to having his questions answered, the caterpillar and Alice might well disagree about the existence of a problem.

Problems in Multiproblem Families. A functional definition which substantiates the subjective and experiential nature of problems, suggests why multiproblem families (who are quite used to undesirable outcomes) so frequently collide with clinicians (who are used to desirable outcomes). Maria, who was beaten by her own parents, does the same with her own children when they fail to comply with her requests. The fact that the beating doesn't improve her children's compliance makes no difference. She has never seen parents who don't use physical punishment and whose children are compliant.

Child abuse is not a problem for her, but it is a problem for the many professionals who have tried to change the way she deals with her children. This difference in perspective about the problem, explains the struggle Maria frequently encounters when she talks with mental-health professionals. In answer to one clinician's question, "Why are you here?", she answered, "I don't know. Some lady told me I have to come." In answer to the question, "Is the problem that you need to work on your physical abuse of your children?", she replied, "Oh, I don't do anything different than was done to me. The only problem is, the workers are on my back."

Crises in Multiproblem Families. Members of multiproblem families voice ample dissatisfaction with the way things go in their lives. But their complaints seem better labeled as crises than as problems. I define a crisis as an event, or a series of events, that is unexpected by the crisis owner, and that is viewed by the crisis owner as unyielding to personal prediction or control. To the crisis owner, the crisis is a pure stroke of bad luck. Thus, Maria's initial dissatisfaction centers on the crisis of being reported to the authorities for child abuse and forced into treatment. Using this definition of crisis, multiproblem families are more accurately termed multicrisis families. Every family encounters unpredictable and uncontrollable crises (e.g., death of a family member in a plane crash). However, the multiproblem family views as crises, events that other families would view as resolvable or avoidable problems. (For example, hospitalization of a father who pulls a knife in a dispute with a landlord and stabs himself and the landlord.)

Solutions and Transitions. Cowan (this volume) proposed a functional definition of individual and family life transitions. For him, a life transition has occurred when people reorganize their world view, change problem-solving strategies, reorganize role arrangements, shift within-system relationships, and shift system-network relationships. I would add that Cowan's transition is a period during which a person grapples with a problem. The transition begins when the person recognizes that a problem exists and ends with that person's habitual, comfortable enactment of a solution for the problem. Thus, a transition is a time period during which a person uses words to portray a solution in the abstract and then enacts the abstract solution portrayal in concrete actions in real-life settings. Concrete actions required to enact solutions involve overt words and actions as well as covert thoughts and feelings.

No problem is ever solved solely through an abstract solution portrayal. The problem owner must live the solution to make it work. Even a solution portrayal involving reappraisal of a problem ("Every child has a temper tantrum once in a while. Sick children often have temper tantrums. A temper tantrum doesn't mean Juanita hates me. So I can ignore her tantrums.") must be followed by solution enactment (e.g., consistent ignoring of temper tantrums).

When Maria entered treatment she did not act or feel like a mother. Maria began her transition into the socially defined role of parent when she recognized that complaints about her parenting constituted a solvable problem not an unpredictable crisis. Later, she began to express an interest in learning how to manage her children's behavior without violence. Her transition was complete when she put into practice relevant behavior-management skills and developed more tolerance for her children's behavior. At this point, she acted and felt nurturant and motherly.

Solution Portrayal and Solution Enactment. The distinction between portrayal of a hypothetical solution and its behavioral enactment is essential for successful intervention, yet is ignored in most theories about behavior change. Experienced clinicians, whatever their orientation, know that there is a difference between abstract discussions of change and the real thing. Realizing that the solution plans most likely to be enacted are those that come from the patient's lips, experienced clinicians refuse to lecture or badger. Instead they facilitate patients' plans for their own solutions. They have often observed the struggles, self-doubt, and anger that are part and parcel of the transition process. Recognizing that the most important, yet most difficult, part of their job is to support patients in transition as they enact solutions, they refuse to lose hope or to become frustrated with slow progress. They realize that patients in transition are like women in labor for the first time. The patients do the painful, creative work, while the clinicians provide encouragement, instructions, and information about what is likely to happen next.

Theories about behavior change rarely reflect clinical insights about transitions. Instead, they tend to focus on solution plans at the expense of solution enactment. In like manner, inexperienced clinicians have little success with seemingly simple behavioral interventions because they assume that the intervention ends with a solution plan. A general tendency to ignore the importance of enactment of the solution during a sometimes lengthy transition or to be extremely impatient with the time and struggle required for successful transitions at the least reflects our ignorance about common features of transitional behavior.

Prerequisites for Successful Transitions. Cowan (this volume) has posed a number of unanswered questions about life transitions. To his list might be added these, "What are the behavioral stages common to all successful transitions?" "What is the best environmental predictor of a successful transition?" "What is the best organismic predictor of a successful transition?"

In my view, the behavioral stages common to all successful transitions are these: problem recognition, solution plan, and solution enactment. In my view, the best environmental predictor of a successful transition is availability of a confidant who has already made the transition successfully or observed the successful transition or both. In my view, the best organismic predictor of a successful transition is communication skill.

Normative Individual Transitions. Alice's rapidly growing body and her concomitant difficulties in self-recognition (reminiscent of the early adolescent experience) suggest a normative set of human problems. Normative individual problems occur with each discriminable change in a person's physical appearance, size, and motor capabilities. Entrance into puberty is an obvious example of a normative, individual problem. Rooted in changes in biological circumstances, these problems make available individual skills obsolete and require from the individual, passage through normative transitions, commonly called developmental stages. During these normative transitions, the individual struggles to acquire the interpersonal and intrapersonal skills their changing bodies demands.

Successful normative individual transitions require recognition of the problematic biological change and an environment which promotes the acquisition of skills needed for the transition. An individual developing in the context of a family system which encourages problem recognition, solution plan, and solution enactment is most likely to succeed with the transition. In such families, more experienced family members recognize the problematic change and provide relevant examples, feedback, instruction, and support. They are tolerant of the difficulties involved in solution enactment. Like experienced clinicians, they act as confidants for other family members in transition.

Normative Family Transitions. Normative family problems occur with each discriminable change in the family group's size, structure, and composition. Birth of a couple's first child is an obvious example of a normative, group problem. Rooted in interpersonal circumstances, these problems make available group skills obsolete and require from the group, passage through normative transitions or stages in the family life cycle. Successful normative group transitions require recognition of the problematic interpersonal change and an environment which promotes the acquisition of skills needed for the transition. A family embedded in a network of extended family and friends which encourages problem recognition and skill acquisition is most likely to succeed with the transition. In such networks, more experienced kin and friends occupy the confidant role, recognizing the problematic change and providing relevant examples, feedback, instruction, and support.

Normative and Nonnormative Problems. A normative problem is an inevitable waystation in the individual or family life cycle. For example, occasional husband-wife disputes about childrearing are a normative problem in couples with young children. A nonnormative problem is the result of failure to resolve a normative problem. For example, perpetual marital strife about childrearing issues in a couple married for 25 years is a nonnormative problem. No family avoids a stream of normative problems and an occasional nonnormative problem. The multi-problem family is distinguished by the sheer number and longevity of nonnormative problems.

The Rigidity of Multiproblem Families. By definition, the multiproblem family is burdened with chronic, unresolved, nonnormative problems because they have not progressed through successful transitions in response to either normative or nonnormative problems. These families get stuck at the waystations through which less troubled families pass briefly. The sociologist Oscar Lewis (1966) actually defines members of the underclass by their absence of transitions into normative social roles such as adolescent, spouse, and parent. Although at first glance multiproblem families appear chaotic and unpredictable, their infrequent engagement in transitions suggest a rigid, inflexible, and static system. Both Patterson (1979) and Gottman (1979) have described the predictably aversive patterns of interaction in unhappy families.

Why are multiproblem families so rigid? Why, even when they seek therapy do they appear to work so hard to resist change? Anderson and Stewart (1983) claim that "irrational as it may seem, resistance is universal." Following an integrative review of systems, structural, and strategic family therapy views of resistance (p. 1), they conclude that "the major sources [of resistance] seem to be a family's natural striving for stability and a family's equally natural, if sometimes irrational, fear of change" (p. 38).

Is resistance universal? In my work, I've found that many families adapt well, even without family therapy (Blechman & McEnroe, 1985). To me, the conclusion that resistance to change in multiproblem families is largely a product of habit and fear fails to recognize that the multiproblem family's communication-skill deficits make these families impervious to new information.

The barriers to change thrown up by communication deficits are (as Anderson and Stewart point out) explicit in the strategic communication theory of Bateson (Bateson, Jackson, Haley, & Weakland 1956) and implicit in the structural family therapy approach to Minuchin. According to Minuchin, "the therapist must make the family 'hear,' and this requires that his message go above the family threshold of deafness (Minuchin & Fishman, 1981, p. 116). Despite their recognition that communication deficits make multiproblem families closed to change, structural and strategic family therapies fail to specify how communication skills open effective families to change.

EFFECTIVE FAMILY COMMUNICATION

The interdependence of family members' thoughts, feelings, words, and actions, forged in ongoing communication, molds individuals into a psychological family. The communication process can be operationalized by focusing on the smallest, meaningful message units sent by one person to others in face-to-face interaction and by coding each message's verbal and nonverbal aspects. Jean Dumas and I (Dumas & Blechman, 1990) have developed the INTERACT/BLISS coding system using this approach.

The INTERACT/BLISS codes listed in Table 1 are clustered in respect to presumed skill. Some codes apparently indicate communication proficiency (e.g., facilitative listening with neutral affective valence), while other codes apparently indicate skill deficit (e.g., aggression with aversive affective valence).

TABLE 8.1
Communication Coding

The INTERACT/BLISS Coding System codes the verbal (content) and nonverbal (valence) aspects of each meaningful message in a face-to-face interaction. This table shows the content codes classified in respect to communication skill (present, absent) and impact (information exchange, behavior management, problem solving). Regardless of content code, any message with an aversive valence code (rather than a positive or neutral valence code) is considered skill deficient.

Impact	*Skillful*	*Skill Deficient*
Information Exchange		
	Facilitative Listening	Disruptive Listening
Behavior Management		
	Request Compliance Approval Affection Disapproval	Request-x Noncompliance Aggression
Problem Solving		
	Target Acceptance	Target-x Refusal

The codes are also clustered in respect to presumed impact on others. Some codes apparently promote (or inhibit) information exchange, behavior management, or problem solving.

To illustrate this perspective on communication, consider this excerpt from a telephone conversation between mother and 26-year-old daughter. Each message from mother to daughter and from daughter to mother typifies skillful communication, with the impact of information exchange. In this case, daughter affirms that mother understands her point of view.

> *Mother:* "What's up? You sound strange."
> *Daughter:* "I'm exhausted. I was up all night working on a report for my boss. I did a fabulous job and he didn't even bother to thank me."
> *Mother:* "Are you sure he saw it?"
> *Daughter:* "Oh, he saw it alright."
> *Mother:* "He sounds really insensitive."
> *Daughter:* "You got it. He sure is."

Communication Impact

In any episode of communication, one person's behavior always has some impact on a second person's behavior (Buck, 1984). Without impact there is no communication. Impact is the product of two kinds of communicative behavior: spontaneous and symbolic (Buck, 1984). Spontaneous communication behavior uses gestures, expressions, and words to convey the speaker's immediate concrete experience to a listener. Symbolic communication behavior uses words, gestures, and expressions to convey a speaker's abstract idea to a listener. (Buck's definition of symbolic communication is idiosyncratic. In common usage, symbolic communication refers to transmission of information via medium rather than via message.)

Spontaneous communication can take place without symbolic communication, but symbolic communication is always accompanied by some degree of spontaneous communication. The two types of communication are not necessarily congruent (Buck, 1984).

Together, spontaneous and symbolic communication behavior have three kinds of impact: sending a message, influencing behavior, and solving a problem (Blechman, 1990). The three types of impact can be envisioned as tiers in a pyramid with information exchange at the base. First-tier communication episodes involve information exchange, in which one person sends a message about personal experience to another person. ("Juanita, isn't it time for your shot?" "Oh ma, I guess so.") In second-tier communication episodes, one person sends a message and influences another's behavior. ("Well then, meet me in the bathroom right away." "O.K. ma.") In third-tier communication episodes, two (or more) people exchange information, influence each other's behavior, and progress toward solving a shared problem. ("Juanita, what do you think about giving yourself the shot this time, the way the nurse showed you?" "O.K., ma, I'll try if you'll rub my back afterwards.")

The three communication tiers overlap sightly, since behavior cannot be influenced without considerable information exchange. Nor can problems be solved without considerable information exchange and behavior management. The largest of the three communication tiers is information exchange, since every communication episode must have this impact. The smallest of the three communication tiers is problem solving, since few communication episodes have this impact.

The Match of Impact and Intent. In any episode of effective communication, the impact of people's behavior matches their intentions. In first-tier communication, the receiver gets the message the sender intended. In second-tier communication, the sender influences the receiver's behavior in the intended direction. In third-tier communication, sender and receiver address a mutually defined problem in a mutually agreeable manner. Gottman (1979) devised the "talk table" as a way of assessing the fit between impact and intent. Using the talk table, spouses signal each other and observers about the intention of messages they send and about the impact of messages they receive. In the course of normal conversation, people let each other know about the fit between impact and intent. In effective communication, family members check out the impact of the messages they send ("How do you feel about what I just said?") and about the intent of messages they have just received ("Tell me more about what you mean.")

The Effect of Affect. All communication between people is emotional so long as they are in physical contact, either face to face or talking on the telephone. Each person is continuously responding to their own immediate experience, reading their experience, and spontaneously reading-out this experience to the other (Buck, 1984). (A letter would not provide for this spontaneous read-out of one's own experience to the other.) Thus spontaneous communication of affect is ever present, even when it is accompanied by symbolic communication. Spontaneous communication of affect is at times accomplished in words, but it is continuously conveyed nonverbally by facial expression, gesture, and tone of voice (Izard, 1977). For this reason it is the nonverbal channel of communication which is generally regarded as the more clinically significant. The nonverbal channel sets the emotional tone of an interaction (Gottman, 1979). The nonverbal channel of communication discriminates best between distressed and non-distressed married couples (Birchler, 1972; Vincent, 1972; Gottman, 1979; Navran, 1967; Revenstorf et al., 1980; Schaap & Jansen-Nawas, 1987). Among friends, it is the nonverbal channel that determines perceptions of openness (Montgomery, 1981, 1984).

The nonverbal channel of communication is the primary route for spontaneous metamessages about feelings. Although some metamessages (messages about messages) come in words, the verbal channel is the primary route for symbolic messages about ideas. The metamessage reveals the speaker's spontaneous feelings about the symbolic message and about the relationship with the listener. Sometimes the spontaneous message is at variance with the symbolic message.

Spontaneous messages are difficult to read when they clash with symbolic messages. However, when information exchange is effective, family members' spontaneous and symbolic messages are sufficiently congruent to achieve the impact they intend.

Effective information exchange is a reciprocal process in which family members skillfully send spontaneous and symbolic messages to match their intended impact and receive messages as they were intended. These family members know how to understand and be understood by each other (e.g., Kahn, 1970). When family members consistently engage in effective information exchange they develop a shared intimate understanding of the innermost subjective aspects of each other's being (Chelune, Robison, & Kommor, 1984). As a result, each feels understood, validated, and cared for (Reis & Shaver, 1988).

Effective Communication and Successful Transitions

Effective communication, at each level of impact, contributes to successful transitions in response to normative and nonnormative problems. The biggest contribution is made by effective information exchange which enables the problem owner to engage in problem recognition, solution plan, and problem reappraisal. In this context, enabling has a purely positive connotation as in Hauser's pursuit of how families enable adolescents' achievement of higher levels of ego development (e.g., Hauser et al., 1987). Information exchange is, at the outset, an interpersonal (not intrapersonal) process engaged in by the problem owner with family, friends, or therapist. Together with these confidants, the problem owner thinks out loud about relevant features of the problem, about ways to confront the problem, and takes a different (more tolerant) view of the problem. After considerable experience with interpersonal information exchange, the problem owner may engage in an intrapersonal self-dialogue mulling over the problem, potential solutions, and alternative visions of the problem.

If information exchange enables the problem owner to embark on a transition in response to normative and nonnormative problems, behavior management permits the problem owner to complete this transition successfully. Effective behavior management enables the problem owner to engage in solution enactment, putting into action the skills envisioned during solution planning. Behavior management is, at the outset, an interpersonal process engaged in by the problem owner with family, friends, or therapist. Under the influence of these confidants, the problem owner avoids unskillful, pessimistic, intolerant behavior and begins to try out more skillful, optimistic, and tolerant behavior. Thus at the outset, effective confidants use component behavior management skills (instruction, praise, and selective inattention to unskillful, pessimistic behavior) to support the problem owner through the struggles of transition. After considerable experience with interpersonal behavior management, the problem owner may engage in a self-directed, intrapersonal stint of self-control trying out new skills, observing the outcome, and planning for future skill enactment.

Interpersonal Problem Solving. While information exchange and behavior management permit the problem owner to move successfully through the stages of a transition, interpersonal problem solving enables the problem owner to put into words abstract conclusions about this process before, during, and after the transition has been completed in the context of an intimate relationship. Interpersonal problem solving involves reciprocated information exchange and behavior management regarding a mutual problem and resides in intimate interaction not in individual behavior. In this relationship, both participants are problem owners. The mutual problem can combine one person's interest in mastering a personal deficiency (dealing with an unsatisfactory parent-child relationship) and the other person's desire to be of help. In contrast, in intrapersonal problem solving, a solitary individual engages in out-loud or covert intrapersonal problem solving. Another person's presence has no impact on this process.

Successful interpersonal problem solving does not take place in one-shot planning of a solution in discussion with a confidant. Instead, it takes place over repeated interactions during which participants move gradually from solution planning, to attempts at solution enactment, to evaluations of solution enactment, to refinement of solution enactment. The process ends only when both participants are confident in the success of solution enactment.

Successful interpersonal problem solving can take place in the context of an intimate two-way relationship between peers or marital partners or parents and adolescents or in the context of an intimate one-way relationship between patient and psychotherapist or parent and young child. In a two-way relationship, participants repeatedly make their own transitions as each responds to new problems. Participants must be relatively equally skilled at information exchange and behavior management so that they can engage in reciprocated problem solving addressing shared problems. In a one-way relationship, the focal transitions are those made by the child or patient. The parent or therapist uses information exchange and behavior management skills to enable the child or patient to make successful transitions. In both one-way and two-way relationships, the confidant provides information and support that would be unavailable in solitary, intrapersonal problem solving.

Ineffective Communication and the Family Climate

If effective communication enables families to cope with normative and avoid nonnormative problems, ineffective communication breeds a stressful, violent climate which obstructs marital satisfaction and socialization of children.

Stress. Information exchange, during which a speaker describes personal feelings and experiences to a listener who shows interest and sympathy without evaluation, is an emotionally soothing process. Reciprocal information exchange, during which two people count on each other as listeners, is the matrix of intimacy, marital satisfaction, and successful socialization of children (Blechman & Tryon, in press-a). Information exchange seems to buffer marital partners against the stresses of the outside world, warding off wives' depression and anxiety and husbands' substance abuse.

In multiproblem families, the absence of skillful information exchange means that bad feelings are generated when members fail to listen nonjudgmentally to one another's point of view, and are heightened when members actively criticize each other (Gottman, 1979). The stressful climate created in this way has been described as "expressed emotion" by Vaughan and Leff (1976) and shown to be associated with a propensity for relapse in previously hospitalized schizophrenic and depressed family members. Women in a marriage lacking in skillful information exchange would seem to be at higher risk for depression than their husbands who tend to have more sources of interpersonal gratifications away from home, particularly at work (Brown & Harris, 1978). Children reared in a family devoid of soothing interpersonal information exchange have little chance to progress to self-soothing interpersonal information exchange in which the child attends to and moderates endogenous negative arousal. The result may be chronic overactivity and an accompanying inability to cope with situational demands.

Violence. Information exchange and behavior management permit family members to understand each other's different perspectives and accommodate to each other's different needs. In the effective family, husbands and wives, parents and children, gain the capacity to manage each other's behavior through information exchange. In the multiproblem family, however, skillful information exchange and behavior management are rare. Since family members rarely hear or comply with each other's requests, they often resort to verbal threats and physical violence to get what they want. Patterson's coercion hypothesis describes how verbal demands, threats, and criticism snowball in unhappy interactions between family members, teaching them to use physical aggression and antisocial behavior inside and outside the family (Patterson, 1979).

Socialization of Children. If information exchange and behavior management are the prerequisites for an intimate, tranquil family climate, problem solving is the prerequisite for successful socialization of children. In my view, problem solving is an outgrowth of prolonged, reciprocal information exchange and behavior management.

Parents in multiproblem families who are unskilled at information exchange, behavior management, and problem solving are ill-prepared to learn or teach the rules governing competent behavior in the surrounding culture (Bandura & Walters, 1963; Hudson & Blane, 1985; Patterson, 1979). Instead of words, these parents often use physical manipulation to influence children's behavior (Aragona & Eyberg, 1981). At times, this results in physical and sexual abuse (Straus, 1983).

Although these parents desperately want to manage their children's behavior successfully, their maladroitness at information exchange obstructs behavior management of children by parents and of parents by outsiders. Parents who don't listen will not be susceptible to anyone's spoken rules, instructions, requests, or to the expert opinions of society at large. Nor will these parents derive any of the usual benefits of a social-support network of friends and family. Such socially insular parents are likely to evidence psychopathology and antisocial behavior and to rear similarly deviant children (Dumas & Wahler, 1985).

COMMUNICATION SKILLS FOR MULTIPROBLEM FAMILIES

On the assumption that multiproblem families, above all else, will benefit from improving their communication skills, my colleagues and I have been developing and evaluating methods of clinical intervention. Earlier, I developed a manualized, operant approach to Family Skills Training (FST) (Blechman, 1985). FST includes modules applicable to the broad range of child presenting behavior problems and psychiatric diagnoses. Although I recognized the importance of communication within the family and between the family and the therapist, I emphasized behavior management and problem solving at the expense of information exchange. In part, that was because I had not yet developed a way of specifying and measuring what I call information exchange and what Patterson calls "soft clinical skills" (Personal Correspondence, G. Patterson, 1987).

Development with Jean Dumas of the INTERACT/BLISS coding system (Dumas & Blechman, 1990), specified information exchange so well that I was able to use the codes in the supervision of therapists engaged in Family Skills Training. My current work specifies how the clinician uses information exchange as the medium for delivery of Family Skills Training to multi-problem families of troubled children and adolescents (Blechman, Tryon, Ruff, & McEnroe, 1989; Blechman, Tryon, McEnroe, & Ruff, 1989; Dumas, Blechman, & Prinz, in press).

In this concluding section, I omit a detailed description of the formal aspects of Family Skills Training, which can be found elsewhere (e.g., Blechman, 1985). Instead, I describe how effective therapist communication provides an informal medium for delivery of the formal aspects of FST.

Effective Communication as the Medium for Behavioral Intervention

The presumption that effective communication is a necessary medium for delivery of any behavioral intervention to a multiproblem family differs from the radical behaviorist approach to parent training exemplified by the Hanff model (cf. Dangel & Polster, 1984). Adherents of this approach presumed that given appropriate therapist-delivered antecedents (e.g., clear instructions and illustrative models) and consequences (e.g., praise) all parents would readily enact behavioral principles, rearranging antecedents and consequences for child target behavior with predictably benign results. However, 2 decades of research have failed to support the presumption that all parents are equally prepared to profit from parent training. All parents are not equally receptive to parent training; parent demographics do predict receptivity (e.g., Blechman, Budd, et al., 1981). The parents least receptive are those who resemble heads of multiproblem families.

The communication deficits of multiproblem families make it impossible for them to respond as radical behaviorists expected. Before these parents can solve their family's problems through better contingency management they must improve their information-exchange skills. And, even relatively well-functioning families do not benefit from an intervention that emphasizes behavior management and problem solving at the expense of information exchange.

Early Socialization Requires Information Exchange and Behavior Management Skills. When the rule a child must learn is clear, consistent, and enduring, and when it is safe for a child to experience all the natural consequences of the rule, the caretaker need only be skilled at behavior management. Without encountering major disasters, a child can deviate from the simple rule: "When bladder is full, use the toilet." Without speaking, parents can teach: "If you wet your bed, the buzzer will wake you up. If your bed is dry in the morning, pancakes for breakfast."

In fact, from early on, many of the rules young children must learn are complex by virtue of adverse natural consequences. Therefore, successful early socialization requires a combination of skillful information exchange and behavior management. As the speaker in information exchange, the parent teaches the consequences of touching fire without getting burned. As the listener in information exchange, the parent learns what words to use to teach the rule "Look both ways before crossing a street."

Later Socialization Requires Information Exchange and Behavior Management Skills. The rules governing behavior in modern society are neither widely known, true, consistent, or invariant. Most of the rules that older children must learn are complex and problematic by virtue of unclarity, inconsistency, evanescence, and lethal consequences. Therefore, successful socialization from middle childhood through late adolescence requires family problem solving in which parents and children reciprocate information exchange and behavior management regarding shared problems. Through repeated immersion in family problem solving, adolescents learn to fulfill their own needs within the constraints of society, they learn self-care, self-control, and sophisticated moral judgment.

Multiproblem Families Can't Solve Problem Without Information Exchange. In multiproblem families, information exchange is not reciprocal. Family members simply don't listen to what each other has to say. They interrupt, or refuse the validity of each other's statements. In addition, family members don't engage in compelling self-disclosure. They wander off the topic and criticize others in a way that provokes disputes. In multiproblem families, behavior management is not reciprocated. Family members don't answer each other's questions, don't respond to each other's requests, don't attend to each other's statements. In these families, a shared problem (e.g., each family member's craving for affection from the others) is not recognized. In this context, interpersonal problem solving is impossible.

Operant-interpersonal treatment strategies have correctly emphasized the improvement of family problem solving as a route to prevention and amelioration of individual psychopathology (via better contingency management) but have mistakenly ignored the family's need to acquire and use information exchange and behavior management skills in preparation for group problem solving. A therapist who imposes a contingency contract on a family (and gives lip service to family problem solving by asking each member to sign) is courting disaster as several studies show (Stuart, 1971; Stuart & Tripodi, 1973; Weathers & Liberman, 1975).

Effective Communication During Family Skills Training

The multiproblem family begins Family Skills Training confused about the reason for the referral, skeptical about the severity of the problem, and convinced that the therapist can be of little help. The therapist acts as confidant to all family members using information-exchange skills to avoid otherwise predictable outcomes: angry exchanges with the therapist, missed appointments, poor adherence to therapist recommendations, and premature termination of treatment.

Enabling the Family's Transition. The therapist, acting as confidant to a multiproblem family, envisions the long, treacherous journey ahead and uses information-exchange skills to insure that family and therapist stay the course. In the early stage of treatment, when most multiproblem families drop out, the therapist uses information exchange to encourage problem recognition. Problem recognition applies not only to the presenting problem (e.g., poor school achievement) but also to specific, concrete, subproblems (e.g., child has no set bedtime and is always sleepy at school). Problem recognition applies not only to the problem as the parent sees it (e.g., "My boy is lazy."), but also as the child sees it (e.g., "My mother thinks I'm dumb."), and as outsiders see it (e.g., the chaos at home interferes with readiness for learning at school). Problem recognition, therefore, is an ongoing process that is amplified as treatment progresses. Evidence of problem recognition comes each time parents indicate that a problem is undesirable and changeworthy and that it is amenable to their control. Until parents show some evidence of problem recognition, the therapist blocks attempts at solution planning or enactment.

Once the parents show some evidence of problem recognition, the therapist uses information exchange to stimulate solution planning. In Family Skills Training, a series of modules details the procedures for solution planning and solution enactment relevant to a comprehensive set of subproblems associated with the broad range of child psychiatric disorders and presenting problems. The therapist works through these modules one at a time, each time using information exchange to stimulate parents' planning and enactment of their own solutions. Work continues on a module until solution enactment is evidently successful.

Recognizing that problem recognition will become more complete as treatment progresses, as therapists work on a particular module they are constantly alert to the need to interrupt solution planning and enactment and to briefly (usually just for a few minutes) focus on problem recognition.

Therapist Skills. The components of *information exchange* are communication-skill codes we call facilitative listening and statement (see Table 8.1). Engaging in facilitative listening, the therapist listens attentively, asks relevant questions, summarizes and paraphrases. In this way, the therapist facilitates the patient's self-disclosing statements. ("So what you are saying is that you want to know how serious Juanita's problem at school really is?" "Did I get that right?") Engaging in statement, the therapist describes goals and procedures for the present and future sessions. (For example, "Today, I plan to give you feedback about the tests you all took last week.") The therapist uses information exchange codes to accomplish the purpose of the current session and to address spoken and initially unspoken questions about treatment.

The components of *behavior management* are the communication-skill codes: request, compliance, approval, affection, and disapproval (Table 8.1). Engaging in behavior management, the therapist insures that during the session, family members wait their turn to speak, avoid physical violence, ignore other family members' interruptions and inappropriate behavior, praise other family members' appropriate and desirable behavior, and comply with the therapist's requests. (For example, "Remember that you agreed to ignore Dolores when she interrupts. Look at me now and keep talking to me even if she interrupts. That's good. Keep it up.")

First Goal: Accomplishing the Formal Purpose of the Session. The therapist's first and foremost goal is to accomplish the session's formal goal (e.g., working on the temper tantrum module). The therapist begins the session by explaining the session's formal goal and procedures (using questions to insure that all family members understand both) and ends the session by summarizing (with the family's help) what happened during the session. Formal goals and procedures are described elsewhere (Blechman, 1985).

Second Goal: Promoting Information Exchange. The therapist's second goal is to encourage information exchange, addressing spoken and unspoken questions relevant to achievement of the session's formal goal. The therapist addresses these questions, most often, by leading family members into clarifying and then answering their questions themselves. When, as often happens, a question asked in a previous session is asked again, the therapist will lead family members into recalling how they answered their own questions the last time and into embellishing on their own earlier answers. The therapist's job is to do this with good humor and without a trace of condescension or irritation.

The therapist engages in information exchange with each family member and each combination of family members in the presence of the entire group. This often requires the therapist to resist pressures from family members to listen to their side of the story in private. Information exchange with the entire family present is a necessity because misunderstandings so easily occur in multiproblem families.

Each time the therapist encounters evidence of confusion, skepticism, or pessimism, the therapist uses facilitative listening (particularly questions followed by silent attentiveness), to encourage family members to describe their state of mind and to check out understanding of their self-disclosing statements. Next, the therapist uses facilitative listening (particularly summary statements combined with questions) to insure that family members realize that the therapist is interested in how they feel and what they think. Third, the therapist uses facilitative listening (particularly leading questions) in combination with statements (indicating what the therapist plans to do) to teach the family (and insure the family understands) what the therapist does and why it is likely to be of help. The therapist relies as much as possible on questions so that family members quickly find themselves stating how the therapeutic process works and why it is worth their while to help it work. In this way, the therapist enables the family to clarify their own confusion, overcome their own skepticism, and provide their own optimistic rationale for full participation in treatment.

Spoken questions include queries about why the parents have to come to the treatment sessions (since the child is the one with the problems), queries about the severity of pathology of other family members (confirming that they are the immutable source of the problem), and statements of disapproval about treatment progress (despite the fact that pretreatment assessment is the current session goal). In response to spoken questions about treatment, the therapist restates the question (or converts the comment into a question), asks a question to establish comprehension, and asks a question to encourage family members to answer the initial question in a manner that will promote treatment participation. All this is done in a pleasant, nonaccusatory manner. A smile, a warm but very audible tone of voice, relaxed but confident posture and avoidance of hand gestures, help therapists be direct and pleasant at the same time. For example, these questions might be asked with ample opportunity for response in between. "Are you asking if your son was thrown out of kindergarten just because of normal boyish behavior?" "Is that the question?" "What's your opinion?" "Let's see, is it normal for a 4-year-old boy to destroy everything in sight if he isn't restrained?" "Well, if it isn't normal, is it worth doing something about?" "Are you sure you're not just wasting your time focusing on a trivial matter?"

Unspoken questions include all the reluctant, unmotivated behavior through which members of multiproblem families express their skepticism, confusion, and pessimism. These unspoken questions may not be intentional but they do obstruct accomplishment of the session's formal goal. For example, a father smiles as his son screams and throws toys around and quietly refuses to help his wife put the boy in time out. A mother's constant crises prevent her from coming to her appointments. A grandmother sends her adopted schizophrenic grandson to the appointment by taxi and can't understand why her presence is important. A mother spends the entire session castigating her son until she provokes an outburst that she blames on the therapist. Parents allow their son to attack each of them with his fists and with dangerous toys. Ignoring the therapist's question, a mother nurses her infant son while berating her adolescent son.

In response to unspoken questions, the therapist uncritically describes the behavior, asks a question to insure agreement about the behavior, asks a question about the impact of the behavior on the session, and asks a question about the intended impact of behavior. For example, "Let's see, your son just interrupted us and you began talking to him." "Did you see yourself doing that, talking to him when he interrupted?" "How will talking to your son each time he interrupts influence the work we do in this session?" "Will it speed up our work or slow it down?" "Is it your intention that we go slow?" "If you want us to make fast progress, what would be a good thing to do when your son interrupts?"

The final question asked in response to unspoken questions move in the direction of behavior management, setting up a mutually agreed upon rule for coping with behavior that might otherwise make treatment impossible.

Leading Questions. In response to spoken and unspoken questions, the therapist is careful to avoid mind reading or imposing a question on the group that they don't intend. The therapist is also careful to avoid answering these questions with a lecture or forcing family members to make guilty or unflattering confessions. The therapist does not ask, "Why do you always pay attention to your son when he interrupts?" "What is your reason for missing so many appointments?" "Do you realize how rude you appear when you ignore my questions and talk to your wife?" "How do you think your mother feels when you talk back to her?" The therapist does not badger the patient, rapidly firing tough questions that are demeaning or confusing.

The therapist does ask leading questions designed to elicit statements related to problem recognition, solution planning, and solution enactment. The questions are phrased so that the patient can understand them and can give the desired response. The therapist provides the patient with ample time to respond and praise for response, even for a fractional response. Instead of the questions just listed, the therapist might ask these. "What would be a wise thing to do when your son interrupts us? Pay attention or ignore him?" "What can I do that will help you keep the appointments you make?" "How do you think I'll feel if you do your best to answer my questions and tell me when you don't understand?" "What would be a smart thing to do when your mother says something irritating? Answer back or say nothing?"

The therapist often conducts an entire conversation with leading questions, as in this example. "Your mother told you your son should be hospitalized?" (Yes.) "Do you want to know if what we do here will make your son better?" (Yes.) "Should we talk about that now?" (Yes.) "So what do you think? How could what we do here be of help to you?" (It could teach me to not worry so much about him. I can't stop worrying.) "So if this treatment is going to work, its going to have help you worry less, is that right?" (Yes.) "Could it also be that your worries could get in the way of treatment. For example, you could get so worried that you'd lose confidence in me and get angry when I ask you to do something new. Could that happen?" (Yes. That's what happened last time I was in therapy.) "So what can you tell me about so that together we can make treatment succeed?" (I can tell you my worries.) "Which worries in particular will be important to tell me?" (My worries that you don't know what to do for me or that you don't care about me.) "Are you willing to tell me when you worry that I can't help you?" (Yes.) "How will I know if you are worried but forget to tell me." (Well, I might cancel an appointment and give you an excuse.) "What should I do then?" (Could you ask me if I'm worried?).

Third Goal: Promoting In-session Behavior Management. The therapist's third goal is to insure accomplishment of the session's first two goals (its formal purpose and information exchange) by promoting successful behavior management in the session. From the first moment that therapist and family are together, the therapist works on this goal using a combination of information exchange and behavior management skills to insure that family members don't interrupt each other, don't engage in physical or verbal abuse of each other, ignore each other's inappropriate behavior, approve of each other's desirable behavior, and comply with the therapist's requests.

Informal behavior management is exemplified by this exchange between Maria and a therapist. The session's formal purpose concerns the Sunday Box module for messiness. In this module, the parent learns to stop nagging or punishing children for messiness and instead, once a day, to silently lock away toys and belongings that are left around the house. The parent returns these items on Sunday without discussion. Items put in the Sunday Box for 2 weeks in a row are returned as Christmas presents next year. In this module, children learn to take responsibility for their belongings without repeated reminders.

Maria's family has passed the pretest and posttest in-session role plays for this module and Maria was discussing her use of the Sunday Box at home. Juanita and Dolores were playing together on the floor. The therapist asked: "So, how do you feel about your progress with the Sunday Box." (Real good. I don't blow up.) "What about the girls, are you happy with how they are doing?" (Yeah.) "Have you told them?" (No.) "Would you tell them now?" ([Mumbles. Eyes averted.] You guys did o.k.) "Could you say that again? This time, use the girls' names, look at them, smile, and tell them exactly what they did that you like." (Dolores, Juanita, I liked that you picked your stuff up this week.) "Good job. You did just what I asked." "What did you do?" (Smiled. Looked at them, Said what I like.) "How about some more practice at praising good behavior. What do you think?" (Yeah, nobody ever did that for me. Just the belt for me.) "You like it when I praise you?" (Sure.) "How does it make you feel?" (Like I'm a good kind of person.) "So would praise be good for your girls?" (I guess.) "Why would praise be good for them?" (Make them feel good about themselves?) "You want that, for them to feel good about themselves?" (Sure.) "Could you find something good that Juanita is doing now and praise her?" (Juanita, you're making a funny picture. Hey, it makes me smile.)

Summary. Normative individual and family problems can be resolved by a transitional process that begins with problem recognition and solution planning and ends after prolonged, viable comfortable solution enactment. Successful transitions require communication skill (at information exchange and behavior management) and a supportive environment composed of family, friends, and experts experienced with similar transitions. In the context of these supportive, intimate relationships, interpersonal problem solving allows participants to experiment safely with problem recognition, solution planning, and solution enactment.

Multiproblem families are distinguished by a deficit in communication skills and the absence of a supportive environment. Skill deficits and a nonsupportive environment conspire to obstruct successful coping with normative problems and engender a host of unresolved nonnormative problems. Under these conditions, family members do not move into normative social roles of adolescent, spouse, and parent. Instead, they suffer from a stressful, violent family atmosphere that hinders marital satisfaction and childrearing. In Family Skills Training, the therapist delivers the formal aspects of training through the medium of effective communication. Therapist-prompted information exchange and behavior management enables parents to move repeatedly from problem recognition to solution planning and enactment. In this way, the therapist removes the usual impediments to successful treatment of multiproblem families.

ACKNOWLEDGMENTS

I thank Tom Wills, Jerry Patterson, and Phil Cowan for their comments on this chapter, Allen Norin and Stuart Hauser for their discussion with me of ideas considered in this chapter. Portions of this chapter were presented at the NIMH Family Research Consortium's Summer Institute, Santa Fe, NM, June, 1987. The case examples in this chapter have been altered to preserve clients' anonymity. Segments of interaction cited within quotation marks are not exact quotes but instead close approximations. Preparation of this chapter was supported in part by NIMH grant DK36519 to the author.

Address correspondence to E. A. Blechman, Dept. of Psychology, Muenzinger Bldg., University of Colorado at Boulder, Boulder, CO 80309-0345.

REFERENCES

Anderson, C. M., & Stewart, S. (1983). *Mastering Resistance: A Practical Guide to Family Therapy*. New York: Guilford.

Aragona, J. A., & Eyberg, S. M. (1981). Neglected children: Mothers' report of child behavior problems and observed verbal behavior. *Child Development, 52,* 596–602.

Bandura, A., & Walters, R. H. (1963). *The social learning of deviant behavior: A behavioristic approach to socialization.* New York: Holt, Rinehart, & Winston.

Bateson, G., Jackson, D., Haley, J., & Weakland, J. (1956). Toward a theory of schizophrenia. *Behavioral Science, 1,* 251–264.

Belsky, J. (1981). Early human experiences: A family perspective. *Developmental Psychology, 17*(1), 3–23.

Bernal, M. E., Klinnert, M. D., & Schultz, L. A. (1980). Outcome evaluation of behavioral parent training and client-centered patient counseling for children with conduct problems. *Journal of Applied Behavior Analysis, 13,* 677–691.

Bijou, S. W. (1984). Parent training: Actualizing the critical conditions of early childhood development. In R. F. Dangel & R. A. Polster (Eds.), *Parent Training: Foundations of research and Practice*. New York: Guilford Press.

Birchler, G. R. (1972). *Differential patterns of instrumental affilitative behavior as a function of degree of marital distress and level of intimacy*. Unpublished doctoral dissertation. Department of Psychology, University of Oregon.

Blechman, E. A. (1982). Are children with one parent at psychological risk?: A methodological review. *Journal of Marriage and the Family, 44,* 179–195.

Blechman, E. A. (1985). *Solving child behavior problems at home and at school*. Champaign, IL: Research Press.

Blechman, E. A. (1990). A new look at emotions and the family: A model of effective family communication. In Blechman, E. A. (Ed.), *Emotions and the family: For better or for worse.* New York: Lawrence Erlbaum Associates.

Blechman, E. A., Berberian, R. M., & Thompson, W. D. (1977). How well does number of parents explain unique variance in self-reported drug use? *Journal of Consulting and Clinical Psychology, 45,* 1182–1183.

Blechman, E. A., Budd, K. S., Christopherson, E. R., Szykula, S., Wahler, R., Embry, L. H., Kogan, K., O'Leary, K. D., & Riner, L. S. (1981). Engagement in behavioral family therapy. *Behavior Therapy, 12,* 461–472.

Blechman, E. A., & Manning, M. (1976). A reward-cost analysis of the single parent family. In E. J. Mash, L. A. Hamerlynck, & L. C. Handy (Eds.), *Behavior modification and families I. Theory and research.* New York: Brunner/Mazel.

Blechman, E. A., & McEnroe, M. J. (1985). Effective family problem solving. *Child Development, 56,* 429–437.

Blechman, E. A., & Tryon, A. S. (in press-a). Familial origins of affective competence and depression. In K. Schlesinger & B. Bloom (Eds.), *Boulder Symposium on Clinical Psychology: Depression.* New York: Lawrence Erlbaum Associates.

Blechman, E. A., & Tryon, A. S. (In press-b). Inner-City Families: Competence, Depression, and Communication. *Journal of Clinical Child Psychology.*

Blechman, E. A., Tryon, A., McEnroe, M. J., & Ruff, M. H. (1989). Behavioral approaches to psychological assessment: A comprehensive strategy for the measurement of family interaction. In M. M. Katz & S. Wetzler (Eds.), *Contemporary approaches to psychological assessment.* New York: Brunner/Mazel.

Blechman, E. A., Tryon, A., Ruff, M. H., & McEnroe, M. J. (1989). Family skills training and childhood depression. In C. E. Schaefer (Ed.), *Parents as co-therapists for children's behavior problems.* New York: Wiley.

Bond, C. R., & McMahon, R. J. (1984). Relationships between marital distress and child behavior problems, maternal personal adjustment, and maternal parenting behaviors. *Journal of Abnormal Psychology, 93,* 348–351.

Breitmayer, B. J., & Ramey, C. T. (1986). Biological nonoptimality and quality of postnatal environment as codeterminants of intellectual development. *Child Development, 57,* 1151–1165.

Brown, G. W., & Harris, T. D. (1978). *Social origins of depression: A study of psychiatric disorder in women.* New York: Free Press.

Buck, R. (1984). *The communication of emotion.* New York: Guilford.

Chelune, G. J., Robison, J. T., Kommor, M. J. (1984). A cognitive interactional model of intimate relationships. In V. J. Derlega (Ed.), *Communication, intimacy, and close relationships.* New York: Academic Press.

Christensen, A., Phillips, S., Glasgow, R. E., & Johnson, S. M. (1983). Parental characteristics and interactional dysfunction in families with child behavior problems: A preliminary investigation. *Journal of Abnormal Child Psychiatry, 11,* 153–166.

Dangel, R. F., & Polster, R. A. (1984). *Parent training: Foundation of research and practice.* New York: Guilford Press.

Dumas, J. E., & Blechman, E. A. (1990). INTERACT/BLISS: A computer coding system to assess small group communication. Unpublished ms., University of Montreal.

Dumas, J. E., Blechman, E. A., & Prinz, R. J. (In press). Helping families with aggressive children and adolescents change. In R. DeV. Peters & R. McMahon (Eds.), *Aggression and violence throughout the life span.* Proceedings of the Twenty-Second Banff International Conference on Behavioral Sciences.

Dumas, J. E., & Wahler, R. G. (1985). Indiscriminate mothering as a contextual factor in aggressive-oppositional child behavior: "Damned if you do and damned if you don't." *Journal of Abnormal Child Psychology, 13,* 1–17.

Emery, R. E. (1982). Interparental conflict of discord and divorce. *Psychological Bulletin, 92,* 310–330.

Emery, R. E., Weintraub, S., & Neale, J. M. (1982). Effects of marital discord on the school behavior of children with schizophrenic, affectively disordered, and normal parents. *Journal of Abnormal Child Psychology, 10,* 215–228.

Fleishmann, M. J., & Szykula, S. A. (1981). A community setting replication of a social learning treatment for aggressive children. *Behavior Therapy, 12,* 115–122.

Forehand, R., Griest, D. L., Wells, K., & McMahon, R. J. (1982). Side effects of parent counseling on marital satisfaction. *Journal of Counseling Psychology, 29,* 104–107.

Forehand, R., Middlebrook, J., Rogers, T., & Steffe, M. (1983). Dropping out of parent training. *Behavior Research and Therapy, 21,* 663–668.

Forehand, R. E., & Wells, K. C. (1977). Teachers and parents: Where have all the "good" contingency managers gone? *Behavior Therapy, 8,* 1010.

Ghodsian, M., Zajicek, E., & Wolkind, S. (1984). A longitudinal study of maternal depression and child behavior problems. *Journal of Child Psychology and Psychiatry, 25,* 91–109.

Gottman, J. M. (1979). *Marital Interaction.* New York: Academic Press.

Griest, D. L., & Forehand, R. (1982). How can I get any parent training done with all these other problems going on?: The role of family variables in child behavior therapy. *Child and Family Behavior Therapy, 4*(1), 73–80.

Hargis, K. R., & Blechman, E. A. (1979). Social class and training of parents as behavior change agents. *Child Behavior Therapy, 1,* 69–74.

Harris, S. L. (1986). A family systems approach to behavioral training with parents of autistic children. *Child and Family Behavior Therapy, 4*(1), 21–35.

Hauser, S. T., Houlihan, J., Powers, S. I., Jacobson, A. M., Noam, G., Weiss-Perry, B., & Follansbee, D. (1987). Interaction sequences in families of psychiatrically hospitalized and nonpatient adolescents. *Psychiatry, 50,* 308–319.

Holahan, C. J., & Moos, R. H. (1987). Risk, resistance, and psychological distress: A longitudinal analysis with adults and children. *Journal of Abnormal Psychology, 96,* 3–13.

Horne, A. M., & Van Dyke, B. (1983). Treatment and maintenance of social learning family therapy. *Behavior Therapy, 14,* 606–613.

Hudson, A., & Blane, M. (1985). The importance of nonverbal behavior in giving instructions to children. *Child and Family Behavior Therapy, 7,* 1–10.

Izard, C. E. (1977).*Human emotion.* New York: Plenum.

Jones, A. P., & Demaree, R. G. (1975). Family disruption, social indices, and problem behavior: A preliminary study. *Journal of Marriage and the Family, 37,* 497–504.

Kahn, M. (1970). Non-verbal communication and marital satisfaction. *Family Process, 1,* 449–456.

Kauffman, C., Grunebaum, H., Cohler, B., & Gamer, E. (1979). Superkids: Competent children of psychotic mothers. *American Journal of Psychiatry, 136,* 1398–1402.

Kohn, M. L. (1973). Social class and schizophrenia: A critical review and reformulation. *Schizophrenia Bulletin, 7,* 60–79.

Lewis, O. (1966). The culture of poverty. *Scientific American, 225,* 19–25.

Lindsley, O. R. (1970). Procedures with language described by a common language. In C. Neuringer & J. L. Michael (Eds.), *Behavior modification in clinical psychology.* New York: Appleton-Century-Croft.

Lutzker, J. R., McGimsey, J. F., McRae, S., & Campbell, R. V. (1983). Behavioral parent training: There's so much more to do. *The Behavior Therapist, 6,* 110–112.

McLean, P. D. (1976). Parental depression: Incompatible with effective parenting. In E. J. Mash, L. C. Handy, & L. A. Hamerlynck (Eds.), *Behavior modification approaches to parenting.* New York: Brunner/Mazel.

McMahon, R. J., Forehand, R., Griest, D. L., & Wells, K. C. (1981, Spring). Who drops out of

treatment during parent behavioral training? *Behavioral Counseling Quarterly, 1,* 79–85.
McMahon, R. J., Tiedemann, G. L., Forehand, R., & Griest, D. L. (1984). Parental satisfaction with parent training to modify child noncompliance. *Behavior Therapy, 15,* 295–303.
Minuchin, S., & Fishman, H. C. (1981). *Family Therapy Techniques.* Cambridge, MA: Harvard University Press.
Montgomery, B. M. (1981). Verbal immediacy as a behavioral indicator of open communication content. *Communication Quarterly, 30,* 28–34.
Montgomery, B. M. (1984). Behavioral characteristics predicting self and peer perceptions of open communication. *Communication Quarterly, 32,* 233–240.
Navran, L. (1967). Communication and adjustment in marriage. *Family Process, 6,* 173–184.
O'Leary, K. D. (1984). Marital discord & children: Problems, strategies, methodologies and results. In A. Doyle, D. Gold, & D. S. Moskowitz (Eds.), *Children and families under stress,* San Francisco: Jossey-Bass.
Oltmanns, T., Broderick, J., & O'Leary, K. D. (1977). Marital adjustment and the efficacy of behavior therapy with children. *Journal of Consulting and Clinical Psychology, 45,* 724–729.
Patterson, G. R. (1979). A performance theory for coercive family interaction. In E. J. Mash, L. A. Hamerlynck, & L. C. Handy (Eds.), *Behavior modification and families* (Vol. 1). New York: Brunner/Mazel.
Patterson, G. R., & Fleischman (1979). Maintenance of treatment effects: Some considerations concerning family systems and follow-up data. *Behavior Therapy, 10,* 168–185.
Reis, H. T., & Shaver, P. (1988). Intimacy as an interpersonal process. In S. Duck (Ed.), *Handbook of personal relationships: Theory, relationships, and intervention.* Chichester, England: Wiley.
Reppucci, N. D., & Saunders, J. T. (1974). Social psychology of behavior modification: Problems of implementation in natural settings. *American Psychologist, 29,* 649–660.
Revenstorf, D., Vogel, B., Wegener, C., Hahlweg, K., & Schindler, L. (1980). Escalation phenomena in interaction sequences: An empirical comparison of distressed and nondistressed couples. *Behavior Analysis and Modification, 2,* 97–116.
Sanders, M. R., & James, J. E. (1983). The modification of parent behavior: A review of generalization and maintenance. *Behavior Modification, 7*(1), 3–27.
Schaap, C., & Jansen-Nawas, C. (1987). Marital interaction, affect, and conflict resolution. *Sexual and Marital Therapy, 2,* 35–51.
Straus, M. A. (1983). Violence in the family. In S. H. Kadish (Ed.), *Encyclopedia of crime and justice.* New York: Free Press.
Stuart, R. B. (1971). Behavioral contracting within the families of delinquents. *Journal of Behavior Therapy and Experimental Psychiatry, 2,* 1–11.
Stuart, R. B., & Tripodi, T. (1973). Experimental evaluation of three time-constrained behavioral treatments for predelinquents and delinquents. In R. D. Rubin, J. P. Brady, & J. D. Henderson (Eds.), *Advances in behavior therapy, Vol. 4.* New York: Academic Press.
Szykula, S. A., & Fleischman, M. J. (1980). Generating referrals to newly established programs: A cost effective comparison of two procedures. *Community Mental Health, 16,* 201–204.
Vaughn, C. E., & Leff, J. P. (1976). The influence of family and social factors on the course of psychiatric illness. *British Journal of Psychiatry, 129,* 125–137.
Vincent, J. P. (1972). *The relationship of sex, level of intimacy, and level of marital distress to problem-solving behaviour and exchange of social reinforcement.* Doctoral dissertation. Department of Psychology, University of Oregon. 96(2), 83–87.
Weathers, L., & Liberman, R. P. (1975). Contingency contracting with families of delinquent adolescents. *Behavior Therapy, 6,* 356–366.
Weissman, M. M., & Paykel, E. S. (1974). *The depressed woman: A study of social relationships.* Chicago: University of Chicago Press.

III METAPHORS AND MODELS

9 Chaos and Regulated Change in Families: A Metaphor for the Study of Transitions

John Mordechai Gottman
University of Washington

In this chapter I outline a general approach to how families change. I draw heavily from a new understanding of deterministic and nonlinear systems in physics and biology that has come to be called "dynamics," and is also known as "bifurcation theory" or "catastrophe theory." Part of this new understanding lies in a new definition of the term "chaos." The ideas of this fascinating new area have recently been popularized in a national bestseller by Gleick (1987).

When Isaac Newton wrote his laws of motion a few hundred years ago, he assumed that, given enough information, the behavior of a dynamic system was completely determined. Indeed, it is possible to predict, almost perfectly, the times of solar and lunar eclipses for the next 300 years. This is a quite remarkable prediction. Newton and his contemporaries assumed that, although things may get increasingly complex, nature and its motions are completely determined by the laws of motion. God in Newton's scheme was the clockmaker and initial winder of the celestial grand clockworks. This has often been referred to as deterministic physics.

Unfortunately, Newton was wrong, even on the nonquantum mechanical scale. Physicists attempting to solve Newton's equation have found two results: (1) there are the solutions of the kind that Newton encountered; (2) but there are also solutions of a very different character with very different sorts of predictabilities, and these solutions have been described as *chaos*.

I propose that there are two kinds of change in families, *regulated change,* and *chaotic change*. In this chapter I explain both kinds of change and provide examples of each kind.

REGULATED CHANGE IN GENERAL

Homeostasis and Periodicity. The concept of *homeostasis* does not imply that the behavior of a system is stable, but merely that there exists a mechanism regulating the limits of the system's behavior. The classical example is the thermostat, which is set to some desired temperature. When the room temperature exceeds or is below some tolerance around the target temperature, the furnace or air conditioner is activated to bring the room temperature back to the acceptable range. A similar process operates in the cardiovascular system and the central nervous system in the regulation of blood pressure during normal functioning (i.e., during nonemergency situations) known as the baroreceptor reflex, or Marey's law of the heart. There are stretch receptors, primarily in the aortic arch and the carotid sinus that send impulses to the brain when blood pressure increases and result in a reduced heart rate and consequent drop in pressure. Because of regulation, things can not keep going up indefinitely; eventually they must come down. Similarly, things can not keep going down; eventually they must come up. Hence a system must be quasi-periodic if it is regulated. This just means that it goes up and down over time and due to a famous 19th century theorem by Fourier, that it can be described with patterns that have rhythmicities.

Embedded in this notion of homeostasis can be a variety of other periodicities. These cycles arise through periodic changes in the input to the regulated system. For example, it may be warmer in a room in the morning and cooler in the evening if the room has an eastern exposure, so that the onset and offset of the heat pump will have a diurnal cycle because of the earth's motion on its axis. In a similar way, the inputs to a regulated system may have several periodicities summed together. However, we should take note of the fact that most inputs to regulated systems produce reasonably regular outputs in the sense that smaller deviations in the inputs produce smaller deviations in the output. In chaotic systems we can not assume that we have this usual kind of smoothness in which small deviations in input produce small deviations in output. In fact, it is possible in chaotic systems that very small deviations in the input can create enormous changes in the output. For this reason chaotic systems are called *deviation amplifying systems.*

EXAMPLE OF A REGULATED SYSTEM: INTRODUCING STATE DIAGRAMS

A classic example of a regulated system is the Lotka-Volterra (1925) model (cited in Abraham & Shaw, 1985, pp. 85ff) of predators and prey from mathematical biology. Imagine a fictitious ecosystem containing substantial populations of two species only, big fish and small fish, and a large population of food for the small fish. Let us imagine a graph that is called a "state space" with the population of big fish at any time, *t,* as the y-axis, and the population of small fish at time *t* as the x-axis. In our first approximation to this set of curves in the state space we can notice (see Fig. 9.1) that there are four regions:

Region A: Both populations are low, and the population of big fish decreases due to the lack of food (small fish) while the population of small fish increases due to the lack of predation. This is shown by the vector A.

Region B: In this region there are lots of small fish but relatively few predators, and hence both populations can increase. This is shown by the direction of the vector B.

Region C: In this region both populations are large. The big fish are multiplying, which results in a dramatic reduction of the number of smaller fish. This is illustrated by the direction of the vector C.

Region D: In this region there are few little fish but many big fish. Both populations must decline. This fact is illustrated by vector D.

As we collect more data points the smooth limit of the vectorfield will be a circle, shown as Fig. 9.2. This is called a "phase diagram" of this ecosystem. Depending on different initial and boundary conditions, a set of parallel circles describe all possible configurations of the Lotka-Volterra vectorfield (Fig. 9.3). The center of this field is a point of total homeostasis, one that is rarely realized in any system that is not closed from outside influences (e.g., on the amount of food available to the little fishes). The conclusion is that every trajectory of this

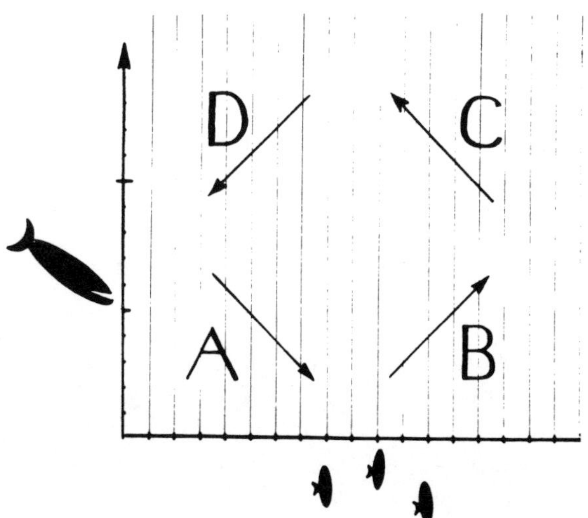

FIG. 9.1. Phase diagram of a stable ecosystem.

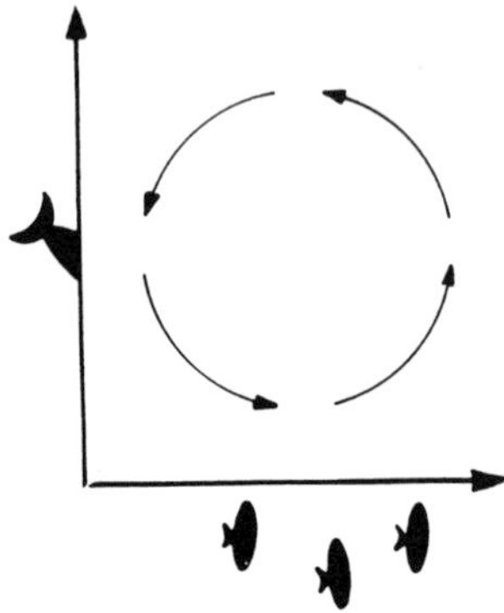

FIG. 9.2. A stable ecosystem can be represented by periodic motion in a circle.

system is periodic, with periodic variability in the population of big and small fish.

INPUTS AND OUTPUTS

We can now consider inputs and outputs in the regulated system. We have assumed that the amount of food available to the small fish was in large supply. Suppose now that the amount of food available to the small fish was merely adequate on the average and varied around the mean with some amount of deviation. Then instead of a circle, a set of trajectories in the state space would transcribe a ring instead of a circle. The width of the ring will decrease if the deviation in the input decreases. This is an important characteristic of regulated systems. In linear systems, by definition, the inputs and outputs will be related to one another in linear fashion. Chaos arises as a possibility in nonlinear systems, even if they are deterministic.

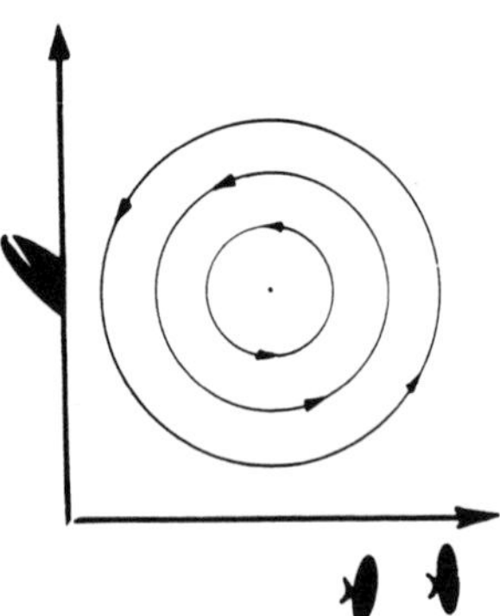

FIG. 9.3. A series of consectric circles represents all the possible states of the stable ecosystem.

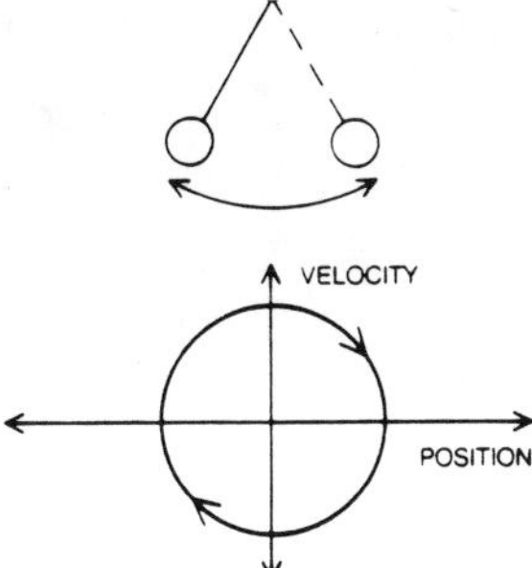

FIG. 9.4. A simple pendulum and its phase diagram.

Attractors. A recent modification of the model that is designed to describe a kind of natural stability includes "ecological friction." Adding this notion of friction leaves only one solution in the state space, depicted as a small circle in Fig. 9.4 toward which all other trajectories are drawn. This small circle is called an *attractor* in dynamics. This notion of an attractor is illustrated in Fig. 9.5 for the pendulum with and without friction. In the case of the pendulum the state space is described by the position and velocity of the pendulum. An attractor need not be a point; it can be a curve or a rather complex surface in multidimensional state space.

The next most complex attractor is called a torus, which is like the surface of a bagel. The torus models two periodicities. We can describe two circles in a bagel, depending on whether we make a horizontal or a vertical slice. Any particular set of data describe only one trajectory on this surface; the surface itself is defined by repeated data sets. This torus surface describes motion made up of two independent oscillations; one frequency determines how fast the orbit circles the bagel in the short direction while the other frequency determines how fast the orbit circles the bagel in the long direction. Higher dimensional tori represent the combination of a series of oscillations. These "multidimensional bagels" are not chaotic solutions to observed motion, but regulated solutions.

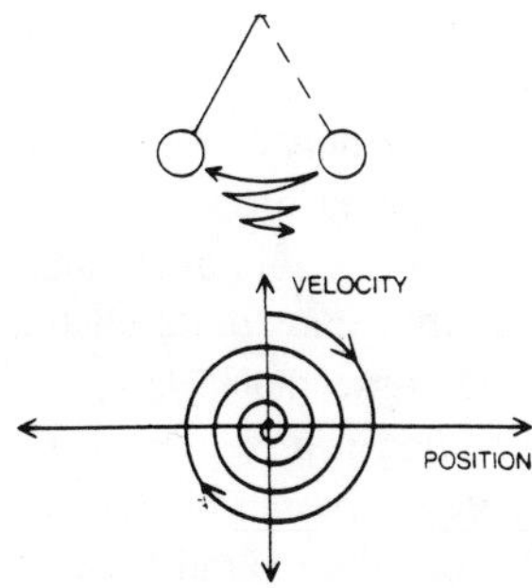

FIG. 9.5. A simple pendulum with friction.

Energy Balance and Homeostasis

Each circle in the state space of Fig. 9.4 represents a particular energy state of the pendulum. An energy state of a pendulum is perefctly represented by the amplitude of its oscillation. The harder the pendulum was initially shoved, the more energy it has. In fact, the energy with which the pendulum was shoved is proportional to the square of the amplitude of the pendulum's oscillation, and, in general, this fact leads to an important generalization of energy in time-series analysis as variance. This is not difficult to prove mathematically. When we compute the variance in the pendulum's displacement over time, we will obtain half the square of its amplitude of oscillation. *Thus, there is a natural mathematical equation between variance and energy.*

A mathematical function called the "spectrum" in time-series analysis is a breakdown of the energy or total variance in the time series into separate frequency bands. In the case of a very regular pendulum all the energy is located at one precise frequency of oscillation, regular as clockwork. More complicated oscillations can be obtained if we hook a second pendulum to the base of the first and give each one separate shoves. By adding pendula we can get the sum of frequencies and very complex motions are possible. In this manner of thinking, we can see that the motion of the energy of a system or its total variance is what we are trying to account for and understand (model) in most of our research.

Applied to Families. In physiology it is possible to show that a simple relationship exists between an organism's weight and the ratio of growth hormone (GH) to insulin (IRI); IRI is an anabolic (or energy conserving) hormone responsible for the storage of fuels as glucagon in the liver or adipose tissue, while GH is a catabolic (or energy expending) hormone whose action can regulate the expenditure of energy (see Woods, Decke, & Vasselli, 1974).

Therefore, I suggest that it makes sense to think metaphorically of social exchanges in a family system as being either energy expending and energy draining, i.e., catabolic, or energy conserving or building, i.e., anabolic. The energic nature of social interaction can be considered a part of the essential transactions between family members, or between family members and the environment outside the family. In the same way I posit in this paper, if we obtain that a particular fixed circle in a family system's state space then this represents a balance between catabolic (energy expending) processes and anabolic, energy conserving processes. The family transactions would be in equilibrium in this case of a circle in the state space. Obviously this concept of "state space" for a family seems quite abstract at this point, but I will soon make it precise.

I argue that in most healthy families there is a balance between energy expending transactions with the environment and within the family such that the state space can be described like a pendulum. Processes in the family are regulated if the overall balance of energy expense and energy storage are equivalent.

In most marriages this probably means that the ration of positive to negative affect will need to exceed 4:1, based on what we know from early research with the Spouse Observation Checklist (Wills, Weiss, & Patterson, 1974). Suppose there is such a critical ratio. This implies that if the emotional interactions in the family fall below this ratio and there are not adequate social supports that resupply energy (confidants, for example), there will be a biological toll. This will probably initially involve diffuse levels of autonomic activation, eventually chronic levels of stress-related hormones, and eventually a compromised immune system. It is likely that these biological conditions will affect social behavior as well.

A system may have several attractors. In that case, different *initial conditions* of the system may eventually move toward the limit of different attractors. This means that the notion of "equilibrium" can be complex. It needn't be the case that the energic nature of the family's interaction is fixed, but it can be composed of complex rhythms over time, just as in the previous example of many pendulums hooked on to one another can describe some very complex motions. This discussion shows that homeostasis is not necessarily a static state, a point that is often overlooked in thinking about regulation in family systems.

So far all the vicissitudes of the systems we have been discussing are predictable or regulated.

Chaos

Much of this field of chaos comes from solving differential equations (which are equalities about rates of change). For example, in predicting the course of a storm a specific set of differential equations (called the Navier-Stokes equations) are solved. Once upon a time it was believed that if one were given the equations and the initial conditions that theoretically the future of the system was completely determined. This is called a deterministic solution. Of course, usually the equations were too hard to solve exactly, but that was not considered important philosophically. The important point was that the set of equations had a deterministic solution.

However, it turned out that many apparently deterministic physical systems had two different solutions, one that was regulated and behaved as it should have, and one that broke all the rules. This second solution was called "chaotic." In the solution of the Navier-Stokes equations for fluid motion applied to the analysis of storms, these two solutions have been called "laminar flow" to describe the regular flow of air masses and "turbulence," "bursts," or chaotic motion to describe another state of the system in which the motions of air masses are much less predictable.

This condition of two kinds of solutions, one that is expected and regulated, and one that is chaotic has been discovered in many fields other than meteorology. For example, in the case of the heart, the analogous two conditions (or "solutions") are the normal beating of the heart under the many biological demands of the adapting organism (laminar flow) and ventricular fibrillation (chaos).

One of the exciting aspects of chaos theory is that it is possible to tell, from the behavior of the system itself, whether or not the system is regulated. One way that this can be done is by estimating a number that is known as the Liapunov exponent. In chaos theory the Liapunov spectrum is also of interest but it is not discussed here.

Chaos and wild unpredictability. We will see how chaos is in fact the limit of the kind of predictability we have been discussing, but with enormous sensitivity to the system's initial conditions that results in the attractor surface folding back on itself, for example as in a Mobius strip (see Kaneko, 1986). What this means can be understood in terms of the concept of energy balance I previously introduced. In the case of homeostasis, we have the system in the Lotka-Volterra example orbiting in state space around only one circle. The same is true for the pendulum's motion. However, when the system folds back on itself, a trajectory crosses from one circle to another, transcribing a kind of figure eight on the attractor's surface. What this means is that different circles become joined and the surface becomes joined, very much like the dissipative pendulum in Fig. 9.5. In fact, dimensionality in the state space is lost. This means that instead of the attractor being a circle in the idealized pendulum, in the pendulum with friction the attractor becomes a point. We have lost a dimension since a circle is a two-dimensional object whereas a point is a one-dimensional object. When this loss of dimension occurs, the torus that described the attractor of a rhythmically stable system in equilibrium is called a "degenerate torus." For example, instead of a bagel (torus) in three dimensional space we might have only one oscillation because the other oscillation (due to friction), degenerated over time to an insignificant amount. The degenerate torus is now represented by a circle in two dimensional space rather than a bagel in three dimensional space.

Let us think of all this in physical terms. What does a "degenerate torus" imply in terms of energy? It means that these energy transitions can happen gradually (as in dissipative cases) or they can happen suddenly. In the case of sudden transitions we have wild unpredictability. The system started to move slowly and smoothly in one place but suddenly it wound up in an entirely new place. Sometimes it is easier to picture this in state space by thinking of weird attractor surfaces. Perhaps the most famous case of these sudden transitions in state space is the well known example of the Mobius strip (Fig. 9.6), which is actually a one-dimensional surface; the Klein bottle is another example of a degenerate torus. What does this mean physically? In terms of the concept of a system's energy balance, this means that the system can undergo wild and sudden shifts in energy balance. These shifts no longer have to be gradual. This is so even though the state space is represented by a smooth although degenerate surface.

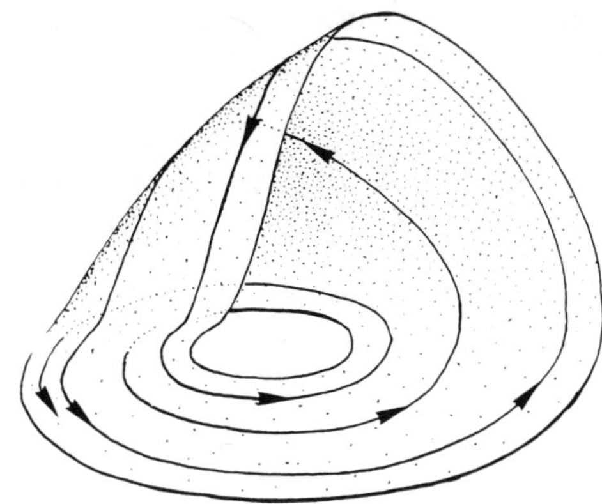

FIG. 9.6. The Mobious strip as a degenerate torus.

The problem with this field for the social psychologist without a mathematical background is that it seems very abstract and it is hard to imagine applying it to any real data. How might we accomplish a translation that has some theoretical appeal? I propose that the notion of an "energy set point" might be an appropriate metaphor for an attractor in state space.

Energy Set Points in Chaotic Systems

Recall that for regulated systems it is possible to describe the system as having an *energy balance set point.* However, for chaotic systems it becomes very difficult to predict the system's ability to adapt to the changing energy needs of its transactional environment, and chaos ensues. Homeostasis is violated.

Furthermore, the disorder has a special nature: Although we can say with certainty that we cannot predict the trajectory of any individual family energy system, prediction in the large (i.e., statistical prediction) of many chaotic families of a similar type is still theoretically possible. Once we have described the nature of the chaos, we can be certain that the accumulated trajectories of families are constrained to describe this degenerate torus in state space. It is in this statistical sense that chaos is predictable. Of course, this kind of discussion is very speculative and it will remain so until we have created a typology of chaotic systems. In this section I try to make these abstract mathematical notions more concrete. To do this, I begin by discussing several physical examples. This discussion leads to a broad suggestion for measurement using observational techniques applied to families.

The Dripping Faucet: An Approach to Measurement. Recently, Crutchfield, Farmer, Packard, and Shaw (1986) analyzed the behavior of a dripping faucet as a function of different rates of water flow (Fig. 9.6a). In their experiment, a microphone was employed to measure the "interdrip interval" or IDI, and the state space is the successive time intervals between drips. We can start with two dimensions. In concrete terms, we get the state space by computing the time between drips (t1, t2, t3, t4, etc.). Then we plot a set of points (t1, t2) and (t2, t3), and (t3, t4), and so on. We also connect the dots, and this describes an attractor surface. If we move to three dimensions, we plot triplets (t1, t2, t3), (t2, t3, t4), and so on, using three coordinates. Again, we connect the dots to see the surface.

This application is analagous to the study of interbeat intervals of the beating heart in which the event of interest is usually the R-spike of the electrocardiogram. When the faucet is dripping relatively slowly, the behavior of the IDI is fairly periodic, much as was the case in our Lotka-Volterra example. However, as the rate of flow was systematically increased, the pattern that emerged in the state space was characteristic of what has come to be called "deterministic chaos" in physics.

Now let us return to the faucet. It has one possible regulated state, in which the time between drips may get larger for a while, but then eventually it gets smaller. But what happens as we close the faucet? The time between drips goes to infinity; that is the faucet will eventually stop dripping if we shut it. What happens as we open the faucet? Eventually the time between drips goes to zero as

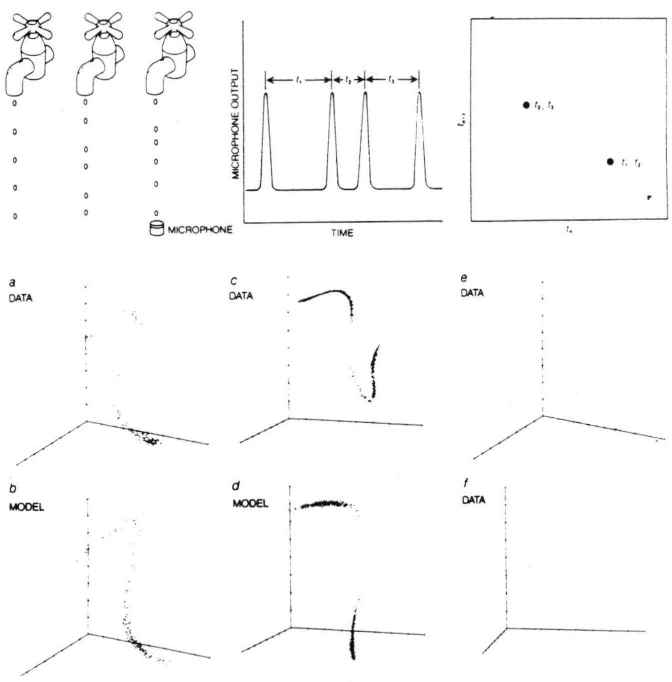

FIG. 9.6a. Phase diagram for the dripping faucet problem.

the flow becomes continuous. In each case (the shut faucet or the flowing one) the time between drips becomes a meaningless concept. Now suppose that we really have no idea if the system is moving toward one or another state. Can we tell simply from the behavior of the IDI what is happening to the system, that is, if it is regulated or not? The answer is, yes.

In fact, I propose that this approach is quite general if we substitute the notion of Interevent Interval for interdrip interval. The events can be anything of interest in a family that can assigned a time (or for that matter any value along some dimension).

DESCRIBING CHAOS IN THE STATE SPACE

Chaos is not the Same as Random. Deterministic chaos need not be described as a featureless blob attractor, which would be the case if the system were entirely random. The attractor in deterministic chaos has a definite shape, but it is one that involves the surface folding in on itself. What makes the system unpredictable, however, is that even small variations in the system's initial conditions can have huge implications for the trajectory of the system on the attractor's surface, and the variations in trajectories may not be predictable. The amount of predictability can be measured by a number called the Liapunov exponent. The transition from periodicity to chaos has also been the subject of investigation in dynamics.

What Chaos Looks Like: The Logistic Map. Figure 9.7 illustrates a widely applied solution to most nonlinear dynamical equations, called the "logistic map." This set of values may predict interbeat intervals of the heart, or the size of a changing biological population. In this map, the (n + 1)-st point is computed as a constant, *a,* times the n th point, times one minus the n th point:

$$x_{n+1} = a * x_n * (1 - x_n)$$

Several aspects of this process are interesting. One can describe the progress of the *n* points in purely geometric terms. The way one proceeds geometrically to determine the next point is to begin with a value on the x-axis, project it up to the curve, then over to the 45° line, then to the curve, and so on, indefinitely. When $a < 1.0$, all populations must decrease to zero, and zero is the fixed point attractor of this state space. When $a = 2.9$, we can see that this process converges to a particular fixed point attractor. When *a* is between 1 and 3 all populations evolve to this fixed point attractor. When *a* becomes larger than 3.0, however, the fixed point becomes unstable. When *a* is 4, in fact, the values of x_n wander around in random fashion. Hence, at $a = 4$ the attractor would resemble a featureless blob characteristic of complete randomness.

What is interesting about this equation is the set of values between 3 and 4.

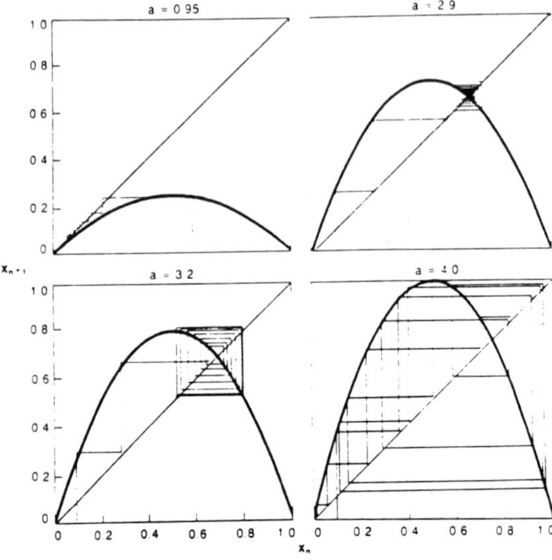

FIG. 9.7. The logistic map with different constants.

First, the fixed point becomes unstable and the population evolves to a dynamically steady state in which it alternates between a large and a small population; for $a = 3.2$ the population cycles between two points on the parabola at about $x_n = 0.5$ and $x_n = 0.8$. For larger values of a this two cycle is replaced by a period-4 cycle in which the population becomes high-low, returning to its original values every four time steps. When a is increased, the long-time cycle finally converges to period-8, -16, -32, -64 cycles, finally accumulating to a cycle of infinite period for $a = 3.57$. This sequence is called "period-doubling bifurcations," and it is usually displayed in a bifurcation diagram. The sequence of regular periodic orbits is the precursor to chaos. Other paths to chaos exist such as "intermittency" and the degeneracy of tori (see Kaneko, 1986 for a mathematical discussion and Glass, Scherer, & Belair, 1986 for an experimental example with embryonic chick cardiac cells).

Quantifying Chaos, and the Deviation Amplifying Property. Figure 9.8 shows that the trajectories of two nearby initial conditions for this system can be seen to diverge after only a few iterations. If the two initial conditions are viewed as the error bar on the beginning state of the system, it can be seen that chaos makes it impossible to pinpoint the error bars on the system's end state. This means, in terms social scientist would understand, that the confidence intervals around a point become stretched from initial to end state. We can't say with any great certainty where the system will wind up, even if there are very small changes in intial conditions. While we expect such a state of affairs if there are large changes, we really don't expect this with small changes.

For example, if we were studying families longitudinally and learned that a particular family had experienced major losses and traumas since our last assessment, we would not be surprised to find that they had changed a great deal on our measures. With a chaotic family, however, small events can lead to huge changes. This is the notion of the deviation amplifying property of chaos. In a group of subjects we can assess the variance at Time One in our longitudinal study and the variance at Time Two and draw these standard deviations as error bars around the means. We can think of the ratio of the two standard deviations as the amount of change the families as a group have undergone. In chaos theory this ratio is called the amount of "stretching." This amount of stretching of the error bar from intial to end states quantifies the degree of chaos in families in our study. If we measure one family frequently, the amount of stretching can quantify the amount of chaos in one family system. (In practice it is defined as as the product of the log of the stretching multiplied by the probability of encountering that amount of stretching, which is an interpretation of the Liapunov exponent.) Chaotic systems are therefore unpredictable because of what is called their *extreme sensitivity to initial conditions* and their average properties need to be described using statistics. I call this the *deviation amplifying characteristic of chaos*. Note that this is independent of whether the equations of the system are deterministic or not. Here we can see why chaos in not the same as randomness. In a random system the next state of the system has an equal probability of being anywhere in the state space; a chaotic system is constrained to amplify deviations.

Liapunov exponents that are negative represent stable periodic orbits; chaos is

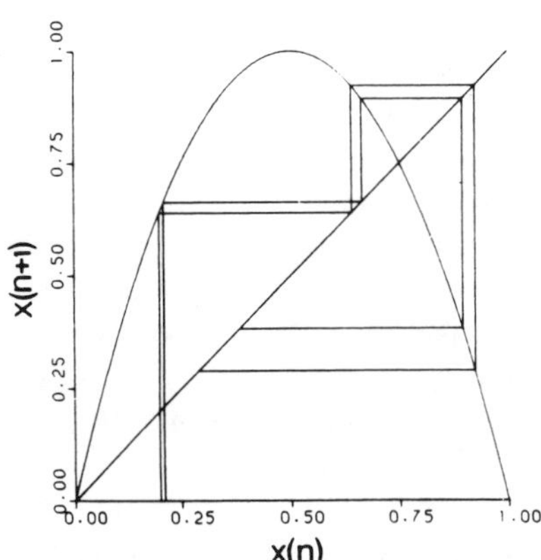

FIG. 9.8. The logistic map is chaotic because small changes in input could result in large changes in output.

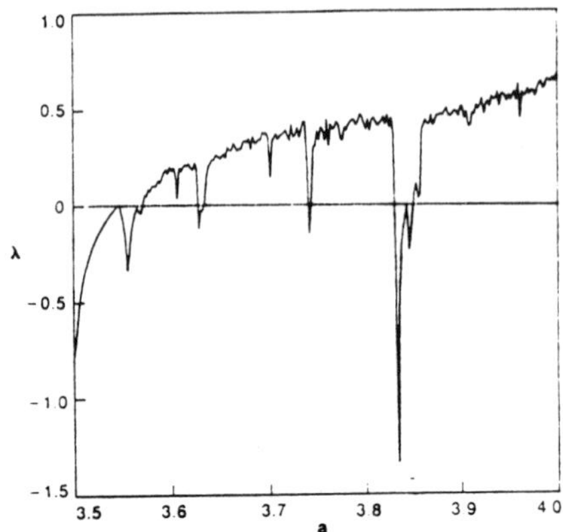

FIG. 9.9. Liapunov exponents for the logistic map.

represented by a positive average Liapunov exponent (it equals 0.693 for $a = 4$ in the logistic map; see Fig. 9.9.[1]

Goal of our Analyses. What we have attempted to accomplish here is that it may be possible to predict, from the behavior of a system, when the future behavior of that system will be unpredictable. In physics this means that prediction only makes sense in the statistical aggregate sense (e.g., in the study of gases, instead of studying the motions of one molecule in Brownian motion, physics introduces statistical mechanics). This means that in the chaotic system I can not predict the behavior of any one realization of the system. However, I can tell you that across many realizations a particular surface in the state space will be described.

Transitions to Chaos: Experimental Data. What has become of interest to chaos theorists is to model the transition of a homeostatic, regulated system to one that is chaotic. If we look around in nature for such objects, we find them in abundance. A volcano is a good example. The actions of the heart provide another example. Hence, some researchers have tried to model how a heart can suddenly go into the ventricular fibrillation that leads to a myocardial infarction. Glass et al. (1986) studied spontaneously beating aggregates of embryonic chick heart cells. They were able to stimulate these cells to model cardiac arrythmias characterized by frequent premature systoles of multiple points of origin (ectopic pacemaker cells, simultaneous atrial and ventricular or A–V node firing) that is a condition premature to sudden death. In the study of families, it may be of interest, for example, to model a type of family's transition from distressed to

---

[1]We can also see an increasing number of negative spikes in the plot of the Liapunov exponent against the parameter a (see Fig. 9.9).

physically abusive. This transition might be an excellent candidate for the change from regulated to deviation amplifying.

Randomness is Not Chaos. We can now mathematically differentiate between chaos and randomness. In the random state the attractor is a blob, not a surface at all; there is no relationship between successive states of the system. In the chaotic system, the state space maps out a surface that contains elements that fold back on itself. This latter statement is admittedly quite abstract, so let us explore it, particularly as it might apply to family change.

APPLIED TO FAMILY CHANGE

In a sense we can think of a regulated system as having two qualities: First, in a regulated system, there is a fixed attractor surface that can be described as a multidimensional torus. In other words, *in a regulated system there is, in a sense, a fixed point* (assuming that we generalize the notion of a fixed "point" to a multidimensional nondegenerated torus). Second, in a regulated system with deterministic laws, the system is determined once we know its initial conditions. On the other hand, *a chaotic system has no fixed point* (in the sense that the attractor either has no shape or folds back on itself). Furthermore, a chaotic system is extremely sensitive to minor perturbations; it is a noise or *deviation-amplifying system.*

Thus, I suggest that we think of the concept of an *attractor* in families as a fixed point. This fixed point is theoretically defined in terms of energy balance in terms of anabolic and catabolic processes. These processes will, in turn, have to do with positive and negative affects.

Let us now speculate on how to apply these notions to the study of families, both normal and pathological.

FIXED POINTS IN FAMILIES

How might these concepts from physics be applied to the study of family change? The key to answering this question, I think, lies in theoretically and operationally defining the notions of a "fixed point" and "deviation amplifying mechanisms" in families. What might be the equivalent of a "fixed point" in families?

I suggest that the key to defining what a fixed point is in families lies in asking the question, "Under which condition is conflict functional in families?" We have noticed in our research with couples using the Oral History Interview that some couples have a sense of "we-ness" that comes from a variety of sources and they can refer to this when resolving conflict. For other couples who lack this sense of we-ness, every conflict seems to challenge their basic beliefs and result in a decrease of cohesion.

Along these lines, I suggest that *a family's fixed points, can be defined as all those things that can be referred to by family members to resolve conflict in such a way that family cohesion increases after the conflict.* These points are the foundations of the family, they create the context in which the family wants to resolve the conflict. Examples of these fixed points would generally revolve around a sense of we-ness. More specifically, the procedures we might employ that could help us measure this construct include: the implicit marital contract, a shared religious or cultural viewpoint, an agreed-upon dominance hierarchy, the family's belief system, shared values, shared goals, shared memories, a shared viewpoint of reality (e.g., seeing the world as a dangerous place), the family's stories, heroes, demons, and myths, and expectations the parents have of their marriage, the family's rules, rituals, beliefs about people, good and evil, nature, etc.

Measurement. How might these things be measured? I suggest that an excellent index of the *absence* of family fixed points is the *loneliness* of family members. This general observation must be qualified in two ways. First, there are many different kinds of loneliness, such as existential, which are likely to be independent of the kind of loneliness that stems from not having a close personal relationship. Second, in adolescence, the loneliness of the adolescent may be an index of conflicts involving closeness to the family and individuation, which is a healthy part of adolescence. In other words, if the cognitive/emotional family schemes held by individual family members overlap and intersect, this provides a frame of reference that helps regulate interaction and also helps regulate change.

I propose that when these family fixed points exist, the family system is regulated. In fact, we can propose that it is precisely the family's fixed points that provide meaning for the microsocial processes we observe that describe this family's interactions. In regulated systems there are ordered mechanisms for change.

However, without these fixed points, every conflict runs the risk of threatening the existence of the family itself. Thus, we can hypothesize that *normative transitions in a chaotic system are likely to be similar to traumatic events in a regulated system.* Chaotic instability during normative change is thus similar to the kinds of change that a regulated family system will undergo when major changes occur, such as finding out that one family member has a terminal illness, or that one parent is in love with someone else. In these cases, the regulated family's fixed points are threatened.

What needs to happen first to avoid chaos is that the family's fixed points need to be reestablished. If this does not occur, the family will continue to change, but in a deviation amplifying fashion that is characteristic of chaos. Chaos will continue until the family establishes a fixed point. There is no guarantee that this will ever occur. Changing inputs within a family can occur with major developmental changes, such as when an infant begins walking. If families are characterized by the deviation-amplifying property, these changes within families can have major consequences.

Energy

Let us now return to the diagram of the pendulum (Fig. 9.4) and propose that the emotions of anger, fear, and sadness, blends of these emotions, and their close temporal sequencing are catabolic, or energy expending emotions, while the emotions of interest, amusement, humor, affection, and disgust (though receiving disgust is not energy conserving, broadcasting it to another family member may be for the broadcaster) are anabolic, energy conserving or restoring emotions. A regulated system with a fixed point is one that maintains a balance between these emotions, probably in a ratio that is greater that 4:1 for anabolic to catabolic. This ratio may vary with the nature of the family's philosophy and expectations. It is likely that the physiological basis of the balance needs to be heavily on the anabolic side; that is, you need a lot of the "anabolic emotions" to balance a little of the catabolic. A system that is dissipative will have an imbalance in favor of these catabolic emotions, and such a system will eventually become chaotic.

I propose that several processes will be likely to accompany blends of these negative affects of fear, anger, and sadness (includes whining). These processes are:

1. *Diffuse Physiological Arousal (DPA).* One result of chronic levels of negative affect blends is a diffuse physiological arousal that leads to increased sympathetic and parasympathetic nervous system activity, increased stress-related endocrine activity (catecholamines and glucocorticoids), and decreased immune response (Gottman, 1990).

2. *Hypothesized Consequences of DPA*. There are a number of hypothesized consequences of DPA, including a reduced ability to process new information, a reliance on overlearned behaviors and cognitions, and a tendency to invoke fight and flight behaviors (e.g., the escalation of aggression and threat, and withdrawal from interaction). Another hypothesized consequence of DPA is its aversive nature. If this is the case, then states of DPA fit an escape conditioning model. Whatever behaviors are used to soothe DPA will become more likely in the subject's repertoire. Gottman and Levenson (1985) suggested this as a model for how marital interaction changes over time.

3. *Flooding*. Ekman (1984) recently introduced the concept of flooding, by which he meant that through emotional conditioning a wide range of stimuli eventually become capable of eliciting blends of anger, fear, and sadness. I

would add that the term "flooding" also suggests that the emotional state becomes disregulating in the sense that a person can attend to or do little else when flooded. In this manner flooding may be highly disruptive of organized behavior.

4. *Hypervigilance*. People in relationships that chronically generate negative affect blends that leads to flooding may become excessively vigilant to potentially threatening and escalating interactions. They may become likely to misattribute threat potential to relatively neutral or positive acts. This could be the mechanism that explains the Dodge, Pettit, McClaskey, and Brown (1986) finding that aggressive boys see threat in relatively ambiguous situations.

HOW CHAOS ARISES IN FAMILIES

Let me suggest that probably the most common way that chaos arises is by the chronic de-regulation of this balance between anabolic and catabolic emotions and their blends. This could be detected by the same sort of process that Glass et al. were modeling in the chaos of embryonic cardiac chick cells. The normal regulation, exemplified in the case of the beating cardiac cells by a more-or-less steady rhythm, became disorganized in the Glass et al. study by period doubling bifurcations. In a similar manner, in families a common path to chaos can be found in the de-regulation of the energy balance between anabolic and catabolic emotions until it reaches chronic levels.

An Example from Marital Interaction. Our discussion of chaos theory should lead us to examine interevent intervals (IEIs). For marital interaction there are many possible behavioral candidates. A likely one to select as an event is negative affect, in part because it has a reasonably high base rate during conflict discussions, and because it tends to be high in dissatisfied marriages. But our interest here is not whether negative affect is high among an unhappily married couple, but whether this system is homeostatically regulated and stable, or whether it is chaotic. Recall that in our earlier discussion of chaos theory I suggested translating the circles of the pendulum into energy dynamics as the balance of anabolic and catabolic processes.

Figure 9.10 is a plot of the IEIs for negative affect in the conflict discussion of one unhappy couple in a study that Robert Levenson and I are conducting. In the Liapunov computation, we need to create a state space of x_{i+1} versus x_i. This is nothing very new, by itself. It is merely the scatter diagram one would use in computing the first-order autocorrelation coefficient. What is different in chaos theory is that *we connect the dots in order*. This is not a standard statistical procedure in the social sciences. Start at the point labeled "1" in the Figure. This is point (x_1, x_2). We then connect this dot to the next point, which is (x_2, x_3), and so on. Figure 9.11 shows a part of this graph. We can see that there is a tendency

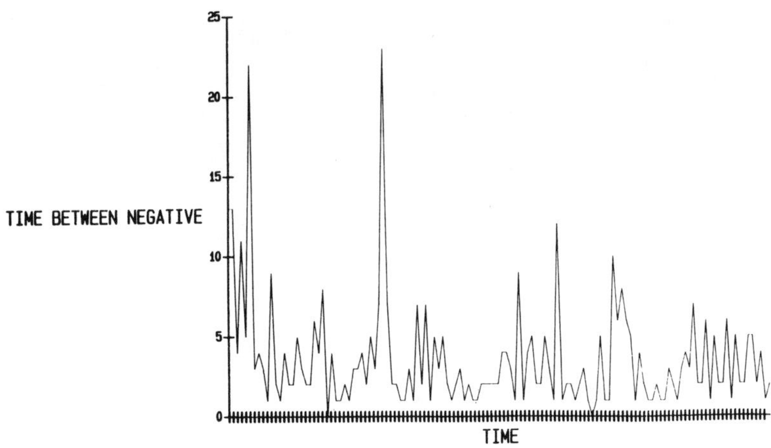

FIG. 9.10. Interevent intervals for negative affect in a marital conversation.

for this system to wander in toward the vertex of a triangle whose apex is at the origin. This can be viewed as a two-dimensional projection of the three dimensional trajectory I have shown as Fig. 9.12. In fact the Liapunov exponent[2] for the first 14 points is 1.7, and for the first 28 points is 2.3, both positive, which is indicative of chaos.

What does this mean? It means that, insofar as we can ascertain from these data, we have a system whose energy balance is not stable, but dissipative. Like the pendulum winding down, this system tends toward one attractor. However, for the consequences of energy balance, this movement toward an attractor of zero interevent interval between negative affect may be disasterous. Specifically, this system tends, over time, toward shorter response times for negative affect.

We can verify this notion using more standard analytic tools, in this case by performing a mathematical procedure called "spectral time-series analysis" of these IEIs (see Gottman, 1981). A spectral time series analysis (see Fig. 9.13) tells us whether there are specific cyclicities in the data, and, if there are, how much variance each cycle accounts for. Note that the overall spectral analysis of

---

[2]To compute the Liapunov exponent, L, one first creates a plot of the time series of interest x_n. Next one plots x_{n+1} versus x_n, with the former on the y-axis and the latter on the x-axis. Next a function, f(x) is fit to these points. Let f′(x) be the slope of this function. Then:

$$L = \lim_{n \to \text{infinity}} (1/n) \sum_{i=0}^{n-1} (\log_2 |f'(x_i)|).$$

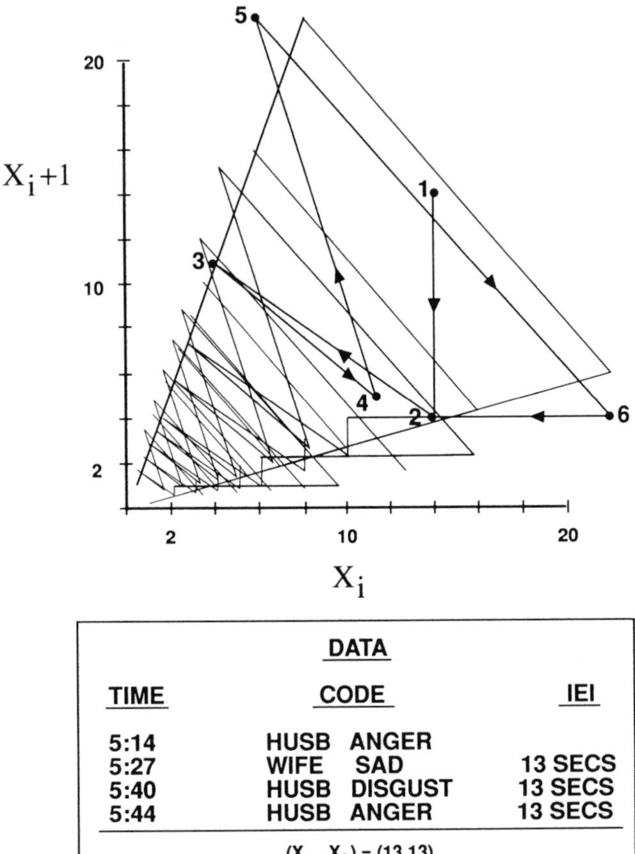

DATA

TIME	CODE	IEI
5:14	HUSB ANGER	
5:27	WIFE SAD	13 SECS
5:40	HUSB DISGUST	13 SECS
5:44	HUSB ANGER	13 SECS

$(X_1, X_2) = (13, 13)$
$(X_2, X_3) = (13, 4)$

FIG. 9.11. A scatterplot of interevent interval times with consecutive points connected.

all the data reveals very little. There seem to be multiple peaks in the data, some representing slower and some faster cycles. However, if we divide the interaction into parts, we can see that there is actually a systematic shift in the cyclicities. The cycle length is 17.5 sec at first, and then moves to 13.2 sec, and then to 11.8 sec. This means that the time for the system to cycle between negative affects is getting shorter as the interaction proceeds. This is exactly what we observed in the state space diagram in which all the points were connected. Hence, we have been led to the conclusion that this system is not regulated, but is moving toward more and more rapid response times between negative affects. From the data we have available, this trajectory seems relentless and unabated. Of course, there

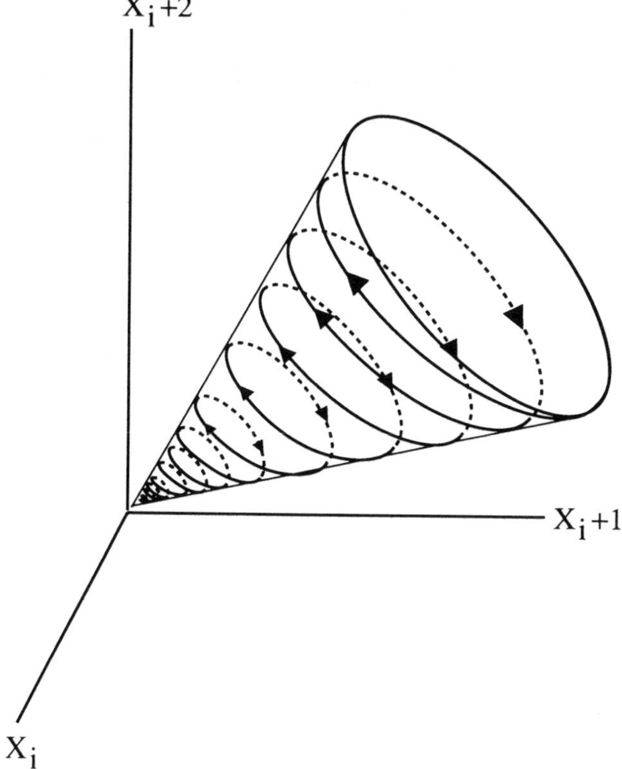

FIG. 9.12. System is being drawn toward faster and faster response times in the IEI of negative affect.

may be a more macro-level regulation that we do not see that will move the system out toward the base of the cone once it has moved in, and it may oscillate in this fashion. But we can not know this. At the moment it seems fair to conclude that this unhappy marriage represents a runaway system.

In my research with Levenson (Levenson & Gottman, 1983), we created a variable we called "physiological linkage." This was the ability to predict one partner's physiological data from the spouse's, controlling for autocorrelation. We assessed this across physiological channels, and employed a standard normal z-score to summarize the significance of the linkage. If we compare the physiological data from this couple with a happily married couple in the same study, we see that there is strong evidence of physiological linkage in this couple (average $z = 7.0$) compared to the happily married couple (average $z = 0.1$). Also, one of our best predictors of change in marital satisfaction over a 3-year period was the husband's heart rate during conflict. The unhappily married husband's heart rate

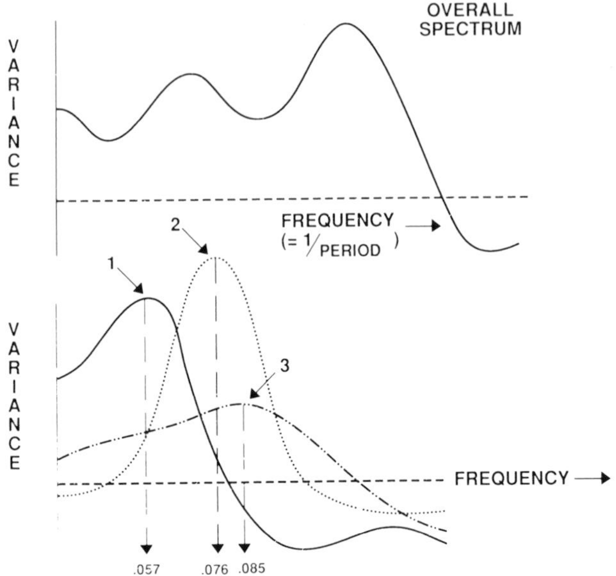

FIG. 9.13. Spectrum for 3 segments showing higher frequencies and shorter periods.

was 85.7 BPM, compared to 72.9 BPM for the happily married husband. Hence it might be reasonable to predict that this marriage should deteriorate in marital satisfaction over time. In our 4-year longitudinal followup of these couples we were, unfortunately, unable to locate this couple. This was highly unusual since we always obtain the names and addresses of three people who will always know the couples whereabouts. It is quite likely, in my opinion, that this couple did not stay together.

What process is most important in predicting from DPA to chaos? I would suggest that it is an inability to soothe:

5. *A general inability to soothe*. Families who have chronically high levels of DPA have a deficit in being able to self soothe or to soothe other family members.

We have also seen instances of couples who soothe one another by using escalations of anger by a spouse who is extremely unlikely to express anger. This is likely to act as a limit-setting brake on a runaway escalation of negative affect. However, it is a risky pattern of behavior, because it invokes an escape conditioning model (escape from the highly aversive state of DPA), and therefore one can predict that the expression of anger will become more probable by this usually nonangry spouse (see Gottman & Levenson, 1986). In many marriages where there is a dominance hierarchy, there are severe negative consequences for this usually non-angry spouse's expression of anger. We can predict that these mechanisms will be invoked more often, probably with more frequent instances of DPA. A similar pattern was described in the marital interactions of couples in which the wife is chronically depressed. Among happily married couples of this type, there is a de-escalation of conflict pattern in which the husband's anger decreases after his wife expresses sadness (Biglan & Hops, personal communication, 1986). Thus, soothing is likely to be critical in saving a marriage in which the expression of negative affect is not regulated.

Prediction in the Face of Chaos. It is has been proposed that chaotic mechanisms have adaptive value (Conrad, 1986), for search and the generation of diversity. Conrad (1986) noted that the "key to chaos . . . . is delicate threshold behavior" (p. 10). Chaotic systems are capable of generating extremely diverse behavior and variety. It may in fact be the case that a family without its usual fixed point will hit upon extremely novel and adaptive behaviors that lead to the reestablishment of new fixed points. However, as attractive as this possibility may seem to those of us who are optimistic, it is, I think quite unlikely for the following reason. I have previously suggested that if it is the case the diffuse physiological arousal (DPA) accompanies threat. Threat should follow logically from the loss of a fixed point, and we would predict that the family's most dominant interaction patterns (i.e., high probability sequences) will emerge while in that unregulated state. In this event we can also predict that the family will be resistant to the processing of new information or the acquisition of new behaviors. Furthermore, most of these behaviors that accompany DPA will involve withdrawal (flight) or the escalation of aggression (fight), designed primarily to provide soothing and control in the chaotic condition.

Response of Chaotic Systems to Inputs. As noted earlier, regulated systems can be characterized by the relationship that if we decrease the error bars on the inputs to the system, we will correspondingly decrease the error bars of the outputs of the system. The opposite is true for chaotic systems. Thus, wheras stress may cause subsequent adjustment, assimilation, and ordered change in a regulated system, in a chaotic system the system's trajectory will be unpredictable.

Probe Messages. There is an unreliability in communication that is inherent in the nature of some communications. These communications may be called *probe messages*. They are low-risk messages sent to be intentionally ambiguous so that the climate of interaction can be tested. For example, in a seductive encounter, these low-risk messages that have double meaning can be taken as sexual invitations to the receptive person, but as something neutral or humorous to the disinterested receiver. Depending on the response, the interaction proceeds

TABLE 9.1
Table of Major Concepts from Dynamics and Their Translation

Concept in Dynamics	*Translation*
Laminar flow	Regulated change
Turbulence	Chaos
Deterministic solution	Homeostasis defined in terms of set point in energy balance and the existence of a fixed point
Noise amplifying property of chaotic systems	Deviation amplifying property
Fixed, noncollapsed tori as attractors	Fixed points in families defined in terms of conflict resolution and cohesiveness and also in terms of energy balance between anabolic and catabolic emotions.
Torus, Mobius strip	Trajectory of data in state space fitting stable energy path or a degenerate (or folded) path
Interdrip interval	Interevent interval
Chaos	DPA and its consequences: Hypervigilance Flooding Inability to soothe

on one course or another. The meaning of particular interactive events in a microsocial process in a family is provided, in part, by the family's fixed points. During periods of chaotic change, when the family's fixed points are undergoing challenge, the frequency of these unreliable low-risk probe messages will increase and new microsocial processes may be established.

Indices of Major Family Transitions. Based upon the reasoning in this paper, we can propose that families undergoing major life transitions will have several properties:

1. *Increased Variance.* This increase in variance may reflect a family search process as the family attempts to adapt to large changes.

2. *Decreased Predictability.* The actual covariance structure among family variables may decrease in predictability during transition periods. This may be a general characteristic of major developmental changes as well.

3. *The Potential for Transition to Chaos.* This potential depends on the family's ability to maintain a set point in energy balance (or to establish a new one). Here we can theorize is where social supports assist. A family can operate on the catabolic end of the scale if there are sources of anabolism in the family's support systems.

SUMMARY

Table 9.1 is a summary of the concept in dynamics that I have introduced and their application to change in families. I began by talking about regulated and unregulated change. The analogue of these ideas in families had to do with two concepts: (1) the existence of a fixed point, and, (2) the existence of a set point for energy balance between catabolic and anabolic processes. I suggested that fixed points have to do with those things that can be referred to to resolve conflict so that cohesion is increased, such as a sense of "we-ness." I suggested that energy regulation had to do with a balance between anabolic emotions and blends (humor, interest, and affection) and catabolic emotions and blends (anger, sadness, and fear). I also suggested that catabolic affect blends result in DPA, which is also induced by perceived threat. DPA has a number of consequences, including a reduced ability to process new information, a reliance on overlearned behaviors and cognitions, a tendency to fight or flee, hypervigilance, and flooding.

Chaotic systems have no energy balance set point. They are also deviation amplifying systems. This has implications for being unable to predict the response of the family system to changes in inputs. Even small changes in input may result in vast changes in output.

Finally, I suggested a way to operationalize these notions in the study of actual family interaction by using the interevent interval, the state space graph, the Liapunov exponent, and the spectral analysis of progressive chunks of the interevent interval time series.

REFERENCES

Abraham, R. A., & Shaw, C. D. (1985). *Dynamics: The geometry of behavior: Part 1—Periodic behavior.* Santa Cruz, CA: Aerial Press.

Conrad, M. (1986). What is the use of chaos? In A. V. Holden (Ed.), *Chaos.* Princeton, NJ: Princeton University Press.

Crutchfield, J. P., Farmer, J. D., Packard, N. H., & Shaw, R. S. (1986). Chaos. *Scientific American, 255,* December, 46–57.

Dodge, K. A., Pettit, G. S., McClaskey, C. L., & Brown, M. M. (1986). Social competence in children. With commentary by J. M. Gottman, *Monographs of the Society for Research in Child Development, 51*(2), Serial No. 213.

Ekman, P. (1984). Expression and the nature of emotion. In K. R. Scherer & P. Ekman (Eds.), *Approaches to emotion.* Hillsdale, NJ: Lawrence Erlbaum Associates.

Glass, L., Scherer, A., & Belair, J. (1986). Chaotic cardiac rhythms. In A. V. Holden (Ed.), *Chaos.* Princeton, NJ: Princeton University Press.

Gleick, J. (1987). *Chaos.* New York: Penguin.

Gottman, J. M. (1981). *Time-series analysis.* New York: Cambridge University Press.

Gottman, J. M. (1990). How marriages change. In G. R. Patterson (Ed.), *Current topics in family research* (Vol. 1). Hillsdale, NJ: Lawrence Erlbaum Associates.

Gottman, J. M., & Levenson, R. W. (1985). A valid procedure for obtaining self-report of affect in marital interaction. *Journal of Consulting and Clinical Psychology, 53,* 151–160.

Gottman, J. M., & Levenson, R. W. (1986). Assessing the role of emotion in marriage. *Behavioral Assessment, 8,* 31–48.

Gottman, J. M., & Levenson, R. W. (1988). The social psychophysiology of marriage. In P. Noller & M. A. Fitzpatrick (Eds.), *Perspectives on marital interaction.* Philadelphia: Multilingual matters.

Holden, A. V. (Ed.). (1986). *Chaos.* Princeton, NJ: Princeton University Press.

Jensen, R. V. (1987). Classical chaos. *American Scientist, 75,* 168–181.

Kaneko, K. (1986). *Collapse of tori and genesis of chaos in dissipative systems.* Singapore: World Scientific.

Levenson, R. W., & Gottman, J. M. (1983). Marital interaction: Physiological linkage and affective exchange. *Journal of Personality and Social Psychology, 45,* 587–597.

Levenson, R. W., & Gottman, J. M. (1985). Physiological and affective predictors of change in relationship satisfaction. *Journal of Personality of Social Psychology, 49,* 85–94.

Wills, T. A., Weiss, R. L., & Patterson, G. R. (1974). A behavioral analysis of determinants of marital satisfaction. *Journal of Consulting and Clinical Psychology, 42,* 802–811.

Wolf, A. (1986). Quantifying chaos with Lyapunov exponents. In A. V. Holden (Ed.), *Chaos.* Princeton, NJ: Princeton University Press.

Woods, S. C., Decke, E., & Vasselli, J. R. (1974). Metabolic hormones and regulation of body weight. *Psychological Review, 81,* 26–43.

10 A Soft Models Approach to Family Transitions

R. Frank Falk
Nancy B. Miller
*University of California, Berkeley**

Transitions in families are frequently marked by specific dates such as birth of a child, marriage, divorce, or death. Such transitions, however, are frequently of long duration, and their effects may be variable over long periods of time. The transition to parenthood, for example, begins before the actual birth of the child and the effects continue to change for at least 18 months (Cowan, Cowan, Heming, & Miller, this volume). Recognition of these over-time processes has lead to increased interest in the use of longitudinal research designs. Data generated by these designs create unique data analysis problems which have been identified as problems in measuring change (Harris, 1963). These problems range from questions regarding the reliability of difference scores to the conceptual definitions of change itself.

Many mathematical and statistical models have been used to analyze over-time studies, including such familiar techniques as: Hotelling's T^2 (Harris, 1985), repeated measures ANOVA (Collier, Baker, Mandeville, & Hayes, 1967; Winer, 1971), repeated measures MANOVA (Harris, 1985), time-series analysis (Glass, Wilson, & Gottman, 1975; Ostrom, 1978), and trend analysis (Kerlinger & Pedhazur, 1973). The logic of experimental research designs motivated much of this work. In this chapter we describe three recent data analytic models from the literature in structural equation modeling which are motivated more by the logic of nonexperimental or observational research designs.

Autoregressive cross-lag (Joreskog, 1979), state variable developmental[1]

---

*Both authors are presently at the University of Akron, Department of Sociology, Akron, Ohio.

[1]Without naming it, Hertzog and Nesselroade present this design as an alternative to the autoregressive model. "State variable developmental" is our label for this design.

(Hertzog & Nesselroade, 1987), and latent growth curve (McArdle & Epstein, 1987) designs provide three distinctive models with which to approach the study of over-time transitions in nonexperimental, i.e., observational, situations. Each of these models asks different questions about the predictive (causal) relationships among variables within a study. Our purpose here is to describe these models and their associated questions through RAM graphic notation (McArdle & Horn, 1986). In so doing, we present an estimation procedure for these designs, called "soft modeling," and illustrate the designs and their estimations with a simplified and simulated example.

We begin by describing the research problem and RAM graphic notation system. Then a series of conceptual models that lead to autoregressive cross-lag, state variable developmental, and latent growth curve designs are presented. The soft modeling estimation procedure with hypothetical data follows the explanation of these designs.

THE RESEARCH PROBLEM

Let us assume that we are interested in the effects of the transition to parenthood on personal adjustment and that we note two demographic trends that may have a bearing on how individuals and couples adapt. First, more women are entering the labor force and establishing occupational careers. Second, more couples are postponing childbearing until later in life than their parents did. These two cultural trends lead us to ask: How does the timing of transition to parenthood affect personal adjustment? Our concern is not just the effects of becoming a parent, but the timing of that event relative to other life activities.

Within the context of this transition, we are interested in two additional concepts—the couple relationship and their parenting style. We would like to know what relationship exists between: (1) timing of transition (TT) and parenting style (PS), (2) timing of transition (TT) and quality of couple relationship (CR), (3) timing of transition (TT) and personal adjustment (PA), and (4) quality of couple relationship (CR) and personal adjustment (PA).

The question of measurement is put aside until the actual example is discussed. For now, simply note that we have specified four theoretical constructs and four relationships that provide the context for our discussion and graphic presentation of the models.

RAM GRAPHICS

McArdle (1980) has developed a generic structural equation model that is highly parsimonious, algebraically complete (McArdle & McDonald, 1984) and provides a graphic notation system that places structural equation modeling within the grasp of behavioral science researchers (Falk & McArdle, 1986; McArdle & Horn, 1986). We briefly describe the graphic notation system here and use it as the primary vehicle for describing the models. It consists of two types of variables and two types of relationships.

First, there are manifest variables. They are the measured variables and are graphically represented by rectangles or boxes. They are indicants, markers, or operational definitions of theoretical constructs, which are the second type of variables. The theoretical constructs may be latent variables (unobserved concepts) or composite variables (weighted aggregates) and are graphically represented by circles.

Single-headed arrows between variables represent an asymmetrical relationship. The arrow points toward the variable being predicted and graphically represents the regression weight or path coefficient. A two-headed arrow is called a span. A span between two variables represents a symmetrical relationship in the same sense as a correlation does. When a span is located on only one variable, it represents the variance of that variable or, if reduced by predictors in the model, its residual variance.

Two additional definitions not related to RAM graphics may be helpful to the reader. Traditionally, variables have been defined as independent and dependent or predictor and criterion. In modeling, variables are frequently referred to as exogenous and endogenous and have similar meanings. However, endogenous and exogenous variables are distinguished by whether they are predicted by other variables in the model. Endogenous variables have predictors in the model, exogenous variables do not.

A CROSS-SECTIONAL DESIGN

Although it is not one of our three over-time models, the cross-sectional design is the simplest baseline model with which to begin the discussion of analytic procedures. Suppose that we used the four theoretical constructs (TT, PS, CR, PA), and we measured 20 families at 6 months after the birth of their first child. The theoretical design of our questions would look like Fig. 10.1.

This design has only circles; all of the variables are theoretical constructs or composites. There are arrows from TT to PS and CR and from TT and CR to PA. These arrows represent our four questions, but they are more specific than just asking about the relationship between these concepts. The arrows are regression coefficients and the questions asked are: To what degree does the "timing of transition" predict "parenting style" and "couple relationship," and to what degree do "timing of transition" and "quality of couple relationship" predict "personal adjustment"?

Each circle in the cross-sectional design has a span on itself. For TT this span is the variance. Since PS, CR, and PA have arrows pointed toward them, their

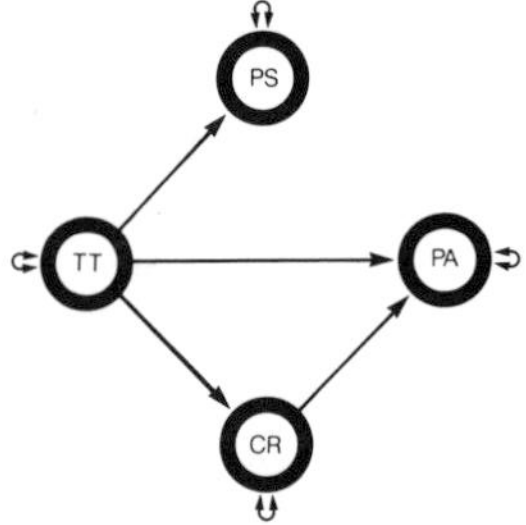

FIG. 10.1 Cross-sectional design where:

TT = timing of transition to parenthood
PS = parenting style
CR = quality of couple relationship
PA = personal adjustment

spans represent the amount of unpredicted variance that remains after the predicted variance is substracted. These are often referred to as residual variances. To aid in interpretation of results, these variances are frequently constrained to the value of one. This procedure scales every composite variable to the same unit variance allowing for comparison of the arrows and interpretion of the residual variances as the percent of variance unaccounted for.

If we had used spans instead of arrows between the variables, the residual variances (spans on the individual circles) would all equal one; and the spans between the variables would be the correlations between the constructs. Again, this design does not include over-time considerations. All over-time designs, however, can be thought of as a series or set of replications of cross-sectional designs.

TRAIT VARIABLE AUTOGRESSIVE DESIGN

In the trait variable autoregressive design, the trait-state character of the variable "personal adjustment" is considered in addition to the over-time measurement of personal adjustment. Let us assume that personal adjustment tends to be stable over time, i.e., given any two individuals their relative position will be the same over time unless something interfers. To the extent that this assumption is true, the variable is described as traitlike. This is distinguished from statelike variables in which the assumption is that individuals' relative positions change from time to time.

For the purpose of examining the over-time measurement of personal adjustment, let us suppose that our study began by identifying families who were in the third trimester of pregnancy at several local obstetric clinics. We asked for volunteers and obtained a 20-family sample. In addition to some background questions, the couple filled out the personal adjustment scales. We now have the measurement of personal adjustment at two time periods. With this additional information our new design is graphically presented in Fig. 10.2.

As in Fig. 10.1, all of the variables are constructs, shown as circles. There is one new arrow added to the model from personal adjustment prior to birth to personal adjustment 6 months after birth of the first child. In all other respects the model appears to be the same as the cross-sectional design, but we have substantively changed the meaning of personal adjustment at time 2 (PA2). It no longer has a variance of 1; it has been reduced by the measurement of personal adjustment at time 1 (PA1). In fact, if everyone in the study maintained the same score on personal adjustment at time 2 or if the same relative rank order of persons was maintained, the span on PA2 would be zero; and there would be no variance in PA2 to be predicted by TT and CR.

If changes have occurred in personal adjustment between the first and second measurement periods, PA2 is said to represent the independent change that occurred in personal adjustment between the two time periods. Let us assume that the personal adjustment scores of some people changed and that the relative rank order of persons between the two time periods also changed. The residual variance that remains in PA2 can be predicted by TT and CR. Autoregressive models are characterized by the reduction in variance of an endogenous variable by its measurement at a prior time. For display purposes the autoregressive relation is drawn as a broad arrow, but it is still only an arrow from the RAM logic point of view.

The question about the relationship between TT and CR and PA2 has now become: How much of the *change* in personal adjustment is predicted by timing

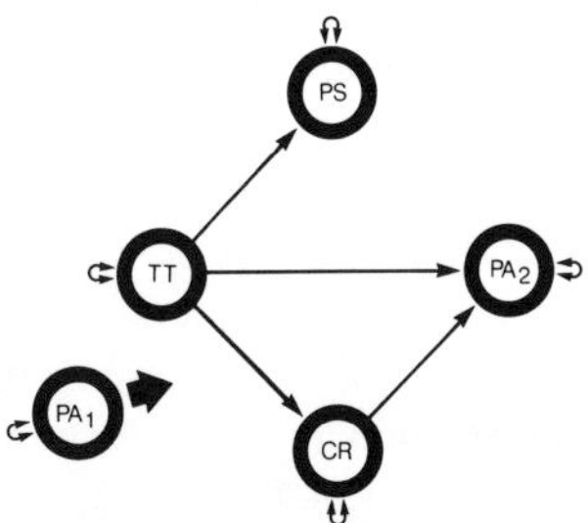

FIG. 10.2. Trait variable autoregressive design where:

PA_1 = personal adjustment prior to the birth of the child
TT = timing of transition to parenthood
PS = parenting style
CR = quality of couple relationship
PA_2 = personal adjustment 6 months after the birth of the child

of transition and quality of couple relationship? It is vital to understand that this notion of change is interindividual. "No change" means that the relative rank order of individuals has not changed although all or many or even a few individual scores may have changed. When change is found in traitlike variables modeled with autoregressive arrows, the change in the relative ordering of individuals is said to be the result of, or is predicted by, the other variables in the model.

Autoregressive models frequently lead to the world of small effects, and researchers should recognize that there may be little residual variance available to be predicted once the variable has been autoregressed. Small increments in variance accounted for may be all that are possible.

Unless altered by the effects of other variables in the model, autoregressive models assume that subjects are in the same relative position from time 1 to time 2.

TRAIT VARIABLE FIRST-ORDER AUTOREGRESSIVE CROSS-LAG DESIGN

As stated earlier, prior research indicates that the effects of the transition to parenthood are evident beyond 6 months and have been reported up to 18 months. Therefore, in the following design we assume that we measured our families at 6, 12, and 18 months after the birth of the first child. Figure 10.3 presents a model of these over-time measurements. All of our variables are constructs, i.e., circles. Timing of transition (TT) occurs only once. Personal adjustment (PA) was measured at 4 time periods—during pregnancy, at 6, 12, and 18 months postpartum. Parenting style (PS) and quality of couple relationship (CR) were measured at 3 time points—6, 12, and 18 months postpartum. Figure 10.3 also shows the first-order autoregressive relationships.

The spans on PA, PS, and CR are reduced by their measurements at the preceeding time period. This is referred to as the first-order effect because only the immediately preceeding measurements were used to reduce the variance. If the first and second time measurements were used to reduce the third, we would have both a first- and second-order autoregressive effect. Once again variables are assumed to be traitlike. This imposes a strong interindividual assumption: The relative rank order of individuals remains the same over time unless altered by the effects of other variables in the model.

To obtain Fig. 10.4 we add the relationships among variables presented in Fig. 10.1: timing of transition affecting parenting style, couple relationship, and personal adjustment at 6, 12, and 18 months postpartum; and couple relationship affecting personal adjustment within each of the measurement periods.

To Fig. 10.4 we add the cross-lag dimension, which represents the fully developed first-order autoregressive cross-lag design shown in Fig. 10.5. The cross-lag dimension suggests that the arrow between couple relationship and

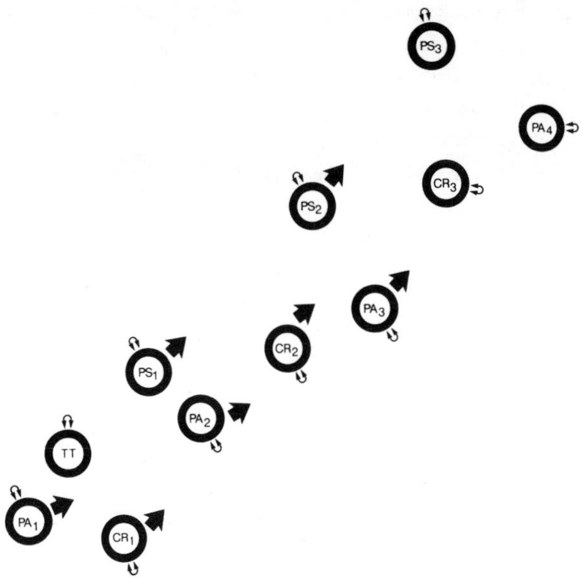

FIG. 10.3. Over time first-order autoregressive design where:

PA_1 = personal adjustment prior to the birth of the child
TT = timing of transition to parenthood
PS_1 = parenting style 6 months after birth
CR_1 = quality of couple relationship 6 months after birth
PA_2 = personal adjustment 6 months after birth
PS_2 = parenting style 12 months after birth
CR_2 = quality of couple relationship 12 months after birth
PA_3 = personal adjustment 18 months after birth
PS_3 = parenting style 18 months after birth
CR_3 = quality of couple relationship 18 months after birth
PA_4 = personal adjustment 18 months after birth

personal adjustment is not just a function of their current situation, but is also a function of the quality of the couple relationship 6 months earlier.

Through the presentation of Figs. 10.1 through 10.5, we have constructed one of the most common over-time designs, the first-order autoregressive cross-lag design. The questions that are posed by this design are variations on those originally stated. In this design we alter the definition of our dependent or endogenous variables to that of a change score. (PS, CR, and PA are all endogenous variables.) We have performed a first-order autoregression on the variables so that they reflect change which is independent of the prior state of the same variable. The relationships between variables reflect a concern with the prediction of change in the relative rank order of individuals. In addition to the predic-

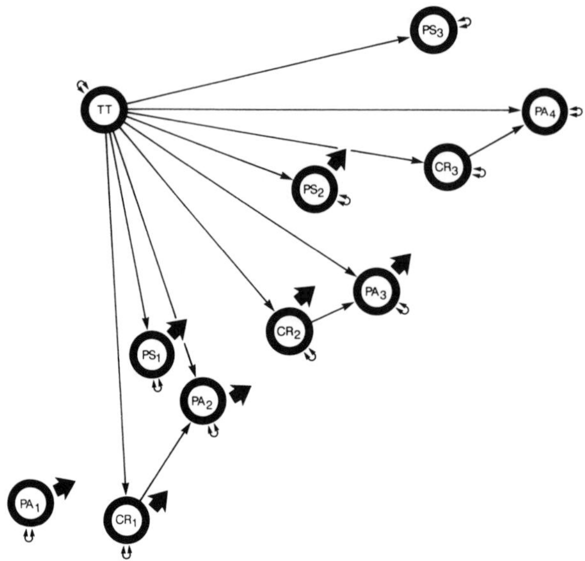

FIG. 10.4. First-order autoregressive relationship design.

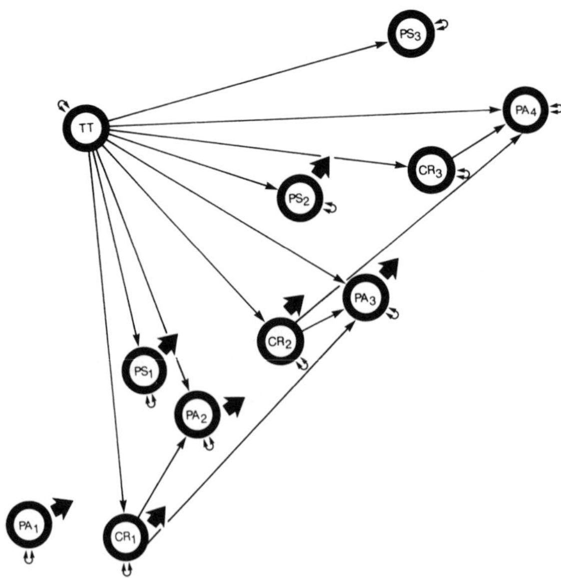

FIG. 10.5. Trait variable first-order autoregressive cross-lag design.

tive relationship between couple relationship and personal adjustment change within a time period, we have asked about the predictive relationship between couple relationship 6 months earlier and personal adjustment change 6 months later. We have also asked: What is the predictive relationship of timing of transition (1) to parenting style and couple relationship at 6 months after the birth of the first child, (2) to independent change in personal adjustment at all three time periods, and (3) to independent change in parenting style and couple relationship at 12 and 18 months postpartum?

It is common for an autoregressed endogenous variable to have 80% or more of its variance absorbed by its own measurement at a prior point in time; that is, the relative rank order of individuals usually remains fairly constant across measurement periods although the level of scores may change dramatically. This leads again to what we call the world of small effects. When only 20% of the variance remains to be accounted for or predicted, the researcher is limited to the interpretation of small effects. Perhaps it is this situation that has lead to consideration of other designs. We now turn our attention to two designs that change our questions and avoid the autoregressive problem—the state variable developmental design and the growth curve model.

STATE VARIABLE DEVELOPMENTAL DESIGN

We emphasized in the autoregressive design that there are two built-in presumptions—that the variables are traitlike and that the design is based on an interindividual model. In the interindividual model, individual change is viewed in terms of the change relative to others. Likewise, in correlational analysis, we understand that although individual scores change from one measurement time to another, if the relative rank order of individuals does not change, there is perfect correlation. The implication for our autoregressive design is that even if the scores of individuals change but the relative rank order remains the same, there will be no change to predict. In terms of our graphics, this raises the question of whether an arrow between time periods on the same variable is desirable.

Hertzog and Nessleroade (1987) questioned these underlying presumptions and proposed a trait-state distinction. They point out that many researchers have an intraindividual notion of change. In such a view the question is not whether individuals change their relative rank order vis-à-vis the other individuals, but whether individuals change. On many of our variables we anticipate that individual scores will change and that these new scores can be predicted by the effects of other variables in the model, i.e., the relationships between the variables at each time period.

In a recent longitudinal study of the effects of health on family contacts and feelings toward family members, this trait-state distinction became an important issue in the data analysis (Field, Minkler, Falk, & Leino, 1990). The study focused on a group of older aged persons who were first interviewed in the late 1960s and then reinterviewed approximately 15 years later. The basic question was how do health problems associated with aging affect familial interactions.

As a longitudinal study, the first reaction to the data analysis procedure was the autoregressive cross-lag design; but before the data analysis began, the stability of variables was questioned. Over a 15-year period, few individual characteristics remain stable, and among an older population many events can be especially disruptive. Health, most obviously, can have dramatic shifts. Family contacts can show marked variability. Death of other family members and decreased locomotion may be expected during this phase of life. Family feelings resemble many "mood" type variables which have been the traditional examples of statelike variables—one day a person is happy and the next anxious. Considerations such as these suggest the use of the state variable developmental design.

This design is shown in Fig. 10.6. Again, all of the variables are composites or theoretical constructs. Three time periods are portrayed. Timing of transition predicts each dependent variable at the separate time periods, and couple relationship predicts personal adjustment within each time period. The added time periods allow the researcher to examine the stability of the predictive relationships. It can be determined then whether the patterns of relationships remain the same over time or, for example, whether the timing of transition loses importance.

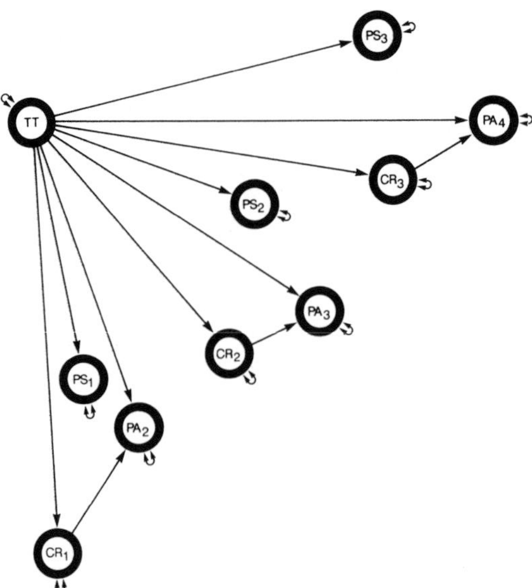

FIG. 10.6. State variable developmental design.

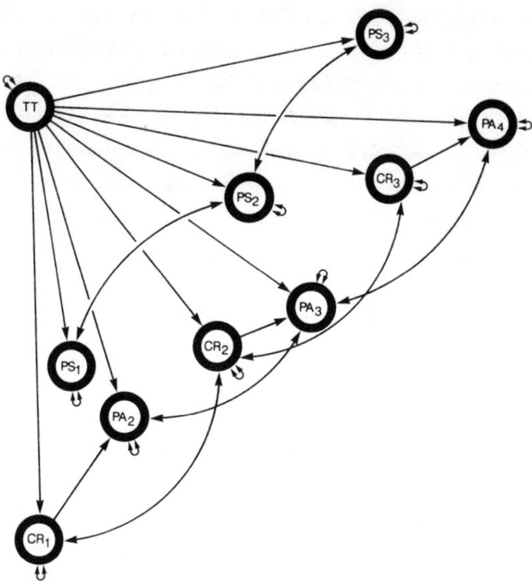

FIG. 10.7. State variable developmental design with cross-time correlations.

Again, arrows pointed toward a variable indicate that it is predicted by other variables in the model and that the size of its span is reduced, leaving only the residual. In this model there is no autoregressive arrow, but we are still interested in the relationship between variables over time. We can express this interest without reducing the variance by drawing spans between the same variables measured across time as in Fig. 10.7. Spans used in this manner are interpreted as correlation coefficients.

GROWTH CURVE MODEL

Spurred by the mathematical work of Meredith on "Tuckerizing curves" (Meredith & Tisak, in press), a different conceptual approach known as latent growth curve models (McArdle, 1986a, 1986b) has emerged. All possible ramifications of these models have not yet been explored, but, we believe, this avenue of data analysis should provoke the interest of researchers. Our third model is an example of this type of analysis.

To present this model we simplify our example and only investigate one aspect of personal adjustment—the self-image of the mother as a parent. (A discussion of the measurement model is in the next section.) In growth curve models, the goal is to describe the dependent variable in terms of the across-time change. This type of change is described as a curve.

To describe a curve, measurement at three or more time points is required. Recall that our personal adjustment measurements were taken prior to the birth of the first child and then at three 6-month intervals after the birth. The model does not assume that the time intervals are equally spaced. Figure 10.8 is a graph, using hypothetical data, of mothers' self-image over the four time points.

One might be inclined to change the caption on Fig. 10.8 from "Growth Curve" to "Decline Curve," but the general nomenclature has been kept. The middle line of this graph depicits the group mean at each of the four time points. The two outside lines describe the variance around each of these means. Note that the curve reveals a slow decline in mothers' self-image over the first 6 months with a more rapid decline between 12 and 18 months. Additionally, there is a continual decrease in the variance of the curve over time.

In latent variable growth curve analysis, we want to capture all of the information contained in the growth curve, as depicited in Fig. 10.8, in a single variable. To do this, we create a new construct variable, which represents the curve. Each time point of the measured variable of interest is treated as one of the manifest variables for a new composite. Raw cross-product moments are used in the calculations (see Appendix).

Additionally a new type of construct is introduced into the RAM logic and diagrams. The new construct is called "unit." The name reflects the fact that the value of one is assigned to every subject on this construct. Its mean therefore is one and its variance is zero. This construct is required for the computation of parameter estimates; it is used to establish the initial value of the curve. In effect it creates the equivalent of an intercept in a regression equation. Since it is not one of the measured variables or composited variables, we give it a special symbol, a triangle.

A description of the diagramatic representation of the growth curve design depicted in Fig. 10.9 is as follows. The circle represents the curve of self-image over time. The triangle is the unit variable previously described. The rectangles are the measurements on self-image at the four time periods. The arrow from the triangle to the circle Csi is the reference mean for the overall self-image curve, and the span on Csi is the variance for the overall curve. The arrows from the

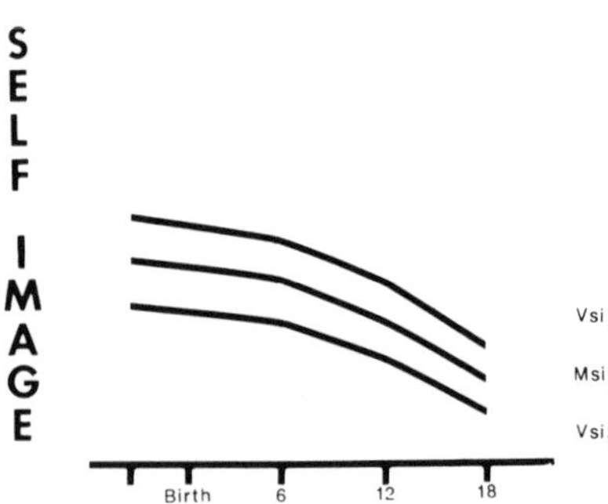

FIG. 10.8. Growth curve of mothers' self-image as a parent.

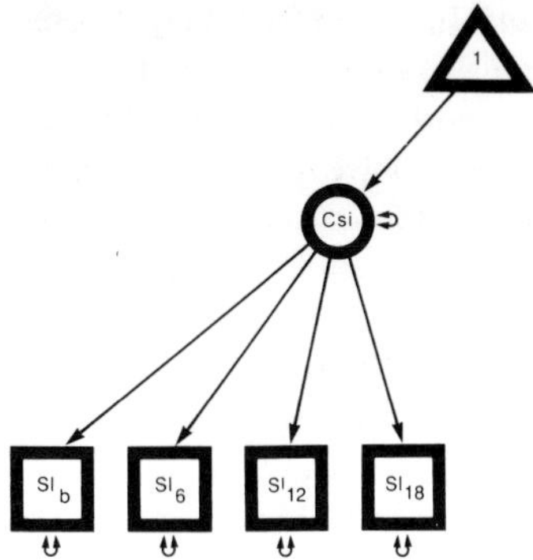

FIG. 10.9. Growth curve design where:

1 = a unit constant variable
Csi = the curve of the self-image over time
SI_x = the self-image measurement at each time

circle to the rectangles are the means for each time period, and the spans on the boxes are the variances of the measured self-image at each time.

After constructing the composited curve variable, timing of transition (TT) can be added to the design and the prediction of the curve (Csi) represented by drawing an arrow from TT to Csi. This arrow stands for the change over time in self-image that is accounted for by timing of transition. The interpretation is that timing of the transition to parenthood influences or predicts the growth curve. The growth curve has been transformed into a variable that describes change over time.

Up to this point we have described a series of model designs and pointed out the questions which each design asks. We have discussed these designs with reference to the theoretical variables without consideration of the specific measurements used in the study. This has been an attempt to establish a conceptual understanding without reference to any procedure by which numerical results are obtained. Our presentation now shifts to the explanation of a set of measurements and an estimation procedure.

MANIFEST VARIABLES

Manifest variables are measured variables. Recall from above that they are shown in RAM graphics within boxes or rectangles. Although our data are simulated, we have tried to select variables that will be familiar to family researchers. The data we generate have the same ranges and distributional characteristics as the measures described. The manifest variables are presented in the order of the theoretical constructs to which they belong. A theoretical construct and its associated manifest variables represent a block.

While recognizing the importance of fathers' as well as mothers' contributions to family processes, for simplicity we include only mothers in our model. Consequently our unit of analysis is the individual.

Block 1: Timing. Our first block is "timing of transition." We are interested in manifest variables that represent "when" the transition to parenting occurs in the life course of new mothers. Age of the mother at the time of birth (MA) is a strong candidate to measure this concept.

Because more women are in the labor force today and many, like their husbands, are attempting to develop occupational careers, number of years in occupation prior to the birth of the first child (YO) might be an important variable. Length of the couple relationship (LR) is used as another measure of timing. These variables are interval level measures.

Finally, mothers' scores on a scale of 20 items measure the timing of transition in terms of committment to other activities in her life (LA). The major areas questioned are commitment to career, education, recreational activities, and hobbies. Commitment is scored from 1 to 5 on each question for a total score range of 20 to 100. This represents an ordered metric level of measurement.

Other variables could be added to this list or substituted. The primary concern in model construction is that at least three manifest variables mark each theoretical construct.

Block 2: Parenting. In the second block called "parenting style," we are interested in how the mother enacts the parenting role. The parent's ideas regarding child-rearing issues are represented by scores from two domains in the "Ideas about Parenting" questionnaire (Heming, Cowan, & Cowan, 1982). Two total scores are used—one for the individuating parent (IP) and one for the authoritarian parent (AP). The first score reflects a parent who encourages the child's autonomy and self-expression, the second a parent who believes in strong control of the child. There are 8 and 6 items on the scales respectively. Each item is rated by the parent on a 9-point scale from strongly agree to strongly disagree.

Observations of the mother's warmth toward the child (MW), including nurturance and affectionate response, represent the third measure of the parenting style latent construct. A global rating of parental warmth on a scale of 1 to 5 is assumed.

Block 3: The couple. A third block, "couple relationship," consists of measures of the quality of the relationship between parents. Mothers' total scores on the Dyadic Adjustment Scale (DAS) (Spanier, 1976), a 32-item measure for assessing the quality of marriage, serves as the self-report measure for this concept. Observations of couple interaction during problem-solving tasks provides scores for quality of the couple relationship in two areas—communication (CO) and affectional expression (AE). Observation scale scores range from 1 to 5.

Block 4: Adjustment. Our final theoretical construct is "personal adjustment." Four scales are used to measure this concept: Reid and Ware's locus of control (LC) (1974), Rosenberg's self-esteem (SE) (1979), Kinch-Falk self-image (SI) (Kinch, Falk, & Anderson, 1983), and Dabrowski's emotional development (ED) (Gage, Morse, & Piechowski, 1981; Miller, 1985).

The internalizing versus externalizing locus of control scale has 32 items: 12 designed to measure a fatalism dimension, 12 to measure a social system control dimension, and 8 to assess a dimension of self-control. Two choices are given for each item—one representing external and one representing internal control.

Rosenberg's self-esteem scale has 10 items with a 5-point Likert response system. The scale is skewed to the low end; few respondents indicate low self-esteem. The range of the total score is 5 to 50. The level of measurement is an ordered metric.

The self-image inventory consists of the 12 adjectives most consistently used to describe oneself and others. The inventory is phrased to apply to a specific role. In this case respondents are asked to rate themselves as a parent. The instrument has a 7-point scale for each adjective. The total score ranges from 12 to 84 with a mean of approximately 48 and a normal distribution. Level of measurement is assumed to be interval.

Emotional development is measured by an open-ended questionnaire. In content analysis of responses, paragraphs serve as the context unit for the rating of themes. Each theme is rated on a 5-point basis to reflect the intentional feelings of the respondents regarding values, self, and others (Miller & Silverman, 1987; Miller & Falk, 1987). Total scores are averaged and range from 1 to 5. The scores are skewed to the high end with 80% of all scores occurring in categories 1 through 3. The level of measurement is assumed to be ordinal.

To summarize, the measurement model has the following characteristics: (1) the grouping of manifest variables has been based on a priori theoretical constructs, (2) each group consists of a minimum of three manifest variables, (3) the levels of measurement range from ordered categories to interval scales and involve observational as well as self-report measures, and (4) several of the measures are not normally distributed.

We believe that the types of variables we have described are representative of those used in many behavioral science research endeavors. Using variables such as these, with varying levels of measurement and nonnormal distributional characteristics, has implications for the estimation procedures used to compute the parameters of structural equation models. Specifically, maximum-likelihood estimation procedures require interval-level measurement and multivariate normality among the variables. For this reason a less restrictive procedure such as partial least squares is appropriate.

PARTIAL LEAST SQUARES ESTIMATIONS

Partial least squares (Wold, 1975, 1980a, 1980b, 1982) is part of the family of component analyses (Meredith & Millsap, 1985) of which principle components is most familiar. Partial least squares or its nontechnical name "soft modeling" is computed with the computer program "Latent Variable Path Analysis with Partial Least Squares" (LVPLSC) (Lohmoeller, 1984, 1989). The basis of the program is principle components analysis and prediction (Horst, 1965, p. 553. See Appendix for the basic formula).

The philosophy underlying component analyses in general and soft modeling in particular is reflected in a calculational approach that is different from that of common factor analysis (Harris, 1985; McDonald, 1985). In soft modeling components or composites are created from measured variables. These new variables are iteratively recalculated so as to create optimal linear correlations between them. In this manner soft modeling closely resembles canonical correlational analysis.

Common factor analysis does not create composite variables. The factors in common factor analysis are called latent or hidden variables to indicate that their effects can be measured without actually calculating factor scores.

Partial least squares (PLS) or soft modeling creates its components, or what has been described as constructs, by extracting the first principle component from the manifest variables theoretically defined as belonging in the same block. The first principle component of a set of variables has maximum variance given the manifest variables. Composited variables are created by weighting the manifest variables and adding them under the constraint that the compositing weights form a new variable or factor score with maximum variance.

There are two additional restrictions placed on the formation of composite variables. The first is that they be standardized so that their variance equals one. This places them in the same variance metric and allows for proportionate reduction in error (amount of variance explained) interpretations. The second is that composites are calculated to optimize the linear correlation among them. In weighting and adding the manifest variables, no assumptions have been made about normality or level of measurement.

To reiterate, in soft modeling new variables are calculated that are composites of the original manifest variables. These composites provide new information that is used in the estimation process. This information consists of the variance of the composite variables and their intercorrelations.

The new variables, shown in the diagram as circles, maximally describe the original variables. By contrast, common factor analysis maximally describes the correlations among the manifest variables. As one might guess, there is a substantial relationship between predicting the scores on the original variables and predicting the correlation among the original variables, but they are not the same.

The common factor analysis approach to modeling most often uses a maximum likelihood estimation procedure. This estimation procedure in particular assumes multivariate normal distributions and interval level measurement. Skewed distributions create special difficulties.

Procedures such as COSAN (McDonald, 1978), EQS (Bentler, 1985) and LISREL (Joreskog & Sorbom, 1985) are based on the common factor structure philosophy that defines common variance, unique variance, and uncorrelated unique variances as separate elements in the analysis. Separating these three aspects of variance in this way forces additional restrictive conditions on the calculation of parameter estimates (cf. Harris, 1985 and McDonald, 1985). The component analysis we are describing does not divide the variance of a variable into these parts. It simply seeks to represent as much of the variance in a group of variables as possible with a single composite variable.

In constructing PLS and labeling it soft modeling, Herman Wold (1980b) had in mind a modeling technique suited to the behavioral sciences as opposed to the "hard" sciences. He wished to create a technique appropriate to the situation where measurements were still in early stages of development and theoretical propositions were not well established. Wold observed that behavioral science research is frequently confronted with many questions and variables, but relatively few subjects. In political science, for example, nation-states are sometimes the subjects. In all they number less than 300.

The concept "partial" in partial least squares addresses this problem in the following way: Estimates are solved a part at a time. The analysis is partitioned by solving for each composite independently, and estimates within each block are made before the relationships between the blocks are taken into account.

As a final technical point, the LVPLSC procedure uses the generalized inverse solution, based on singular value decomposition, to solve for the inverse of the data matrices, an integral part of the mathematical calculations of regression weights (Green, 1976; Horst, 1965). This is a direct eigenvalue eigenvector solution that avoids many problems encountered by utilizing the determinant to solve for the inverse.

In summary, four conditions make soft modeling a powerful tool for behavioral science research. By creating composite variables, information or data for analyzing the model is increased. Optimal linear relationships between composites are obtained. The analysis is partitioned, and a generalized solution for the inverse of a data matrix is used.

These conditions have practical implications for the researcher. First, it is possible to have more variables in the model than subjects, although subjects must outnumber variables within a block. Second, stable estimates of the relationships between the variables are obtained; the problem of underidentified models (inadequate information to estimate the number of parameters specified) is avoided. Finally, variables with nonnormal distributions and varying levels of measurement may be used in the analysis.

To explore the models presented in this chapter, partial least squares estimation procedures in the computer program LVPLS are used. Instructions for the use of the program can be found in the program manual (Lohmoeller, 1984) and in a primer for soft modeling (Falk, 1987).

PRODUCING RESULTS

Up to this point we have discussed the conceptual basis for analyzing a set of data within a research problem. We now turn our attention to the process of obtaining results. This is accomplished through a 5-stage process known as the ISEER steps (Horn & McArdle, 1980). The steps are: initialization, specification, estimation, evaluation, and reevaluation. They provide an ordered sequence of steps to guide the process of analysis.

Initialization. In the initialization phase, the adequacy of the theoretical blocking of variables is established. Variables are selected to define constructs on an a priori basis. In the initialization phase these ideas are tested with the LVPLS program.

In this study we have proposed four theoretical constructs: timing of transition to parenthood (TT), parenting style (PS), couple relationship (CR), and personal adjustment (PA). We have identified three or four manifest variables as indicants of each construct.

The four variables selected to mark TT are: age of mother at birth of child (MA), years in occupation prior to birth (YO), length of couple relationship (LR), and commitment to other life activities (LA). Parenting style (PS) is measured by mother's scores on an individuating parent scale (IP) and an authoritarian parent scale (AP) plus an observation of maternal warmth (MW). Quality of the couple relationship (CR) is indicated by mother's dyadic adjustment score (DAS) and observational scores on communication (CO) and affectional expression (AE). Personal adjustment (PA) is measured by the following four variables: locus of control (LC), self-esteem (SE), self-image (SI), and emotional development (ED).

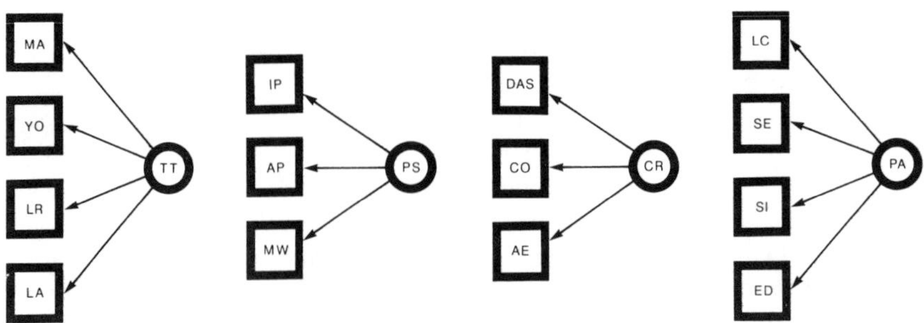

FIG. 10.10. Manifest markers of theoretical constructs.

In the initialization stage, we must evaluate the degree of common variance shared by the manifest variables for each construct. This is done by examining the relationship between each manifest variable and the theoretical construct. Traditionally, pattern loadings are used to judge the contribution a manifest variable makes to the composite variable. Harris (1985), however, points out that the compositing weights can also be used. In this paper we use the more familiar loadings (see Table 10.1 for examples), but the weights are also available from the LVPLS program. In either case, the higher the weight or the loadings on a

TABLE 10.1
LVPLS Component Loadings and Residuals for Both Trait Variable First-Order Autoregressive Cross-Lag and State Variable Developmental with Cross-Time Correlations Designs

					Composites						
Manifest Variables	*PA1*	*TT*	*PS1*	*CR1*	*PA2*	*PS2*	*CR2*	*PA3*	*PS3*	*CR3*	*PA4*
MA		.91									
YO		.86									
LR		.89									
LA		.83									
IP			.88			.82			.87		
AP			-.90			-.88			-.78		
MW			.92			.91			.84		
DAS				.90			.87			.85	
CO				.92			.90			.83	
AE				.88			.87			.89	
LC	.79				.82			.88			.85
SE	.82				.82			.82			.79
SI	.87				.87			.79			.85
ED	.73				.71			.71			.67
					Residuals						
	PA1	*TT*	*PS1*	*CR1*	*PA2*	*PS2*	*CR2*	*PA3*	*PS3*	*CR3*	*PA4*
MA		.17									
YO		.26									
LR		.21									
LA		.32									
IP			.23			.33			.25		
AP			.18			.23			.39		
MW			.15			.16			.29		
DAS				.18			.24			.28	
CO				.15			.20			.24	
AE				.23			.24			.20	
LC	.37				.32			.23			.27
SE	.33				.32			.32			.37
SI	.25				.23			.38			.27
ED	.47				.50			.50			.56

manifest variable, the more that variable defines the composite variable. Manifest variables with near zero loadings contribute very little to the composite variable, and the researcher should consider dropping such variables from the analysis.

Some manifest variables may have negative loadings. These are important variables that help to define the negative pole of the composite variable. When all the manifest variable loadings have the same sign, the composite variable is unipolar. When the manifest variables have both negative and positive loadings, the composite variable represents a bipolar concept.

Occasionally, a manifest variable may have been placed in the wrong block of variables. This can be detected by examining the correlations between the residuals of the manifest variables. This is referred to as the correlated error term. If there are moderate to highly correlated error terms between manifest variables in different blocks, the manifest variables have been incorrectly assigned to the composite variables and adjustments should be made. These residual correlations are reported by the computer program.

When the researcher is satisfied that the blocks of manifest variables adequately define the composite variables, the initialization process is completed.

Specification. Specification is the process of deciding on the order of the composite variables and the direction of the arrows that are drawn between them. Some composite variables will be exogenous, predictors of other variables; others will be endogenous, predicted variables. Some variables will be predictor as well as predicted. These are also referred to as endogneous and are sometimes called mediator variables. The order of the variables and the arrow schema represent the specification. One's theory, prior findings, hypotheses, and the research question determine this specification. In general, the ordering of the variables will be the most definite, the arrow schema the most tenuous. The more powerful the theory, the more specific the arrow schema will be.

Two extremes of the arrow schema are the full model and the null model. Once the order of the variables is determined these two models may be defined. In a full model every preceeding variable predicts all the variables that follow it. The null model has no arrows at all between composites. These two models are not very interesting, but they can serve as reference points. The full model provides the highest possible prediction of the endogenous variables given the ordered sequence of the variables. The arrow schemata presented in Figures 10.1–10.9 are examples of specifications.

Estimation. Estimation is the application of a particular algorithm to the data. The estimation procedure utilized in this paper is partial least squares as discussed in the previous section.

Evaluation. The evaluation of a soft model is based on how well the endogenous variables are predicted. The prediction estimate is evaluated by using the squared multiple correlation coefficient R^2 familiar to researchers. The specified model should have R^2 values on the endogenous variables that are higher than the null model but not less than the R^2 for the full model. The first condition is equivalent to the null hypothesis that there is no prediction of the endogenous variables, i.e., $R^2 = 0$. The second condition is equivalent to the hypothesis that there is no change in the R^2 by adding relationships beyond those specified by the theory.

Additionally, the overall model may be tested by examining the average correlation between the residuals on the manifest variables and the residuals on the composite variables. This value is given as the RMS Cov (E,U), which stands for the Root Mean Square of the Covariance of the manifest and composite residuals: The higher this number, the less adequate the model is in representing the data. A value of .20 or greater signifies a poor model, a value of .02 or less an excellent model.

Reevaluation. With large models and weak theoretical specification, comparisons between the specified model and the full and null models frequently lead to a new, respecified model. Some paths thought to be important may not contribute to the predictions; others may be discovered that do. One criterion to use in judging the importance of a path in the full model is whether the path (or arrow) coefficient, multiplied by the correlation coefficient between composite variables, equals 10% of the R^2 of the endogenous variable. If this is not the case, the model should be respecified without this path. The new model is then reevaluated using the same criteria.

EXAMPLES

We present the results of the data analysis from the three models that represent the central focus of this paper: trait variable first-order autoregressive cross-lag, state variable developmental with cross-time correlations, and the growth curve. The purpose is to demonstrate the type of results that might be produced by each of these models.

Table 10.1 presents the loadings between the manifest variables and their associated construct. In this particular example the loadings are all above .5, which represents a preferred cutting point. The residual variances for the manifest variables are therefore small.

In Fig. 10.11 note that while the R^2 values on the criterion variables are substantial, the contribution of the nonautoregressive variables (TT and CR) is relatively small. This is the effect of autoregression. In comparison, the individual predictor variables (TT and CR) in Fig. 10.12 have a greater influence; however, the R^2 values on the endogenous variables are lower.

The RMS Cov(E,U) values in both Figs. 10.11 and 10.12 are very small indicating models that have an excellent fit to the data. It is not likely that models

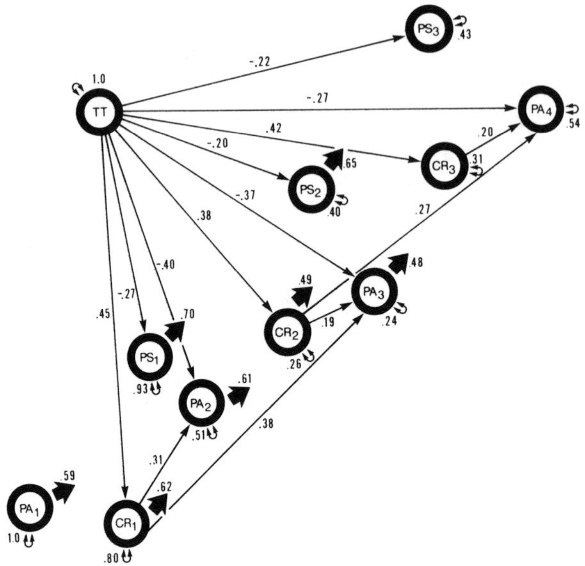

FIG. 10.11. Trait variable first-order autoregressive cross-lag design.
R Squared Values for Endogenous Variables

PS1 = .07	PS2 = .60	PS3 = .57
CR1 = .20	CR2 = .74	CR3 = .69
PA2 = .49	PA3 = .76	PA4 = .46

RMS Cov(E,U) = .0103

with actual data will show such a match. The small differences between these values in Figs. 10.11 and 10.12 are the result of simulated data.

The growth curve model provides two graphs shown in Figs. 10.13 and 10.14. Figure 10.13 is produced by the estimation procedure. The arrow from the unit triangle to the circle predicts the average height of the curve or its intercept. The span on the circle represents the standard deviation of the curve and was set to equal 1. The arrows from the circle to the squares represent the regression weights in raw score form. The regression weights multiplied by the intercept equal the mean value of the measured self-image score at each time period, and the spans on the squares represent the standard deviations.

Using the formulas provided in the appendix, values obtained can be used to generate Fig. 10.14 which describes the curve, represented by Csi, in Fig. 10.13. In general, the curve shows a steady decrease in self-image from time 1 to time 4 with a slightly more marked decrease between means at time 3 and time 4. The variance around these means also decreases over time. Table 10.2 provides the actual values for Fig. 10.14.

In Fig. 10.13, the timing of transition has a regression weight of .45 on the

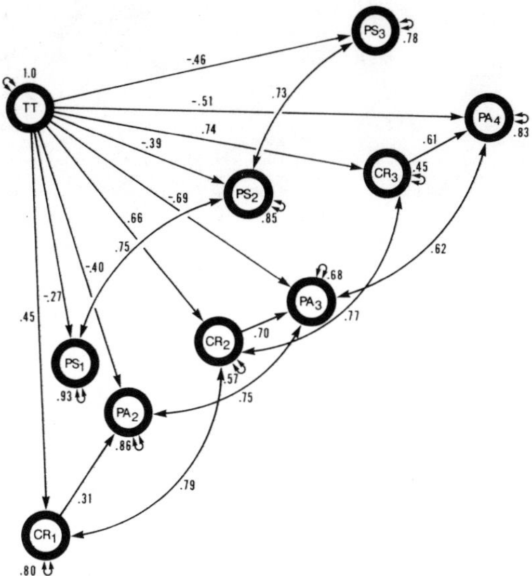

FIG. 10.12. State variable developmental design with cross-time correlations. R Squared Values for Endogenous Variables

PS1 = .07	PS2 = .15	PS3 = .22
CR1 = .20	CR2 = .44	CR3 = .55
PA2 = .14	PA3 = .32	PA4 = .17

RMS Cov(E,U) = .0108

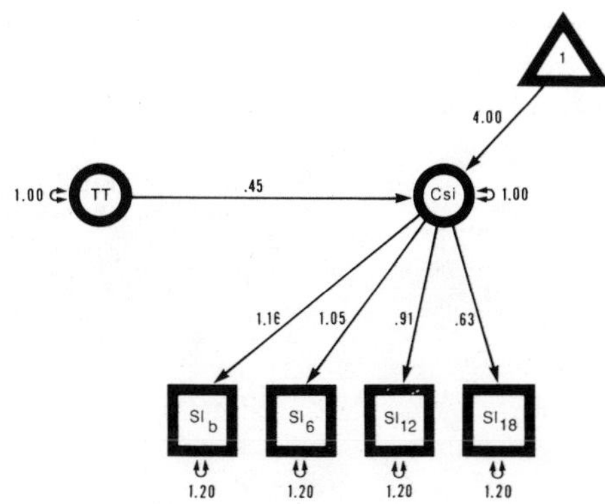

FIG. 10.13. Growth curve model.

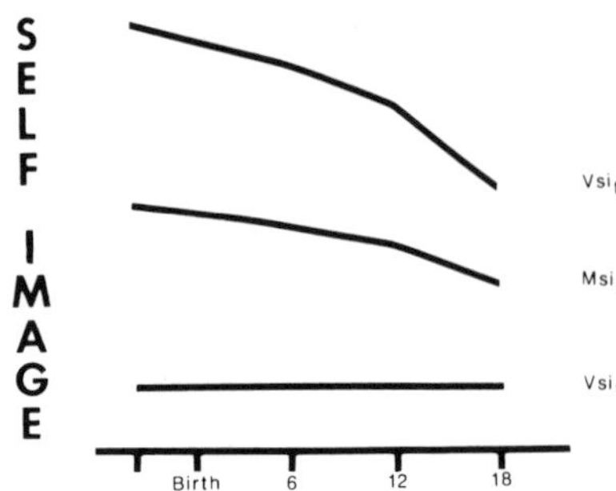

FIG. 10.14. Growth curve of mothers' self-image as a parent.

curve Csi. This indicates that the shape and height of the curve, depicted in Fig. 10.14, are influenced by timing of transition—the higher the regression weight the greater the influence. Examples of additional curve analyses can be found in the work of McArdle (1986a, 1986b; McArdle & Epstein, 1987).

CONCLUSION

In concluding, we note that analyzing transitions in families creates one of the most challenging problems facing researchers today. There is no definitive solution to the problem of measuring change over time though several different approaches exist. We have presented three models in this chapter based on nonexperimental or observational designs from the structural equation modeling field. We have specified the assumptions on which each design is based and the implications for the research problem under consideration here.

In both the autoregressive cross-lag and the state variable developmental designs, composites are created as weighted combinations of variables, each variable representing an attempt to gain information relevant to that concept by a different measurement. Change, or the lack thereof, is represented by either the autoregressive relationships, in which the variance of an endogenous variable is decreased by its prior measurement, or the cross-time correlations of latent variables.

The growth curve model, on the other hand, utilizes the measurements of the

TABLE 10.2
Calculated Values for the Growth Curve

Observation	*Mean*	*Variance*	Vsi_t
SI_1	4.65	1.44	$\pm$ 2.79
SI_2	4.20	1.44	$\pm$ 2.54
SI_3	3.65	1.44	$\pm$ 2.27
SI_4	2.50	1.44	$\pm$ 1.84

same variable over several time periods to calculate the curve or composite variable that represents change over time in the dependent variable. Then the effect on the growth curve of independent latent variables of interest, such as the timing of transition, can be examined.

We have recommended LVPLS or "soft modeling" as an estimation procedure for each of these designs. Because of its robustness in regard to measurement and distributional assumptions, it is most appropriately used when manifest variables lack precision (i.e., come in different sizes and shapes) and theory is in an emergent stage (i.e., struggling to keep pace with data).

In addition, we have taken the reader through the process of initialization, specification, estimation, evaluation, and reevaluation to obtain numerical results. Suggestions regarding the usefulness of the null and the full model as reference points are made and a measure of the overall fit of the model to the data is suggested. Finally, examples from similated data give the reader an idea of the type of information produced by the estimation procedure given the research problem.

ACKNOWLEDGMENTS

Sections of this chapter were presented by the first author as an invited contribution to the Family Research Consortium, Second Annual Summer Institute, June 2–6, 1987, Santa Fe, New Mexico. During the preparation of this chapter, the second author was supported by an NIMH Post Doctoral Fellowship in Family Processes and Psychopathology (1 T32 MH18262).

APPENDIX

In the appendix we consider a few more technical aspects of the procedures discussed in this chapter. Our intention, however, is to make this section comprehensible to the researcher.

Cross-Products, Covariances, and Correlations

Traditionally in soft modeling, the correlational metric is used. To calculate growth curves, however, the raw cross-products metric is required. The following procedures distinguish three types of product moments.

We begin by considering the simple multiplication of two variables. If, after multiplying two variables, you sum or add their products (scores) and divide by the number of cases, you have the average cross product of the two variables. This is referred to as the *raw cross-product moment* of the two variables.

If you subtract the mean of each variable from the variable score, multiple the two variables and then sum their scores, this is referred to as the cross-product deviations. If you further divide the cross-product deviations by the number of cases, you have the *covariance.*

If you subtract the mean of each variable from the variable score as before and then divide each score by its standard deviation, you have created standard score variables. If you multiply the two standard score variables, sum their scores and divide by the number of cases, you have the *correlation.*

In all three cases (i.e., correlations, covariances, and raw cross-product momemts) you have multiplied two variables, summed their products, and divided by the number of cases. Adding the products and dividing by the number of cases creates an average or a mean or a moment. Multiplying creates a product. The product moments of two variables may be correlations, covariances or raw cross-products. In all three cases, these product moments describe the way in which two variables covary. What you do to the variables before you multiple, sum, and divide distinguishes the three.

Correlations ignore two pieces of information about each variable, the mean and the standard deviation (or variance). Covariances ignore one piece of information about each variable, the mean. Raw cross-products maintain the information about both the mean and the variance of both variables.

Formulas for the Growth Curves

A full discussion of the mathematics and application of growth curves can be found in several recent publications (Meredith & Tisak, in press; McArdle, 1986a, 1986b; and McArdle & Epstein, 1987). Here we present only the formulas that allow a researcher to compute and draw the growth curve from the modeling equation results:

$$Mr_t = B_t Mc$$

$$Vr_t = B_t Vc B_t{}' + Vd$$

Source: McArdle and Epstein (1987)

These terms are defined with reference to Figs. 10.8 and 10.9. Mr_t and Vr_t are the means and variances for the growth curve of Fig. 10.8. The other values come from Fig. 10.9. B_t are regression weights on the arrows from the circle of the curve to the rectangles for each of the time points. Mc is the mean of the curve and is the value of the arrow from the unit triangle variable to the circle of the curve. Vc is the span on the circle of the curve, Vd the span on the rectangles.

Principle Components and Prediction Formulas

The concept of using principle components as a data reduction representation of a number of variables is an old tradition (Horst, 1965). Utilizing these components as variables in a prediction equation is also a familiar procedure. The combination of these procedures in an iterative program which minimizes all residuals provides the basis for the LVPLS program (Lohmoeller, 1984). Here we reproduce the basic formulas for these procedures (Horst, 1965, p. 553). The reader is reminded that a data matrix may be partitioned into any number of submatrices representing different combinations of exogenous and endogenous variables. The basic formulas are as follows:

$$R_{pp} = x_p{}'x_p \;/\; N$$
$$R_{pc} = x_p{}'x_c \;/\; N$$
$$QD^2Q' = R_{pp}$$
$$b = Q(m)^{D}(m)^{-1}$$
$$B = b(b'R_{pc})$$

Where: x is a matrix of standardize scores on all measured variables

R_{pp} is the correlation between the exogenous variables or predictor variables

R_{pc} is the correlation between the exogenous and endogenous variables or the predictor and criterion variables

B is the matrix of regression coefficients

Q and Q' are the basic orthonormals of R_{pp}

D^2 is the basic diagonal of R_{pp}

$Q_{(m)}$ is the first m vectors of Q

$D_{(m)}{}^2$ is ithe first m elements of D^2

REFERENCES

Bentler, P. M. (1985). *Theory and implementation of EQS: A structural equations program.* Los Angeles: BMDP Statistical Software.

Collier, R. O., Baker, F. B., Mandeville, G. K., & Hayes, T. F. (1967). Estimates of test size for several test procedures based on conventional variance ratios in the repeated measures design. *Psycometrika. 32,* 339–353.

Falk, R. F. (1987). *A primer for soft modeling.* Berkeley: Institute of Human Development.

Falk, R. F., and McArdle, J. J. (1986). *Latent variable path analysis using RAM graphics.* Paper presented at the annual meetings of the Pacific Sociological Association, Denver.

Field, D., Minkler, M., Falk, R. F., & Leino, E. V. (1990). The influence of health on family contacts and family feelings in advanced old age: A longitudinal study. (Submitted for publication).

Gage, D. F., Morse, P. A., & Piechowski, M. M. (1981). Measuring levels of emotional development. *Genetic Psychology Monographs. 103,* 129–152.

Glass, G. V., Wilson, V. L., & Gottman, J. M. (1975). *Design and analysis of time-series experiments.* Boulder: Colorado Associated University Press.

Green, P. E. (1976). *Mathematical tools for applied multivariate analysis.* New York: Academic Press.

Harris, C. W. (1963). *Problems in measuring change.* Madison: University of Wisconsin Press.

Harris, R. J. (1985). *A primer of multivariate statistics.* New York: Academic Press.

Heming, G., Cowan, P. A., & Cowan, C. P. (1982). *Ideas about parenting: Self-report questionnaire developed for Becoming a Family Project.* University of California, Berkeley.

Hertzog, C., & Nesselroade, J. R. (1987). Beyond autoregressive models: Some implications of the trait-state distinction for the structural modeling of developmental change. *Child Development. 58,* 93–109.

Horn, J. L., & McArdle, J. J. (1980). Perspectives on mathematical/statistical model building (MASMOB) in research on aging. In L. W. Poon (Ed.), *Aging in the 1980's: Psychological issues.* Washington, DC: American Psychological Association.

Horst, P. (1965). *Factor analysis of data matrices.* New York: Holt, Rinehart & Winston.

Joreskog, K. G. (1979). Statistical estimation of structural equation models in longitudinal-developmental investigations. In J. R. Nesselroade & P. B. Baltes (Eds.), *Longitudinal research in the study of behavior and development* (pp. 303–352). New York: Academic Press.

Joreskog, K. G., & Sorbom, D. (1985). *LISREL-V program manual.* Chicago: International Educational Services.

Kerlinger, F. N., & Pedhazur, E. J. (1973). *Multiple regression in behavioral research.* New York: Holt, Rinehart, and Winston.

Kinch, J., Falk, R. F., & Anderson, D. (1983). A self-image inventory: Its theoretical background, reliability and validity. *Symbolic Interaction. 6,* 229–242.

Lohmoeller, J. B. (1984). *LVLPS 1.6 program manual: Latent variable path analysis with partial least-squares estimation.* Cologne: Universitaet zu Koehn, Zentralarchiv fuer Empirische Sozialforschung.

Lohmoeller, J. B. (1989). *Latent variable path analysis with partial least squares.* New York: Springer-Verlag.

McArdle, J. J. (1980). Causal modeling applied to psychonomic systems simulations. *Behavior Research Methods and Instrumentation. 12,* 193–209.

McArdle, J. J. (1986a). Latent growth within behavior genetic models. *Behavior Genetics, 16,* 163–200.

McArdle, J. J. (1986b). Dynamic but structural equation modeling with repeated measures data. In J. R. Nesselroade & R. B. Cattell (Eds.), *Handbook of multivariate experimental psychology, Volume II.* New York: Plenum.

McArdle, J. J., & Epstein, D. (1987). Latent growth curves within developmental structural equation models. *Child Development. 58,* 110–133.

McArdle, J. J., & Horn, J. L. (1986). *A simple graphic model for moment structures.* Unpublished manuscript, University of Denver.

McArdle, J. J., & McDonald, R. P. (1984). Some algebraic properties of the Reticular Action Model for momemt structures. *British Journal of Mathematical and Statistical Psychology. 37,* 234–251.

McDonald, R. P. (1985). *Factor analysis and related methods.* Hillsdale, NJ: Lawrence Erlbaum Associates.

McDonald, R. P. (1978). A simple comprehensive model for the analysis of covariance structures. *British Journal of Mathematical and Statistical Psychology. 37,* 59–72.

Meredith, W., & Millsap, R. E. (1985). On component analyses. *Psychometrika. 50,* 495–507.

Meredith, W., & Tisak, J. (in press). Latent curve analysis. *Psychometrika.*

Miller, N. B. (1985). *A content analysis coding system for assessing adult emotional development.* Unpublished doctoral dissertation, University of Denver.

Miller, N. B., & Falk, R. F. (1987). *Intentional value-feelings: An adult developmental perspective.* Paper presented at the annual meeting of the American Sociological Association, Chicago.

Miller, N. B., & Silverman, L. K. (1987). Levels of personality development. *Roeper Review. 9,* 221–225.

Ostrom, C. W. (1978). *Time series analysis: Regression techniques.* Beverly Hills: Sage.

Reid, D. W., & Ware, E. E. (1974). Multidimensionality of internal versus external control: Addition of a third dimension and non-distinction of self versus others. *Canadian Journal of Behavioral Science. 6,* 131–142.

Rosenberg, M. (1979). *Conceiving the self.* New York: Basic.

Spanier, G. B. (1976). Measuring dyadic adjustment: New scales for assessing the quality of marriage and similar dyads. *Journal of Marriage and the Family. 38,* 15–28.

Winer, B. J. (1971). *Statistical principles in experimental design.* New York: McGraw-Hill.

Wold, H. (1975). Path models with latent variables: The NIPALS approach. In H. Blalock (Ed.), *Quantitative sociology: International perspectives on mathematical and statistical model building* (pp. 307–357). New York: Academic Press.

Wold, H. (1980a). Model construction and evaluation when theoretical knowledge is scarce—Theory and application of partial least squares. In J. Kmenta & J. G. Ramsey (Eds.), *Evaluation of econometric models* (pp. 47–74). New York: Academic Press.

Wold, H. (1980b). Soft modelling: Intermediate between traditional model building and data analysis. *Mathematical Statistics 6,* 333–346.

Wold, H. (1982). Systems under indirect observation using Pls. In C. Fornell (Ed.), *A second generation of multivariate analysis* (pp. 325–347). New York: Praeger.

Author Index

C

F

G

Y

Z

Subject Index

A

B

C